To Adrian,

with all good wishes
and thanks for all your
support.

3 March 1997
[The 38th anniversary
of the declaration of
the State of Emergency].

State of Emergency

INTERNATIONAL LIBRARY OF AFRICAN STUDIES

State of Emergency:
Crisis in Central Africa,
Nyasaland 1959–1960

COLIN BAKER

Tauris Academic Studies
I.B.Tauris Publishers
LONDON · NEW YORK

Published in 1997 by Tauris Academic Studies,
an imprint of I.B.Tauris & Co Ltd, Victoria House,
Bloomsbury Square, London WC1B 4DZ

175 Fifth Avenue, New York NY 10010

In the United States of America and in Canada
distributed by St Martin's Press
175 Fifth Avenue, New York NY 10010

A full CIP record for this book is available from the British
Library

A full CIP record for this book is available from the Library of
Congress

ISBN 1 86064 068 0

Library of Congress catalog card number: available

Set in Monotype Ehrhardt by Ewan Smith, London

Printed and bound in Great Britain by
WBC Ltd, Bridgend, Mid Glamorgan

Contents

Plates

1. Sir Robert Armitage
2. Sir Patrick Devlin
3. Dr Hastings Kamuzu Banda
4. Assistant Commissioner Philip Finney
5. Leading Congress detainees, and Counsel (H.B.M. Chipembere, D. Chisiza, F.W.K. Nyasulu, G. Mills-Odoi, D. Foot, Dr H.K. Banda, T.O. Kellock)
6. The British South Africa Police 'Yellow Scarves'

Introduction

The 1959–60 crisis in Central Africa – the state of emergency in Nyasaland – was brought about by attempts to resolve a major dilemma in which the British and Nyasaland governments were in conflict with those they governed and for whom they were responsible; with the Nyasaland people being represented and led by Dr Banda and the Congress Party. In simple terms the conflict was that the governments wanted the Central Africa Federation, of which Nyasaland had become one of the three component territories in 1953, to persist, succeed and flourish, whereas Congress wanted to secede from it and preferably bring about its demise.

The crisis represented a remarkable turning point in the history of Nyasaland and of Central Africa as a whole. Before the emergency the British government was adamant that the Federation was a permanent institution; after the emergency they recognised that its survival was in the gravest doubt and then decided to abandon it. Soon after the emergency was declared Lord Perth said the rapid advance to independence was being halted; well before the end of the emergency Macleod made it clear that it was to be accelerated. Before the emergency independence for Nyasaland appeared to be at least a decade, and probably longer, away; after the emergency it was clear that it would follow in a matter of a very few years. Before the emergency Banda was generally seen by the governments concerned as representing relatively few, ambitious, self-seeking political activists, separated by a great gulf from the aspirations of the politically more apathetic majority; after the emergency he was clearly recognised as the undisputed leader of a committed mass movement involving almost the whole of the African population of Nyasaland. Before the emergency Banda refused to condemn violence; just before its end he publicly appealed to his people to be peaceful. Before the emergency the governments and much of the press were convinced that Nyasaland did not have anywhere near enough 'cabinet material' for Africans to form a meaningful part of the executive council; after the emergency Africans quickly filled half the ministerial posts.

Before March 1959 the gap between Congress demands and what their European political opponents and the British and Nyasaland governments were prepared to concede was enormous. From the governments' point of view the essential question that needed to be answered in order to resolve the dilemma in which this conflict placed them was how to advance Nyasaland to a position of full self-government within the Federation. It was vital that the people of Nyasaland accepted the Federation because only then could Britain withdraw its protection, and the Federation – with Nyasaland voluntarily remaining part of it – continue in existence and hopefully flourish. Indeed, the task given to Armitage when appointed Governor in 1956 was to win the Africans over to acceptance of the Federation. Getting to that position would require, on the way, methods to be found to progress Nyasaland towards full self-government while somehow inducing her people to stay within the Federation: enough progress for them to be satisfied they were advancing sufficiently towards their goal, but not enough to enable them to secede. From the Africans' point of view, the question – if they were to stay within the law – was how to secure a sufficient majority in the legislature both to have a dominant role at the 1960 federal review conference and influence the deliberations there, and also to secede from the Federation by powerful resolutions in the Nyasaland legislative council. That is why Banda wanted an immediate African majority in the legislature and why his opponents and the governments did not. Whatever their feelings about a majority in the legislature and when this should be granted, it was precisely this reason of Banda's for wanting an immediate majority that was his European opponents' and the British and Nyasaland governments' argument for adamantly refusing it: they wanted the future pattern of the Federation settled first. The Europeans wanted this in order to secure greater control through a stronger federation, preferably with a dominion constitution, and the British and Nyasaland governments wanted it – with a redistribution of responsibilities in favour of the protectorate – in order to see how far and in what ways they could advance the Nyasaland constitution after 1960.

Yet 18 months after the emergency was declared all the parties involved – Banda and Congress, other African parties, the United Federal Party in Nyasaland, the chiefs, the Nyasaland and British governments – agreed to a very early constitutional change which would give a large African majority in legislative council. And they agreed this before the federal review conference, indeed before the preparatory commission prior to that conference had reported.

During the emergency over 1300 Africans were detained; 51 were killed and many more wounded; 31 women were widowed and 68 children orphaned; over 3000 soldiers and police officers were brought in from neighbouring countries; the Conservative government faced and escaped defeat in the Commons in July 1959 and in the country at the October 1959 general election; the British government's relationships with the federal, Southern Rhodesian and Nyasaland governments were stretched almost to breaking point; a near fatal split between the Commonwealth and colonial secretaries opened up; the chief secretary of Nyasaland was removed; the Governor was told of his own imminent departure; relationships – formerly always enviably harmonious – between Africans and Europeans in Nyasaland were severely strained and in some cases deeply damaged; the economic and social development of the country was distressingly slowed down; and the chances of the Federation's survival, with all its economic and potential race relations benefits, was cast into the gravest doubt.

Still, out of all these unfortunate happenings emerged hope: hope from the Africans' point of view of rapid and smooth progress to independence; hope from the British and Nyasaland governments' perspective that this prospect could be achieved in a peaceful environment. Nyasaland's motto was *Lux in tenebris*: it was the 1959–60 crisis that showed there was light at the end of the political darkness into which the country had been plunged.

It is the purpose of this book to examine what happened during the emergency in Nyasaland in 1959 and 1960 which brought about a complete change in the British and Nyasaland governments' policy in Nyasaland, and therefore in Central Africa as a whole and wider afield. Its focus, naturally, is on Nyasaland itself but often it shifts to what was happening in Whitehall and Westminster. It shifts occasionally, too, to Southern Rhodesia: to Salisbury, the seat of the federal and Southern Rhodesia governments, and to Gwelo and Khami prisons, where Banda and 120 of his Congress colleagues were imprisoned. Although much of the detail is about other people, especially the Governor, Armitage – upon whom rested the practical burden of handling the emergency – behind all the events stands the short, mercurial figure of Banda, wearing dark spectacles, dressed in a British-tailored three-piece suit and carrying a flywhisk: determined, unbending, resolute yet, once the crisis had broken, patient – knowing then that he could not fail to secure self-government for Nyasaland and secession from the Federation.

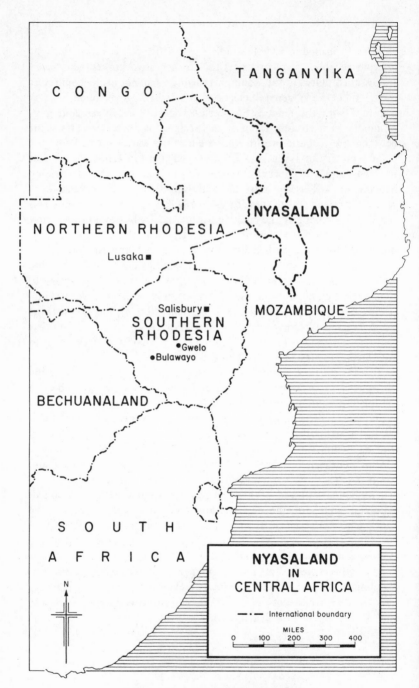

Map 1 Nyasaland in Central Africa

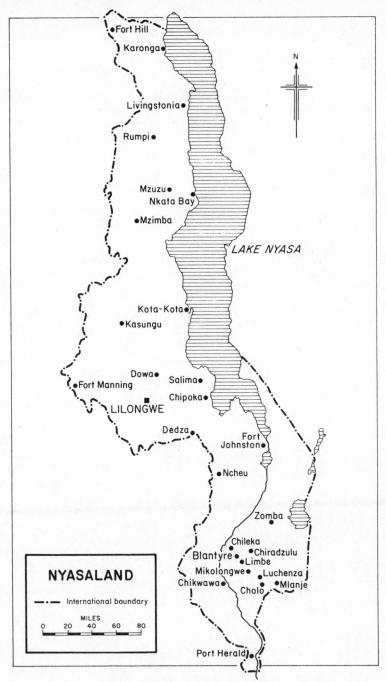

Map 2 Nyasaland

I

The seeds of crisis

Nyasaland may have federation imposed upon it but it will not be by the choice of any of the Protectorate's native population.

The steps taken to achieve closer association between the three British territories in Central Africa were hesitant and protracted.[1] Pushed by Southern Rhodesia and the non-official Europeans of Northern Rhodesia and Nyasaland except the missionaries, they were resisted by the Labour Party, the Nyasaland Governor Sir Geoffrey Colby[2] and – overwhelmingly, persistently and unequivocally – by the Africans of Nyasaland. As the *Nyasaland Times* said: 'Nyasaland may have federation imposed upon it but it will not be by the choice of any of the Protectorate's native population.'[3] The turning point came with the report of the officials' conference in June 1951 – set up by the Labour government – which concluded that the need for action was urgent and recommended that closer association should be brought about by a federation rather than amalgamation.[4] The point of no return had come with the decision by Lyttelton, Conservative secretary of state, in November 1951 that federation should be pursued.[5] Thereafter things were driven fast and the Federation came into existence on 1 August 1953.

With the Federation accomplished, the secretary of state – now Lennox-Boyd – turned his mind to altering the Nyasaland constitution so as to increase African representation. In announcing a new constitution on 15 June 1955 he said the executive council would remain unchanged but that the new legislative council – with a life of four years – would comprise 12 official members including the Governor, five African non-official members elected by the African provincial councils, and six non-African non-official members elected on a non-African electoral roll by constituencies. He hoped the various communities in Nyasaland would get together and see if they could agree future changes in the constitution so as to avoid a racial approach to politics.[6]

In elections held in March 1956 – the month Colby was succeeded by Sir Robert Armitage – Congress candidates secured all five African seats: M.W.K. Chiume in the North, J.R.N. Chinyama and D.W. Chijozi in the Centre, and H.B.M. Chipembere and N.D. Kwenje in the South. Only Chiume had a majority of votes cast although Chipembere almost received a majority.[7] These two were much younger than the others and much more extreme in their views. By their attacks in legislative council and adamant opposition to federation: 'the Governor was left in no doubt that he could not succeed in his policies and that he was dealing with a new group of African militants that could not be contained by traditional methods of being nice to the Africans'.[8]

Despite their outspokenness and exploitation of Hansard as a means of widespread free publicity – 'virtually a mouthpiece for Congress' – Chiume and Chipembere were frustrated that they were making no impression on the British or Nyasaland governments in their demands for self-government and secession from the Federation, and they felt their militancy was causing Armitage to 'harden' in his attitude towards their demands: 'he became more and more anti-Congress'.[9] At this point, too, the secretary of state made great play of announcing that the Federation was permanent.[10] Faced with these rebuffs, Chipembere, strongly supported by Chiume, pressed Banda – for long an adamant opponent of closer association and now living in West Africa – to return to Nyasaland and lead Congress. Others, including Doig of the Church of Scotland, also encouraged him to return to Nyasaland.[11] Chipembere felt that Banda, a man of maturity, a medical practitioner and with a Western education, could be built up to become a powerful leader despite having left Nyasaland over forty years earlier and having lived in the meantime in Southern Rhodesia, South Africa, the United States of America, Great Britain and Ghana.[12] Banda was initially cautious and reluctant to return, but changed his mind in April 1957. The 1953 Order in Council creating the Federation provided for a review of its provisions between seven and nine years later.[13] In April 1957, at the insistence of Welensky, federal prime minister, the British government announced the review would take place at the earliest time, in 1960, and would consider a programme for attaining a status which would enable the Federation to become a full – dominion – member of the Commonwealth.[14] Banda's deep worry now was that, since the existing legislative council in Nyasaland was not due to be replaced until 1960, Nyasaland Africans would not have majority representation which could make their views prevail at the federal review conference.

At its annual conference in August 1957 Congress expelled the two

Nyasaland African members of the federal parliament, W.M. Chirwa and C.R. Kumbikano, because continued membership was inconsistent with opposition to federation, and – repeating a request made 11 months earlier by the Salisbury branch of Congress and more recently by T.D.T. Banda, the Nyasaland Congress president – invited Dr Banda to return to lead the struggle for self-government and secession.[15] The following month Congress sent a delegation (T.D.T. Banda, Chisiza,[16] Chiume and Chipembere) to the Governor to seek constitutional reform, with a legislative council of 40 – 32 Africans and six non-Africans elected on universal suffrage and two ex-officio members – and an executive council of two officials with the remainder elected by the legislature. Armitage felt these proposals were too advanced and impracticable, although he neither accepted nor rejected them.[17] When the delegation pressed him for his own proposals he refused, saying he needed first to consult other communities and it would be better – as Lennox-Boyd had asked in 1955 – if Congress met with European political leaders and tried to reach agreement between them.[18]

On 6 March 1958 the secretary of state announced that the Nyasaland government itself was unlikely to come forward with proposals before the late summer, and when a Congress delegation saw Armitage a month later he said he had early 1959 in mind. This alarmed Congress because they felt such late proposals, even if accepted, could not lead to legislation and elections early enough for Nyasalanders to have a strongly representative voice at the 1960 federal review conference. They thus sent a delegation to see Lennox-Boyd on 13 June, this time led by Dr Banda, accompanied by Chief Ntaja, Chipembere and Chiume.[19] At the delegation's meeting with Lennox-Boyd they reiterated the proposal given to Armitage and emphasised, now even more clearly, their deep anxiety for early constitutional reform to enable the Nyasaland African viewpoint to be made strongly at the 1960 federal review conference. Lennox-Boyd assured them that he understood their anxieties and added that he expected Armitage's recommendations after his return to Nyasaland from leave in August. The secretary of state said 'there were going to be constitutional changes which would enable the Africans to get political advantage'.[20] Three days previously, Armitage and Banda had met at the flat which Armitage had taken in St. James' Court while he was on leave. The Governor found the doctor 'a fanatic on wanting Nyasaland independent [but] pleasant to talk to and good mannered'. The meeting was at Banda's request and Armitage welcomed it because, knowing of the doctor's 'intense political opinions', he felt it important to find out whether they 'were going to be able to work together'.[21]

Arriving back in Nyasaland, Chipembere – who for some time 'had taken pains to paint Banda as a supernatural Messiah'[22] – found his fellow Congressmen very keen that Banda should join them as soon as possible, and he telegraphed the doctor asking him to return on 29 June. This he failed to do, to the consternation of the crowd assembled at Chileka airport to greet him.[23] However, the following Sunday, 6 July 1958, Banda did return.[24] Chiume made the introductory speech at Chileka in which he said Banda had come to lead them but he had come to carry out the wishes of the people, and he, like anyone else who did not follow the wishes of the people, would have to go if he did not do so.[25] Chiume repeated the point the same day at Soche: 'Dr Banda should be our leader so long as he toes the party line.'[26] On the evening of Banda's arrival Chiume, Chipembere, Chisiza and other Congress leaders met in secret and agreed that Banda would remain their leader as long as he accepted their policy, but no longer.[27]

2

The crisis gathers

Which was going to prevail? Constitutional talks and ordinary arguments on political reform here, or a pattern of disorders making a state of emergency inevitable?

At its annual conference on 1 August 1958 Congress elected Banda president-general with exclusive power to appoint officers and executive committee members. He chose Chipembere as treasurer, Chiume as publicity secretary and Chisiza – not yet returned to Nyasaland from studying in Britain[1] – as secretary-general. In doing this he ignored the older, more moderate elements in Congress in favour of the younger, more vigorous and extreme elements.[2] The other members of the executive committee were Rose Chibambo, Chakuluka, Lawrence Makata and Lali Lubani, the latter two being mature and moderate businessmen. Probably under the influence of the less moderate leaders, Banda now began to eschew social contact with Europeans.[3]

Two weeks later the Governor returned from leave and stated that he had no announcement to make on constitutional changes but wished to complete his discussions with all political parties and then come forward with proposals. Congress were disappointed: encouraged by overseas press reports, they had assumed when Lennox-Boyd said he expected the Governor to produce proposals after his return from leave, this had meant immediately on his return.[4]

In the following three months, in addition to settling into his medical practice, Banda had a number of meetings with the Governor, the secretary for African affairs, the acting chief secretary and heads of department. He also made speeches all over the country and his audiences 'hung on his every word'.[5] Since this was an agriculturally inactive period, before the rains, and thus a period of relative leisure for rural dwellers, he commanded very large audiences – up to 20,000 in the north – with time to listen and react to his rhetoric.[6]

The government quickly became aware of the effect of Banda's return, his reorganisation of Congress and his speeches. As early as

August Armitage gave Lennox-Boyd a 'definite warning that disorders were virtually certain in or before 1960' and there would have to be a 'show-down' with Congress. Within a month of his return from leave he commented privately on 'an intensity of African political activity' although at this time he felt W.M. Chirwa was 'making the public running' and not Banda who 'seems to be biding his time'. He also said: 'I am afraid that the African politicians are going to get obstreperous soon, so we are going to be kept busy.' Chisiza later said that for Congress 'August to November was a period of understandable suspicion, conspicuous suspense and anxious waiting' and he attributed this to the government not coming forward with constitutional proposals and Banda's inability to inform his people of any progress.[7]

At a Nyasaland intelligence committee meeting on 7 October Youens, acting chief secretary, set out government's assessment of the security situation and gave clues as to their tactics for combating it.[8] They thought Banda would resort to specific action against the government in order to maintain the interest and support of the African population, but would not divulge his tactics until Armitage announced constitutional changes early in 1959.

> Government considered it advisable to hit Congress with all possible provocative measures in order to force Banda into taking some unconstitutional action. In this respect it was being contemplated whether to announce the federalisation of non-African agriculture, should the Government decide to accept the federal government's proposals, at the same time as [the Governor] announced his constitutional revision – which proposals will in no way satisfy the Congress extremists.[9]

Youens also dealt with the action to be taken against pro-Congress chiefs possibly by deposing them in the south and centre, but in the north all the chiefs were anti-federation and it would be highly dangerous to adopt any preventative measures against them 'in case the whole country were set aflame'. Indeed, the Federal Intelligence and Security Bureau (FISB) officer present gathered that the government was apprehensive about taking any action in the north.[10]

At a meeting with Ingham, secretary for African affairs, later in October,[11] Banda complained about the injustice of having only five African members in the legislature and none in executive council, but declined the offer of a seat for himself on executive council which he was then offered.[12]

> He said he conceived his task as being that of organising the people ...
> to bring about the degree of pressure required to right the basic wrong regarding political rights for the Africans of Nyasaland.[13]

Bloodshed did not form part of his programme, and when Ingham countered by saying a mass movement such as he was trying to organise was liable to get out of hand, the doctor said the Nyasaland people were basically peace loving and most unlikely to get out of hand. They did not discuss federation or any details of territorial constitutional advance. The discussions were amicable and devoid of any bitterness. Banda did, however, decline an invitation to lunch, but looked forward to a more formal meeting with the chief secretary.[14]

Some of Banda's public speeches were followed by demonstrations, including stone-throwing by Africans against Europeans. The *Nyasaland Times* made a big issue of one of these incidents, referring to 'a raw display of racial hatred without parallel in the country'. They criticised the government for not allowing the police to break up the crowds and they demanded a public inquiry.[15] Armitage was convinced the criticism was a campaign to get the police placed under federal control since 'the extremist Europeans' felt they would thereby get better protection.[16] Banda's speeches – in which he would often begin 'quietly and urbanely' but later speak more loudly, 'blustering', 'forceful and bombastic' and finish up shouting[17] – everywhere raised great enthusiasm and expectations among his African audiences, many of whom now felt that constitutional advance, self-government and secession were inevitable and imminent. 'The frenzy into which he worked himself was almost embarrassing ... but the hysterical displays were undeniably effective.'[18] Armitage privately acknowledged that the doctor was 'a clever spell binder'.[19] It was felt by Europeans with long knowledge of the country that 'the natural cheerfulness and courtesy of the [African] people began to disappear – probably due to intimidation'.[20] Many also observed that 'the rallies caused an immediate sense of expectation and excitement among ordinary Nyasalanders. Civil disturbances and aggressive bloody-mindedness became the norm.'[21] District commissioners noticed that:

> After Dr Banda had addressed a few rallies, the mode of his followers changed noticeably from one of exuberance to that of aggression [and] raised clenched fists were much in evidence for the first time.[22]

More and more requests were received for the police mobile force (PMF) to support local police to cover the increasing number of political meetings. Banda's main meetings were in the townships, typically at a market, and normally at weekends. The usual problems of policing were exacerbated by these meetings and although Chiume believed the PMF were used 'on the flimsiest of pretexts', Armitage thought Mullin, commissioner of police, was 'going to have a very difficult time'. Congress women's groups baiting the police were especially difficult to handle. The Youth League were always present in force and tried to usurp the crowd control duties of the police. Police vehicles for observing and recording the speeches were often surrounded by crowds who rocked them and tantalised the men in them to distract the recording. The speeches caused great alarm among the non-African communities who criticised the government for not taking more effective and tougher action against the demonstrators.[23]

In fact the government was not inactive as the local press alleged but was taking the early steps needed for more effective action later. These steps were taken in consultation with the head of special branch, Thomson, assistant commissioner of police. He had been in Nyasaland since 1949, having previously served in Palestine, Tanganyika and Germany. He left the protectorate in December 1958, three months before his fiftieth birthday. Armitage considered him 'most competent' in collecting information but was doubtful as to his analysis of trends, and consequently did not try to dissuade him when he asked to retire because the Governor did not agree to his request to be given a higher status and be consulted more frequently. He was succeeded by Finney, who had arrived in Nyasaland in September 1958. Finney was then approaching his fifty-fourth birthday and, having been in the Indian Police from 1924 to 1947 – much of his work being concerned with security, intelligence, terrorism and detainees – had spent 11 years as a salesman with Guinness before being asked (he did not apply) to take the job in Nyasaland. Armitage considered Finney to be 'in the top rank of special branch officers'. The Nyasaland special branch liaised closely with other intelligence agencies including the FISB, whose director, de Quehen, reported directly to Welensky.[24]

In November, Finney revised the lists of those to be arrested in the event of trouble. These, known as 'Sunrise' lists, had existed since at least 1954 and were reviewed annually. The new revision was undertaken because the intelligence committee contemplated trouble in May or June 1959. Of the names on the revised lists 268 were in the northern, 218 in the central and 131 in the southern province.[25]

For the first three weeks in December Banda was away from Nyasaland attending the All-African People's Conference held at Accra in Ghana. The conference declared

> full support of all fighters for freedom in Africa, to all those who resort to peaceful means of non-violence and civil disobedience as well as to all those who are compelled to retaliate against violence to attain national independence and freedom for the people.[26]

This was a compromise between those drawing the line at peaceful means and those advocating violence, and was taken by Chiume to mean that 'while advocating peaceful means to the achievement of independence, [it] did not rule out the use of force when peaceful means would not yield results'.[27] FISB sources reported that Banda had secret meetings with the Russian delegates, other Congress leaders from Central Africa, and the Rev. Michael Scott, who advised that a Central Africa Congress should be set up. The conference also called for the formation of an African legion of volunteers who would be ready to protect the freedom of the African people and break up the Federation of Rhodesia and Nyasaland.[28] 'Nkrumah held the center of all attention when he attended a session, and Tom Mboya ran second in adulation. In the huge gathering, no leader was quite as ignored as Banda.'[29]

While the doctor was in Ghana, legislative council granted additional powers to the government to control crowds and punish the stoning of vehicles.[30] Armitage authorised special branch to tap Banda's telephone in Limbe, and for the following three months incoming and outgoing calls were automatically recorded. Although some interesting background information was picked up, the interceptions were not of much use to special branch.[31]

Banda returned via Salisbury and intended to fly on to Nyasaland the following day, a Sunday, but at the Nyasaland government's request – fearing weekend demonstrations – the airline withheld his booking until Monday. Additionally, customs officials subjected his baggage to a minute inspection lasting over an hour. Furious, he gave vent to his feelings the following day when he addressed a mass meeting in the African township of New Highlands, urging Africans to go to prison in their thousands 'singing Hallelujah' and vowing to break the 'stupid and hellish' Federation.[32] On Monday his arrival at Chileka was a quiet affair because the police had refused his followers permission to meet him at the airport or to line the streets. Even so, up to 5000 awaited his arrival in Blantyre during their lunch break to greet him and shout Congress slogans.[33] At a public meeting on 28 December he repeatedly expressed his readiness to be arrested and again told his audience they must be ready to be imprisoned in their thousands for the sake of freedom.[34] A few days earlier in a television interview he had said that he would fight federation, not with violence but he could not exclude violence if they were not allowed to secede from the Federation,[35] and Chipembere had warned his own audience that in times of violence those who sided with the Europeans would be destroyed.[36] Chiume left Accra 'elated that [they] were part of the continent's struggle for emancipation' and the conference had 'tremendously rejuvenated' them.[37]

By the very early part of January 1959, although Armitage privately, but unconvincingly, said he hoped Banda would spend so much time on his medical practice that he would have little time for 'touring around', he and his colleagues were taking very seriously the possibility of grave trouble. The doctor had, of course, already toured a great deal and stimulated much excitement and expectation in his audiences. Armitage was convinced there would be 'more trouble than games in the next few months'.[38]

One of the steps the Governor now took was to call for a report on emergency prison and detention accommodation from Cameron, the federal director of prisons, and Theunissen, the operations officer in Nyasaland. A review had been made in July 1958 'from which it became evident that should circumstances arise when any substantial number of persons had to be arrested, additional prison and detention accommodation would certainly be required'. Meetings between Nyasaland and federal officials were held in September and November to discuss additional accommodation.[39] The problem with which they dealt was:

> To provide prison and detention accommodation for 250 persons (subsequently revised up to 500 persons) immediately detained in the event of an emergency and for up to 4000 persons who might have to be taken into custody at a later stage and held either on remand or as convicted persons.[40]

In their report they were particularly careful about responsibilities because, as they noted, otherwise 'there will inevitably arise faults of omission and commission'. The federal authorities insisted the responsibility for detention centres – as opposed to prisons holding detainees – should be that of the Nyasaland government. Theunissen felt this made Nyasaland 'stool pigeons': if anything went wrong, they would be blamed and the federal prison service would not be responsible. The target date for stockpiling barbed wire and poles, for completing detailed planning and organisation, and for constructing non-secret works, was 28 February. In fact, action was being taken while their investigation was in progress, because it became clear that additional accommodation would be required sooner than they had thought.[41]

Banda met Youens on 5 January[42] and when asked if he was prepared to compromise on any aspect of Congress's constitutional proposals the doctor remained firm on an overall African majority in the legislature. He was, however, prepared to compromise on executive council with three ex-officio members, two European and six African non-officials with the Governor as president.[43] Youens got the impression he might also compromise over legislative council by agreeing to a rather larger official representation than the three proposed by

Congress. Each alternative proposal Youens put forward, however, was rejected. Youens received two particular impressions. First, Banda was determined to go to gaol and he repeated this point: the acting chief secretary lost count after the sixth repetition. Second, the doctor had staked more than he could afford or wished to lose on the chance of 'quick returns'.

> Financially and maybe politically, he sees himself in 'Queer Street' unless he delivers the goods at an early date. He sees perhaps one way of buying time is to go to gaol.[44]

Youens shrewdly detected the dilemma in which Banda found himself. The doctor had stomped the country raising his followers to a fever pitch of anticipation but Armitage was not coming forward with the statement on constitutional advance which had been expected on Armitage's return from leave. Chisiza shortly said:

> But August and September came and went without any statement. So did October and November. In the meanwhile Dr Banda continued to have with [the Governor] constitutional talks the exact nature of which the anxious masses were not permitted to know ... there was a time when people were tempted to think that Dr Banda was making a clandestine deal with [Armitage] which would leave them worse off than before he came.[45]

Chisiza and other members of the central executive also became worried about how they were to explain to Congress any compromises which Banda might have to make.

Youens in fact had a number of meetings with Banda[46] and he subsequently recalled, concerning the rising violence:

> I asked Dr Banda to come and see me and he would say, well, it was all very regrettable because, of course, he didn't believe in violence; he wanted to get his way by constitutional means. So I said, 'Well, why don't you tell your people this, and stop them doing what they are doing?' He said, 'Oh, their feelings are too strong for me to do that'. And I looked at him and he looked at me, and he just burst into laughter. He was quite cynical about the situation really.

Youens believed Banda created a lawless situation 'quite deliberately although of course paying lip-service, with a sort of grin in his eyes, to the fact that it was not his aim to achieve his ends by violence but by what he described as constitutional means'. He was convinced – and told Armitage – that by the time Banda returned to Nyasaland he had worked out that the quickest way to persuade Britain to give him what he wanted was to produce a situation in which the country became ungovernable and which would lead to his incarceration.

Armitage's general feeling at this time was that the government were 'going to have [their] work cut out to avoid trouble'.[47] He was concerned particularly about the increasing violence over the past few months:

> Agricultural legislation ... came under attack by Congress and Dr Banda said that with self-government such irksome legislation would be abolished. Following a public meeting held by Dr Banda in Fort Johnston District in September 1958, Government officers encountered serious opposition and threats of violence by the villagers.

Agricultural legislation was widely disobeyed and in October, while police were trying to make arrests, they met with strong resistance and were attacked by a crowd. The riot proclamation had to be read and the crowd was dispersed with tear smoke and batons. Similar incidents were reported from Kota Kota. In Cholo, Congress leaders incited people to disobey the agricultural rules, saying that they had instructions from Banda that all the rules had been withdrawn.[48]

> Trends toward violence had been noted for some time in speeches by Congress leaders. In December reference was being made by Congress supporters in the Northern Province, to violence and Mau Mau. During January there were open demonstrations of hostility towards Europeans and Asians by Africans in the urban areas. Six illegal meetings and two unlawful processions took place in the Zomba District alone and illegal Congress meetings took place elsewhere also. Twice crowds attending Congress meetings in Zomba were incited to go and release persons in police custody, and on the second occasion ... the Riot Proclamation had to be read, stone throwing took place and the police had to use force to disperse the crowd. At Blantyre, following a meeting addressed by Dr Banda on the 18th January, three cars were involved in incidents of stone throwing.[49]

During January the Governor discussed hospital and school security with federal ministers, and noted that all European nurses had been withdrawn from outstation hospitals.[50] He was conscious his deliberations were taking place against a background of very sensitive European opinion, frightened by riots in the Congo and recollections of Mau Mau in Kenya, which believed the government was doing nothing to maintain law and order. His immediate priorities were, first, to 'clean up the trouble spots and then prevent disorder' and, second, to hold talks on a new constitution and 'have it in force by May 1960'.[51] On 12 January he wrote to the Colonial Office suggesting that constitutional advance could best be dealt with by a personal visit by Lennox-Boyd.[52] The secretary of state agreed and said that since he would be visiting Somaliland and Aden in mid-February, he proposed to travel on to Nyasaland, arriving on Saturday 21 February. He would then have initial talks with the Governor and discussions 'with all concerned' so that on the last day they could 'decide ... what we ought to do subject to the consideration of the representations by the federal government', which he would consult on 27 February. He would then return to London on 28 February.[53]

Armitage replied that the visit was 'most welcome', but it would be unwise to arrive on a Saturday and via Salisbury. As on many occasions, he tried to avoid risking disturbances at weekends and preferred potentially troublesome events to be scheduled for Mondays when many people, especially in the townships, would be at work. Presumably, too, he did not want Welensky to speak with the secretary of state in Salisbury before discussions had taken place, and views had been formed, in Nyasaland. In any event he wanted the announcement of the visit to 'be delayed as long as possible ... in order to curtail the period of possible demonstrations'.[54]

Lennox-Boyd cabled Armitage on 2 February saying he had to be back in London by 19 March and if he came at all he must reach Nyasaland on Saturday 21 February; he hoped to do so direct from Nairobi. He concluded: '[I] assume your objections to arrival on 21 February are not so serious that you would prefer me not to come at all.'[55] With this implied threat, Armitage quickly agreed to his arrival on 21 February.[56] Whether Lennox-Boyd was irritated by Armitage's reluctance over the date of arrival is not known, but he did minute to the prime minister on 4 February, saying he wished Perth, his minister of state, to make an early visit to East Africa during the first three weeks of March, adding:

> I had hoped to go to Nyasaland but I have dropped this plan because of the need for me to be back in London while you are away. This will be a bit of a blow to the Governor of Nyasaland and also to Roy Welensky. I therefore think that it would be a good idea if Perth went a little earlier than he would otherwise have to and spent a week in Nyasaland and Southern Rhodesia ... leaving the U.K. about 21 February and returning back 22 March.[57]

Macmillan agreed, saying he was pleased Perth was going and 'It may be necessary to deal with Dr Banda. If so, the ground must be well prepared.'[58]

It is likely the words 'deal with Dr Banda' were taken to mean 'handle him firmly' or 'put him in his place', although a year later they could more certainly be taken to mean 'treat with him' or 'have dealings with him'.

The change of plans was indeed a blow to Armitage but he hoped they would still 'provide for a very early consideration of constitutional changes'. Anxious to announce the visit, he cabled the Colonial Office on 13 February: 'Time presses'; and was further disappointed two days later when told the visit might be postponed for a week and no announcement should yet be made. On 16 February, however, Perth's arrival date was agreed as 26 February and he would stay until 5 or 6 March. Armitage strongly urged an immediate announcement and steps to avoid Welensky meeting him in Salisbury on the way; to do otherwise would be a tactical error and he also wanted the maximum time with him in Zomba.[59]

While arrangements were being made for the visit, Armitage and Dixon – the senior non-official member of executive council – saw Banda at Government House on 20 January. This meeting was Banda's response to the government's wish that Congress should consult with European opinion concerning constitutional advance. Banda told Youens on 5 January that he had always been willing to consult in this way and was prepared to meet with Armitage and Dixon. Armitage hoped very much that Banda would meet European politicians and 'make a rapprochement with the other races', but the only way he could get this done was to be present himself when Banda saw Dixon.[60] Banda was surprised that the Governor opened this meeting by saying he had called it to get the doctor's views on constitutional reform, because he had already told him what his views were.[61] He was surprised too that Armitage was still having to consult with the Europeans, and thought he had finished these consultations. When asked for his views Dixon said he had heard about Congress's demands and the people he represented could not accept them; the most he would accept was eight Africans on legislative council and two on executive council, with an official majority in both. Banda recalled:

> The Governor suggested that the number of European officials should be reduced to about eight, so that there would be ... eight African and eight official members and six Europeans, and I did not accept that, because Congress wanted 32, and I told them I was willing to go half way. I did not care whether we had 18 or 20 as long as we had the majority.

Armitage supported Dixon and gave Banda the impression – correctly – that the reason he opposed a majority was that 'we might vote ourselves out of federation'. When in a speech a few days later Banda appealed for patience, he was hoping that having discussed matters and come to no agreement, the Governor would now make his own recommendations:

> I was hoping that after the Governor had made recommendations and there had been ... some official announcement I would still go back and negotiate on the basis of what they suggested.

Earlier that day Armitage talked with Greenfield, federal minister of law and in charge of discussions on constitutional change, and found him 'equally as stubborn' as Banda, 'in other directions'. The day had been one of the most exhausting and frustrating he had ever had,[62] but it was not yet over.

When Banda left Government House he addressed a public meeting and gave two indications that he might be prepared to compromise. First he said, 'We will not accept anything that is not reasonably near our demands' and, second, 'We insist on having at least a majority in Legislative Council' – he said nothing about executive council. After this public meeting a large crowd – incited by Chipembere – marched on Zomba police station to try and release some women who were held there. They threw stones, damaged buildings and were dispersed only after the riot proclamation had been read and tear smoke and batons had been used.[63]

On the same day Armitage wrote to Gorell Barnes about the action he might take if, as he believed, 'disorders and trouble' occurred in the coming few months when they announced the federalisation of non-African agriculture and the proposed constitutional changes.[64] Offering the former of these may have been designed to secure non-African acquiescence in the latter, but more likely, as Youens had hinted, it was a 'provocative measure' to force Banda into 'some unconstitutional action'. Armitage did not think a 'fairly violent, but short-lived, eruption' could be handled by arresting Congress leaders and charging them with criminal offences so as to bring about a fairly sudden collapse of opposition as in 1953. Now, Congress was much better organised, emotions would be 'far more deeply stirred' and trouble more widespread, with an undercurrent of dissatisfaction and opposition to law and order which could readily be exploited by those left in control of Congress. He thought too that Chipembere and Chiume would definitely not put themselves in jeopardy of arrest but he was less sure of Banda. He then turned to a number of alternatives. First he could declare Congress an unlawful society, a solution he would have to consider 'in the light of the circumstances then prevailing'.[65] Second, he could place restriction orders on the Congress leaders,[66] but Nyasaland was not a large country and did not have well-defined inaccessible areas, which ruled out any comprehensive use of restriction orders. In any event, the three people still restricted after the 1953 disturbances were 'at liberty to meet [and did meet] a variety of agitators'. These difficulties could be overcome by the third possibility, detention, but introducing detention legislation 'would give advance notice of [his] intentions and action under its provisions would carry its own complications'. Although he asked Gorell Barnes's views on introducing a Detention Bill 'if and when trouble seems imminent', detention was not Armitage's preferred option, which was deportation:

> Clearly, the most effective and clean-cut procedure in our circumstances would be to deport the few top-level leaders who might remain at large after disorders had been quelled.

He asked if the British government would agree to deportation[67] and if so, whether they would 'make arrangements with, say, the Government of the Seychelles for such agitators to be placed with them'. He added, 'Dr Banda has already suggested that we may want to do this to him, so if we had to, it would not come as a great shock.' He did not at this stage suggest handling matters by declaring a state of emergency.

By the end of January, however, the declaration of a state of emergency had become very much part of Armitage's thinking: the necessary regulations were prepared and ready for use, and Footman, the chief secretary, was 'going hard on getting the emergency prepared for'. As Armitage wrote privately, 'We are busy coordinating [Royal Rhodesian Air Force] and military moves if the Congress ever get too excited and try to push things to the point of civil disobedience.'[68]

Welensky, significantly worried by events in the protectorate, now asked Armitage whether it would embarrass him if army reinforcements were moved to Nyasaland from Lusaka. The Governor did not want this yet but he discussed with his security advisers what reinforcements might be required 'to be ready for a security situation being sparked off prematurely'. Three days later he felt they were now 'fairly clear' about their requirements.[69]

Civil servants returning from overseas leave early in 1959, having been away for several months, noticed a different atmosphere – 'an unfamiliar air of apprehension'[70] – and even in the north the change was 'palpable':

> Instead of the sleepy outpost, where there had really been nothing to note in [our] monthly political intelligence report, we now had frequent political meetings held throughout the district, and incidents of truculence and intimidation ... The old style trust [of] European officers was too often replaced by fear, provocation and dispute.[71]

This change was obvious to missionaries as well. At Livingstonia there was 'a strange change of atmosphere [and] some of the students ... were not quite so friendly as usual'.[72] Private employers in commerce noticed 'a sullenness amongst the work force which was previously not evident'.[73] Lord Salisbury, visiting Southern Rhodesia at the end of January, experienced 'a feeling of intense anxiety about the situation in Nyasaland, which was very noticeable':

> I met an old friend in the streets of Salisbury who spoke with the gravest anxiety about the safety of his wife and children who were in Nyasaland. There was no doubt about his sincerity. He was really in a state of torture.[74]

When Kettlewell, director of agriculture and a member of executive council, returned from leave in January 1959, having been away since July 1958, he noticed the great and 'very apparent' difference and was so concerned that he and Ingham saw the Governor and

> suggested that some special organisation should be set up to handle [the security situation]. We had little confidence in [the chief secretary's] ability to cope with it: he didn't know the country well enough and seldom left Zomba. [Armitage] did not comment much on our proposal at the time ... but he evidently considered it and later set up the [Nyasaland] Operations Committee.[75]

Other criticisms came from the commissioner of police, Mullin, who, when he arrived in April 1958, was told by Thomson that he anticipated security trouble and did not have confidence in the upper reaches of the secretariat to accept responsibility for how it was handled.[76] Mullin recalled:

> I was soon to discover that a deep rift existed between [the chief secretary] with other senior administrative staff and myself as Commissioner and my Special Branch officer. This invariably arose during the compilation of the monthly intelligence report under the chairmanship of [the chief secretary] who ... displayed a tendency to exclude or reduce the impact of unfavourable developments [and] we reached the stage that he declined to complete the signing of the report stating that he wished to consult His Excellency first.[77]

It may be that to the chief secretary's natural caution and tendency to play down unfavourable developments was added a desire to protect the Governor after Armitage's experience in Cyprus, and not highlight difficulties unless it was necessary to do so.[78]

Illegal processions and meetings – including those held under the guise of religious meetings in African churches[79] – became more common after December and, although the police gained a good deal of experience in dealing with them, the experience showed Armitage that 'if trouble was caused regularly and spread widely, the police would not have the men and the equipment to deal with it'.[80]

Early in January 1959 Chisiza secured Banda's agreement to call an emergency meeting of chairmen and secretaries of Congress branches for the weekend 24–25 January to 'charge them with enthusiasm and inspire them to new and higher administrative goals', to secure a vote of confidence in Banda's leadership which had been criticised by W.M. Chirwa and others, and to discuss fund raising since there was a threat that Congress branches in Southern Rhodesia, the source of much of their funding, would be banned.[81] During the Saturday meeting in Ndirande hall a crowd of 2000 gathered outside and listened to the proceedings inside relayed through loud speakers. Afterwards groups collected in Blantyre and 'had to be chased away by police'. These events were noted in Armitage's private diary on the day they occurred.[82] He also noted on 25 January:

> Dr Banda had a conference of Congress branch delegates and I hope we shall hear later what plan they have. I can't believe he will want to spark widespread trouble which might involve the leaders of Congress and so prevent it from carrying on while they were absent from the scene.[83]

Armitage's reference to 'absence from the scene' suggests he already had in mind detaining, deporting or restricting Congress leaders although he believed that any trouble Banda caused would not be sufficiently widespread to merit arresting all the leaders. His inability to believe Banda would spark widespread trouble suggests that others did believe it or at least the possibility had been mooted. His hope to hear what plan Congress had suggests he fully expected the meeting to have a plan; they, of course, would take steps to ensure he did not learn about any plan they might have.

On Sunday the venue provisionally decided on was too small and an alternative, an open site in the bush – the former site of Chief Kachapila's village – just outside Limbe, was selected at very short notice. It may also have been the case that, after the disturbances of the previous evening, Congress officials 'decided to hold their meeting in an unrecognisable place solely for public safety', feeling that if the location were known to the police a clash would be inevitable: 'this was not in the interests' of Congress. One hundred and forty delegates were taken to the new site in a lorry by a Congress employee who was paid as a 'freedom fighter'. Although all the other Congress leaders were present, Banda did not attend, but Armitage believed it was held at his direction. All present were required to preserve the secrecy of the proceedings – special branch believed they were sworn to secrecy under threat of death – and so effective was this requirement that it took some time before Armitage could learn much about what had taken place.[84]

The Governor gave his provincial commissioners preliminary details of the meeting on 7 February.[85] Welensky learned of the meeting from his own sources three days later.[86] It took Finney time fully to receive, check, collate and analyse the reports from his sources but by 13 February this task was sufficiently complete for him to report:

> At this secret meeting ... it was decided by the Congress High Command, and instructions given to delegates accordingly, that there should be illegal meetings and processions from then on until the announcement of the Constitutional Reform. It was also decided that there should be a widespread campaign of assassination of Government officials, murder of European men, women and children and wholesale sabotage in the event of Dr Banda's arrest. A general strike ... was to be staged if Dr Banda did not agree with the Constitutional Reform.[87]

The illegal meetings were not intended to be violent: people were encouraged to offer themselves for arrest 'in a passive manner'. Congress was appointing 'security detectives' to denounce loyal Africans; setting up an 'intelligence school' to train members to get information about government forces and police informers; placing someone in the police camp to report on police movements; and setting up an organisation to secure information on European habits, arms and ammunition. If Banda were arrested, Chipembere, Chisiza, Chiume and Rose Chibambo should run Congress in his absence, notify all branches of the arrest, and fix a day, 'R-Day', 10–21 days after the arrest, when violence was to begin. It seems that Congress, like Armitage, while expecting Banda's arrest, did not anticipate all the other leaders being arrested. The plan for 'R-Day' violence included widespread sabotage, murder of the Governor and other senior civil servants, missionaries, and other Europeans and Asians, including women and children. This plan, which came to be known as the 'murder plot', was to be taken to Congress chairmen and secretaries throughout Nyasaland by the conference delegates.[88]

On 18 February, Mullin asked for the Governor to be informed of his conviction that:

> the Nyasaland African Congress has prepared plans for the mass murder throughout the Protectorate of all ... Europeans and Asians, men, women and children, to take place in the event of Dr Banda being killed, arrested or abducted ... [T]his plan ... will be put into operation only in the event of something happening to Dr Banda, but the seeds of violence

have been sown and there is a great danger that action of this nature might be sparked off by an unfortunate incident.[89]

He felt immediate action had to be taken to avoid this grave trouble. Congress were claiming that three-quarters of the police and King's African Rifles (KAR) would defect if the plan were put into action and this possibility, with the smallness of the Nyasaland police force, persuaded Mullin that they should be immediately strengthened by flying a 'fire brigade' battalion from Britain. Unless such reinforcements were secured and action taken against Congress, they might be faced with a security situation beyond their control 'which we know would result in widespread murder, looting and destruction of property'.

Officials in the Colonial Office intelligence and security department were concerned about the reports from Nyasaland, and a senior officer on secondment from Uganda was sent to the protectorate to assess the position. He thought:

> Finney's analysis of the information about the 'plot' was probably correct. It seemed to fit the current attitudes of the main characters concerned. Obviously, one can never be certain of the veracity of an informant or the reliability of his reporting; but the Special Branch had to err, if anything, on the side of caution (in the sense of not underestimating the dangers) especially when the security situation was so tense. Finney himself was keen and energetic.[90]

On his return to London, he reported to the secretary of state that 'there was evidence for the plot coming from secret sources which could not be quoted', but he was 'not entirely happy about the handling of the situation in the field'. His contacts in Nyasaland were solely 'at the government level'. He would have liked to talk with some Africans but he encountered 'a sense of distance between Government House and the people, a feeling very different from that which existed in the era of Cohen's governorship of Uganda'.[91]

The federal government too was apprehensive of the developing trouble in Nyasaland and early in February senior officers of the federal army were told of the likely escalation. They established an operations room in Salisbury for federation-wide operational troop movements and communications, and for reinforcing the Zomba battalion of the KAR if it became necessary.[92]

Discussions on constitutional advance continued parallel with the rising lawlessness and the Governor's attempts to deal with it, and many suggestions for increasing African representation were proposed. In January, the United Federal Party, of which Blackwood and Dixon were the leading Nyasaland figures, worked on proposals through a committee chaired by Greenfield and agreed that their goal should be to form an elected and responsible government. They were unable to agree on either the composition or the size of the official or nominated groups in the legislature. It is not surprising that Armitage saw the party as being 'very un-united' and he was thus engaging in 'a process of trying to wear them down to come closer to realities'.[93]

In addition to these United Federal Party views, Armitage invited 'all groups in Nyasaland' to put forward suggestions for a new constitution, and received three – widely divergent – major proposals in response.[94] Banda stuck to the proposals given to the secretary of state over a year earlier: a legislature of 40 of whom 32 would be Africans, six European non-officials and two officials. This suggestion, with its massive African and non-official majority in the legislature, was far removed from what the British government and Armitage had in mind and were prepared to accept.[95] Sacranie, of the Asian Convention, suggested equal representation for Asians, Africans and Europeans, on both councils, which infuriated Banda who felt that Sacranie should have mentioned this when they met just before Sacranie flew off to London to make his proposals. Banda believed the Nyasaland government had suggested the parity proposals and encouraged Sacranie in them in order to combat Congress's demands for an all-African government, and he warned the Asians not to meddle in politics – which Armitage thought 'rather silly' because he ran the risk of alienating Nehru and 'nations of colour' whose support he would need in due course.[96] The third set of suggestions came from 'moderate groups of the European, African, Asian and Coloured communities' who worked together at the invitation of the United Federal Party. These groups suggested an equal number of Europeans and Africans on legislative council with an official majority; they saw no objection to Africans being members of executive council nor to non-official members holding portfolios. This suggestion coincided with government views of retaining an official majority in the legislature but was otherwise vague.[97] The *Manchester Guardian*,[98] noting that the chances of compromise between the widely varying suggestions were negligible and that the Governor must already realise this, succinctly stated Armitage's dilemma and thought he would have to come forward with his own proposals – as Congress had asked him to 18 months earlier and as Banda was expecting – and see what support they could win:

> The Nyasaland Government almost certainly recognises that Nyasaland must be an African State and ... ultimately have an African majority in its legislative council. [But] an African majority in 1960 is impracticable,

first because there is not sufficient 'Cabinet material' in Nyasaland to form an African Government, and secondly because in their present mood the first action of an African majority in the legislature would be to pass a motion demanding Nyasaland's secession from the Federation [which] would make it wellnigh impossible for the Federation to continue to operate in its present form.

It would be equally difficult ... to agree to the kind of set-up proposed by the United Federal Party ... whereby European unofficial members and Colonial Office officials between them would command a majority [because] on ... all the important issues of Federation itself, the officials would inevitably vote with European unofficial members thereby giving rise to accusations by Africans that officials were ruling only with the consent of 'white settlers'.

Armitage described his general approach during these negotiations, especially his approach to Congress:

There was such a conflict between European, Asian, coloured, [and] a variety of African views. The secretary of state had made it quite clear ... that the present constitution was going to run its four years unless there was agreement between all concerned, so that my job was, as I saw it, to go on and on and on until possibly one might have got some measure of agreement ... We could have brought in changes earlier [and] with the appearance of Dr Banda it did look as if there might be a chance ... I had to give him as much time as I could to make up his mind to see in fact whether he differed from the original Congress proposals put up by quite different people ... hence my view that this was something which one had continually to plug on and on until time was running out.[99]

Banda himself, at least up to October 1958, 'did not want to hurry [the Governor] or embarrass him' by asking for a meeting to discuss constitutional advance.[100]

Armitage's strategy with Banda was one of delay and persistence: 'We kept going at him ... and we were able to keep talks on constitutional matters going for several months.' His idea was to 'go on and on and on' trying to get the various interests to agree proposals and if this did not come about, to produce his own – but at the very latest time which would enable the new constitution to be in operation before the 1960 federal review. He knew such proposals would not be to Banda's liking but felt that maybe, at such a late stage, Banda would acquiesce to them as being something gained and the best offered. Banda, on his side, may have recognised Armitage's strategy, planned to let it take its course and hoped to negotiate a somewhat better deal out of the Governor's last minute offer. His adamant demands would then stand him in good stead because he would appear to be reasonable in European and government eyes in accepting less than his demands, and a successful leader in African eyes in wringing concessions out of the government after their final offer.

With so many conflicting political interests and proposals, Armitage was in 'somewhat of a flap', and unclear of the way ahead: 'The fancy franchises involved and completely irreconcilable views put forward, leave us in rather a muddle.' Ingham also confessed that events were moving so fast that he could 'only just keep [his] head above water'.[101]

The great variety and quantity of views put forward and 'the fancy franchises involved' are indicated in a seven-page summary of proposals made to him which Armitage prepared towards the end of February.[102] In this document he gave details of proposals by the Nyasaland African Congress, African Progressive Association, Asian Convention, Euro-African Association, Coloured Community Welfare Association, Non-party Africans, W.M. Chirwa, Nyasaland Association, Blackwood and Dixon, Congress Liberation Party, United Federal Party and 'certain elected non-African members of legislative council', as well as his own proposals. Some of the proposals were exceedingly complex.

The Governor's difficulties were exacerbated by the Colonial Office not formulating and expressing views of its own. As he recalled:

> I was in extreme difficulty ... because I found that Her Majesty's Government in London had no idea what constitutional advance would be suitable for Nyasaland ... [T]he officials in the Colonial Office were unable to agree to present a unanimous picture to the Secretary of State, which he could get cabinet approval for, for the advance which should be made in Nyasaland.[103]

Notwithstanding this difficulty of eliciting and recommending the various views on a future constitution, Armitage – as the alternative to mutually agreed proposals – made fairly definite proposals to the Colonial Office late in January 1959.[104] He envisaged a legislature of 29 made up of 14 elected members and 15 ex-officio and appointed members. Of the 14 elected members, eight were to be elected on a general roll and in effect would be African; and six were to be elected on a selective roll and in effect would be European. Among the 15 on the 'government' side, Armitage would consider some non-official nominated members if the need for this emerged during negotiations. He envisaged an executive council – over which he would preside – of five officials and four appointed, elected non-officials, two of whom would be non-Africans and two Africans – if willing to serve. The non-official members of executive council would be advisory only and there would be no ministerial system. Beyond this, although he did not say so, he could not go without prejudicing the work of the commission – which was being considered in the Colonial Office – to produce a formula before the 1960 conference. The plan, it seems, was to go as far as he could now and indicate that his proposals would be in operation by May 1960 and in the meantime the commission would come up with suggestions for further territorial advance within a framework dealing with the longer-term future of the Federation as a whole.

Banda continued to demand an overall African majority in the legislature, and on the executive council the least he would accept was six African non-officials, with three ex-officio members and two European non-officials. He argued that this would provide parity between Europeans – the Governor, three officials and two non-officials – and Africans. Armitage felt there was no possibility of giving way to these demands and recommended they should be rejected.[105] Chisiza was shortly to reveal that by mid-January Congress was prepared to accept a bare majority in the legislature:

> instead of demanding that we should have 32 Africans in the Legislative Council we had come down to a bare majority in number, and ... in the case of our demands not being accepted we would have to take such action as would make it possible for us to bring about that state of affairs ... we felt this action was absolutely necessary.[106]

By mid-February, unrest was widespread: disturbances in schools; strikes in hospitals, post offices and other government offices; malicious damage to an airfield putting it out of operation; assaults on government officers; stonings; forceful release of prisoners; arson; looting; widespread breaking of soil conservation laws; arrests, and police use of tear-gas and firearms.[107] The police were aware that the Youth League were

> perpetrating acts of intimidation and assault on their own people [but] very little police action could be taken as victims and witnesses were generally too frightened to come forward to give evidence or to report crimes.[108]

The unrest was particularly acute in the Karonga district where previously the atmosphere had been peaceful, race relations good and government officers able to carry on with their normal field duties.[109] The government believed that after the 25 January bush meeting Chisiza told delegates from the north that they should not be put to shame because people in the north had not yet taken any action, and this goaded them into causing disturbances.[110]

For some time Armitage had believed that trouble would break out

in 1959 but not early in the year. He planned that his various constitutional talks would be concluded in February and he expected
disturbances to be delayed until then and to emerge as a reaction to
his proposals.[111] His precautions to handle the disorders were planned
in anticipation that they would be needed after the proposals were
announced and, presumably, rejected by Banda. Even in the middle of
February he reported:

> the situation ... is uncertain and complex; but so far as we can assess it,
> though we shall continue for the time being with isolated disorders, Dr
> Banda will not himself seek to cause his arrest just yet and that is the
> essential factor calculated to spark off violence.[112]

He continued to hope Banda would not 'carry through with disorders'.
Having had discussions with the doctor he felt he was keen to have
constitutional talks. He did not, however, know – nor could he have
guessed from Banda's intransigent stance – that the doctor was also
hoping for proposals to be published and then to negotiate on them.

By being so implacably obstinate and adamant in his demands, and
not shifting an iota from them, Banda risked having all his demands
refused and also risked imprisonment or banishment for a long enough
period to allow other, including more moderate, leaders to emerge and
displace him. He needed to be recognised by all as the undisputed
leader before it became obvious that he was not having the impact on
the government which his speeches led people to believe he was having.
In the eight months following his return to Nyasaland he secured no
concessions and no promises of concessions from Armitage and, since
he was naturally reluctant to admit to this failure, he could not tell his
followers about his talks with the government. 'Why can't he tell us
what he discusses with the Governor?' they understandably asked.[113]
Chisiza claimed that Lennox-Boyd announced early in December 1958
that he would make a statement on the country's constitutional future
before parliament's Christmas recess. 'People sighed with relief but
became tense' and when no statement was forthcoming the relief
disappeared and the tenseness increased. Matters were then made worse
when the Governor 'entered into another round of secret talks with
Dr Banda'.[114] As Youens had perceived, time was running out for the
doctor because he was not able to 'deliver the goods at an early date'.
Banda had to plead with his followers to be patient, an emergency
meeting had to be called for 24 and 25 January 1959 to secure a vote
of confidence for him, his lieutenants were becoming uneasy and
perhaps disillusioned, and he kept the sympathy and support of his
followers by expressing a preparedness to go to gaol and, if necessary,
die for his country.

As a consequence of the fast-mounting trouble, Armitage met with the chief secretary, attorney-general, secretary for African affairs and commissioner of police on 17 February:[115]

> The basic position was that Congress had African support from North to South. We would have to rely on the King's African Rifles, including the battalion from Lusaka. These were all Nyasas, but we were dependent on them. We were in the middle of various discussions on the constitution ... Presumably, if he did not like the proposals [Banda] would at least order strikes and disturbances. We had little idea of what the alliance of Chipembere and Chisiza was thinking. Chiume was out of the country. So we would have to have powers to detain. This led us to consider whether we could detain all the ring leaders excluding Banda. This might make things more difficult for him.[116]

The idea that all other leaders should be arrested but Banda left free came from Youens, who advised Armitage to adopt this course because Banda had always said he was against violence and was relying on constitutional means to achieve what he wanted and to be left free 'would have embarrassed him to a considerable degree'.[117]

Armitage had been discussing with the Colonial Office since mid-January ways in which he might deal with the increasing unrest, and he felt that if he were to have any chance of maintaining order 'drastic measures' would be inevitable and it might be necessary to deport the doctor and 'one or two others such as Chipembere'.[118] In response to this idea the Colonial Office feared it was 'not possible to be encouraging': 'owing to the very considerable legal, administrative and practical difficulties entailed, it must now, generally speaking, be regarded as impracticable'.[119] The Governor said he was 'quite satisfied' the time for effective restriction – an alternative to deportation – was passed, and in any case there were no suitable places to which to restrict people against whom he made orders. He felt, too, that it would be dangerous to enact a detention ordinance – another alternative – because if the legislature met for this purpose there would be a 'grave risk of serious disorder' and the ordinance itself would create a situation in which it would be necessary to proclaim an immediate state of emergency. Consequently, he concluded that 'rapid executive action', declaring a state of emergency, might be necessary despite recognising that this could only be a temporary solution, and a more permanent detention ordinance could be enacted during the emergency. He reported:

> I am advised that the present situation would justify declaring a state of emergency but have not reached any decision to take that step yet ...

Intelligence sources show Dr Banda is looking forward to discussions on
constitutional proposals. [The] danger is that one of his extremists may
provoke violence.[120]

On 19 February Armitage concluded that conditions in the north
were so bad that they must send for the 1st Battalion of the KAR from
Lusaka and two platoons of the Northern Rhodesia PMF.[121] The
following day he travelled to Salisbury and met with Dalhousie, the
Governor-General, Benson, the Governor of Northern Rhodesia,
Welensky, Barrow, the federal deputy prime minister, and Whitehead,
premier of Southern Rhodesia.[122] Armitage reported on the severe and
increasingly disturbing situation in Nyasaland, and 'it was decided to
send federal troops to Nyasaland to keep the peace ... Sir Robert
accepted, though reluctantly, the necessity'.[123] He emphasised that these
measures were taken to protect life and property and 'in [the] hope
that [a] genuine show of force will stop [the] situation deteriorating'.
He was sorry to have to take these steps just before Perth's visit but he
could see no option because he could not release further forces from
the Southern Province.[124]

At the Salisbury meeting Armitage gave the impression he was
'very worried about the situation' in Nyasaland but that it was not
desperate.[125] Whitehead was 'dreadfully worried' about draining Southern Rhodesia of soldiers to send to Nyasaland because he was thinking
of declaring an emergency in Southern Rhodesia and would need as
many troops as possible.

> The right thing, he said, was for him to clear up all the subversivists in
> Southern Rhodesia first and get them inside, at which time he would
> then be able to agree to further reinforcements going to Nyasaland.

Benson reported that although there had been 'intensely violent and
seditious speeches' by a few nationalists, there was 'no question whatsoever of an emergency in Northern Rhodesia'; he had, however,
planned to arrest the Zambia party leaders on charges of sedition that
morning but had not done so because the KAR had been sent to
Nyasaland and 'deprived him of that degree of internal security support'.[126] It was little wonder that he was irritated.

The Salisbury meeting did not discuss whether Armitage should
declare a state of emergency: 'That was my affair', as he later said.[127]
He still hoped Perth's visit would have a calming effect and felt that
'there was still just a chance that the announcement of the visit might
in itself help to restore the situation and enable the talks to take place
in something like a reasonable atmosphere'.[128] He was convinced, however, that he would have to declare a state of emergency 'unless there

could be some miracle on the constitutional issue with the arrival of Lord Perth'.

> Which was going to prevail? Lord Perth and the chance of constitutional talks and ordinary arguments on political reform here, or a pattern of disorders making a state of emergency inevitable? I took five days more to make up my own mind on that.[129]

In reporting the meeting to the Colonial Office, Armitage[130] said Welensky, Whitehead and Benson had all agreed to assist to the limit of their police or military capacity.

> As a result of reinforcements we appear to have contained the situation. When further reinforcements can be spared to me we will be able to arrest those responsible for disorders in Northern Province and to secure position better in Southern Province.

He added that everyone at the meeting was aware of his difficulty in immediately dealing more forcefully with Congress when he did not have adequate forces, and when Perth was about to arrive for talks with Congress and other political parties. When these two restraints were removed he hoped to 'take complete control' of the situation, but he was aware that in the meantime others would think him inactive:

> You will appreciate [the] need for this phase of apparent inaction, the difficulty of reassuring rather militant pressmen and a public which cannot be fully informed of intentions. The result is that the general impression is that this Government is concealing information.

At this stage, the situation was 'quiet but tense', 'contained but still anxious'.[131]

The Governor sent Footman to Salisbury to finalise the details of reinforcements. Although Welensky had earlier not seen the need to accept outside reinforcements he now partially changed his mind – largely because some outside forces could get to the northern province more quickly than could internal forces – and said 'All right. Get your reinforcements where you can.' When Footman asked the chief secretary of Tanganyika whether he could, if needed, send in police reinforcements, he received the initial reply: 'You haven't a hope. We are getting into serious trouble ourselves.' A little later the Governor of Tanganyika did agree to send in his police and they re-took Fort Hill airfield – which was being held by rioters – from a position close to the border to which he had already moved them. Indeed, Tanganyika now seemed very willing to help – partly to avoid disorder spreading into their own country.[132]

In thanking Welensky for his help to Footman,[133] Armitage said he had decided to declare a state of emergency at midnight on 2–3 March and 'those on the list' would be arrested and flown out of Nyasaland. He would welcome one company of the Royal Rhodesia Regiment (RRR) to be flown to Chileka on 27 February and another company on 28 February. He asked 'most earnestly' that the three platoons of British South Africa Police (BSAP) should be flown to Chileka on 2 March – their transport being provided, as arranged, by train – because Nyasaland police officers had been working very long hours for several months and needed support.[134] Also, the Governor was anxious to get the correct balance between military and police forces which had become 'unbalanced', and he was 'using the military forces far too much in the role of police and [he] therefore wanted more police'.[135] It was the case, too, as the Governor-General later recalled, that

> Sir Robert was concerned by the presence of federal troops in Nyasaland. Not because of maintaining security so much as because of the unpopularity of the Federation ... and the danger of the presence of these troops increasing the unpopularity.[136]

Later Armitage was criticised for having insufficient proper forces for dealing with unarmed crowds. This criticism was based on the perception that the police, with their training in riot control, were absent and the army, incorrectly thought[137] to be untrained in these techniques, had to handle the crowds – and that the army's normal way of dealing with such circumstances was to open fire. It was precisely this danger which Armitage hoped to avoid by altering the balance between police and army in favour of the former.[138]

The relationships between the military and the civil authorities, including the police, were invariably good but the – quite proper – differences between the role and procedures of the army on the one hand, and the police on the other, could have led to major difficulties despite the army having been trained in security operations (both rural and urban) and despite their troops having been drilled in the procedures of crowd control and minimum force.[139] For example, in an incident on 27 February after the riot act had been read, a KAR company commander, Caine, was confronted by an African who refused to move when told to disperse. The commander 'turned him round and gave him a jab with a bayonet in the buttock'[140] or, as the commander recalled he 'tackled the ringleader and in the skirmish ... pricked his backside with the bayonet'.[141] It appears, however, that Banda complained about the incident to the police who proposed to question the commander with a view to charging him with grievous bodily harm.

General Garlake instructed Brigadier Anderson to tell the Governor that
if the Nyasaland Police continued with the so-called assault by Captain
Caine, he would pull out every soldier in Nyasaland.[142]

Though not proceeded with, the case highlighted the difficulties that
may be encountered when the military are engaged in internal security
operations. There was another, similar, case this time involving the
federal prime minister:

> When the matter of an African being shot ... was reported to the
> Nyasaland Operations Committee, Donald King, the Attorney-General,
> was very clear and insistent that the [soldier] shooting him should be
> prosecuted. General Long, federal army, said that he would have to
> report this to his prime minister, and Welensky's quick and firm answer
> was that if the person were prosecuted he would immediately withdraw
> all his troops from Nyasaland. Although King's legal right to make the
> decision is unquestionable, he was made to climb down and the prosecu-
> tion was not proceeded with.[143]

By the fourth week in February feelings in the Shire Highlands –
where trouble had started in 1953 and where the combination of dense
African population, significant European settlement and land hunger
was potentially explosive – were becoming tense. Numerous European
parents took the opportunity of sending their children out of the
country, troops were stationed at schools and children's hostels and
the parents of children at township schools but with homes in the
rural areas were advised to leave them at school at weekends because
protection in the rural areas could not be guaranteed. In Limbe there
was a 'laager' or 'beleaguered' feeling as if a 'last stand might have to
be taken'.[144] Privately the Governor said it might be necessary virtually
to encircle Blantyre with security forces although the provincial commissioner felt this was unnecessary.[145] In Cholo,

> Europeans [took] precautions such as 'doubling up' and evacuating out-
> lying places before 3 March. Violence was proposed at an illegal meeting
> of Congress at Luchenza on the 25th February; reports were circulated
> that Asians at Luchenza had been warned by Congress members on the
> 28th February that they would be killed; a watchman at Makanda Estate
> near Luchenza was murdered for no apparent reason on the lst March,
> and large numbers of people were seen moving from Bvumbwe area
> towards Blantyre on the 28th February and the 1st March to guard Dr
> Banda's house.[146]

Under the pretext that an attack might be made on the Luchenza fuel
storage tanks, the security forces in the Cholo area were reinforced to
reassure the numerous European families living there. Elsewhere in

the Shire Highlands, for example Mlanje, European families 'doubled
up' or moved into the district headquarters, and stocks of foodstuffs
were laid in. Armitage hired a Beaver aircraft ready to evacuate families
if necessary. Barrow ensured that his own family from Cholo flew to
the relative safety of Salisbury.[147]

The press – 'a mob of reporters looking for trouble', in Armitage's
view[148] – had naturally become deeply interested in Nyasaland's problems. The *Rhodesia Herald* said:

> The forces of law and order must not hesitate to take whatever action is
> necessary to preserve life and property; they must once and for all put a
> stop to the criminal activities of those persons who are leading their
> fellow men into disaster.[149]

Taking a concurring but broader view of events occurring simultaneously elsewhere in Africa, *The Times* agreed that: 'The first duty
of the parent countries concerned – Belgium, France and Great Britain
– is quite clearly to restore order.'[150]

Other newspapers were critical of what they saw as Armitage's
inactivity.[151] Having described Banda as 'fanatical ... a loud-voiced,
gnome-like figure who yells that Nyasalanders must fill British prisons
singing alleluia', David Wise of the *Daily Express* asked:

> But what is being done about the Congress and its leaders? No arrests.
> No state of emergency. I've never before been in a British possession
> where government servants displayed such little confidence in their
> Governor. All I hear from Africans is he will make this another Cyprus.[152]

The *Manchester Guardian*, on 26 February, reported that the position
in Nyasaland was beginning to clarify 'through the fog of official
communiques'. The situation, it felt, was 'complex, difficult and
dangerous', but also 'near absurdity':

> The federal government thinks the best course is immediate and firm
> action to bring back under control an area [north Nyasaland] within the
> Federation and yet cannot take this action without being asked to do so
> by the Nyasaland Government which, in its turn, would also prefer to
> wait a while.

> It is equally apparent that the Nyasaland Government hopes that it may
> sometime or other be able to persuade Dr Banda to align himself on the
> side of the authorities in stopping further trouble, while the federal
> government on its side considers that ... Dr Banda and his fellow
> Congress leaders ... have passed beyond the point where negotiation
> within the existing framework is possible.[153]

Members of Parliament, too, were worried by the Governor's apparent inactivity: Shinwell claimed that Armitage was treating the matter 'somewhat lightly', with complacency and not very seriously, adding 'we do not want a repetition of the events of Cyprus and to discover we have acted rather belatedly'.[154]

The result of Armitage's discussions with his senior advisers and with the heads of government was that the 2nd Battalion of the KAR was sent from Zomba to the north of the protectorate, and was joined there by the 1st Battalion from Lusaka and by police reinforcements. Dakota aircraft of No. 3 Squadron of the Royal Rhodesian Air Force (RRAF) flew 120 European soldiers of the 1st Battalion RRR to Chileka in the south to safeguard the airport and the Shire river crossings, while a platoon was also sent north to guard Mzuzu airfield, and a rear party of medical teams and support staff travelled by road via Northern Rhodesia to Lilongwe. Two companies of the 2nd Battalion KAR were stationed at Limbe, and officers and men of the Rhodesia African Rifles (RAR) went to Ncheu and Lilongwe. Troop movements into Nyasaland were made at very short notice. For example, since the senior company of the RRR was on exercises in Southern Rhodesia, the second senior company was given only 24 hours to prepare and move to Nyasaland and others were given even less notice. The 3rd Battalion RRR, formed earlier as a force to support the civil power in the event of unrest on the Copperbelt, was mobilised and held in reserve at Ndola with preparations made to fly to Nyasaland if needed. They were not needed, which was fortunate since there was a feeling that the large South African element among the tough European troops would not have been particularly sympathetic in Nyasaland.[155]

The outbreak of violence in Nyasaland took the federal government somewhat by surprise because they had anticipated trouble first in Northern Rhodesia, where elections were taking place, but they quickly shifted their security forces to Nyasaland. Welensky made his determination clear: he intended to use 'the most rigorous methods legally at [his] command' to maintain law and order and to make things 'thoroughly unpleasant' for those who persistently broke the peace.[156]

Within Nyasaland the outbreak of trouble in the north took Armitage by surprise:

> We were expecting [trouble] but not to start in the extreme north, where there are no towns, no developments and as a result few police. We think the affairs were sparked off prematurely. We had feared major troubles in the south and the north making diversions.[157]

The reinforcements were naturally very unwelcome to Banda who wrote to Armitage and said local forces could have maintained law and order – 'Nowhere in the country has law and order been so broken down as to necessitate the calling in of troops from Southern Rhodesia, either territorial or federal' – and that the reinforcements simply confirmed the people's fears about federation. The reaction of the Nyasaland government, he argued, revealed clearly that it was not a free agent, not even an agent of the United Kingdom, but 'a mere puppet of the European Federal and territorial politicians in Southern Rhodesia, Northern Rhodesia and Nyasaland'. Copies of the letter were handed out by Youth Leaguers to the African public in Blantyre.[158]

Despite pressure to do so, Armitage was deeply reluctant to proscribe Congress because of Perth's imminent arrival for discussions in which Congress would be the most important African political party. To ban or severely restrain them would defeat the visit's purpose. He had hoped Lennox-Boyd would visit Nyasaland because he 'wanted his clear and forthright approach to [their] problems [and] to demonstrate how [they] were not going to be deterred from putting new constitutional proposals into effect' by Banda's adamant refusal to accept anything which the government was prepared to propose. Disappointed that Lennox-Boyd was unable to come, Armitage was none the less pleased at the prospect of Perth's visit on 26 February. When on 20 February, while in Salisbury, he first learned of the date, he remarked 'at last!'[159] and asked Footman to see Banda immediately, tell him of the visit, explain that constitutional talks could take place only in a calm atmosphere and warn him 'not to provoke trouble'.[160] Although Footman saw Banda straight away and told him how important 'it was for constitutional talks to take place in a favourable atmosphere',[161] Congress none the less held a private meeting on 22 February, at which:

> Inflammatory speeches were made to delegates attending and [a] programme for disorder was set up. When [the] meeting dispersed, [the] crowd which had gathered invaded parts of Blantyre, [and] stoning of cars ... continued for two hours necessitating major police action.[162]

The situation in Central Africa, and particularly in Nyasaland, now became even more tense. In Southern Rhodesia the territorial army was mobilised and Stonehouse, a visiting Labour member of parliament, was making what the government saw as provocative speeches. Violent incidents – including the stoning of Europeans – continued in Nyasaland, where police and military forces killed two Africans when dispersing rioting crowds; field officers found it impossible to carry out their normal duties; loyal African staff were placed in an increasingly invidious position; forestry field staff, especially in sensitive areas, were advised to 'go easy' with their work lest they provoke villagers into violent reactions. The situation was causing the British government considerable concern and Butler – acting prime minister in Macmillan's absence – asked Perth if he was satisfied about security arrangements in Nyasaland and the number of troops available. He asked for an up-to-date note for his audience with the Queen on 24 February and for a report to take to cabinet two days later, adding that he was 'very ready' to help Perth in any way he could 'in handling the rather difficult situation which seems to be developing in Nyasaland'.[163]

Perth cabled Armitage on 25 February saying he hoped he would not feel restrained from taking whatever security steps he felt necessary 'out of regard for [his] visit or the fact that such action may make constitutional talks, as originally planned, difficult or even impossible'.[164] In the prevailing troubled circumstances Welensky and Armitage separately concluded that the visit should be postponed. On 25 February Welensky cabled this advice to the Commonwealth Relations Office and copied his cable to Armitage:

> In view of developments in Nyasaland, I am of the opinion that you should give serious consideration to postponing Perth's proposed visit to Nyasaland for constitutional discussions. I have not had an opportunity of discussing this matter with Armitage, but am sending him a copy of this telegram, so that in the event of his disagreeing with my opinion he can let you know at once. [165]

Welensky's advice was immediately considered by a small group of ministers, chaired by Butler, who decided not to postpone the visit.[166] A little later the same day Armitage, whose private correspondence only two days earlier had been written in terms of confidence that Perth was about to visit Nyasaland and whose official correspondence earlier on 25 February was to the same effect, cabled him at the Colonial Office:

> Situation now makes early declaration of State of Emergency inevitable. In these circumstances constitutional discussions with you could not take place in calm atmosphere and might well be accompanied by serious disturbances. I had always hoped that constitutional discussions which would have been with representatives of all races and opinions would have been possible before drastic action was necessary. I much regret that this is no longer the case. I am forced to suggest that your visit should be postponed.[167]

When this cable was received in London it was immediately decided that the visit should indeed be postponed.[168] Perth cabled Lennox-Boyd in Aden telling him of the postponement[169] and Lennox-Boyd replied: 'Very sorry but sure decision to postpone is right.'[170] Reporting this decision to the cabinet the following morning,[171] Perth told his colleagues the situation in the Federation was confused, Southern Rhodesia had declared a state of emergency that morning 'and similar action might shortly become unavoidable in Nyasaland'.

> In discussion the Cabinet was informed that there was some reason to suppose that the recent riots in the Federation had been carefully planned and had been deliberately directed against Europeans. The white people in Nyasaland, whose safety remained the direct responsibility of the United Kingdom Government, might be in some danger; and steps should be taken urgently to ascertain what reinforcements could, if necessary, be made available to the security forces.

The cabinet approved Perth's decision to postpone his visit, and Amery, Colonial Office minister of state, explained to the Commons on 27 February:

> There is of course no question of the situation being too dangerous for [Perth] to go. The problem is that his visit may have given rise, so we are advised, to the dangers of further disturbances and loss of life.[172]

Armitage had advised that there might be serious disturbances but he had said nothing about loss of life. Perth had simply told the cabinet that the Europeans might be in some danger.

Now the question of his visit had been disposed of, Armitage told Perth he would probably declare a state of emergency at midnight on 2–3 March, to which Perth replied: 'Your plans have our fullest support. Good luck. Hope the birds won't have flown.' A little later, on 1 March, on his return from Aden, Lennox-Boyd also cabled the Governor, saying he had been brought up to date on his intention, adding 'All good wishes'.[173]

On 27 February Armitage told the Colonial Office he now considered it inevitable he would have to declare a state of emergency within the next few days, and – looking to the future – added:

> I must have a bill ready for enactment before that state of emergency is terminated. I naturally hope that such determination will take place within a relatively short time and this factor increases the urgency of the enactment of a bill [dealing with detention outside a state of emergency].[174]

As he had forecast at the Salisbury meeting, Whitehead declared a state of emergency in Southern Rhodesia on 26 February – the intended day of Perth's arrival – to control any disturbance while he freed troops and police to go to Nyasaland. He proscribed Congress in Southern Rhodesia and detained its leaders.[175]

Conditions remained peaceful in Southern Rhodesia. Not so,

however, in Nyasaland where Armitage believed the 'Government was in serious danger of losing control'.[176] Riots, disorders and personal attacks on Europeans, Asians and African court staff continued and another African was shot dead by the army in dispersing rioters,[177] although the weekend of 28 February and 1 March was – contrary to Armitage's expectations – fairly quiet. This lull enabled further reinforcements of troops and police to arrive by train and by RRAF and requisitioned civilian aircraft – some being flown to Chileka, others to Lilongwe[178] – and to be deployed without taking positive security action.[179] Welensky ordered the call-up of all territorial reservists in both Northern and Southern Rhodesia.[180] Over one thousand troops were moved by Dakotas of No. 3 Squadron RRAF to Nyasaland. Their transport and armoured cars came by road through Portuguese East Africa, crossing the Zambezi at Tete at night,[181] while the RRR rear party also travelled by road but through Northern Rhodesia to Lilongwe.[182] The additional forces now in Nyasaland were the 1st Battalion RAR less one company, the 1st Mashonaland and 1st Matabeleland Battalions and two supporting companies of the RRR, the 1st Battalion of the KAR, the Northern Rhodesia Rifles (NRR), two depot companies of the RRAF, and a contingent of BSAP.[183] The NRR and both Battalions of the KAR were African soldiers under European officers; and the RRR comprised young European territorials, mainly farmers, miners, lawyers, architects, accountants and small businessmen,[184] with a four-year commitment with the active forces – an annual training camp and weekly training sessions – after which they were posted to the reserve.[185] Reconnaissance and flag-showing flights by RRAF aircraft over parts of the country were increased.[186] An additional emergency operating theatre was set up in the main hospital at Blantyre – but not used – and two extra surgeons were brought up from Salisbury.[187] The general atmosphere was tense. For example, a senior RRAF officer returning to Southern Rhodesia by air from Nyasaland reported a large gathering of Africans in the bush near the perimeter of Chileka airport.

> Alarm bells rang in Salisbury and the opinion was expressed: 'If Chileka falls, Nyasaland falls.' All hell broke out. [A] company was sent to Chileka to give support to European troops. [They] patrolled the perimeter most of the night and returned to Blantyre early the next morning after a quiet night. The large gathering referred to, and the cause of the 'flap' [turned out to be] the usual beer drink in the area![188]

The Governor had originally asked that the BSAP contingent should be flown to Chileka on 2 March but they in fact came by train, leaving Salisbury on the afternoon of 28 February, and travelling via the Lower

Zambezi, the Lower Shire and the Cholo escarpment. They left the train at Luchenza and were taken by road to Blantyre. This breaking of the journey at Luchenza instead of continuing by rail was fortunate because it appears that eight Congressmen, briefed on the troop movements by African railway telephonists, were 'ready in the lower section between Limbe and Mikolongwe to set back ... the last train before the emergency'. The whole contingent was under the command of a senior assistant commissioner. The Alpha section, who flew yellow pennants from their Land Rovers and adopted, informally but proudly, yellow cravats, were known as 'The Yellow Scarves' and considered an élite unit from then on. The Bravo section adopted red cravats but less successfully and were much less well known than their yellow-scarf-sporting colleagues.[189]

On 2 March, Orton Chirwa, a barrister, wrote a letter to a friend that indicates the prevailing situation as seen through African eyes. Until shortly before Chirwa had rarely spoken of politics to this correspondent, but now he said:

> We are going through a very difficult time here. Admittedly there is some violence and the Nyasaland Africans are in very bad humour. Yet the position has been exaggerated beyond measure and has received publicity out of all proportion. The result is that settler feelings have been worked up to such a degree that Southern Rhodesia has sent us her troops: so have Tanganyika. The whole country is at present a battlefield in that you meet a soldier at every corner in Blantyre and Limbe. Already about a dozen Africans have been shot for doing nothing other than refusing to leave what the police allege to be an unlawful assembly. There is ample provision in the law of Nyasaland for dealing with a thing like that. Nor are the troops very scrupulous ... This action by the government has killed stone dead whatever little sympathy there may have been for Federation on the part of the Africans.[190]

With the obvious security forces activity, members of the now very large media corps in Nyasaland[191] asked Armitage on 25 February for a press conference, and he agreed to give one on 2 March. When he agreed to the conference and its date he had not made up his mind about declaring a state of emergency. He gave the conference, as agreed, on the afternoon of 2 March.[192] He assured them he intended to 're-create conditions of law and order so that the life of the country [could] go on as usual in peaceful circumstances'; also he stated that he intended to arrest those who had committed offences and created disorders. He could not tell them what, precisely, he intended to do and he expected them not to press him on this. Although there were attempts to make much of it later, Armitage was only once drawn into

referring to a state of emergency, a matter on which he was determined
to stall:

> *Question*: Can I turn to the question of the use of troops? In Cyprus no
> troops ever fired on the crowds.
> *Answer*: If conditions arise that ordinary police forces cannot handle the
> situation and lives are put in jeopardy, you can always use force.
> Normally the Riot Act is read.
> *Question*: You don't need a state of emergency to act in this way?
> *Answer*: Not necessarily.

In a separate question he was asked: 'Is it possible to say whether the
laws of Nyasaland give Government the power to act against Congress
– to proscribe its members – without the declaration of a state of
emergency?' Armitage replied, 'Yes. Nyasaland laws do give powers to
proscribe Congress. Any association of persons can be proscribed as
unlawful.' Armitage was speaking of general acts of violence and
powers of proscription for which emergency powers were not necessary,
but he thought afterwards that *The Times*, which reported the press
conference the next day, may have read into his remarks a specific
inference that it was not necessary to declare a state of emergency in
existing conditions in Nyasaland. *Time Magazine* claimed – incorrectly
– that he 'had flatly stated that no such drastic action would be
needed'. In any case, he successfully avoided being drawn on how he
would act in the future, even the immediate future. He certainly did
not say he would not declare a state of emergency – even though some
took his words to mean this, including the federal broadcasting cor-
poration whose news relay that evening was found by many to be
'reassuring' and a 'great relief'.[193]

About three-quarters of an hour before he started this press conference Armitage sent a telegram to Lennox-Boyd saying he proposed to
declare a state of emergency at a quarter past midnight and to arrest
and detain about 180 active office holders of Congress and its branches,
plus known 'brave and bad men'.[194] During 2 March Armitage signed
the documents to bring the state of emergency into force ready for use
just after midnight. During the preceding few days, he told Lennox-
Boyd in a separate telegram,[195] his intelligence sources had reported
widespread activity by Congress branch officials encouraging the crea-
tion of disturbances to 'prepare for the general plan of violence'. He
thought the riots in Karonga were part of this plan and were designed
to draw security forces away from the south of the protectorate.
Already there were rumours that Banda had been or was about to be
arrested, but there had been no disorders during the previous 24 hours.
There were also rumours of a planned mass gaolbreak from Zomba

Central Prison during the night of 2–3 March and frequent police patrols were carried out near the prison throughout the night.[196] Armitage was aware Banda was heavily guarded and believed his arrest would require force. He thought too that reaction to the arrest would probably depend on the 'speed and secrecy of the pick-ups', and the reaction in the urban areas would probably be intense but, he hoped, 'sharply smothered' in most areas. Because he thought the reaction would be 'intense' he had arranged for most of the 180 detainees to be flown immediately to Bulawayo; there they would be interrogated since, due to Congress's security arrangements, he felt that few documents would be found. 'Separate V.I.P. attention' would be accorded to Banda, Chipembere and the Chisiza brothers. He had already recorded a broadcast message about the declaration, briefly giving the reasons for it, and he had pamphlets ready to be air-dropped on all district head-quarters with a message to chiefs and African civil servants. In his telegram sent just before the press conference – his last detailed communication with the Colonial Office before declaring a state of emergency – he said:

> Planning by all Provincial Operations Committees appears detailed and satisfactory and designed to ensure speedy arrests and to contain any reactions following. In Central Province indications are these will be slight in most places. In Northern Province uncertain. In Southern Province there are 42 platoons of troops alone and practically every area is covered.

The weather was bad, and he ended his telegram with the words: 'we want a dark night and a clear morning'.[197]

3

The crisis breaks

It all seemed an uncouth invasion ... on a quiet African night.

Just after midnight, on 3 March, Armitage declared a state of emergency over the whole of the protectorate and proscribed the Nyasaland African Congress and its affiliated bodies; leaders, including Banda, were arrested and placed in detention. Out-going telegraph traffic was monitored, including press telegrams, and night curfews were imposed in the townships and outstation headquarters. 'Blue Band Radio', using police equipment, was set up to keep the public informed of developments and to reassure people in outlying areas, as it had been in 1953.[1]

By the time Armitage made the declaration, arrest parties throughout the country had already been briefed on the arrests they were to make in the exercise, known as Operation Sunrise, to detain leading members of Congress. These parties were usually quite small, consisting typically of an administrative officer, a police officer – often a European special constable – and two or three African constables. In many cases African special branch officers, briefed as to the identity and location of those to be arrested, accompanied the party.[2] In the more remote areas parties often had to travel long distances – on foot, by vehicle or by boat – and arrest people in widely separated villages.

The extent to which government officers and others knew of the murder plot before Operation Sunrise was mounted varied both between and within districts and so, therefore, did the extent to which their actions could have been influenced by that knowledge.[3] There was a general awareness, communicated to all district commissioners during February, of the Congress's plans for disruption including the possibility of violence. As to knowledge of more precise details, the position varied between districts. For example, in the southern province districts where a large number of European settlers lived – Zomba, Blantyre, Cholo and Mlanje – the district commissioners knew the details of the plot before 3 March, but only in Zomba and Blantyre was this information passed on to pick-up team leaders and even then not to all leaders. In the remaining four, 'non-settled' districts of the southern province the district commissioners did not know specifically of the plot before 3 March and so neither did their pick-up teams. Indeed, the assistant district commissioner of Chikwawa recalled:

> When the emergency was actually declared on 3 March, the [district commissioner] was away in Blantyre, I think, and the first we knew of what was happening was a plane circling over the boma dropping pamphlets telling us that an emergency had been declared. Even this unusual event didn't cause much excitement.[4]

Similarly, at Fort Johnston:

> We had an odd Sunrise. There was a detachment of Rhodesia Rifles ... near the town and one of them dropped in at the boma during the course of the morning and mentioned that he had heard on the radio that a state of emergency had been declared in Nyasaland. That was on March 3. No one had told us! We had planned for the emergency, but started 24 hours late.[5]

Few army officers and fewer of their men knew of the plot until after 3 March.[6]

After intensive probing, the commission which shortly inquired into the disturbances concluded that there was only one 'clear case' where belief in the plot had had a 'significant effect on the course of events' and that was at Nkata Bay. They claimed that 'from first to last [the district commissioner's] chief fear was for the safety of the European women and children'.[7] Yet this was a misunderstanding of what the district commissioner, a bachelor, had told them:

> My main concern was to prevent bloodshed and to do all I could to contain the situation until the promised troops arrived to break up the crowd without opening fire. In giving evidence, I expressed support for [the police officer's] decision to use his small police contingent to protect the European residential area rather than attempt to break up the crowd from the rear, and this, I believe, gave the commission the wrong impression.[8]

It is unlikely, then, that knowledge of the murder plot affected any actions by government officers and security forces during Operation Sunrise.

Naturally, Banda's arrest was extremely carefully planned. He was living in a house at Limbe and a fairly large number of people were staying in the grounds to protect him. The operation was led by the officer in charge of police at Limbe, Superintendent Bevan, who was in charge of six groups.[9] There was a diversion group under Inspector

Cotton accompanied by four special constables, a driver – Special Constable Dagnell – and a vehicle guard; a PMF assault group under Assistant Superintendent Gorham; a snatch party led by Detective Inspector Davis with a special constable, two African detective sergeants, a driver – Inspector Bowery – and two special constable vehicle guards; an escort group of three special constables for the snatch party; a search group led by Assistant Superintendent Humphrys and a special branch detective; and a support group of three platoons from D Company of the 2nd Battalion, KAR, commanded by Captain Caine.

The PMF and KAR were briefed separately but all the others were assembled at the forestry department offices to avoid too much activity being noticed at the Limbe police station. They were summoned there by telephone at about 11 p.m., told that a state of emergency was to come into effect an hour later and that Banda was to be arrested.[10]

> The news was greeted with quiet jubilation and relief and seen as a solution to the long hours [they] had all been working and an opportunity to restore law and order.[11]

After a final briefing at 3.30 a.m. they moved off an hour later and joined the PMF and KAR at the tobacco producers' warehouse. They formed up and, led by the diversion party, all moved off at 4.35 a.m. with their vehicle lights extinguished and their engines turned off so that they coasted downhill to Banda's house.[12]

The task of the leading party was to create a diversion at the house, drawing any bodyguards' attention away from the main party or containing them for as long as possible to prevent interference with Banda's arrest.[13] They drove into the grounds from the back roadway while the other vehicles went in from the front. Dagnell drove straight into the back yard and all others in the vehicle immediately debussed. One of the young special constables was so nervous that he accidentally discharged a round from his rifle as he got out of the Land Rover. There was no opposition to their arrival but several Africans ran away from the house shouting '*Kwacha*' and 'Freedom'. Cotton and his men surrounded the servants' quarters and arrested the people in them, using tear gas to ensure that no one was still hiding in the quarters. It is probable that the speed and stealth with which the diversion party acted maintained the element of surprise and prevented a drum, located near the house, being beaten to give the signal to Congress supporters – to be relayed by other drums – that Banda had been arrested or attacked by the police.[14]

The PMF party, led by Gorham and accompanied by Bevan, drove to the front of the house which was well lit up. They found about sixty people around the house. They used a five-ton open truck with the sides down so that the entire unit was able to sit around the edges ready to leap off and into action immediately. They jumped off and charged the twenty or so bodyguards on the verandah, encountering little resistance.

During the afternoon of 2 March the support group were placed on standby. The commander reported to the special branch operations room in Blantyre at midnight and was told of his task: to support the unit arresting Banda. The deployment was left to Caine save that one platoon, led by Captain Wallace-Jones, was to accompany the pick-up team. He placed his other two platoons to act as road blocks near Banda's house.[15]

The leader of the snatch party, Davis, struck the door of the house one blow with an axe as instructed. As this had no effect, he turned the handle, the unlocked door opened, and he and his three colleagues entered.[16] Inside they saw lying on the settee in the lounge, Yatuta Chisiza, Banda's personal bodyguard, who said, 'I suppose you are looking for the doctor.' When Davis replied 'Yes', Chisiza led them into Banda's bedroom. The doctor was awake but still in bed, possibly having just been awakened by the sound of the vehicles, and Davis removed the mosquito net, told him that he was being arrested under the state of emergency that had just been declared and asked him to get up. Banda put on his dressing gown and, since Davis refused him permission to get dressed, his clothes – including a suit but inadvertently no underclothes – were collected by one of the detectives, placed in a suitcase and taken to the Land Rover outside. Banda's own account says:

> When I was arrested I was not allowed to touch anything at all, not even my clothes to dress ... I was led out to the truck in pyjamas. I left everything in the house, cash, my watch, clothes ... including an overcoat which was lying on the chair.

The only comments made by Banda in the house, apart from asking if he could get dressed, were to ask why shots had been fired outside, adding that there was no need to use arms, and to remonstrate with Humphrys who, since Banda could not produce a key, barged down one of the interior doors with his shoulder. The doctor was very calm and quiet throughout the incident and Davis formed the view that he had been expecting to be arrested and therefore was not surprised. He behaved 'peacefully, quietly and no force was used'.

The get-away vehicle was driven by Inspector Bowery,[17] a former driver in the Metropolitan Police, with training and experience in high speed driving. Banda and Yatuta Chisiza climbed into the back of the Land Rover outside the house under the control of Detective Sergeants

Laja and Wemusi, Detective Sub Inspector Banda and Special Constable Evans. Immediately Bowery, with observer Special Constable Smith sitting next to him, drove off at high speed from Limbe through Blantyre, negotiating the first military road-block while it was still dark to the cheers of the army and police personnel manning it when they realised who Bowery's chief passenger was.

> The drive through to Blantyre was uneventful and I drove through to the Chileka Road which is a ten mile downhill run from Blantyre to the airport ... The road was a mere twelve foot tarmac and just wide enough for two vehicles to pass one another. On the downhill run ... I was travelling very fast indeed when I saw two lights approaching from the opposite direction. I pulled over to the extreme left but remained at speed. Only at the last minute, due to it still being dark, did I realise that it was a military Saracen armoured car with its small headlights set inside massive one meter armoured wings. I recall flicking the wheel of the Land Rover sideways then back again and missed the Saracen by fractions. I reached Chileka in near record time ... and the aircraft which was to take the Doctor to Gwelo stood waiting. Dr Banda looked at me as he got from the vehicle and remarked that it was a rather rough ride. I apologised, saying that I had a time element to consider. He nodded and was then escorted through to the aircraft. Dr Banda had no idea how close he had come, along with myself and the others, to a horrendous accident.[18]

In declaring a state of emergency, the Governor also declared a number of locations to be prisons, including Chileka where a barbed wire holding cage was erected. On arriving at Chileka, the Land Rover carrying Banda entered the cage and the doctor was handed over to Captain Swart and taken to a small office where he was seated by himself. Swart recalled:

> I remember him well. He was very subdued, did not offer any resistance and looked rather forlorn. He carried himself with dignity, poise and a beaten, far away, look in his eyes. I would say full marks for his behaviour and attitude pattern. He was then air-transported from Chileka to Gwelo [in Southern Rhodesia].

He was flown, with Chipembere, in a separate plane from that in which other detainees were taken.[19]

While Banda was being driven to Chileka, his house was searched by Humphrys and Sub Inspector Banda, assisted by Cotton.[20] The search was very thorough and a quantity of papers was taken away. At about 7 a.m. a crowd of about five hundred, which had gathered at Banda's surgery, was dispersed by the police.[21]

Although there had for some time been widespread rumours that

Banda would be arrested – because many believed that W.M. Chirwa, Chinyama, Chijozi and Kwenje had advised the Governor to do so[22] – and although Banda himself had said he might be arrested and in many ways had courted arrest, it is possible he did not believe that he would be arrested at the precise time the arrest took place. Some ten weeks later he said:

> where people were telling these stories I told them I did not believe that, I did not think the Governor would act on Chinyama and Kwenje's advice. He was too intelligent a man ... and he had assured me ... they had nothing against me, and there was no question in their minds of arresting me. Not only that, but Mr Youens had told me that they would not be so stupid as to arrest me as they knew I had the people with me, and Mr Ingham said they wanted no head on collision with me, and these were his words.[23]

On the other hand, Banda said, 'On the day of my arrest, I had my suitcase and another bag all packed, as I knew I was going to be arrested', and he had spent part of the previous evening, 2 March, with A.C. McAdam of the Blantyre Scottish Mission who shortly afterwards recalled:

> Dr Banda ... on the night of 2nd March ... had in fact given me some personal cash that he had in hand in the house that night. He did tell me that he was going to be picked up, and I could see arrangements were being made to tidy the house, medicines were being packed away carefully [and] stored, and [also] clothes.[24]

Banda also asked the journalist, George Clay, to visit him at his house at 10 p.m. on 2 March, and shortly afterwards Clay recalled:

> Speaking softly and quietly, Dr Banda ... told me that he expected to be arrested next morning. He had heard on the radio an account of a press conference at which ... Sir Robert Armitage had said that the government planned to make a number of arrests in connection with the recent disturbances. This had been followed by the announcement that next morning an important statement would be made about the Nyasaland situation.[25]

It is possible that a fairly large number of others anticipated arrests would be made because of this announcement. A number of people 'thought that made it a dead cert [that an emergency would be declared] and was an astonishing breach of security',[26] although others took the broadcast itself to mean that there would be no declaration. Furthermore, one of the Africans guarding Banda's house said:

I was a guard on Dr Banda's house. I was not on duty on the night of Dr Banda's arrest. At about 8 p.m. I was in my house and another guard came and said that an official telephone message had come to Dr Banda stating that he was going to be arrested and I went to Dr Banda's house. There were a lot of people, more than a hundred, who carried no weapons. Somewhere between 4 and 5 [a.m.] we were awake. We were as witnesses that Dr Banda had been arrested and had not been killed. There were about a hundred of us in the Doctor's garden when the troops arrived. Before they arrived they fired tear gas and it affected our eyes and we got out, and we stood some way off and waited until he was arrested.[27]

A week earlier Banda had written to Fenner Brockway saying there were rumours he was to be arrested 'any time now' and, while he was ready to be taken, he shuddered at the thought of the day he would be arrested: 'What the settlers do not know is that I am the main restraining influence here. Well, let [the settlers] have their way.'[28]

While Banda was being arrested, special branch officers searched and cleared the Congress secretariat and the doctor's clinic.[29] There were reports that the clinic had been used to indoctrinate patients and to gain information about the employers of those who worked for Europeans.[30] They removed a large quantity of documents and anticipated that it would take two to three weeks before they could be fully examined; two special branch officers spent long hours 'methodically going through the hundreds of kit bags stored in the Registrar-General's strongrooms, sifting through the papers seized'.[31] All documents after 23 January 1959, that is from the bush meeting onwards, had been destroyed in the Congress secretariat before special branch officers searched the premises.[32] As Armitage reported at 'Vespers' that evening, 'there were no signs of stocks of arms or explosives etc. being held' there;[33] this gave the impression that while he was not surprised no arms were found, neither would he have been surprised had some been discovered.

During the morning RRAF Vampires 'buzzed' Blantyre and Limbe and flew the length of Nyasaland at a low level in a display of force which frightened many people, especially African villagers, and re-assured others who thought 'an aerial display of power would have a salutory effect on those who make trouble'.[34] Other aircraft 'dive bombed one village after another, dropping ... bundles of leaflets', and on some of these sorties the pilot was accompanied by an administrative officer, acting as a guide but feeling distinctly airsick.[35] All schools in Blantyre, Limbe, Zomba, Cholo and Lilongwe were closed, and parents warned to keep their children at home and not leave them unattended.[36] In the townships the great majority of Africans stayed away from work, and some who had gone to work left quickly when the RRAF planes flew over. In Limbe several vehicles were overturned and set on fire.[37] In each of the urban areas, administrative officers toured in Land Rovers, using loud hailers, told people about the emergency and the arrest of Congress leaders, encouraged them to return to work, and gave them assurances of the safety of their families and of themselves.[38] In most cases they returned to work the next day or a few days later.[39]

Many years later one of the African detainees, the Livingstonia branch secretary of Congress, recalled his own arrest.[40] At 1 a.m. on 3 March he heard a knock on the door of his house:

> When I opened the door I found a pistol directed at my head and a deep voice saying you are arrested, Dr Banda has been arrested and a state of emergency has been declared ... and I give you two minutes to get dressed. When I went into my bedroom he followed me and my wife shouted at him why are you entering my room? ... [He] told my wife if she was going to shout ... she would be shot. When we came outside the house I found so many policemen. I was handcuffed and taken in a nearby Land Rover.

He was taken in the back of the Land Rover, 'surrounded by policemen', to Rumpi, picking up the branch chairman on the way. From Rumpi he was taken to the Mzuzu holding centre where he found 'all political leaders' from five districts. He was later flown to Khami prison near Bulawayo, where the Nyasaland detainees were separated in a two-storied block from the Southern Rhodesian detainees.

The arrests of Chipembere and Lubani were successfully and peacefully accomplished but not in the manner intended. A special constable recalled:

> The African [special branch officer] showed us the house which [we] quietly entered but it was empty. Similarly the second house was also empty. [The inspector] knew of a Congress house on the Chileka road and we decided to visit the area. As we drove quietly up the drive [the inspector] recognised an African walking along the drive as Chipembere. He was arrested and put under guard in the truck whilst [the inspector] quickly searched the house – no other persons were found. We immediately took Chipembere to Chileka airport. We then drove back towards Blantyre and on the way passed Lubani walking along the main road. [The inspector] recognised him, arrested him and we took him to Chileka.[41]

Both Chipembere and Lubani seemed surprised to be arrested – possibly because the warning drum in Banda's garden had not been sounded – they offered no resistance, were given no reason for their arrest at the time, and gave the strong impression that they were on their way to a meeting of some sort.[42]

One of the few national leaders of Congress who was not arrested early in the day on 3 March was Dunduzu Chisiza, who was staying with another Congress official at a bungalow outside Blantyre at Chirimba, and who telephoned the assistant commissioner of police, Long.

> Chisiza stated that he was ready to give himself up and requested Mr Long to send a vehicle and come personally to collect him. This, Mr Long declined to do, then notified the Special Branch. It transpired that there was a plan for press build-up.[43]

Chisiza was shortly arrested and when pressmen were refused entry to the Blantyre police station they attempted a forced entry, were stopped by a special constable whose language 'was not exactly tasteful and left nothing to the imagination'.[44] One photographer, attempting to film the 'surrender', was told: 'If you don't go back I will blow a hole through your guts.'[45] A full apology was quickly given 'since a more experienced police officer would have used more temperate language and exercised more restraint and tact'.[46] A special branch officer interviewed Chisiza who started to give details of the plan of violence but with the rider that they felt they had no other way to achieve independence. Finney, however, insisted on Chisiza being sent quickly to Southern Rhodesia where other expert interrogators would complete the interview. In the event, no further information was forthcoming when Chisiza arrived in Gwelo. The special branch officer long remained convinced that Chisiza would have revealed many of the details of the plan for violence had he been able to pursue his interview.[47]

By 6 a.m. on 3 March, 22 people had been arrested; by 10 a.m., 60; by 1.30 p.m., 90; by 5.30 p.m., 120; and by 9 p.m. on 4 March, 130, together with a further 44 detained on 28 day orders. By 5 March 263 had been arrested, over three-quarters of those on the 'Sunrise' lists, and 87 remained at large.[48] Some who were arrested on 3 March were almost immediately released because they had not been at the 24–25 January emergency meeting, and the Governor very quickly let it be known to those detained that they were able to make representations to him on their detention; this made Chisiza, at least, 'regain faith in the British sense of justice'.[49] In all, 72 detainees were flown to Southern Rhodesia on 3 March.[50] Chileka was the collecting point for the southern province detainees to be flown out of the country and Lilongwe performed a similar function for those from the central and northern provinces. Detainees from the northern province were taken by road to Nkata Bay, then by lake steamer to Chipoka and then by rail to Salima, from where they were taken by road to Lilongwe airport.

At the two airports the detainees were handed over to the federal prison authorities.[51] Except for the five detainees in Gwelo – Banda, Chipembere, the Chisiza brothers and Kapombe Nyasulu – all other Nyasaland detainees in Southern Rhodesia were 'held in the most modern prison accommodation in the Federation with experienced staff and maximum security' at Khami.[52]

Operation Sunrise was, on the whole, efficiently conducted. District pick-up teams effected their arrests with the minimum of trouble and difficulty. In the actual pick-up arrests, 120 people were detained within the first 12 hours and only five were injured; no one was killed.[53] Although in a few cases excessive restraint – in the sense that more restraint than proved necessary in the event – was probably used, generally the arrests were made peacefully and with the cooperation of those arrested. Fairly large numbers gave themselves up.[54] The potential for resistance and counter-attack by those arrested was high since their homes were peremptorily entered – in the dark, without warning and often without explanation – by armed strangers, and they were hastily removed while their houses and property were searched. The transfer of those arrested to prisons in Southern Rhodesia was also efficiently conducted and in a peaceful fashion, the detainees generally suffering little physical discomfort in the process.[55] The same was largely true of those detained in Nyasaland although the journeys to the detention camps, especially when long distances, rough roads and lake transport were involved, were uncomfortable – sometimes extremely so.

Nearly all government officers involved in arresting detainees thoroughly disliked what they had to do. The general feeling was recalled by one of them:

> I personally felt a strong distaste for the whole episode ... Clearly we had to take out the trouble-makers who had been intimidating peaceable villagers, challenging our authority, burning bridges and houses etc., but I did not know the man [I was arresting] and it all seemed an uncouth invasion of his village on a quiet African night.[56]

District commissioners were relieved that the vast majority of arrests were made without opposition and attributed this to a willingness to be detained with their leaders, and a number of others who were not arrested seemed to be 'disappointed on discovering that they were not considered important enough to be picked up'.[57]

The worst problems experienced at the very beginning of the emergency were not encountered in effecting the pick-up arrests but in dealing with the crowds that gathered as a result of those arrests. The commissioners shortly inquiring into the disturbances pressed witnesses to agree that these crowds gathered, and did so naturally and spontaneously, simply to inquire of the district commissioners the reasons for the arrest of their leaders. They were reluctant to accept that the crowds were deliberately gathered by Congressmen who had avoided arrest, in order to demonstrate against the arrests made, to try to release the prisoners and to stir up greater disturbances, although this was clearly so in many cases. It may be that in some instances, when encouraging people to go to the bomas, those inciting them to go said they must do so in order to find out the reasons for the arrests, but they should have known very well the result would be further disturbances and attempts to release those arrested.

In five cases throughout the country resistance to the arrests was such that five detainees were injured; however, in two other incidents 21 people who were not being arrested but demonstrating against the arrests were killed and 29 injured. Of these, 20 were killed and 28 injured at Nkata Bay in by far the most serious encounter of the whole emergency.[58] A large crowd gathered at the Nkata Bay dock area at the instigation of a Congress leader who had not been arrested.

> This leader went round the villages very early in the morning after the emergency had been declared. He told the people to stop their daily business and get to Nkata Bay and ask why their leaders had been arrested. This leader told them that the leaders had been arrested because the Government wanted to impose Federation by force. This call to people who are strongly opposed to Federation was very effective. Many people flocked to Nkata Bay including school children ... At the Bay they first went to the prison [where] they demanded the release of their leaders ... During this time the unarrested leader had gone to call the people from a distance where he was arrested by the Chombe tea estate manager.[59]

The gathering of crowds, whether to inquire as to the reasons for arrests, to attempt the release of those arrested or to cause further disturbances, had been anticipated by Armitage[60] but the arrangements and precautions for dealing with it were not as efficiently made or executed as were those for the actual pick-ups. Thus Brock, district commissioner at Nkata Bay, was faced with a terrible situation without the security force back-up needed to handle it. Since all northern province detainees were to be evacuated through Nkata Bay; since, too, the northern province Sunrise arrest list contained more names than those of either of the other provinces; and since by mid-February disturbances in the north were more serious than elsewhere, it is surprising that major precautionary steps were not taken in good time to strengthen the security forces at the Bay. The reason for this was later given by the district commissioner:

Nkata Bay, by the standards of the country at the time was [a district] in which ... I enjoyed friendly relations with most of the people. I was very unwilling for that relationship to be impaired in any way and when we were informed that an emergency was to be declared I realised that it would bring a change in the general atmosphere but I did not want to bring about that change earlier than was necessary. And I was unwilling for troops to be brought into the district earlier than I considered really necessary because I thought that the local people would not understand the reason for it, and the happy relations that existed between us would be harmed ... I realised that troops would be necessary at Nkata Bay on that particular morning ... therefore it was arranged that they should come in at dawn on the morning of March 3. In the event they were delayed on their way up through Nyasaland.[61]

A small team of Nyasaland police interrogators flew to Southern Rhodesia on 2 March and were awaiting the detainees when they arrived: Senior Desk Officer Hodder, Superintendent Chevalier, Assistant Inspector Gombera, Sergeant Chaca and Detective Sergeant Kampa.[62] Questioning started on 4 March – of 'as many as possible ... before they could concert their defence'.[63] Two detainees, Thomas Karua and Origin Kaigine, sent messages saying that they wished to speak with the officers. Altogether 30 detainees were interviewed, six statements were taken, and others were deterred by 'the ringleaders ... shouting threats from their cells at night that anyone squealing would be murdered together with their wives and families'. These shouted threats became so severe when a small group of new detainees – the 'second eleven' – arrived on 7 March that two ringleaders were placed in segregated single cells. When the chief prison officer, Stokes, was told by Hodder that Karua was an informer he was removed from his cell to another two floors up, together with several other detainees to avoid suspicion.[64] Of the others who made statements, two were current agents of special branch and one more had previously been an agent.[65] No statements were forthcoming after 6 March and by 9 March it was clear further interrogation would not be fruitful, so the team returned to Nyasaland.[66]

Some interrogation in Nyasaland was neither as well organised nor as successful as that in Southern Rhodesia, although inexperienced interrogation teams received brief training and in many cases were accompanied by a special branch officer.[67] For example, an officer of considerable experience in Nyasaland recalled that he and his colleagues in an interrogation team at Kanjedza, Blantyre, did not work to any particular guidelines: 'We just wanted to know generally what they could tell us. The interrogation teams were very much in the dark.' He complained that he was given no guidance or briefing before starting the questioning and 'had to get all the information out of the detainee himself'.[68] In another case a special constable, a former Palestine police officer who had been in the country for several years, interrogated detainees in Lilongwe, with little to no guidance initially:

> I complained about the fact that we did not have any line to go on ... and then they allowed us to read a document about the murder plot and they asked us to investigate on these lines, which we did.[69]

Thereafter the interrogators met with some success, especially when they used African police officers to do the interrogations, although a good deal of valuable time had been lost in the meantime. Even the interrogation of Chaloledwa, who had been at the 25 January bush meeting and in whose house had been found a document covering the points made at the meeting, was not particularly firmly carried out despite its seriousness.[70] Several field officers were asked to be members of interrogation teams because of their knowledge of local African languages.[71] One such officer recalled that the interrogations of the Northern Rhodesia police were 'altogether a tougher proposition' than those of the Nyasaland police. Other officers also commented on the Northern Rhodesia police 'who had a reputation for being tough and having a fondness for using their pick helves'.[72] Most probably this applied to one platoon only.[73]

The Governor, like many others, was now working very long hours. He arrived in his office at 7.30 a.m., worked all day and – after 'Vespers' attended by senior civil servants, police, army and air force officers at 9 p.m. – left at about 11 p.m., if he was lucky. He rarely got to bed before 11.30 p.m.[74]

Armitage set up the Nyasaland Operations Committee – in response to Ingham and Kettlewell's worries – comprising General Long, the officer commanding the army in Nyasaland, Mullin and, as staff officer, Kettlewell whom the Governor appointed because of his long service in, and knowledge of, the protectorate and because of his close contacts with district commissioners and chiefs.[75] Mullin was uncomfortable about Kettlewell whom he believed, incorrectly, had been appointed because Mullin himself was under stress and, presumably – but also incorrectly – felt to be unable to cope as well as expected.[76] Kettlewell later recalled:

> Unfortunately neither Mullin (brand new) nor Long knew much (if anything) about Nyasaland. But they had command of Intelligence and considerable forces. I spent much of my time travelling round to keep in touch with the Provincial Commissioners, and, on the information thus gleaned and discussed with Mullin and Long, drafted the operation

orders which were submitted to the Governor. He outlined them at 'Vespers' if appropriate to the discussions of the evening.[77]

Theunissen kept a record of the committee meetings which was 'approved at the highest level'. It was agreed at one of the first meetings to keep no minutes so as not to inhibit discussions. If any matters required further attention a note was made by the member responsible. The records were not submitted at subsequent meetings for approval and the way was open, therefore, for individuals to disclaim.[78]

The day the emergency was declared Lennox-Boyd reported it to the House of Commons, emphasising that Armitage had taken action himself, freely and at his exclusive discretion, without any outside pressures from, for example, the federal government, but with the full support of the British government. This support is indicated by the recollection of Amery:

> I was aroused at two in the morning, or thereabouts, by the Permanent Under-secretary to say that Armitage wanted to declare a State of Emergency and arrest Banda and other Nationalist Leaders. Lennox-Boyd was away at the time, I think in Aden. I said we must support the man on the spot. The Permanent Under-secretary then asked whether I thought it necessary to consult the prime minister. I could see no point in adding to his burdens by spoiling his night's sleep. I accordingly said no, and we gave Armitage a free hand to take emergency action as he thought fit.[79]

The secretary of state had not been able to visit Nyasaland earlier when the Governor had hoped – and Armitage later wondered if Lennox-Boyd's presence on the spot would have altered the chain of events. At this point, however, on Sunday 1 March, returning from Aden and Cyprus, Lennox-Boyd was met at London airport by Amery who had kept him informed of developments while he was away and who now told him of the current situation,[80] including showing him the special branch report of the Congress meeting of 25 January.[81] Lennox-Boyd later recalled:

> I first heard of the crisis in Nyasaland when Julian Amery met me at London Airport ... Julian told me that in January 1959 the African National Congress in Nyasaland had decided to embark on a policy of defiance and sabotage, including violence. I think now that I should have taken longer to make up my mind about how to handle this. The possibility of very serious violence and murder was a real one. I wish I had turned straight round and gone back to Heathrow and told the prime minister I wasn't going to report on my previous visit, I was going straight out to Nyasaland. I wish I had done that.[82]

Lennox-Boyd was very conscious, that Sunday evening and throughout Monday, of the serious nature of the information he had received and was also aware that the situation had for some days justified the declaration of a state of emergency. It could be claimed too that he and Armitage had failed in their duties by not taking action earlier if Europeans, Asians and loyal Africans were murdered. The reason action was not taken earlier was the need to have security forces in place to protect people in remote areas when Banda was arrested – which he felt the disorders would make necessary – and the real risk of violence, including murder, which Armitage believed would follow.[83]

It was with these considerations in mind that Lennox-Boyd went to the Commons on 3 March and told the House that 'the Governor was compelled this morning to declare a state of emergency'.[84] He added that once order had been restored, the government and the Governor would 'consider what constitutional reforms may be appropriate'. He was closely questioned, particularly by Callaghan, about what *The Times* and Callaghan took to be the Governor's statement, made only the previous day, that a state of emergency was not necessary. The opposition was convinced that Armitage, against his better judgement, had been pressed by the British government – who were, in turn, greatly influenced by the federal government – to declare a state of emergency and at the last moment had given way. Callaghan then moved the adjournment of the House to 'discuss a definite matter of urgent public importance, namely, the declaration of a state of emergency in Nyasaland'.

The debate took place that same day from 3.30 p.m. to 10 p.m.[85] Callaghan, whose view was that 'British Ministers at the time were determined that federation should succeed at almost any cost',[86] opened for the opposition and was so emotional that Lennox-Boyd asked him to calm down. He took the point and said 'If I speak with heat, I ask the pardon of the House. I will endeavour to contain myself.' There was the suspicion that his 'heat' was histrionic; as Amery suggested: 'It is always fairly easy to restrain fictitious emotion.' Callaghan appealed to the government, as had Banda and his colleagues, to make an early statement of their proposals for constitutional advance so that when the 1960 conference on the Federation was held, Nyasaland would be represented by 'a delegation which will comprise a majority of their own people'.

Replying to Callaghan's taunts about the influence of the federal government on the British government to press Armitage into declaring a state of emergency and so change his mind about not doing so, Lennox-Boyd said:

Some days ago information came to the notice of the Governor of Nyasaland which was of a very serious kind. I have seen the information. I am not in a position to disclose it nor its source ... That information made it clear that plans had been made by Congress to carry out widespread violence and murder of Europeans, Asians and moderate African leaders: that, in fact, a massacre was being planned. It was essential for the Governor ... to strengthen the security forces, so he asked the Federal Government for troops. He asked the Northern Rhodesian and Southern Rhodesian Governments for police reinforcements and the Tanganyikan Government for assistance at Fort Hill. It was becoming increasingly clear that the disturbances would make the declaration of a state of emergency inevitable.

Colonial Office officials were 'somewhat taken aback' when the secretary of state mentioned the information about murder and a planned massacre 'not because [they] were uncertain about the intelligence' but because they feared they might be unable to satisfy the House without revealing the source and this they could not do. Lennox-Boyd conceded to his officials that he had 'overstepped his brief'. This was the first time the plans for murder had been mentioned in public and Armitage was 'staggered' when he learned what Lennox-Boyd had said.[87]

The secretary of state, in addressing the Commons, went on to say that under the circumstances:

the Governor of Nyasaland decided that it would be inopportune for [Perth] to go to Blantyre for constitutional talks ... It was a ridiculous suggestion [from Callaghan] that the Federal Government said [Perth] should not go. That was utterly without foundation.

This was not strictly true as Welensky had in fact advised postponing the visit, advice which the British government did not accept although they did accept identical advice from Armitage very shortly after. Lennox-Boyd emphasised that the Governor personally and exclusively took the decision to declare the state of emergency, without pressure from Welensky or the British government, and the British government 'approved fully' of his action. As for what Armitage had said to the press the previous day, Lennox-Boyd had spoken to him by telephone just before the debate started and was assured that, in saying 'no state of emergency was needed in Nyasaland to act against dissidents', Armitage had meant that such a declaration was not necessary before he could take certain action against certain individuals – the power to take some action already existed. Lennox-Boyd reiterated that they had arranged Perth's intended visit so as to bring the constitutional discussions to a conclusion 'this month', and once order was restored they would resume the talks.

Closing for the government, Amery dealt with the four main charges made by the opposition: the major cause of the crisis was delay over constitutional discussions; there were no real grounds for declaring the state of emergency; it was wrong to introduce federal forces into Nyasaland; and what had happened was the result of 'a conspiracy or machination' on the part of the federal government.

On the question of constitutional progress, Amery stated Banda had refused to reach agreement on any proposals put forward. 'He was determined to set very high terms and, when these were refused, to lead a campaign of speeches and then of disturbances with the deliberate purpose of courting arrest.'

> There is no question of delay here. There was no chance, as is now clear, of reaching agreement on the constitutional issue. We hoped until the very last minute that it would be possible to reach agreement on that basis. That is why the minister of state was to go out. The truth is that Dr Banda did not want it.

At this point, presumably to support what the secretary of state had said earlier under pressure, Amery dealt with 'a still more sinister feature' and, reminding members of the Mau Mau atrocities, said that in Nyasaland 'there was a conspiracy of murder ... if we had not taken appropriate action at the right moment there may well have been a massacre of Africans, Asians and Europeans on a Kenyan scale'. Colonial Office officials seem not to have been sufficiently 'taken aback' by Lennox-Boyd's statement on this matter to have persuaded Amery to 'go easy' and not repeat it.

Dealing with the need to declare a state of emergency and bring in federal troops, Amery detailed the way in which 'the situation had been building up over the last ten days ... which at any stage in the last week would amply have justified the declaration of an emergency'. If sufficient forces had not been available 'there might well have been the bloodbath which we feared', and since the army was the federal army, the troops were inevitably federal troops.

Finally, he dealt with the 'conspiracy or machination' allegations:

> It was the Governor of Nyasaland who asked for the troops to come into Nyasaland ... it is a travesty to say that [the federal or other governments] were in any sense creating an emergency or urging the Governor of Nyasaland into the emergency ... It would be a complete travesty to suggest that there had been pressure from Salisbury.

When the House divided, the government received 259 votes, the opposition 201. Lennox-Boyd cabled Armitage to reassure him:

Parliamentary situation at this end all under control. Its main importance of course is the possible adverse effect on your position but no need to worry.[88]

Turning his attention from the debate in the Commons to urgent practicalities in Nyasaland, Lennox-Boyd discussed with Home, the Commonwealth secretary, the adequacy of security forces in the two northern territories and discussed requirements with the chief of air staff, who alerted British troops in Kenya because they thought Welensky 'unduly optimistic' about the adequacy of federal forces. Benson feared he might lose his Northern Rhodesia troops for redeployment in Nyasaland as part of a campaign by Welensky to force a state of emergency on Northern Rhodesia. Home telegraphed Welensky about the danger of denuding Northern Rhodesia of troops and stressed that he must give full warning to Britain before taking any such action.[89]

The secretary of state and Armitage were extremely anxious to avoid using firearms if they possibly could and Lennox-Boyd cabled the Governor:

I hope your police and forces are not being prevented from avoiding shooting by any lack of other means. For example, have you sufficient supplies of riot weapons, for example, tear gas and fire hoses (how applicable?). Grateful to learn position and whether I can help in any way.[90]

Armitage had already ordered flame throwers and dye from Britain, and Lennox-Boyd told him they would very shortly be despatched.[91] The situation in some areas in the very first days of the emergency was sufficiently worrying for the Nyasaland Operations Committee to raise the question of firing on crowds from the air.[92] Although RRAF Provosts 'attacked rioting crowds with tear gas bombs',[93] Armitage was immediately and very firmly opposed to firing from the air and ordered that under no circumstances should air firepower be used 'whatever the situation on the ground'.[94] When the brigade commander in the northern province sought permission to use Vampire aircraft, this was refused:

At one stage there were riots and burning of shops at Mzimba with no troops within 80 miles of the place. I made a request for an 'air strike'. This was turned down.[95]

The Governor asked the Colonial Office for 'immediate advice' and received the qualified reply that 'in no (repeat no) circumstances should aircraft fire on crowds who do not carry firearms'.[96] The Committee returned to the question, however, and – presumably bearing in mind the lethal nature of weapons other than firearms – asked whether the order should be altered so as to permit fire from the air in cases 'where a small garrison is in extremis and clearly about to be over-run with the inevitable massacre of all in it'.[97] The Governor, in these circumstances, was prepared to permit fire from the air. He did, however, check his view with the secretary of state who also agreed, but added, 'There is no need for me to emphasise the kind of difficulties into which actions of this kind might lead us.'[98] In supporting the Governor's view,[99] Lennox-Boyd also made it clear that his consent to fire from the air was extremely restricted and did not in any event extend to the use of bombs, cannons or rockets.[100] Such was his caution that he consulted the prime minister, Macmillan, who asked for the question to be raised in the cabinet.[101] He approved of Lennox-Boyd's ruling but added:

> In a situation where aircraft fire may be used as a last resort in the circumstances envisaged ... it would be possible to make some preliminary dummy runs of a menacing kind which might frighten and disperse the mob without actually opening fire and inflicting casualties. It might even be possible to open fire in the first instance in such a way as not to cause casualties as, for example, in the old days troops 'fired over the heads of the mob'.[102]

Although Macmillan's response was somewhat Kiplingesque, he and his colleagues were deeply conscious of the political dangers. For example, the minister of defence was 'much concerned' about aircraft fire being 'used to quell civil riots' and the 'grave embarrassment which this would cause at home and abroad'. None the less, in the extreme circumstances envisaged he did not see how they 'could allow the security forces or the white settlers to be massacred' if they had the means of preventing it.[103]

The British government contemplated the need to fly in British troops if the Nyasaland situation seriously deteriorated, but were concerned on two counts. First, Welensky might claim the situation amounted to an emergency involving the defence of the Federation as a whole and might then feel free to set aside territorial responsibilities for law and order. Alport, minister of state in the Commonwealth Relations Office, had no great confidence that the federal forces would be adequate to contain the situation or that Welensky understood the full gravity of it. Second, they were concerned about discord between Welensky and Benson over the ultimate responsibility for calling in British troops in the event of an emergency in Northern Rhodesia.[104] Presumably similar doubts existed over Nyasaland.

Once Armitage had detained the leaders of Congress on 3 March their direct power was removed, and people who had noticed a change in African attitudes over the preceding months now found it 'extra-ordinary how, on the morning following Operation Sunrise, the courtesy and friendliness seem to have suddenly returned'.[105] Even so, the Governor was worried about others taking over Congress activities and plans in their absence. He noticed that a number of well-educated Nyasalanders had had frequent meetings with the leaders before they were detained and he suspected – on the basis of documents seized since 3 March – that they had 'taken control of the next phase'.[106] On 7 March, therefore, early in the morning he detained: David Rubadiri, an education officer, and Mrs Rubadiri; Dr Bwanausi, a medical prac-titioner; Orton Chirwa and Mrs Chirwa; Moir Chisuse, a principal laboratory assistant in the agricultural department; and Vincent Gondwe, an education officer, and his wife.[107] The Gondwes were personal friends of the district commissioner, who was not consulted and who was 'appalled' by their detention.[108] The arrests were peace-fully and cooperatively carried out at a gentle pace and, at least in the Chirwas's case, appeared to be expected, since they were quite 'chirpy' about it. These new detainees were flown to Southern Rhodesia to be detained at Khami prison or, in the case of the women, Salisbury prison.[109] Much concern was expressed in Britain over the arrest of these graduates, particularly Orton Chirwa, and questions were asked in the Commons.[110] Armitage stressed how important it was not to disclose to the House the grounds for any particular detention, but he explained to the secretary of state that Chirwa:

> was known to have been in close association with Dr Banda while in U.K. and since [his] return here. He is strongly suspected accordingly and recent statements indicate that he was to be a member of [the] controlling body of Congress on Dr Banda's arrest.[111]

A similar arrest was made a few days after the emergency was declared: that of John Msonthi, a graduate teacher in Zomba. When he was arrested – an amicable and good hearted operation on both sides – he said, 'It's no good looking for the letter. I've eaten it.'[112] A little later Msonthi explained that he had received a letter on 2 March asking him to take over the secretary-generalship of Congress if Chisiza were arrested.[113] The letter, signed by Makata, Lubani, Chisiza and Chipem-bere, was sent on the evening of 2 March and taken to Zomba by Karua since 'it was evident that Dr Banda was about to be arrested'. Karua delivered the letter to Msonthi at Tennyson Limbe's bar where he was found with Rubadiri and others.[114]

The Governor noted that while Congress activities did not stop when Banda and other leaders were arrested, the disorders had 'markedly declined' after Orton Chirwa and others were arrested on 7 March. None the less severe trouble continued, especially in the north, where government forces 'held on grimly' and were fully stretched in dealing with it. Colonel Putterill, brigade commander, initially set up his headquarters at Lilongwe, but soon after Operation Sunrise was completed and a 'firm military presence' established in the central province, he moved to the northern province at Mzuzu with the 1st and 2nd Battalions KAR, and B Company of the 1st Battalion NRR under his command – all African troops under European officers, the white territorial soldiers being confined to the southern and central provinces. Since Mzuzu airstrip could handle only light aircraft, he used Central African Airways Beavers flown by civilian pilots to transport him and his staff to Karonga, Fort Hill and Nkata Bay. Their task in the north was to stabilise the position there, particularly at the Fort Hill airfield and customs post and in the Misuku Hills. The journey north took some time because many bridges had been wrecked and bailey bridges had to be sent up from Blantyre. They were also troubled by the ease with which people who were to be arrested and detained were able to cross into Tanganyika, and Putterill unsuccessfully sought the help of the Tanganyika police in preventing 'this migration'. The battalions saw themselves as showing the flag simply by their presence and not as being engaged in a mopping-up exercise. Kettlewell made frequent visits to the north, had many discussions with the provincial and district commissioners, and thought 'things seemed to be under control'.[115]

The account of a Livingstonia missionary adds to the picture of widespread disorder in the north:

> there had been burnings and beatings at Deep Bay ... when it was found that the local Congress leader had been taken. The [African] postmaster had been attacked and beaten and his motorbike smashed, and the post office broken into and the telegraph wires cut, so that Karonga was cut off from the rest of the country ... [T]he [African] headmaster of the school ... had his house burned down and some of his cattle killed. Other houses were also burned ... the crowds were talking of killing two informers, and coming up to wreck the [Livingstonia] post office.[116]

For Armitage matters in the north were considerably complicated by the Church of Scotland Livingstonia Mission. There was evidence that teachers and pupils from Church of Scotland schools in the north were seen damaging roads and bridges, and Armitage had a growing suspicion that at Livingstonia – and at Blantyre – 'people and papers concerned with Congress may be concealed' and felt the security forces would have to search buildings there, but he warned the police and military to exercise great care because 'protests will be extreme'.[117] It is unlikely the Governor was fully aware of the pressure the Livingstonia Mission was under at the time: African members of the church, including ministers, were severely intimidated to join Congress, being threatened with death, assault and arson. European members were also threatened with death.[118] The missionaries feared, with good reason, that a large mob was marching on the mission station from the lake shore below:

> they could be up at Livingstonia in an hour ... It was very scary ... but we had to make plans and act quickly ... It was decided that all missionaries, and wives and children, should be gathered together at the Stone House ... and should sleep there that night.[119]

Bedding, food, letters, diaries and other possessions were gathered and taken to the Stone House, the principal's house. Some kept watch all night but the mob changed its mind and set off for other targets. The missionaries debated whether to evacuate the women and children. In the event, however – despite the administration making plans for their evacuation by lake transport and encouraging them, for their own safety, to leave – the missionaries decided to stay with their African brethren, reached an accommodation with Congress leaders, and remained there safely.[120] Although peace had returned to Livingstonia trouble continued elsewhere in the north.

In the period of 8 to 19 March, security operations in the northern province resulted in two deaths and three woundings, and in the central province four deaths and two woundings. There were no deaths or woundings in the southern province.[121] Armitage was, however, concerned about the dangers which might erupt from squatters in settlements around Blantyre, and he agreed to them being ordered out by a given date or 'the bulldozers would go in at sunrise. Then the troops would ... clear the areas and be free to move to the North' to deal with the trouble there.[122]

On Sunday 8 March Armitage met with Welensky, Whitehead, Metcalf and staff officers at Chileka, 'to discuss the operations situation ... and get some more British South Africa Police'. This meeting was called at Welensky's suggestion and lasted for three hours.[123] As the Governor shortly reported to Lennox-Boyd,[124] his request for up to an additional 120 BSAP was countered by Whitehead saying that for the next six to twelve months at least, agreed areas of the southern province could be handled by a much larger number of BSAP which he would make available so as to release Nyasaland police for duties elsewhere in the protectorate. Armitage impressed upon Whitehead that the needs were for short-term BSAP operations and the political implications of his suggestion were considerable. This proposal was 'talked out' and, instead, Whitehead agreed to supply 75 extra BSAP personnel. The meeting ended amicably and Armitage thought it worthwhile because it disclosed Whitehead's views, which he felt Welensky considered to be 'politically impossible'. Welensky did ask Armitage, however, if he thought he could get Lennox-Boyd to support Whitehead's proposal, to which the Governor retorted that he would not even try.[125] Although he would very much have liked the support of Northern Rhodesian police officers, Armitage defended Benson against the criticism that they had not been supplied to operate in Nyasaland by pointing to the likelihood of early disturbances in Northern Rhodesia. When the meeting was told that a British battalion had been alerted on 24 hours' notice in Nairobi and offered to the federal government, Welensky stressed that he still had large forces which could be mobilised in the Rhodesias. Whitehead and Welensky, in different ways, seemed keen to use the troubles to put a stop to Nyasaland Congress activities in the future and to extend their own influence in the protectorate. Throughout the discussions, they emphasised how deep Congress indoctrination was in Nyasaland, how major a task it would be to prevent violence being started again with political agitation and 'how important it was that steps should be concerted to ensure that disorders of this nature should not occur again'. When the secretary of state was asked in the Commons on 19 March why Armitage had called this 'secret conference', he replied that it was to discuss police assistance from Southern Rhodesia; but, as his officials said, 'it seemed best to avoid indicating that [the] first suggestion of [a] meeting came from Welensky'.[126]

On 13 March, 75 additional members of the BSAP arrived in Nyasaland by train and Benson promised four mobile platoons of police after 22 March if the Northern Rhodesian situation permitted.[127] The new arrivals were men from the districts and from the depot, and they were given the simple instruction that their role was 'to show the flag'.[128] They spent their time in the rural areas helping with tax drives and search operations and generally patrolling in fairly rough conditions. At this time Armitage reported that the first shock of arresting Congress leaders in the central and southern provinces had subsided but, since the presence of troops from outside Nyasaland had been 'unwelcome' to Congress supporters, he felt that agitators might refrain from further disorders so that the troops should leave quickly and not be called in again.[129] He added that:

There is no doubt that the return of Banda and Congress leaders arrested is expected. No one will believe that they will be detained for long.

Until we can show that Banda and Company will not be seen for many years, we shall not get neutral and uncommitted people to come and take their place as moderate leaders.[130]

Once the immediate Sunrise phase was over, Armitage embarked upon the second phase which included a 'campaign of harassment' in which chiefs' messengers accompanied patrols to help identify the 'bad hats', and headmen were encouraged to seek out and prosecute illegal immigrants and tax defaulters.[131] The operations in this campaign were given code names: Wet Dawn, Triangle, Jambo, Fisherman and Herringbone.[132] He noted that 'punishment [was] meted out' to trouble-makers and felt: 'many will remember this'.[133]

It was decided that there should next be a vigorous policy of harassing and breaking up Congress organisers, supporters and hoodlums at a lower level, an aggressive policy being needed to break up the existing pattern of intimidation, threats and truculence and to demonstrate the Government's determination to break the Congress organisation ... The objectives of the new operation were to arrest leaders still at large, to make propaganda, to give firm but friendly displays of force in quiescent areas and to take tough, punitive action in areas where lawlessness and acts of violence were being perpetrated or planned. In pursuit of this last objective ... swift and offensive retribution [was] meted out to convince that lawlessness did not pay; such areas [were] dealt with firmly but without brutality, leaders [were] arrested and searches made for arms and offensive weapons.[134]

The general pattern used in this campaign – broad details of which he reported to the Colonial Office regularly, particularly shootings and arrests[135] – was one of 'cordoning and searching' villages. Security forces would surround a village at night and then police or soldiers would go into the village, knock on doors – breaking them if necessary – and order all the men into the centre of the village. They would then be questioned under guard while the houses were searched – often in a rough manner – and documents and weapons, including agricultural implements, seized.[136] In a number of cases Congress activists gave themselves up rather than risk further damage to their relatives' and their own property.[137]

Armitage said that a number of civilian special constables in this campaign were an 'unruly lot, exceeded their legal powers and were weeded out'.[138] A number were heard to brag about having 'laid into' those they arrested.[139] Mossman of the *Daily Herald* spoke of the 'hostile attitude of the white settlers [many of whom] enlisted in the special police and ... newspapermen frequently had heated exchanges with them in the course of [their] duty'.[140] A number of administrative officers felt that some of the excesses of the settler special constables were linked with previous relationships on their estates, especially labour disputes.[141] In the north:

> The [provincial commissioner] intervened to forbid ill treatment ... Nevertheless, [he] said this kind of violence was inevitable when troops went through the villages.[142]

Experiences of harassment varied a great deal and in the north, for example, a number of reported cases were found to have been exaggerated when missionaries investigated: 'On the whole, what we had found was rather different from the rumours we had got that houses had been smashed up.' On the other hand they encountered a number of allegations of beatings by the security forces which they believed to be true, although the provincial commissioner considered their reports to be exaggerated and biased. Whenever abuses of this sort were brought to the attention of senior officers the practices were immediately forbidden.[143]

In most districts the field operations following Operation Sunrise took the form not of harassment but of mopping up and 'showing the flag'. Showing the flag was felt necessary to restore the authority of the chiefs, 'to show that there was a legitimate government running the country and ... an administration in place to ensure the maintenance of law and order', and to restore people's confidence in the authority of the government.[144] In a number of cases 'the mere sight of the military was enough to send the local villagers off into the bush at a rate of knots'.[145] Other officers felt that if prompt, effective and firm mopping-up action had not been taken at this time 'there would have been a considerable risk of greater violence from the local population [which] would have needed larger forces to contain it'.[146] Police officers also felt the mopping-up exercises helped them:

> Local policing ... had not been possible for some time. There were a number of people who were wanted for criminal offences but who had not been previously dealt with for fear of starting a disorder that could not at the time be contained. There had been non-payment of hut tax on a large scale, encouraged by Congress speakers and members. Breaches of agricultural rules had been widespread. These follow-up operations enabled a number of wanted persons to be dealt with. Most tax payments accelerated, and compliance started with other laws. It had ... a calming effect and it enabled the local police to begin to function as normal again. There was very little trouble ... after the end of March 1959.[147]

One of the flag-showing exercises was a 'grand tour' from Blantyre, covering most of the southern province and ending at Chileka where the 1st Battalion RRR boarded planes and flew back to Salisbury. The full column consisted of the 1st Battalion RRR, a detachment of BSAP, a company of RAR and a battalion of the KAR.[148] Serious as these exercises were, there were elements of humour in them. At Mikolongwe a well-planned exercise involving dropping tear gas from the air was momentarily halted when a message was seen to be dropped from a circling aircraft. A BSAP trooper crept quickly through the bush to recover it only to find that the very senior officer who had dropped it had simply ditched his sick-bag.[149]

This showing the flag, mopping up and harassment was a politically dangerous exercise. There could be little objection to flag-showing in the sense of demonstrating the presence and authority of government and their support of the chiefs in the rural areas simply by the security forces spending time in various districts, especially when accompanied by members of the administration. Benson in Northern Rhodesia might well have done it in full dress uniform accompanied by police or military bands![150] Similarly there could not be much objection to mopping up in the sense of ensuring that those who were supposed to have been arrested earlier were now located and apprehended nor, indeed, in the sense of making sure that Congress cells – now legally banned – were not still operating. But the danger of flag-showing and mopping up was that they could so readily assume some of the less attractive and less acceptable attributes of harassment exercises. It was the campaign of harassment itself which was not entirely wise; even the expression was open to criticism. Both the expression and some aspects of the operation smacked of vindictiveness and a determination to inflict punishment – including, in troublesome areas, punishment of the innocent as well as the guilty. A good deal of the criticism about security force activities, and especially damaging property and seizing weapons including agricultural implements, arose from the harassment campaign.[151]

The intense tightening up of law and order following a period of lawlessness resulted in a significant increase in the number of cases heard by the courts. By the end of April the number of convictions for rioting, unlawful assembly and wounding since the beginning of January was 945, with a further 304 cases awaiting trial. The number of convictions for these offences for this four-month period compared with 208 in the preceding six months and 136 for the six-month period before that. In 1959 the number tried for tax default was 11,021 compared with 6580 and 5862 for the two preceding years; 174 were tried for arson in 1959 compared with 102 and 85 in the preceding two years. The total number of cases tried by magistrates in 1959 was

23,205 compared with 16,007 and 15,785 in the two preceding years.[152] Additionally, during the post-Sunrise operations, further detentions – numbering over a thousand in total – were ordered.

The criticisms made in parliament and much of the British press – which Armitage saw as a 'campaign' – concerned the Governor, partly because he felt that a 'personal witch-hunt [was] clearly on' but, more importantly, because he feared a 'very serious deterioration' in the relations between a large number of people in Britain, including the press, and the Federation.[153] The press were critical of the government's relationships with them not least because of the delays which monitoring caused to the despatch of their cables, including urgent ones.[154] Mossman, who had worked 'in conditions of revolt and riot' in the Lebanon, Syria, Iraq, Jordan and Cyprus over the previous seven years, found the difficulties of newspapermen in Nyasaland greater than in any other place he had worked.[155]

Armitage expressed his fears about a rift between the British public and the Federation to Welensky on 14 March, and explained that the many enemies of the Federation believed they had been given:

> a heaven-sent opportunity to prove that the action which we have taken is nothing more than a Federal Government plot of political suppression in which the arch-plotter is Sir Roy Welensky, that Sir Edgar Whitehead is his willing servant and Sir Robert Armitage is his pawn. They also clearly believe that the disclosure of an assassination plot ... is nothing more than a smoke screen behind which we, including the secretary of state, are trying to hide our political scheming.[156]

He was convinced they would never persuade those intent on injuring the Federation that their actions were justified, and any attempt at forthright statements by himself, Welensky or Lennox-Boyd would only strengthen the belief among their opponents that 'a dastardly Federal plot is being covered up'. The assassination plot was something 'almost outside the ken of the man in the street in Great Britain and therefore viewed by him with suspicion'. Armitage concluded that the most effective way to 'support the action' taken and 'to kill the opposition in the United Kingdom' – an unfortunate term – was for him to issue a statement setting out in a 'completely straightforward manner' what the Congress policies were, the evidence for knowing that these were their policies, and the action taken by Congress to pursue those policies.

> In other words ... I should reveal to the world the way in which the Nyasaland Congress was endeavouring to direct the course of events here [and] the circumstances in Nyasaland which made that course of events so dangerous and necessitated the action which I took.

Consequently he proposed to write a despatch along these lines which he hoped Lennox-Boyd would publish immediately. He preferred a despatch to a White Paper – 'a much more elaborate and fully documented affair' – which would take much longer to prepare. In effect he was trying to divert prime attention away from the murder plot, which he saw as simply a part of Congress's policy, and to publicise the whole spectrum of their opposition and lawlessness.

Welensky, on the other hand, preferred a joint White Paper explaining the 'build-up of Congress subversion culminating in [the] massacre plot' and proposed that they publish full details of the plot. He asked the FISB and the Office of Race Relations to prepare material and send it to Armitage who, he hoped, would also prepare material explaining the action he had taken. He thought this proposal 'would have greater and wider impact than any further individual statements' they might make.[157] In the event Armitage prepared his own despatch rather than pursue the option of a combined publication.

Armitage was urged to write his despatch by the Colonial Office following a meeting – one of several at this time – of the inter-departmental Central Africa committee with representatives from the Colonial and the Commonwealth Relations Offices. On 10 March Alport told the committee:

> From the lobby and from recent questions in the House there was a general feeling that the 'plot' in Nyasaland had been 'cooked-up' especially since no Europeans had been killed. To contain this it was vital to procure quickly as much concrete evidence of the 'plot' as possible. Mr Amery thought that the position in the House could be held until next week but no longer.[158]

They then agreed that the Colonial Office should ask Armitage for any circumstantial evidence suitable for publication. Like Welensky, Alport and his committee (and indeed the cabinet), 'perturbed by the widespread disbelief' in the murder plot even among their followers, were pushing Armitage – whose marked 'lack of enthusiasm' for the story was immediately obvious to pressmen[159] – to give the murder plot greater prominence than the Governor thought either justified or wise.

Armitage sent his despatch to the Colonial Office on 18 March and it was published on 23 March.[160] In it he reviewed the events and the Congress actions which had finally led to his declaring a state of emergency, proscribing Congress and its affiliated bodies, and detaining Congress leaders. He also described the position which had developed since 3 March. Very early in the despatch he said:

The Government of Nyasaland is responsible for law and order in the Protectorate. Faced with the policies and actions of the Nyasaland African Congress described in this despatch it was obliged either to take firm action or to condone lawbreaking, intimidation and violence.

He then described the changes in Congress policy and actions in the following periods: first before Banda returned to Nyasaland, secondly between his return and the Accra conference, and thirdly the period from the Accra conference to 3 March 1959. In his report on this third period Armitage dealt with the Congress meeting of 24–25 January, including the plan for violence on 'R Day' involving murder. In dealing with his reaction to these events Armitage went on to say that by 18 February he 'was faced with a rapidly deteriorating situation [which] clearly called for firm action by Government' if law and order were to be restored. Although justified in declaring an emergency then, he had had to defer doing so until sufficient security forces had been deployed to 'deal with every kind of contingency which the existence of [the Congress emergency meeting] plans made possible'. He concluded:

> By the 2nd March I had completed the necessary build up of reinforcements. I declared a state of emergency in the early hours of the 3rd March ... No Governor wishes to be placed in a position of having to declare a state of emergency. But the events which I have described speak for themselves.

The period preparing the despatch was 'a ghastly week' and the 'flurry' involved a great deal of work and contact between London and Zomba, including many telephone calls over poor lines which caused him to 'strain to hear and yell to be heard, [with] intelligent conversation ... impossible'.[161] It was written in great haste, under pressure from the British government, and without all the documents being available; a few slips in proofreading were made which were later to be picked up and exploited by others. He supported his despatch by sending with it a 161-page document elaborating every page and almost every paragraph in it.[162] In writing the despatch Armitage, in some ways, made himself a hostage to fortune because a commission of inquiry was shortly to use it and the *ipsissima verba* as the basis for much of their inquiry.[163] Later, when speaking of what he perceived as inaccuracies in the despatch, Banda said he was convinced Armitage had not written it:

> I am sure ... he did not write it himself ... No, he is too good a man for that. I have great faith in him. I think somebody wrote that, and he just signed it.[164]

Within three weeks of declaring the state of emergency, Armitage reported to Lennox-Boyd that all three provinces were 'generally quiet'[165] and that even in the Karonga district, although the people were frightened, they were beginning to assist the security forces.[166] The Karonga district commissioner recalled that 'there was a build-up of security forces after the disturbances at the end of February and quite a bit of showing the flag by army and police especially after 3 March. But we seem to have been getting back to normal by early April.'[167] Armitage told the secretary of state that, outside Karonga, conditions were improving in all provinces and 'evidence of still active Congress support was coming to light': 'Very active sweeping and patrolling of last fortnight has had an excellent calming effect and restored order widely.'[168] Consequently he felt the time was right to withdraw the RRR and, although he recognised there would 'inevitably be eruptions in some areas', he was confident the remaining military forces and the police would contain them. He felt too that with the trials of arrested rioters proceeding, others were discouraged from creating disorder.[169] He was, however, dealing with only the immediate situation – restoring law and order – and acknowledged that deeper and longer-term problems continued to exist:

> I cannot report that there is any less anti-Federation feeling or that if Dr Banda reappeared there would not again be a surge of pro-Congress support. Dr Banda must be kept out of the way until some other political leaders have been able to get support for policies unconnected with violence.[170]

He was now able to release most of the federal troops and there was much less of 'a rush of operational planning'.

The Governor felt that there was now a 'political vacuum' and both T.D.T. Banda and W.M. Chirwa pressed him to make interim constitutional changes so that the vacuum could be filled – presumably by themselves. Also the United Federal Party was stepping up its organising and recruiting among Africans, and if they built a fairly substantial membership 'that would certainly alter the whole complexion of African political thinking'. Armitage felt strongly about a bi-partisan approach to Central African affairs: 'anything that can remove federal matters from party politics would have my heartiest support'.

> One comes back to the first priority ... and that is a bi-partisan statement in the House of Commons that the Federation will continue with its three component territories, although there may be various adjustments in the actual links of these territories with the Federal Government.[171]

The BSAP contingent returned to Southern Rhodesia on 9 May, having inflicted no injuries during their service in Nyasaland.[172] At this time, too, Armitage wrote to Kettlewell and said that, although law and order had by no means been fully restored, a great deal had already been achieved and the visiting forces were being run down; he thanked Kettlewell for all he had done 'particularly in connection with the overall planning of operations'.[173] By the very beginning of May he reported that 'the country has been fairly quiet for the last week, people going more normally about their business and few acts of violence' occurring, adding they had 'very few extra troops and police left here now'.[174] He had released 225 detainees in March and a further 275 by the end of April.[175] In Dixon's view the withdrawal of federal troops had left insufficient forces in the protectorate 'for all the necessary mopping-up operations'.[176]

Despite the tough action the Governor was prepared to take he was far from happy at having to take it. The Governor-General was clear that Armitage felt the presence of federal troops in Nyasaland, while necessary for security purposes, would only increase the unpopularity of federation in African eyes. He was also clear that Armitage 'did not think the use of force in any way was a solution to civil disorder':

> On one occasion [during the emergency] I visited the Federal troops in Nyasaland, when of course I met Sir Robert. He was rather concerned at my presence and asked me what I was going to do. On being told I was visiting the troops he seemed to accept it as part of my duties, but I still felt he did not like the situation as it was and would rather not have it emphasised by my presence.[177]

Another indication of Armitage's views on the efficacy of force was given in his press conference the day before the state of emergency was declared when, in answer to the question, 'Do you feel that troops would be able to hold Nyasaland against the wishes of three million Africans?', he replied promptly, 'I doubt it.'[178]

Soon after the emergency was declared Lennox-Boyd quickly agreed with Home that Perth, in East Africa at the time, should be asked to travel from Zanzibar to Central Africa.[179] Lennox-Boyd had already warned Perth he may have to undertake this visit at very short notice, and telegrams were drafted to Welensky, Armitage and Benson saying they thought it would be a good thing if Perth went straight away to the three capitals.[180] The secretary of state told his Colonial Office colleagues:

> It is not for the purpose of formal constitutional talks that Lord Perth is going – the fact that so many of the leaders are in detention would make

this impossible – but in order to get first-hand information and to report to HMG. The real purpose, of course, would be to make sure that there is proper co-ordination machinery between the two Northern Governments and the Federation, to see that the views of the Northern Governors carry proper weight, that prejudices pro and anti the Federation are not interfering with security needs, and generally to knock all their heads together.[181]

Lennox-Boyd telephoned Perth: 'David, you've no idea how much trouble we're having over Nyasaland. Go there and find out what's happening.'[182] In a follow-up telegram he said:

What I think is needed is firstly to make sure that the two Governors and the Federal prime minister are all working in harmony and concentrated on dealing effectively and wisely with the immediate emergency. Secondly, to satisfy yourself on the adequacy and distribution of the police and military forces available in the Federation. Thirdly, to look into the question when and in what form it will be desirable to take up again the question of constitutional changes in Nyasaland.[183]

He added that Perth should return to Britain immediately after this visit and resume his East Africa tour later.

Following an impression Callaghan had given to Home that something on the lines of their intended constitutional proposals might be acceptable to Banda, Lennox-Boyd toyed with the idea of trying them out on the doctor:

Perhaps Lord Perth's visit would be a good opportunity. It would not, of course, be impossible to get messages to Banda in Bulawayo, though this would raise very great difficulties and charges of negotiating while under duress etc.[184]

When Perth arrived in Zomba, Armitage took him straight to the operations room where he noted that 'everything was conducted like a military operation with maps showing the trouble spots'.[185] He attended a meeting of the operations committee and the following day a meeting of executive council.[186] It was clear to him that the Governor and his officials feared widespread insurrection and that Armitage had not yet regained control of the protectorate.[187] An official who attended meetings of executive council at this time noticed that Armitage, while remaining completely under control, none the less frowned a great deal and winced occasionally, which suggested that he was, under the surface, worried and nervous.[188] The minister of state was taken to Kanjedza detention camp where the detainees asked, 'Who are you?' When told they said, 'Oh, you're the one we want to see. We've been waiting for you. Why didn't you come before?'[189] This conversation suggests that these detainees, few of whom had been leaders in Congress, had been looking forward – as Armitage had felt Banda had – to Perth's visit and to constitutional talks. Perth reported:

> The improvised arrangements for looking after the men reflect much credit on all concerned. The authorities running the camps need have no fears of whatever the press may say.[190]

Perth stayed with Armitage from 12 to 17 March before flying on to Salisbury, where he had 'valuable discussions' with Welensky and members of his government.[191] While in Nyasaland he spent a day in each of the northern and central provinces and in Blantyre, and two days in Zomba. He met a wide variety of people: provincial and district commissioners; African, European and Asian politicians; African civil servants; school teachers; detainees; villagers; African businessmen; missionaries; and many others.[192] He also visited a number of places where trouble had occurred and had talks with the provincial commissioner of the southern province, Nicholson, who particularly stressed that 99 per cent of African civil servants were 'utterly embroiled in Congress and probably helping to keep the flame of Congress alive'. This was an opinion also given by James Johnson, a Labour member of parliament, to the secretary of state,[193] and Morgan in the Colonial Office commented on 27 April:

> It seems to me that as soon as the Governor has reached a position of general control of the situation there may have to be a severe purge of the African Civil Service – something which will of course give rise to indignation in certain quarters in [Britain].[194]

Perth thought African civil service loyalty to Congress 'could greatly change' if they could remove the fears of federation in 1960.[195] On his return to Britain his report to the cabinet dealt with three main points: security, constitutional progress and African fear of federation.[196]

In dealing with the security position the minister of state said the situation in the southern and central provinces was improving but the northern province, where the people were 'tougher' and the terrain more difficult, might take many months to be brought fully under control. He found cooperation between the Nyasaland and federal governments good, as was that between the Nyasaland administration and the military authorities. The reinforcements from other governments had been 'indispensable' but the federal government was anxious to withdraw its forces soon – the timing of this would be for the federal and Nyasaland governments to agree. This wish of the federal government for the early withdrawal of its forces may have been in response to Armitage's fear that their presence would lead to the greater unpopularity of federation. Also, the absence of so many civilians while serving with the territorial RRR, plus the general costs, would sooner or later have economic effects on the Federation. Perth was concerned that with one police officer to every 1500 inhabitants, Nyasaland's ratio was much worse than that of the two Rhodesias: 'A lot of money needs to be spent in strengthening the Nyasaland Police Force.' He found 'a widespread feeling of relief' among Africans that firm action had been taken against intimidators but there was also apprehension that the Congress leaders would soon be released from detention. Since the government could prolong detention by only 28 days by using control orders, Perth emphasised the importance of the bill for which Armitage was pressing to permit detention beyond the end of the state of emergency:

> I am convinced that we must support this measure. It is most important that the Bill should be passed very soon in order to set at rest the apprehension [that Congress leaders are to be released shortly].

He made a particular point of saying how impressed he was by 'the evidence of the persistent fomenting' of opposition to federation by the Church of Scotland and he stressed the need for 'their missionaries as well as the Africans whom they have misled' to be convinced of the value of federation. He did not say how this might be done.

Thus, in terms of the security position, it is clear that Perth was extremely supportive of the Nyasaland government.

Perth then dealt with the constitution and told his cabinet colleagues he agreed with Armitage that there should be no change in the Nyasaland constitution until 'some constitutional step' had first been taken 'on the federal plane':

> To such an extent does Federation dominate the African mind that constitutional advance for Nyasaland now would not only fail to mollify them but would be bitterly opposed by the Europeans and by many Asians, and in addition would appear to them as being an unwarranted concession to violence.

He believed they needed to bring the protectorate to a state of 'complete pacification' and to advance the federal constitutional review. In the meantime it was essential to restore the authority of the chiefs, accelerate African advancement in the civil service and support Armitage in his proposals to appoint two Africans to executive council – which he could do without altering the current constitution.

Again, in dealing with constitutional progress, it is clear that Perth was very supportive of the Governor.

Finally, he turned to the fears of federation which he found to be almost universal among Nyasaland Africans and particularly in the civil service, where it was 'a specially grave problem'.

> The fear of Federation, and of Sir Roy Welensky in particular, is held passionately, unreasoningly and apparently with an unshakeable tenacity. The increased wealth which Nyasaland and individual Africans have gained since 1953 counts for little or nothing in their minds; they believe that it will all be handed over to Europeans from Southern Rhodesia in 1960. There is a widespread belief that H.M.G. will fail to stand by their pledges and will sacrifice the Africans to the ambitions of the Federal Government. At the same time there exists an equally strong, if less irrational, fear among Europeans that we are going to sell out to the Africans too quickly.

Perth's visit[197] was very full and thorough and he was able to give the British government a firsthand, up-to-date and perceptive appreciation of the situation in Nyasaland.

4

The Devlin Inquiry

To inquire into the recent disturbances in Nyasaland and the events leading up to them.

Within two days of the declaration of a state of emergency, the British cabinet, in Macmillan's absence on a visit to Russia, decided to set up a commission of inquiry into the disturbances.[1] They were anxious to accompany the announcement of this decision with a pronouncement that they intended to set up a royal commission preparatory to the 1960 federal review. It was the hope that there would be agreement to set up a preparatory commission before the review which would enable Lennox-Boyd deliberately to exclude the underlying causes of the emergency – particularly federation – from the written terms of reference of the inquiry into the disturbances. Although the cabinet thought the combined announcement 'highly desirable' and 'would clearly help everyone including the federal government', they realised they could not make it if Welensky or Whitehead had not already been persuaded that the preparatory commission was desirable.[2] Officials expressed doubts – shared by Lennox-Boyd – about the wisdom of an inquiry specifically related to Nyasaland. At an interdepartmental meeting on 12 March Gorell Barnes said one of the findings would almost certainly be that among the causes of the disturbances was the Nyasaland Africans' distrust of federation and this would prejudice the 1960 review. He thought it best to decide at the present time on a wider inquiry, into the problems that would arise in 1960, by a commission which could also be asked to make an interim report on Nyasaland. The committee agreed to advise the secretaries of state that any commission should be related to the wider issues of 1960, 'leaving the immediate inquiry into the disturbances to be mounted locally perhaps as an administrative inquiry'.[3]

The government came under opposition pressure to involve parliament closely in the Nyasaland inquiry and to send out a parliamentary delegation 'at once'. Lennox-Boyd replied that it was necessary to restore order before an inquiry of this sort was contemplated.[4] In considering appointing privy council parliamentarians from the two major parties to the commission of inquiry, the government told Armitage their decision would:

> turn partly on whether ... it is felt possible to say something sufficiently forthcoming about HMG's intention to fortify themselves before [the] future of Federation is decided with all relevant information acquired as a result of some form of enquiry on the spot.[5]

The opposition continued to press for a parliamentary commission but the cabinet's view was that the first step was for Perth to make his postponed visit to the protectorate. They did not, however, rule out the possibility of a parliamentary commission 'at a more seasonable time'.[6]

Although the government initially considered including parliamentarians, Lennox-Boyd and Home agreed as early as 9 March 'that it was essential to knock on the head the idea of an immediate parliamentary mission'.[7] Subsequently they decided against having any parliamentarians even as members because it would be extremely difficult to prevent them inquiring into the wider – federation – issue.[8] Having an opposition member on the commission ran the risk of an adverse report being produced either unanimously or by a minority, and this, with a general election in the offing, was too great a risk to take. They hoped to 'buy off' the opposition in respect of the Nyasaland inquiry commission by, in effect, offering them parliamentary places on the federal review commission. Perhaps sensing the early, if gentle and scarcely perceptible, movement of an air of change in their political nostrils, they were already not entirely averse to the possibility of criticism of federal operations by the review commission, a possibility which Kilmuir indeed hinted at in respect of the inquiry commission.[9]

When Perth left Nyasaland he visited Welensky, met the federal cabinet and reaffirmed the British government's determination to preserve the Federation.[10] To do this, however, they needed to overcome opposition in Britain and consequently the government had decided to set up a preparatory commission. He gave five reasons: Conservative and church opinion was worried about events in Central Africa and it was essential to retain their support; the Labour Party must be dissuaded from breaking up the Federation; the federal issue had to be removed from the forthcoming British general election; ignorance of the Federation in Britain must be dispelled; and the preparatory commission would help to confine the inquiry into the Nyasaland disturbances within its proper bounds. He also said: 'So far as our general colonial policy is concerned, a halt is being called to the rapid advance of colonial territories to independence.' None of Welensky's cabinet colleagues could see a single argument in favour of a preparatory commission, and all doubted whether its findings would dispel opposition ignorance in Britain and whether federation could be prevented from becoming a general election issue. They opposed being 'put on trial' and having any shortcomings highlighted. Faced with these strong objections, 'Perth rallied gamely enough [and] concluded by asking that no final attitude be taken up and that the proposal should be kept open.'

Of more immediate importance, although it was thought to be of less ultimate significance, was the commission of inquiry into Nyasaland's disturbances. The cabinet decided to keep this inquiry 'on a narrow front' and without parliamentarians, but they emphasised to Welensky that they would get general consent to this only if they could indicate to the opposition that 'the proper time and place for parliamentarians to come into the picture would be as some members of the [preparatory] Commission' – that is to say, only if Welensky would agree in principle to such a commission and to include parliamentarians on it. Immediately after Perth had reported to the cabinet on his return from Nyasaland, Butler spoke with Gaitskell, leader of the opposition, and 'found the basis for an agreed approach to the short term problem of an inquiry into the riots in Nyasaland and the longer term question of preparing for the 1960 review'.[11]

Home also visited Salisbury and tried to persuade the federal cabinet to accept the preparatory commission.[12] He spoke of his deep fear that if Labour won the election they would allow Nyasaland to secede, after which the same right would have to be given to Northern Rhodesia.

> We are trying to persuade [the Labour Party] not to [permit secession] but up to now they haven't accepted our arguments ... In order to hold this position, we must appoint some kind of Commission. One of the big difficulties with British public opinion is that all the five governments concerned are thought to have some axe to grind. We feel that the findings of a Commission will carry much greater weight than even the continued efforts of all the governments.

Welensky found Home's arguments 'formidable' and he gave 'cautious acceptance in principle' to the proposal that there should be a conference at official level, followed by a commission, and ending with a review entirely in the hands of the governments. 'There, for the moment, [their] discussion ended.' A few days later Welensky received a letter from Macmillan 'as soothing as cream and as sharp as a razor' in which it became clear that Welensky's very limited acceptance of Home's ideas had been 'converted by some magic in ... Macmillan's mind into willing – indeed enthusiastic – alliance with him'.[13]

The cabinet was 'certain that [they] must take the opportunity afforded' by the understanding with Gaitskell.[14] They needed his co-operation in not having parliamentarians on the inquiry commission, and Welensky's in having parliamentarians on the review commission. Ideally, they wanted to announce the two together and, having gained Gaitskell's initial cooperation, they were much relieved when Welensky also agreed – albeit reluctantly and with reservation. Welensky asked that the words used in parliament announcing the two commissions should be cautious, and as a result the cabinet agreed to say:

> Her Majesty's Government are ... considering the best way of preparing for the 1960 Review of the Federal Constitution. We shall at the proper time be putting forward proposals for the machinery for this purpose with which Parliament will no doubt wish to be associated in an appropriate way.[15]

This, they told Welensky, would give them time to work out the details and consult him about the composition and other elements of the review commission. They emphasised how grateful they were for his 'tolerance and understanding'. He was, in fact, helping to save their bacon and somewhat lessen the risk of an adverse inquiry report, but he was also giving ground on the review commission issue.

A number of interdepartmental meetings suggested that the announcement of the wider review commission could profitably be delayed, especially in order to emphasise the difference between the two commissions. In the event other arguments prevailed, including the view that 'in particular it would be unfortunate if decisions had to await a general election in [Britain]'.[16]

Armitage 'was opposed to having the Commission [of inquiry into the disturbances] at all and foretold adverse consequences'.[17] He was 'very concerned' about the possibility of appointing members of parliament on the grounds that it defeated the political advantages of a completely parliamentary inquiry and the objectivity of a completely independent inquiry, and their addition to other members would make the commission 'unnecessarily unwieldy'.[18] Benson strongly supported him in this opposition[19] and, in the event, the British government accepted their advice that parliamentarians should not sit on the commission of inquiry.

In order to give the commission at least the air of impartiality and make it publicly acceptable, the government wished to appoint 'a judge as chairman and two or three other members with judicial experience'.[20]

They wished, it seems, to take advantage of the deep-rooted British belief that members of the judiciary are more impartial than other disinterested people, and are better able to discover the facts of a matter than are others more experienced and knowledgeable in the field of inquiry. A number of names were suggested, among them Ronald Sinclair, a New Zealander and then president of the East Africa Court of Appeal, who had been an administrative officer in West Africa and later chief justice of Nyasaland; but it was quickly realised that with his background he might not be seen as entirely impartial although clearly experienced and knowledgeable in both the field of inquiry and its territorial location.[21]

On 17 March, the cabinet formally decided that the inquiry 'should not be carried out by a Parliamentary Commission but by a Commission of three persons presided over by a judge'.[22] Their first choice as chairman was Lord Morton, a judge about to retire who was most strongly recommended by the cabinet as 'a thoroughly sensible person'.[23] Lennox-Boyd tried very hard to persuade him to accept, but failed; many years later he was 'inclined to think that a different report would have emerged' had Morton accepted.[24] In considering the members of the commission, the cabinet said that if Morton accepted they wished to appoint Sir Evan Jenkins, former Governor of the Punjab, and E.T. Williams, the son of a clergyman and Warden of Rhodes House, who had been Montgomery's chief of intelligence during the war.[25] Williams's name was suggested by Macpherson, permanent secretary in the Colonial Office since he knew him as a member of a number of appointment committees.[26] Just after the Second World War, he had worked in the United Nations security council secretariat 'analysing documents and sorting and condensing evidence'[27] – the sort of work now to be undertaken in Nyasaland.

The secretary of state sought the Governor of Kenya's opinion on whether to ask Sir Donald MacGillivray, a former district officer and ex-governor of wide and distinguished experience, to join the commission.[28] Baring advised against the appointment because, excellent a man as MacGillivray was, his future usefulness to the governments of East Africa might be seriously prejudiced. As Baring wrote, he was

> afraid that however reasonable [the] report on Nyasaland may be, and however distinguished the judicial chairman, emotional African national-ists may attack its report. As a consequence, rightly or wrongly, a member of the commission will in their eyes be labelled as someone who supports settler European against African.[29]

That the commission's report might be pro-African and anti-settler European does not seem to have entered Baring's consideration – any more than it is probable that it entered those of others in government at that time.

So, attempts to secure Morton, Jenkins and MacGillivray having failed, and the wish to secure parliamentarians having been abandoned, Sir Patrick Devlin was approached.

Devlin was the son of a deeply religious Irish architect and Scottish mother, and was raised in Aberdeen. Two of his sisters became nuns, one brother became a Jesuit priest, whilst the youngest became an actor … Devlin himself was a Dominican novice, although he abandoned the priory after a few months to go to Cambridge, where he became President of the Union.[30]

He was born in 1906, called to the bar in 1929, built up a successful commercial practice and, at the age of 42, became the youngest high court judge of the twentieth century. Devlin resigned from the bench in 1963 and in his retirement chaired a number of major inquiries and campaigned for the 'Guildford Four'. He was a member of the Carlton Club, 'a Conservative party stronghold'.[31] Though in his later years he lost his faith, before he died he returned to the church.

He believed passionately in justice as well as the rule of law, and that all men, of whatever condition, had the right to equal treatment.[32]

Perth had known Devlin all his life, considered him 'very sensible' and assured Lennox-Boyd that they 'could not have anybody more sensible';[33] they had been at Cambridge together and had become close, life-long friends.[34] In addition, Devlin was a cousin of the wife of Sir Peveril William-Powlett, Governor of Southern Rhodesia.[35] Macmillan, who disapproved of Devlin's appointment by Kilmuir and Butler in his own absence, but who at the time simply 'shrugged his shoulders',[36] later asked in his diary, 'Why Devlin?'

The poor Chancellor [Kilmuir] – the sweetest and most naive of men – chose him. He was able; a Conservative; runner-up or nearly so for Lord Chief Justice. I have since discovered that he is (a) Irish – no doubt with that Fenian blood that makes Irishmen anti-Government on principle, (b) a lapsed Roman Catholic.[37]

Macmillan felt that Devlin had been 'bitterly disappointed at [his] not having made him Lord Chief Justice'.

Butler lunched with Devlin on 20 March and took the opportunity to discuss the commission with him[38] although it is most likely he had been asked to be chairman, and had agreed, two days earlier when Kilmuir spoke with him. Of Kilmuir's meeting Devlin recalled:

He said it was an important inquiry, and that was why he was anxious that a judge should do it. He said it might involve finding to what extent Federation was a cause of the disturbances. He was perfectly frank about what the Government's policy was. He said: 'We believe in Federation, but of course it's open to you to find that the ordinary African does not. We hope you won't make that finding, but if you do, we shall have to accept it.'[39]

The real position, of course, was not simply that the government hoped Devlin would not find federation a cause of the disturbances but that he would not inquire into the Federation and its effects at all. It was precisely to avoid any inquiry into the Federation at this stage that they were so anxious to announce the wider commission at the same time. It was dangerous for Kilmuir to go as far as he did in saying that Devlin might have to find the extent to which federation was a cause of the disturbances. Of his own meeting, Butler reported that Devlin was 'quite taken' with the idea of having as his members Williams and Sir Percy Wyn-Harris, a former administrative officer from Kenya and Governor of the Gambia, an Everest mountaineer of considerable distinction whose name had recently been suggested, and was 'quite in favour' of having two members of parliament to join them.[40]

The idea of having a former African Governor came from either Devlin or Williams when they met Lennox-Boyd and pointed out:

> We couldn't use Government interpreters for obvious reasons so it might be a good idea to have an 'old Africa Hand' – that is how we came to get P. Wyn.[41]

Quite what the connection was between not using government interpreters and having a former Governor who had served in Kenya is unclear unless, like his predecessor Lyttelton,[42] Lennox-Boyd – and Devlin or Williams – believed, incorrectly, that the people of Nyasaland spoke Swahili as the lingua franca. Despite their pure intentions and the 'obvious reasons' against it, the commission did in fact use government interpreters when in Nyasaland in addition to at least two district commissioners and at least one leading member of Congress.[43] Wyn-Harris was approached after it was decided that MacGillivray should not be invited and after Butler's luncheon conversation with Devlin.[44] He accepted on 22 March, at considerable personal inconvenience. Recently retired, Wyn-Harris had spent the winter preparing 'for a long sailing cruise of some years' duration'. He had intended to set out on the first leg on 7 May and had already settled a number of crews for different parts of the voyage over the coming year or so.[45] Subsequently, between 1962 and 1969, he circumnavigated the world.[46]

Wyn-Harris felt it his duty to accept appointment to the commission, a reaction much appreciated at the Colonial Office.[47] He was viewed by other commissioners as the man to ask difficult questions, although this in no way emerges from the transcripts of the questioning in which he took part.[48] He told Devlin soon after his appointment that 'having been mixed up in Africa for the whole of [his] life [he was] possibly not the best person to be on a Commission of a judicial nature'.[49] It was, of course, precisely because he was an 'old Africa hand' that he was appointed, and many would have seen his African experience of particular value especially since similar experience was lacking in the other commissioners. The commission was not a judicial commission although, with a judge as chairman, it was likely to turn out to be 'of a judicial nature'.

Wyn-Harris found himself in a rather odd position – not that it seemed to worry him unduly – because his and Armitage's roles might well have been reversed since he could well have been appointed Governor of Nyasaland instead of Armitage. In privately reporting 'a personal interest' to Devlin, of which he saw no need to apprise his fellow commissioners, he said:

When I was home on leave in 1955, Sir Thomas Lloyd, then Under Secretary [at the Colonial Office], asked me if I would like to be considered for the Governorship of Nyasaland and I replied that I would. Possibly mistakenly I considered the appointment settled and I was somewhat disappointed to see in the Times [sic] that when the present Governor, Armitage, was removed from Cyprus to make way for Lord Harding, he had been appointed Governor [of Nyasaland]. Fresh information came to me a few days later when Sir Thomas Lloyd wrote me a letter explaining that he had been on holiday in Majorca and it had come to him as a complete surprise first of all that there had been a change in Cyprus and a few days later of Armitage's new appointment.[50]

He did not think that this incident would consciously affect him but 'unwittingly [he] might be less objective than [he] should be'. Others too – but not, it seems, Devlin – might have wondered whether his disappointment at Armitage having taken his place as Governor of Nyasaland might, even 'unwittingly', affect his general approach to the commission's work.

Armitage was told of the proposed appointments of Devlin, Williams and Wyn-Harris on 19 March; the question of parliamentarians being added was still open until 23 March.[51]

A few hours before announcing the setting up of the commission and its membership, on 24 March, the British government decided that, 'with Scottish opinion in mind', they should appoint Sir John

Ure Primrose.[52] Also the son of a clergyman, Primrose was a former Lord Provost of Perth, had served in the Royal Navy during the First World War and had been a sergeant-major in the Intelligence Corps serving with MI5 during the Second World War; he had also been a justice of the peace for 15 years.[53] He was, in Williams's view, 'the personification of decency and fairplay'[54] and, in the commission secretary's assessment, a man of 'broad experience, a massively sensible, practical farmer'.[55] He was 'warmly recommended' by Home and Lennox-Boyd's other colleagues – presumably Perth and Kilmuir.[56] 'Scottish opinion' must have been very pleased with Primrose's appointment. He, like Banda, was an elder of the Church of Scotland. He displayed a pro-Church of Scotland partisanship – which Congress counsel and others played on – and he 'obviously felt very much at home with his fellow Scots around him' and 'was especially friendly and at home with fellow Scots' when he visited Livingstonia.[57] Certainly a number of missionaries there, trading on their Scottish and Perth connections, wrote directly and personally to him when making representations to the commission, rather than writing to the chairman or the secretary,[58] and he revealed to some of them that 'he was just waiting until [the commission] had made their report when he would be free to talk, and then he would talk'.[59] Later in Nyasaland, visiting a detention camp, he met the only minister of the Church of Scotland to be detained there. Primrose was deeply offended by, and could not comprehend, his appearance in singlet and shorts – instead of the clerical garb he would normally have expected to see him wearing – and looking, he thought, as if he had just had the handcuffs taken off him.[60] (He had not in fact been handcuffed.) Primrose's concern seems to have been because this man was a Church of Scotland minister rather than for any other reason.

Only Williams[61] said, and maybe no one else noticed, that the commission was now apparently composed of an Englishman, a Scotsman, a Welshman and an Irishman. It had all the makings of a good, if ultimately sad, story. Williams was the one person, of those eventually forming the commission, who had been suggested from the very beginning. Devlin, Wyn-Harris and, at the very last moment, Primrose, were suggested only after others had declined or been subsequently considered less suitable. All were Conservatives.[62] None knew any of the others before being appointed, although in the course of their work in Nyasaland they became a harmonious team and long-term friends.[63]

Between 16 and 24 March, the composition, after a number of false trails had been followed, was settled and the secretary of state announced it in the Commons on 24 March, the day after Armitage's despatch was published as a White Paper. Simultaneously, the Nyasaland government also announced the appointment of the commission although they erroneously stated that it was appointed by the Governor instead of the secretary of state, an error which was not publicly corrected for almost two months.[64]

The government must have been extremely confident of the correctness of their case to subject it to the examination of a commission which appeared so obviously impartial, authoritative and above party politics as that now comprised of Devlin, Williams, Wyn-Harris and Primrose. With a majority of 59 in the Commons, the British government could have resisted setting up a commission or they could have given in to pressure to set up a parliamentary inquiry, the partiality and lack of African experience of which they could, if necessary, later use to reject unpalatable findings. Instead they selected a judge of formidable renown to head the inquiry, and one whose conclusions – for good or ill – were bound to command widespread support; such was their confidence in the correctness of their case.

The commission's terms of reference were short and undetailed: to inquire into the recent disturbances in Nyasaland and the events leading up to them, and to report thereon.[65] On 31 March, Devlin asked for a start to be made putting papers together under various heads, the first of which was 'the plot and decision to declare emergency',[66] and when, at the Colonial Office two days later,[67] he asked whether the terms included inquiry into the declaration of a state of emergency and whether there was a murder plot,

> The Secretary of State confirmed this. He said it was difficult to widen what had been said in Parliament but they could agree mutually on its interpretation.

Notwithstanding the secretary of state saying 'the terms of reference purposely avoided phrases such as inquiring into the underlying causes of the emergency', Wyn-Harris asked if they 'would be entitled to look at the causes of the emergency including' dislike of the Federation.

> The Secretary of State said it was difficult to lay down hard and fast rules. They clearly might have to make reference to these things but it would take too long to go into them thoroughly and in any event there might well soon be an announcement about the wider inquiry he had mentioned. There was agreement with the view that it should be the aim not to inhibit the finding of the truth in Nyasaland, but equally not to prejudice finding the best solution for the Federation as a whole in 1960. The latter had to be looked at in the light of a wider context than Nyasaland alone.[68]

Devlin, too, wished to inquire into the causes of the disturbances –

including African dislike of federation – and he made it 'quite clear' that he wished to go beyond inquiring just into the disturbances and the events leading up to them:

> not merely as to what happened but as to what was the cause of the disturbances as well because [he] had by that time ... appreciated enough to know that there was a political difference of opinion about federation and to that extent [they] might have to go into politics and therefore [he] wanted to be quite clear that it was intended to cover that as well.[69]

Failing sufficiently to clarify the terms of reference risked falling into the very trap Macmillan had hoped to avoid in having both a Nyasaland inquiry and a federal preparatory commission – reserving to the latter, matters concerning the Federation and its future, and to Devlin the much narrower question of the disturbances in Nyasaland. Kilmuir had already gone too far in discussing the terms of reference with the chairman, and Lennox-Boyd should have been much firmer and rejected Devlin's and Wyn-Harris's wishes to include federation in the inquiry as a cause of the disturbances. He ought to have made it clear that 'events leading up to' did not mean 'causes of' the disturbances. As things worked out, the Church of Scotland was able, in many respects, to turn the Devlin commission into a referendum on the Federation. It is clear that large numbers of African members of the Church thought that this was indeed the purpose of the inquiry, and the Livingstonia missionaries were successful in ensuring that an enormous amount of evidence was forthcoming condemning federation and exclusively blaming it for the disturbances.[70]

From the outset, then, a fortnight before leaving Britain and before receiving any evidence, the commission showed a significant interest – based presumably on newspaper reports and on debates in the Commons – in three particular issues: the declaration of the state of emergency, the murder plot and African dislike of federation. Devlin closely linked the first two of these.

The *Daily Telegraph* hoped the inquiry's scope would be very wide and thought there ought to be two inquiries, one to 'satisfy the doubts that still persist in the public mind about the genuineness of the Nyasaland "plot" and the implication of the Nyasaland African Congress', and the other to investigate 'the background of the trouble'.[71] Whereas the *Daily Telegraph* was inclined to accept the existence of a 'murder plot', the *Manchester Guardian* was less convinced, saying 'there must ... still be some uncertainty about the truth' of what Armitage claimed in his despatch about the plot. The *Manchester Guardian* also quickly perceived the immense dangers if the inquiry confirmed Armitage's allegations:

If all that the Governor of Nyasaland reports ... is true, the situation there is even more of a nightmare than it appeared before. By his account Dr Banda and the principal leaders of the Nyasaland African Congress are deeply implicated in a plot which provided for the murder of a large number of Africans, Asians and Europeans. If that is the case, what hope can remain of political reconciliation and of ever securing the consent of Africans in Nyasaland to their staying in the Federation?[72]

The Times, reporting on Armitage's despatch, was concerned to defend him as much as possible. It felt it effectively disposed of two allegations made against him:

The first is that there never was any real threat of violence and that the whole business of declaring an emergency was simply a put-up job to get rid of Congress and Dr Banda. This charge never was one which could reasonably be sustained by anyone with recent experience of Nyasaland. The second charge is that he was jockeyed into taking action by Sir Roy Welensky and others outside Nyasaland. Anyone who reads this report will quickly become convinced that, whether or not he himself believes the story of the murder plot, Sir Robert Armitage certainly did and all his subsequent actions were directed at foiling the plan. The second charge can also be unhesitatingly dismissed.[73]

The *Sunday Times* also was concerned to defend the Governor. It emphasised that whatever the reliability of the evidence, Armitage and his advisers believed the substance of it and even if he were subsequently shown to have been mistaken 'that would not make the slightest difference to the situation that confronted him'. It felt that he could be criticised only for not declaring the emergency sooner, and that Banda's return was a 'disaster for his people'.[74]

Already the 'murder plot' – an expression which Armitage had not used and which throughout he studiously avoided – was the aspect of Nyasaland's troubles which was paramount in the minds of the press in Britain, as it was in Devlin's mind.

Now that the commission and its membership had been announced, Devlin was keen to get on with the job; he wanted the inquiry to be completed by Whitsun[75] – 17 May – and Wyn-Harris wanted to start his cruise. As soon as they decided to set up an inquiry, the Colonial Office selected its secretary: Anthony Fairclough, a principal aged 35 years, who already had the necessary security clearance.[76] Yet, despite the urgency, a number of matters needed to be discussed and clarified and the formal legal documents, the order in council and the warrant, had to be agreed. Most of the legal work was done in the Colonial Office by Sir Kenneth Roberts-Wray, legal adviser. Much discussion took place in the Office and with Armitage, and the draft order and warrant were sent to Devlin for his comments.[77] Four major issues were particularly important: the general nature of the evidence and the extent to which it would be accepted, both quantitatively and qualitatively, whether this was seen in terms of admissibility, standard of proof or weight of evidence; the protection of witnesses; obtaining evidence from Nyasaland government detainees held in federal prisons in Southern Rhodesia; and the confidentiality of inter-government communications.

The British government was clear from the outset that the commission was not a judicial commission, although they asked a judge to chair it and appointed others with judicial experience: Primrose was a justice of the peace, and, as a colonial administrative officer, Wyn-Harris had been a magistrate. In later years Devlin repeatedly insisted that it was a judicial inquiry and likened it to a coroner's inquest.[78] The danger of adopting too judicial an approach to matters such as those they were to study, particularly when headed by a high court judge with no experience of practical government especially in Africa, was that the standard of proof demanded – to establish, for example, whether or not a 'murder plot' had existed – might be too high, maybe even far too high. Perhaps the most important question of all, and certainly one of the most difficult, was the extent to which evidence accepted quantitatively – that is, 'How much can be admitted?' which covers the various aspects of admissibility – should be accepted qualitatively. This qualitative aspect covers the standard of proof, that is, 'How much does one need to be satisfied?' overall, taking all the pieces together – whether beyond reasonable doubt or on the balance of probability or on an innovative approach based on the degree of possibility. It also covers the weight to be attached to individual pieces of evidence accepted: 'How satisfying is this evidence?' For example, how should one choose between the view, 'I have quite deep doubts about all the individual pieces of evidence, so no matter how numerous they are, I will reject them all and attach no weight to them', and the view, 'I have quite deep doubts about all the individual pieces of evidence, but there are sufficient of them pointing in the same direction that I will accept the direction in which they collectively point'? Or how should one choose between the view, 'This witness has changed his stories so often that I will not accept any of them: I will attach no weight to them', and the view, 'Although this witness has changed his stories so often, I will none the less decide which one is true'? In civil actions judges have to decide one way or another between the conflicting stories of the parties: they cannot simply say they cannot decide. What is the difference between selecting between different stories given by two people and different stories given by one person?

Furthermore, there is – at least in principle – a lower standard of proof which in some circumstances could be accepted, based not on near certainty, nor on the balance of probability, but on possibility. Possibility ranges from utterly inconceivable, through virtually inconceivable, remotely conceivable, barely conceivable, just conceivable, distinctly conceivable to very distinctly possible. The commissioners' minds were not used to descending below or probing deeper than the 51:49 level of the balance of probability, so it is not surprising that they did not contemplate a lower level of qualitative acceptability of evidence. The defect of using either of the standards of proof used by members of the judiciary, whether the result is 'I am sure this happened' or 'On balance I accept this happened', is that the result is a finding of 'fact' and therefore in most people's minds it actually happened. In reality, of course, the finding of a fact by a judge makes it neither more nor less of a fact in actuality. If one could use a 'degree of possibility' test for finding facts, especially in non-judicial proceedings, at least the result could be: 'On balance I think this happened but it is entirely possible that it did not.' It would then be more possible for others, including those with greater detailed knowledge and experience of the field of inquiry, to reach conclusions which differ from those of the tribunal without being accused of ignoring the 'facts'.

From the outset the question of the standard of proof required and the particular weight to be attached to evidence was confused with, and blurred by, the question of admissibility of evidence. When Morton was being considered as chairman, Armitage raised the question of admissibility, and the secretary of state reassured him by saying, 'the Lord Chancellor will make sure that the judge appointed as chairman [understands] the importance of the points made', and that he and his colleagues on the commission 'should not stick to the rules of evidence'. When he was asked how best to get this over to the chairman, Roberts-Wray suggested:

Perhaps it would be as well to explain ... that this is not meant to be a judicial enquiry ... [A] member of the judiciary is accustomed to dealing with testimony which is given on oath and admissible under rules of evidence whereas it is not proposed that witnesses should take the oath and I have little doubt that the Commission would be asked to receive and take into account evidence which though it would not be acceptable in a court of law would be regarded as relevant by the man in the street. I would hope that Lord Morton would not find this distasteful.[79]

When Colonial Office officials discussed the matter with Devlin they asked him if he would find difficulty in receiving evidence which, though considered relevant by the man in the street, would not be acceptable in a court of law. Devlin laughed and said he had had a good deal of experience of this in his restrictive practice court.[80] Both Roberts-Wray and the other officials in the Colonial Office were directing their minds to the question of admissibility of evidence and were confining it to relevance and not to the equally important questions of the standard of proof required and the weight to be attached to evidence. The first of these three questions was relatively simple to answer since if the strict rules of admissibility were demanded very little evidence would be forthcoming as the rules relating to hearsay, opinion and corroboration would rarely be met, even if a slightly blind eye were turned to the relevance of evidence. Given the question's focus – admissibility and relevance rather than standard of proof or weight of evidence – it is not surprising Devlin readily agreed to adopt the position of the 'man in the street'. What is somewhat surprising is that no one, including Devlin, seems to have raised the questions of the standard of proof and weight. In the event they adopted the balance of probability standard.[81] The weight to be attached to the evidence admitted was not discussed before the hearings or explained afterwards. It is likely that Devlin considered this a matter exclusively for himself: his view, expressed later, was that for sifting facts and giving each its due weight 'there must be a trained mind' and 'a judge is competent to evaluate' second-hand evidence.[82]

The second major issue was that of protecting witnesses, and this, from different perspectives, was important to both the commission and the government. Devlin wanted to ensure that no one who might otherwise give evidence would be deterred from doing so, either, in the case of those who might testify in favour of the government, by intimidation, or in the case of those who might testify against the government, by fear of prosecution or detention. He was particularly concerned about the latter possibility. Armitage wanted to ensure protection also by prohibiting the publication of memoranda or evidence given to the commission, so as to avoid embarrassing government and the commission through people seeking publicity by making public what they said or wrote to the commission.[83] Lennox-Boyd rejected these arguments claiming that, once published, the statements would no longer be privileged and would be open to legal action.[84] He did not say how this would remove the potential embarrassment.

Devlin voiced his concern at an early stage and the secretary of state told Armitage of this on 25 March:

He will wish at an early date to reach an understanding with your Attorney-General on the way in which he will be placed in a position to

assure persons giving evidence before his Commission that they need
have no fear that any evidence so given would be made the basis of a
prosecution or used for purposes of a prosecution. I gather that what he
rather hopes is that the Attorney-General will be able to say that after
the Commission has commenced sitting there will be no prosecutions of
any persons who give evidence before it – which would presumably mean
the Attorney-General would have to have set in train before the Commission starts work any prosecution of anybody likely to be asked to
give evidence before the Commission.[85]

Although Armitage could see that the early appointment of the
commission had advantages, he could also see disadvantages: primarily
that his and his colleagues' efforts were of necessity concentrated on
preparing the case for the commission – 'what a sweat it is going to be
to get all the documents and correspondence for them!'[86] Consequently
they were not yet ready to commence any major prosecutions for, for
example, conspiracy; and the nature and sources so far available made
the likelihood of such prosecutions remote. Prosecutions for arson,
rioting and sabotage could go ahead. Until it had been decided that
evidence was not to be given on oath, the secretary of state simply
wished to exclude perjury from the withholding of prosecution of
witnesses.[87] Save for this – and in the event evidence was not given on
oath so the concern disappeared – Armitage and the British government had no problem giving an 'absolute assurance' that no charge
would be preferred against anyone which arose from what they said to
the commission, and they were happy for Devlin to make this
'absolutely clear'.[88] The matter of prosecution was thereby cleared up
even though the agreement fell short of what Devlin 'rather hoped':
no one giving evidence would be prosecuted once the commission
began its hearings. The chairman none the less felt that it was an
additional assurance they could give witnesses:

> You can speak freely because even if it gets out what you are saying
> we've got this undertaking [from] the Governor.[89]

Had what Devlin 'rather hoped' been agreed, it would have made his
finding the truth even more difficult because the police would have
had to stop investigating suspected criminal actions, knowing that very
shortly they would not be able to bring the results before the courts.
In the absence of continued police investigation – which in principle
is as capable of uncovering the facts as is the judicial process – the
government's ability to assist the commission in arriving at the truth
was seriously weakened.

Detention was a more difficult matter and such was its importance
that it was considered not only by officials in the Colonial Office but

also personally by Lennox-Boyd, Kilmuir and Manningham-Buller, the attorney-general. When Devlin first mentioned the matter it was suggested the best solution might be to agree that no transcript of evidence would be shown to the secretary of state or to the Governor; Lennox-Boyd said he would think about this and discuss it with his colleagues.

> [The] more [he] thought about it the less [he] liked it because of [his] continuing responsibility for the good government of the territory and the possibility to defend *with conviction* some of the Commission's conclusions.[90]

Kilmuir suggested they could make it clear that no one would be detained on grounds of any act done before giving evidence, but Lennox-Boyd countered that this put 'a large premium' on volunteering evidence simply in order to avoid the consequences of past actions. Lennox-Boyd then suggested that Devlin should assure everyone who might ask him – and, if he wished, to say so in public – that no one would be detained on account of what they said to the commission.[91] Lennox-Boyd was also concerned that his privy counsellor oath required him to disclose information which came to his knowledge that prejudiced the welfare of any part of Her Majesty's dominions.[92] Since, however, the oath is confidential nothing seems to have been done about this concern and presumably Devlin simply noted it.

On 6 April Gorell Barnes told Devlin the secretary of state hoped Devlin would find his formula a satisfactory solution, and, although it would be difficult to prove that what was said to the commission would not be taken into account in reaching a decision on any detention, he hoped the judge would agree that 'this is a matter in which it would not be unreasonable to expect that the word of the Governor would be accepted'. Devlin, not entirely happy with this suggestion – although it was virtually identical to that which he accepted in the case of prosecutions – agreed merely that the transcript of evidence given to the commission should be exclusively for its members' information and to help them in preparing their report, and stated that he would inform witnesses of this when necessary.[93] Devlin must have been confident of the security and secrecy of all the evidence to be given before him, and the transcripts of it, and concerned only with the prosecution and detention use to which Armitage might put the published report. Since the government would not know who had given evidence there was no way in which they could avoid the risk of detaining or prosecuting someone who, without their knowledge, had already given evidence. Indeed there was at least one case in which a witness was subsequently arrested.[94] It seems to have passed unnoticed, save by Lennox-Boyd and his senior officials, that not having access to transcripts of the evidence deprived the secretary of state of the ability 'to defend with conviction some of the Commission's conclusions'.

Whereas Devlin was primarily concerned with protecting witnesses against the government, Armitage was concerned with protecting witnesses for the government. In his report, when explaining the necessity to hold all hearings in private, Devlin did not mention the need to protect pro-government witnesses against intimidation but only to safeguard those who expressed pro-Congress and anti-government views. Indeed his view was:

> [In Nyasaland] it is not safe for anyone to express approval of the policies of the Congress party ... and ... unwise to express any but the most restrained criticism of government policy.[95]

It was because of this view, he said, that all the commission's hearings took place in private. In responding to the Governor's concerns, the secretary of state wrote to him on 2 April[96] about protection through not disclosing the names of witnesses and those submitting memoranda, and divided the concerns into two categories. First, those who did not wish their own names to be revealed should be assured that they would not be disclosed; he mentioned this to Devlin and was sure that he could rely on him and his colleagues not to disclose the names. This reliance was misplaced because Devlin on at least one occasion revealed to Banda and his legal representative the identity and evidence of a district commissioner who had appeared before him; and in the case of a particularly sensitive and crucial African witness who was 'promised faithfully' that the commission would never write down his name in 'any documents lest it fell into the wrong hands', the transcripts of his and other evidence (and a number of other documents) very frequently mentioned his name in full.[97] Devlin also published the names of a number of other witnesses and there is no evidence that he sought their agreement to this.[98] Second, Lennox-Boyd turned to others who might wish to reveal the names of witnesses and those submitting memoranda, and felt it was

> not a matter for legal prohibition but for administrative arrangements to ensure that no one who would disclose names would be in a position to learn of them. This presumably would be secured either by police watch on approaches to Commission offices or by special arrangements for one or more of its members to see certain witnesses elsewhere.[99]

He was clear as to the purpose of private hearings: to protect witnesses wishing to avoid publicity and to ensure, as far as practicable, their willingness to give evidence.[100]

Devlin seems largely to have ignored this concern over privacy in practice and to have done so in three ways. First, by demanding that district commissioners leave the commission 'entirely to itself', he excluded the only practical means of preventing anyone who wished to know who was giving evidence from knowing. Second, by accepting such a large quantity of joint evidence, especially that given *in coram publico*, the identity of hundreds of witnesses became public knowledge. Finally, by accepting memoranda which the Livingstonia missionaries had retyped, the identities of those submitting the memoranda became known to a wide range of people.[101]

From the beginning Armitage argued that if the commission had power to subpoena witnesses this 'would have a disastrous effect on the special branch' whose 'agents should not in any circumstances appear before [the] Commission since, if they did, [the] whole special branch Intelligence Service would collapse'.[102] Lennox-Boyd accepted this view and excluded the power from the commission's warrant.

> Mr Justice Devlin said it clearly would not be easy to pronounce on whether there was a plot without hearing the original sources in person ... he thought the Commission should, after discussion with the Governor, accept his judgement as to whether they should, or should not, seek to see any particular witness of this kind, but the final decision on what the Commission put in their report should be left to the Commission, who would however take fully into account any argument affecting security which the Governor wished to put forward.[103]

These views suggest that Devlin was finding it difficult to break away from the normal rules of evidence – he wanted to hear the original sources in person no matter how strong other sources, including corroborated sources, might be – and that he was placing major emphasis on the murder plot.

At a very early date Devlin made it clear he wished to examine 'all (repeat all) documentary evidence on all (repeat all) matters referred to in the White Paper including the complete relevant files of the Administration, the Police and the military'.[104] These wishes suggest he intended to place considerable emphasis on Armitage's despatch – published three days earlier – and that he harboured doubts whether the Governor intended, or was willing, to produce all the documentary evidence on every matter referred to in it. The Governor had, of course, submitted 161 pages of supporting documentation covering virtually every paragraph in the despatch. While Armitage could not let the commission see the government's working files he was keen that they should see the Nyasaland Intelligence Committee reports since Banda's return to the protectorate because these would be of 'inestimable value to [him] in presenting coherent evidence'. He had new files made up containing all the relevant material from the main files, including secret and top secret documents, but he was going through the material with the 'greatest care' to see if any problems might arise, in which case he would consult the secretary of state. He was particularly keen that potential difficulties should be ironed out before the commission left Britain.[105] He was concerned not only to protect government witnesses giving evidence but also to protect those who might be identified in the material produced to the commission to which its members might refer in their report; he did not want them to be damaged as individuals or sources of information. He asked if he could claim privilege not to produce documents, but Lennox-Boyd concluded that if Armitage were even to mention to the commission the possibility of claiming privilege 'the outcome might be highly unfortunate and embarrassing'.[106] The secretary of state also discussed the general question with the commission and was satisfied that it would be 'safe to rely on them not to publish or make use of any material ... which would in [Armitage's] view prejudice the workings of the Special Branch or bring agents or sources into danger'.[107] He asked the Governor, therefore, to let the commission see all material they asked for but to reach a clear understanding with them about the use of any which might prejudice special branch operations or endanger agents and other sources. Devlin agreed they would use their discretion about publishing any documentary evidence that they received.[108]

The question, then, of protecting witnesses against the government was satisfactorily resolved but that of protecting government witnesses acting covertly seems to have been somewhat left hanging in the air. Partly as a consequence of this scarcely any special branch sources appeared before Devlin.

The third major issue discussed with Devlin was how to receive evidence from people detained by the Nyasaland government but held in federal prisons in Southern Rhodesia, since the British government had no power to compel either the federal or the Southern Rhodesian government to allow access to them. The day after the Commons announcement setting up the commission, Devlin said he assumed it would be possible for him to hear evidence in these circumstances and 'would like to know how [the Governor] propose[d] that this should be arranged'.[109] Momentarily, and not unnaturally, flummoxed, Armitage dismissed transferring detainees to Nyasaland but immediately suggested their temporary transfer to Northern Rhodesia. Benson, equally quickly, dismissed that suggestion because it 'would unquestionably provoke sharp reaction'.[110] As an alternative he suggested detainees be transferred to Bechuanaland and examined there, but the federal director of prisons objected, as he had no power to do this.[111] Benson then asked Armitage to consider detainees being flown from Khami prison in Southern Rhodesia to Fort Jameson in Northern Rhodesia and then transported by road the short distance to Fort Manning, in Nyasaland, under guard.[112] Armitage could not contemplate the detainees' return to Nyasaland – even to a remote corner of the protectorate and even for a very short period. Instead the British High Commissioner in Salisbury, Sir Ralph Hone, approached the prime minister of Southern Rhodesia about the commission taking evidence there. The Colonial Office assumed that Whitehead would object and were pleasantly surprised when he immediately agreed to enact a bill giving the commission the necessary powers, on the 'absolutely clear understanding' they were confined 'in principle and as matters of law' to access to persons detained on Nyasaland government orders and not to others such as those detained under Southern Rhodesian orders.[113] Whitehead was a good deal more cooperative than the British government had expected, and Lennox-Boyd thanked him 'for all [his] help [and] extremely helpful attitude'.[114] The secretary of state was relieved since no other acceptable solution had been proposed to the difficulty in which Devlin's assumption of access had placed them. Witnesses were later examined in Bulawayo.[115]

The sensitivity of matters involving the federal and Southern Rhodesian governments, and Devlin's inadequate appreciation of the difficulties involved, are also illustrated by his proposal that the commission should ask to interview Welensky and Whitehead. Hone's advice was immediate: Devlin should be 'headed away' from it and 'drop it altogether':

> Devlin's proposal leads us straight towards the very dangers we have worked so hard in recent weeks to avoid i.e. confusion between facts of Nyasaland disturbances and basic justification of Federation's achievements and future ... any hint of anything in nature of U.K. inquest into Southern Rhodesia activities in relation to Nyasaland disturbances would have disastrous effects ... any approach to Federal and even more to Southern Rhodesia Government will have to be delicately handled.[116]

Hone, however, diplomatically told Welensky he was sure Devlin would like to meet him on a personal basis and 'also like to see Whitehead if Welensky would bring him along', a suggestion that Welensky accepted.[117] Hone's caution and his protection of Devlin were well founded because in Devlin's mind Welensky was 'a party to the inquiry in that his conduct was being investigated'.[118] Armitage, too, warned of the danger and tried to protect Devlin from it:

If the Commission of Inquiry take evidence from Welensky and, or, Whitehead on anything other than military and police matters respectively, they may get into deep waters ... In any other circumstances [the] Commission of Inquiry may well come under criticism that once more Her Majesty's Government are being influenced by Federal Government – 'It's that man again'.[119]

There remained the fourth major issue – the confidentiality of communications from other governments – and this, in one form or another, persisted as a worrying concern for the British government throughout most of the period the commission existed. The question first arose late in March when Armitage asked about claiming privilege from producing documents.[120] In reply the secretary of state said:

If the Commission were to ask for a communication addressed to you from some Government other than HMG [the] right course would be to seek the agreement of the Government concerned ... and to explain to the Commission that you thought it necessary to do so before complying with their request. If the other Government concerned were to oppose disclosure of the communication in question you would no doubt consult me as to your further action.[121]

At this time, Armitage was thinking in terms of crown privilege and the Colonial Office in terms of communications from other governments. It was Shannon, assistant secretary in the Commonwealth Relations Office, who narrowed the question to Commonwealth governments and first perceived that it raised 'a much more serious issue than that of crown privilege, namely the secrecy of communications between commonwealth governments'. This was 'a potential constitutional issue and not merely a legal one'. They had always refused to disclose such communications because it might prejudice confidential and frank consultations between Commonwealth governments.[122] Although apparently restricted to Commonwealth government communications, the concerns were even narrower and were confined to communications from the federal government, as Lennox-Boyd revealed in a cable to Armitage:

Question of attitude to be adopted if Commission should ask for copies of communications from Federal Government raises an important issue going beyond that of Crown privilege which is being further considered. If you are asked for copies of such communications before I can give you further guidance I shall be grateful if you will consult me and not, repeat not, approach the Federal Government before you have done so.[123]

The Colonial Office was being extremely cautious. Yet in reality the concerns were still narrower and were confined to a single document:

Welensky's telegram to Perth on 25 February advising him to postpone his visit to Nyasaland.

The British government feared that if Devlin found out about Welensky's advice he might conclude – as the opposition in the Commons had strenuously alleged – that they and Armitage were seriously influenced by the federal prime minister in declaring a state of emergency. Officials and ministers considered a number of ways of preventing Devlin knowing about Welensky's telegram, including a suggestion by Lintott that they delete the opening paragraph – 'Reference Welensky's telegram' – of a telegram from Armitage to which Devlin would undoubtedly have access: 'the Governor's telegram is self contained without this reference'.[124] Macpherson was in favour of deleting the phrase but Home was very doubtful about the suggestion, Gorell Barnes was 'extremely unhappy' about it, Shannon 'imagined that it would not be possible' and the attorney-general was 'strongly in favour of not withholding any relevant documents'.[125] It took a meeting of the secretaries of state for the colonies and Commonwealth relations and the attorney-general to decide not to alter the telegram,[126] largely because copies had already been 'fairly widely' distributed and would need to be called in very quickly if the opening paragraph were to be deleted.[127] Commonwealth Relations Office officials argued that Welensky's telegram should not be produced and were prepared to advise their secretary of state along these lines.[128] This view was accepted by the Colonial Office who telegraphed Armitage saying the commission was not entitled to demand, and should not be offered or permitted to see, any communication between the federal government and the British government.[129] They told the Governor to show his telegram to Devlin privately, not to other members of the commission unless Devlin asked, and to explain that Welensky's message could not be made available because of its 'absolute confidentiality' as a communication from a Commonwealth government. They thought that Devlin would 'readily understand the situation and not press the matter further', but if he did Armitage was to consult the secretary of state again.[130] Armitage had already given a copy of his own telegram, including the reference to Welensky's telegram, to Fairclough.[131]

When Armitage gave evidence before the commission on 15 April he was asked for a copy of the Welensky telegram and he told them that Lennox-Boyd had now authorised him to show it privately to the chairman. Consequently he immediately sent Devlin a copy and said that if he wished to show it to other members or use it in his report, Lennox-Boyd would wish to be consulted.[132] Two days later Devlin returned the telegram and on 18 April wrote to Armitage saying: 'I cannot say yet whether I shall want to show it to other members of

the Commission or to use it in the Report. If I do I shall let you know
so that Lennox-Boyd may be consulted.' Armitage assumed he would
indeed want to show it to the commission.

Devlin raised the matter with Welensky when he met him in Salisbury and on 29 April wrote to him saying:

> In a telegram to Armitage on 25 February you suggested that he should
> give serious consideration to deferring the projected visit of Lord Perth.
> We shall make it clear in the report that the Nyasaland Congress is
> closely associated with similar bodies in Northern and Southern Rhod-
> esia; this makes it plain that the way in which it is dealt with in one part
> of the Federation must be the concern of the Federation as a whole.[133]

The point of this was to show that the federal prime minister did
have a legitimate interest in Nyasaland political affairs and Perth's
visit to the protectorate. Welensky agreed with the way the chairman
proposed to deal with the matter,[134] and on 10 May Devlin asked
Armitage if he also agreed.[135] Since, however, Armitage thought
Lennox-Boyd should none the less be consulted – presumably because
the crucial point was not whether Welensky had a legitimate interest
in Nyasaland's political affairs, but rather whether he had applied
pressure to postpone Perth's visit – it was left that Devlin would
discuss it with the secretary of state on his return to Britain.[136]

Devlin assumed or claimed, contrary to the clear evidence already
in his possession, that Welensky's telegram had been addressed to
Armitage. He also – and again manifestly incorrectly – wished to state
in the report that the federal prime minister had urged Armitage to
give serious consideration to deferring Perth's visit.[137] In fact, Welensky
had simply sent Armitage a copy of his telegram to the Commonwealth
Relations Office. Devlin was quite wrong in saying Welensky suggested
to Armitage that he should consider deferring Perth's visit. Indeed,
Welensky stated clearly that he had not discussed the matter with
Armitage and Devlin knew this. Welensky was urging Perth, not Armitage, to postpone the visit – a view with which Armitage independently
concurred. It was upon Armitage's advice that the British government
postponed Perth's visit, not on Welensky's, nor on joint advice from
Welensky and Armitage. By concentrating on, and confining himself
to, Welensky's legitimate interest in territorial government affairs,
Devlin neglected the opportunity – presumably deliberately since the
concerns were well known to him – to show conclusively that the
federal prime minister, in his cable of 25 February, had not put pressure on Armitage and that his advice to Home had been rejected.

So concerned was Perth about this telegram that he asked the
attorney-general whether he should volunteer evidence on it.[138]

Manningham-Buller's response was clear: 'I can see no advantage to be gained by ... volunteering evidence about this and I would have thought it undesirable.'[139]

On the commission's return to Britain, Fairclough told the Colonial Office that Devlin would formally ask to show Welensky's telegram to the rest of the commission.[140] Welensky agreed but Devlin now said he would not need to show them the telegram if he could refer to it as agreed with Welensky;[141] this Lennox-Boyd accepted,[142] notwithstanding the grave and obvious error of fact which the agreed statement contained – probably because he had told the Commons the allegation that the federal government had said Perth should not go to Nyasaland was 'utterly without foundation'. When Perth discussed with Devlin whether what happened when Welensky's telegram arrived in London was pertinent to the story generally, Devlin's feeling was that it did not matter very much one way or the other, although he thought 'there might be some merit' in recording what had actually happened.[143] The following day Perth discussed this conversation – about referring to the telegram – in the Colonial Office where it was 'thought that it probably introduce[d] an unnecessary complication'. He told Devlin this and concluded: 'If you are happy we are happy to leave it at that.'[144] Devlin replied that he was 'happy to go along on those lines'.[145] Even so, in his report Devlin said in a single paragraph:

> On 25th February Sir Roy Welensky asked the Governor in view of the further developments in Nyasaland to give serious consideration to deferring Lord Perth's projected visit ... On the same day the Governor telegraphed to Lord Perth suggesting that he should postpone his visit ... On the next day the Chief Secretary flew to Salisbury in order to make final arrangements for the despatch of troops ... on 27 February it was announced in the House of Commons that the visit of Lord Perth had been postponed because it would provoke disturbances.[146]

In doing this Devlin repeated the error – that Welensky had asked Armitage to postpone Perth's visit – and gave the impression, presumably deliberately, that as a consequence Armitage had suggested to Perth that he postpone his visit, and also that Footman's visit to Salisbury was connected with the postponement which was then announced in the Commons. The following paragraph[147] says that Devlin was satisfied that 'the only contribution which Sir Roy made was the expression of opinion' to Armitage that he should seriously consider postponing Perth's visit – which was untrue and did not remove the impression that it was on Welensky's advice that Armitage suggested postponement. The whole matter could have been much more simply, briefly and clearly stated.

In these ways, then, the four major issues bothering Armitage, the British government and Devlin – the extent to which evidence should be accepted, protection of witnesses, evidence from detainees held in Southern Rhodesia, and the Welensky telegram – were handled and resolved, to the extent that they were indeed resolved.

There was, however, an underlying difficulty to the task which Devlin and his colleagues were undertaking, but one which they did not raise or discuss: the fundamental nature of their proceedings. The English system of justice – that to which Devlin was accustomed and in which he was deeply experienced – is the adversarial system, in contrast to that common in other European countries, the inquisitorial system. Devlin himself described the difference:

> one [the adversarial] is a trial of strength and the other [the inquisitorial] is an inquiry. The question in the first is: are the shoulders of the party upon whom is laid the burden of proof ... strong enough to carry and discharge it? In the second the question is: what is the truth of the matter? In the first the judge or jury are arbiters; they do not pose questions and seek answers; they weigh such material as is put before them, but they have no responsibility for seeing that it is complete. In the second the judge is in charge of the inquiry from the start ... it is for him to say what it is that he wants to know.[148]

In the inquisitorial system, of which English judges generally have little if any practical experience, the 'centrepiece is the dossier', the 'backbone' of which is formed by full written statements of the cases of the two sides, setting out evidence rather than issues; covering all the facts upon which each party relies and indicating how they propose to establish them; 'The rest is made up under the supervision of the judge.' In this system there are usually three judges, one of whom is the judge in charge who decides whether any witness should be orally interrogated and, if so, will do this himself in the presence of the parties. He adds his note of this evidence to the dossier, and then completes the dossier with a summary or perhaps a draft judgment.

> The other judges study the dossier and the three will discuss the case. They decide whether a hearing ... is necessary or desirable. If there is one, the advocates will be allowed a limited time; even in a heavy case it is unlikely to last for more than half a day. The judgment will be expressed briefly and in writing.

Devlin's undertaking in Nyasaland inevitably followed much more closely the inquisitorial system rather than the adversarial but it lacked a number of essential elements of the inquisitorial system which made it extremely difficult, and probably impossible, satisfactorily to fulfil its purpose: arriving at 'the truth of the matter'. What was missing was the full dossier, 'the centrepiece'; while the government produced a large volume of documentation and to it were added numerous memoranda submitted by members of the public, together with transcripts of the oral evidence taken, the 'other party' – the Congress leaders – deliberately did not submit any documentation. The dossier became one-sided and to that extent was defective: it lacked a large part of its 'backbone'. Nor did Devlin have the power to call for evidence of what was missing; he could not 'say what it [was] that he [wanted] to know'. Furthermore, whereas the inquisitorial judge hears oral evidence simply to complete the dossier, Devlin placed great importance on hearing the oral evidence of many witnesses, and presumably benefited – or suffered – from being able to assess their evidence from their demeanour, a possibly dangerous technique with witnesses from a vastly different culture, tradition and set of mores from his own.[149] The procedure adopted also allowed counsel, skilled in courtroom oratory and tactics, to examine many of the witnesses whereas in the inquisitorial system proper, examination is conducted by the judge. As a consequence of all these factors and difficulties the system adopted was – possibly inevitably – a mishmash, the ramifications of which were not considered in advance or, it seems, at any other time.

Fairclough and one of the stenographers arrived in Nyasaland a week before the full commission arrived on 11 April.[150] Footman met the members at the airport and gave them lunch,[151] and Armitage noted:

> They are being wary of approaching me. I suppose they want to make certain that no one can accuse them later of having been influenced or intimidated by me![152]

The extent to which Devlin and his colleagues wished to isolate themselves from government officers, and the reason they gave for this, is shown by a minute Fairclough wrote to Richardson, the Nyasaland government liaison officer, on 28 April:

> The Chairman has asked ... if you would be kind enough to get in touch with all District and Provincial Commissioners ... and make it plain to them that without in any way intending any discourtesy, the Commission would be grateful if the District Commissioners would ensure that the Commission is left entirely to itself at the agreed meeting place, and that they do not in any way attach themselves to the Commission or appear with the Commission unless and until they are called to give evidence ... The point of course is that the District Commissioner is in his District Government authority personified and if he is

seen with the Commission from the moment of the Commission's arrival until its departure, as has occurred in some places, it must be understandably difficult for the more simple souls in the populace to understand that the Commission is in fact an impartial, independent body and not something which is in the pocket of Government.[153]

This overlooked the need, as Lennox-Boyd had pointed out, for administrative arrangements – which could only be made by the district commissioner – to prevent those who wished to learn who was giving evidence from doing so.

With this sort of problem in mind, soon after the commission was appointed Armitage discussed with the secretary of state, who consulted Devlin, the accommodation to be provided for them:

In regard to nature of enquiry could it be criticised if accommodation is arranged either in Government House or in houses of senior officials in Zomba? As you will appreciate alternatives do present difficulties in Zomba where much of Commission's work will be ... Same difficulty is not likely to arise in Blantyre and Lilongwe had Commission wished to spend time there. Grateful for your advice. I would be delighted to accommodate at Government House if appropriate.[154]

Devlin's response to this seeking of advice and sensitive offer of hospitality was that 'the Commission should be seen as clearly as possible to be independent of Government and therefore it would be a mistake for [the] Commission to stay at Government House or with officials' or, indeed, to accept invitations to meals even when extended by old friends and former colleagues – as in the case of Armitage and Wyn-Harris.[155] So concerned was he not to accept hospitality from Nyasaland government officers that Devlin proposed to fly to Mbeya in Tanganyika to stay overnight between visiting Karonga and Fort Hill.[156] The Governor in Dar es Salaam, however, said that it would 'be preferable for the Commission not to enter Tanganyika if this [could] possibly be avoided' because his government had already been considerably criticised for sending in Tanganyika police and he did not want that controversy revived.[157] It appears that the Governors of both Tanganyika and Northern Rhodesia were anxious not to have Devlin and his colleagues in their countries if they could possibly avoid it.

In practice, while in the south the commission, rather than stay in Zomba, preferred to stay at Ryall's Hotel in Blantyre (where Congress counsel were also staying) and travel 80 miles a day to and from Zomba. None the less, in Zomba they lunched daily at the gymkhana club of which they became members, whose membership was almost entirely composed of civil servants and exclusively European.[158] In the north, they spent a night at Livingstonia with the Church of Scotland missionaries – some of whom had their houses 'quite transformed with new curtains and cushions' for the event[159] – and seem to have had no qualms about accepting their hospitality. The mission staff – as Devlin well knew – were openly partisan, and both critical and resentful of the government. They were very active in soliciting and encouraging memoranda from a very wide area of the north and gathered together very large crowds of Africans at the mission and elsewhere to make representations to the commission. The mission clerks were instructed to type out any of the large number of memoranda 'that needed greater legibility'.[160] The missionaries found the commissioners 'gracious guests, patient listeners and courteous questioners'.[161]

On their arrival in Nyasaland Armitage invited the commissioners to dine with him at Government House. They felt that even this invitation was insensitive, were deeply embarrassed and sent Fairclough to get the invitation withdrawn so as to avoid declining it formally. They felt this incident revealed Armitage's unawareness of the commission's role and his part in it.[162] Devlin's understanding of protocol was that the correct course was to assume that the invitation had never been extended. He would have liked to write 'a polite letter to the Governor and explain that [they] didn't feel that it would be a good thing as ... people would say that [they] had gone to receive [their] instructions'. He hoped they did not cause offence but recognised that by declining the invitation they 'very much got off on the wrong foot'. The other commissioners did not dissent from his views on isolating themselves and, partly by way of compensation, Devlin was careful, under Wyn-Harris's guidance, 'to observe all the proper formalities' when Armitage gave evidence.[163] The wife of the acting chief justice of Nyasaland also invited Devlin to dinner: she appreciated he might not wish to join the company of anyone with political associations but hoped he might perhaps feel that this objection did not apply to the judiciary. She had in mind inviting also an Irish judge, the French Consul, and the Roman Catholic Bishop of Blantyre.[164] Devlin politely but firmly replied that although this invitation tempted him more than most, the volume of work compelled him to make a rule to refuse all social invitations.[165] He also shunned contact with other lawyers:

> I thought that as a bencher of Gray's (my Inn of Court) Devlin would not object to social and professional contact. I asked for a meeting through ... his Clerk who spent the night with us. Devlin and I met on the Boma lawn. He shook my hand, murmured an embarrassed greeting and then made off. I think the Nyasaland judiciary considered that his refusal of contact went too far.[166]

If Armitage was unaware of the need for the commission to shun social contact, so also was the Colonial Office because they agreed that Devlin should be paid an allowance, part of which was 'to cover the cost of any official entertaining'.[167] The commission felt, too, that Armitage was embarrassed by their presence and attributed this to his not being accustomed to having to defer to anyone in the protectorate – a natural and proper stance for the Sovereign's personal representative – and possibly to his having been junior to Wyn-Harris during their service in Kenya.[168]

It is unlikely that Devlin paid much regard to the effects of his 'stand off' attitudes to government officers. As a district commissioner remarked:

> It was [a surprise] that, for the first time, I ... would not be entertaining distinguished visitors to the district. It was adding insult to injury that we were still expected to provide their meals, which were taken to them in the government rest house a short distance from our house. This ... suggested to any locals who were aware of it that we were already considered guilty of some misdemeanour. We ourselves understood the desire of the Commissioners to be seen to be completely impartial, and ... we were allowed to give their stenographers a meal in our house.[169]

Another district commissioner was, however, able to make some social contact with Wyn-Harris:

> We were told by Zomba that we were to have no social contact with them – we were clearly regarded as the miscreants! I *did* call round the evening before the hearing started and was ushered in by [Wyn-Harris] and had a whisky with him in secret – 'not supposed to talk to you, old boy'. He seemed a pleasant old boy but never opened his mouth at the hearing – nor did any of the others [except Devlin].[170]

Footman also reported that the commission 'kept themselves largely to themselves'.[171] They started their inquiry on 11 April, spent five weeks in the protectorate, travelled extensively and received evidence in all three provinces. They were based at Mzuzu for a week in May, spending one night away at Livingstonia. Since, unlike Blantyre and Lilongwe, Mzuzu had no hotels, they were accommodated as guests in the houses of civil servants. Had they wished to maintain their stance and not accept the hospitality of government officers, they could have been accommodated, quite comfortably, in tents. Devlin and Wyn-Harris stayed with the provincial commissioner and were accommodated in the thatched guest house. Although these were relatively luxurious conditions for district officers – most of whom spent half their time touring, usually on foot and sleeping under canvas – Devlin,

Williams and Primrose received their first, albeit gentle, taste of conditions in the rural parts of Africa. They took their meals with the provincial commissioner and by tacit agreement the inquiry was excluded from all conversation. The provincial commissioner found his guests extremely interesting people 'whose conversation on a wide variety of subjects was enjoyable and interesting'. He felt he saw a different side of Devlin from that seen by almost everyone else, including probably the Governor himself.[172]

The commission also sat for a week in the high court in Bulawayo, Southern Rhodesia, and four days in the high court in London. They finished their hearings on 26 June. In all they received evidence from 455 individual witnesses and about 1300 witnesses in groups; they also received 585 memoranda[173] – including a petition bearing 1800 signatures collected by Livingstonia missionaries from a wide area around Deep Bay[174] – and the Nyasaland government assembled for them 127 separate documents, many of them bulky,[175] and later gave them 'either by oral testimony or documentary evidence, every piece of information for which [they] asked'.[176] This was an average each week of nearly 100 individual witnesses, 260 witnesses in groups, 117 memoranda and at least 25 Nyasaland government documents – a vast amount of work to get through in a short time. The memoranda were of great variety and overwhelmingly from Africans. They displayed no signs of copying or of concerted action. They were highly individualistic, some were quaint, and they were often written by hand and in duplicate. Many blamed the delay in announcing constitutional advance for the disturbances and nearly all blamed federation. Nearly all, too, utterly disbelieved stories of a murder plot. Although overwhelmingly written by Africans there was a great variety of people submitting statements: Africans, Europeans, Asians, chiefs, non-officials, civil servants, missionaries, honorary consuls, trade and other associations; very few indeed were anonymous.[177]

Despite the many witnesses examined, 1755, Devlin initially intended to hear evidence from a very much larger number, including all Nyasaland government officials, members of the federal army and BSAP who were 'involved in any way in dealing with incidents during the disturbances'.[178] This would have at least tripled the number of witnesses he heard. Once the impracticality and sheer magnitude of the task was appreciated the commission decided to restrict themselves largely to incidents in which severe injuries and fatalities had occurred as a result of using firearms.[179] This was a more manageable undertaking but a severely damaging self-imposed confinement of their terms of reference that, inevitably, gave a much distorted picture of the disturbances into which they were inquiring.

Even so Devlin may have believed that a number of others were deterred from appearing before the commission by the intimidation of the security forces. A Livingstonia missionary recalled:

> Devlin told me personally of clear and menacing action by soldiers and police to stop African witnesses entering the Commission's meeting place, in particular at Kasungu, but also at other points on the Commission's journey north from Blantyre ... we were not at all surprised and indeed expected intimidation to be intensified, though covertly, to interfere with the Commission's work.[180]

Rumours were already 'rampant' at Livingstonia that 'fear of the army was preventing many witnesses from meeting the Commission, and this was borne out by the commissioners themselves on arrival at Livingstonia'.[181] There is no evidence that Devlin or his colleagues expressed this fear to Armitage or to anyone else and it is extremely unlikely to be true, particularly of Kasungu where the district commissioner said:

> I am certain that the Livingstonia missionaries are wrong as far as Kasungu was concerned in their belief that soldiers and police tried to stop African witnesses entering the Devlin Commission's meeting place. In fact it was Chief Mwase and his cohorts who made every effort to prevent anyone from seeing the commission and giving evidence. If anyone made menaces it was Mwase and [Congress].[182]

It is possible that Devlin was confused as to where, if at all, this interference had occurred or – more likely – that he was misunderstood. Williams recalled another district commissioner on their way north marshalling and organising the witnesses outside the building in which the hearings were held.[183] He thought this was Dedza and this may have been the case because the district commissioner there was well known as being a man who was always most anxious to have everything orderly and everyone well organised in his district. The Livingstonia missionaries also said that at Karonga 'there were police at the door and the [district commissioner] said that all must give their names'.[184] Again, the district commissioner is quite clear that this did not happen as 'the whole operation was run in a "hands off" way as far as the [district commissioner's] office was concerned'.[185]

The day after the commissioners arrived in Nyasaland, Devlin had a meeting with King, attorney-general, and Roberts, acting solicitor-general, about how to deal with special branch agents.[186] King was concerned lest the agents be compromised and hoped Devlin would not ask them to appear before him; he had, of course, no power to compel their appearance. The special branch consisted of eight European and thirty to forty African police officers, each one of them recruiting his own informers who reported directly and exclusively to him. Since they owed their loyalty to individual officers, King doubted if they would agree to say anything at all to the commissioners. Even if they did they would be recalling from memory information several months old and might not, therefore, be able to accurately reproduce their original reports. Devlin would be prepared to be 'really un-orthodox' in how he heard them, and would not ask to see them unless he felt he really needed to do so, in which case he would leave them until he had seen all other witnesses. In his report he would not refer to them by name. King thought that if they were to be seen, Finney should be told which agents were required so that he could advise on how dangerous each individual case would be and how safe meetings might be arranged. He also thought the special branch officer to whom each agent reported should be present at any meeting of the agent with the commission. In the event, neither Finney nor other special branch officers were present when agents and informers appeared before Devlin, although Roberts was.[187]

Originally, the decision to hear witnesses in groups was taken in order to allow, for example, the chief secretary to be present when the Governor was questioned.[188] In fact, the chief secretary did not accompany the Governor when Armitage appeared before the commission,[189] nor did he give evidence himself,[190] and Youens, who had acted as chief secretary during Footman's absence on leave, was long puzzled as to why he himself was not called to give evidence, since he had several important meetings with Banda enabling him to get to know the doctor probably better than anyone else in government.[191]

A number of examples of group evidence may be given. First, in the north, six American missionaries gave evidence together. Clearly terrified, they had armed their mission station and were ready to open fire to defend themselves.[192] Second, when the commission arrived in Karonga by air to hear the six witnesses who had asked to give evidence, they found over two thousand people waiting for them. Many, perhaps most, had been assembled at the behest – and with the encouragement and assistance – of missionaries from the Church of Scotland. Fairclough promptly, but with trepidation, divided the crowd into four sections according to the matters about which they wished to speak, and then the commissioners individually heard evidence from smaller groups taken from each section.[193] In this way they heard evidence from 17 spokesmen and nine groups averaging 57 each, including one of 138 witnesses.[194] Third, Wyn-Harris by himself interviewed a number of Africans at Mlanje who wanted to give evidence. He met about one hundred and twenty and soon concluded that 'about half of them were merely onlookers'. These onlookers retired and Wyn-Harris then discovered that only 53 wished to give evidence and they jointly said that 'the whole cause of the troubles in Nyasaland was due to federation'. Wyn-Harris listed their names and later advised Devlin that he 'did not consider that any useful purpose would be served in the Commission hearing them'.[195] Fourth, a number of Scottish Church clergymen appeared together having submitted a joint memorandum, and even when they had submitted separate papers at Livingstonia they appeared together as representatives of synod.[196] Fifth, at Bulawayo Wyn-Harris (but not the other commissioners) interviewed 20 detainees together, including five of the Congress 'second eleven'.[197] Sixth, groups of three to nine detainees were examined in Blantyre;[198] 44 detainees from Kanjedza and 46 from Mzuzu detention centre also asked to see Devlin.[199] In the vast majority of cases where evidence was given in groups, that evidence was simply the opinion that federation was to blame for the disturbances.

During the course of the commission's travels Footman wrote to the Colonial Office:

> Our general impression is that in their dealings with Officials they have concentrated on the details of the disturbances themselves and have not been quick – indeed they have seemed almost reluctant – to invite evidence on the events which led up to and precipitated the emergency. This ... has caused us some concern.[200]

The secretary of state's warrant entitled witnesses to have their legal representative present when giving evidence if they wished.[201] Thus Roberts was present during the evidence given by many government employees. Dingle Foot, T.O. Kellock and G. Mills-Odoi were present when the members of Congress they were advising gave evidence; in several cases all three were present. Soon after the commission had been set up, Banda wrote to Armitage from Gwelo:

> In connection with the Commission of Inquiry now visiting Nyasaland I have the following to say. (1) Dingle Foot Q.C., M.P., is representing me and my colleagues and the Congress. (2) We are not giving any evidence in writing. We want to see the Commission and give our evidence orally. (3) I demand the right to face my accusers before the Commission and in public because (4) whatever information now in your hands is false and given you by my political opponents and others for money as paid informers to the security police.[202]

Chiume claimed that 'a lot of messages were smuggled to and from our colleagues through sympathetic prison officers. Dingle Foot and other lawyers who were allowed to interview them on our behalf ... was very useful in this respect.'[203]

All hearings, except some group evidence, were in private; the representatives of one side were not present during the giving of evidence by witnesses of the other side, and 'no one had the right to hear the whole of the evidence against him'[204] although Banda and Chipembere were shown extensive lists of the allegations made about them by the government.[205] There being no cross-examination by legal representatives, this task fell to the commission itself – almost invariably Devlin personally when he was present, although he was absent in a surprising number of cases including some important witnesses – and they recognised later that witnesses may consequently have felt they were being singled out for criticism.[206]

The transcripts of the evidence taken strongly suggest that the two 'sides' were treated very differently. Part of this was almost inevitable and arose from the fact that the government submitted a great deal of written evidence prior to the appearance of its own witnesses, whereas Banda and other Congress leaders, advised by Foot, gave only oral evidence and submitted no documents. Although the secretary of state's warrant empowered the commission to call for the production of documents, they did not need to call for them from the government because government documentation was voluntarily produced in great abundance; and they did not, even in a single case, call for documents from Congress. Consequently, in the case of government witnesses Devlin was able to study the documents – including the witnesses' own reports – in advance, identify any apparent weaknesses, inconsistencies and lack of clarity, and be well prepared in his questioning. In the case of Congress witnesses, however, in advance Devlin had next to nothing to contemplate and examine or upon which to plan his questioning apart from evidence the government had produced. It is much easier minutely to dissect a written than an oral presentation, and the transcripts of evidence taken at interviews with government and Congress witnesses clearly show this difference. On the other hand, there were many cases where it was clear that the commissioners – less frequently Devlin himself – had not read the documents in advance. For example, they said in a number of cases that they had the memorandum in front of them 'and it will, of course be studied carefully'.

It was not only in the production of documents that the two sides were treated differently but also in the appearance of witnesses. Devlin had no power to compel their attendance but in practice he was able to hear and cross-examine all those government witnesses he wished to, and any attempt not to produce a government witness undoubtedly would have been the subject of severely adverse comment. In the case of Congress witnesses, however, Kellock carefully filtered them and, save possibly for Yatuta Chisiza, whose appearance clearly could not be safely avoided, he did not produce any 'unsteady' witnesses. He marked the statements he took from Congress witnesses, which the commission neither saw nor indeed knew about, with such comments as 'not very steady', 'strike, not intelligent', 'poor' and 'N.B.G.' (no bloody good). The deponents of such statements were not brought before Devlin. Furthermore, a number of original documents addressed to the commission were handed over to, and retained by, counsel for Congress whereas no case has been found of commission documents being handed over to the government. Additionally, Congress counsel need not – and indeed did not – reveal to Devlin inconsistencies between statements made to the police and statements made to Kellock. It followed, therefore, that Devlin was able to probe deeply into statements made by government officers and to ignore virtually all statements made by Congress officials and members to the police and all to counsel.[207]

Foot took his witnesses through their evidence in the form, but without the normal restrictions and safeguards, of an examination-in-chief – asking questions, many of which indicated the answer required and some of which revealed that he had previously discussed the question – and answer – in detail with his clients. In those cases Devlin allowed the examination to proceed with scarcely an interruption and only when Foot had finished his questioning did Devlin 'cross-examine', in some cases not asking any questions at all. One glaring example is that of Chiumia, who was an important witness because he had been present at the Congress bush meeting and had been closely interrogated by the security forces. The vast majority of Foot's questions were answered either 'Yes, Sir' or 'No, Sir' and at the conclusion none of the commissioners, not even Devlin, asked a single question.[208] Roberts did not take his witnesses through their evidence, and the questioning was done by Devlin very much in the form and tone of a cross-examination, on the basis of documents already produced by the government. Roberts was then invited to ask questions – and as such was put in the position of cross-examining his own witnesses – and in a surprising number of cases he asked no questions at all. The effect of this procedure was that Congress witnesses had the advantage of opening and closing examination by Foot whereas government witnesses did not have this opportunity; they were, in effect, subjected almost exclusively – and in many cases exclusively – to Devlin's cross-examination. In a large number of cases when Foot appeared he did so in company with Kellock and Mills-Odoi. In no instance was Roberts accompanied by other counsel even though the attorney-general, like Foot a Queen's Counsel, was present in

Nyasaland.[209] In very many cases Congress witnesses were assured that nothing they said to the commission would ever be revealed to other people but in scarcely any cases – if any – was this assurance given to government witnesses.

The first witness to give evidence before the commission was Captain Caine of 2 KAR. A company commander, Caine had been involved in an incident on 27 February in which an African had been shot. Devlin asked nearly all the questions, Williams a few – about military statistics – and the other two members asked none. It may be that Devlin and his colleagues sensed that the witness – who felt he was fairly treated – was not impressed by the experience of the members of the commission:

> I formed the opinion that all members were completely out of touch with the reactions of a hostile crowd ... some of the questions were amazing and naive ... Dear old Devlin, a most learned legal man for whom I had a lot of respect was most disturbed that our troops had to open fire on unarmed civilians. Did he think that once they had over-whelmed the troops it would lead to happiness and goodwill? They were totally out of touch with conditions prevailing at the time ... intelligence people [such as were Williams and Primrose] were pretty ignorant of the workings of troops in the 'front line'.[210]

Not a good start! Virtually without exception, the view of the army officers who gave evidence was: 'without any doubt that Devlin's main purpose was to discredit the Nyasaland Government and Armitage in particular'.[211]

Armitage gave evidence to the commission for an hour on the afternoon of 15 April.[212] They asked him almost exclusively about the talks he had, and the arrangements he made, with Welensky and Whitehead to get reinforcements to Nyasaland[213] and they quite quickly concluded that he had acted independently in declaring and conducting the emergency. Earlier that day he had replied to a letter from Devlin helpfully asking if there were points into which he felt the commission should inquire.[214] Armitage believed there were five points. In respect of the Nyasalanders' desire to leave the Federation he suggested they inquire into the ways in which the Africans had suffered from federation, since he would be supplying a good deal of evidence showing its benefits. He also thought it would be valuable if Devlin ascertained what effects the presence of Rhodesian troops in Nyasaland in the early days of the emergency had had on the African population since he had been criticised for bringing them in. Next he thought that

> it would be desirable if [the] Commission could clarify the position of the Church of Scotland Mission ... as regards Congress and the

influence of Congress on the Mission [because Devlin] will have received evidence of the damage caused by school children, at times accompanied by their teachers, in the vicinity of schools in the Mission areas.

He felt it likely there were other Church of Scotland missionaries whose 'views would not accord in all respects with those who would probably be the first to make submissions' to the commission. Armitage believed another material point would be to determine how Congress got its following, whether by intimidation and spurious promises, 'or whether it depends on personalities or other factors not easily apparent'. One such 'other factor' was explained a little later by a leading Congressman to a district commissioner when accounting for Banda's large following:

> The trouble with you Europeans is that you forget that we Africans are used to having a Chief who tells us what to do. Dr Banda is our Chief and we do what he says.[215]

The Governor's final suggestion to Devlin was that he try to discover the extent to which the numerical weakness of the administration and the police contributed to the support given to Congress and the extent to which its members resorted to violence. At his interview Armitage was asked briefly about these points. Wyn-Harris then asked if he intended to make a reappraisal of the 'murder plot', to which he replied:

> No one has ever made any suggestion to me that there was any reason to look at the plan for the disorders, and the plot, in a new light ... I would say myself ... that the plot was part of a pattern of disorders to take over the government ... For better or for worse these people appeared to think that they could so disrupt life here that they could ... in fact take over the government, or make the government here so impossible that you had to accept what Congress wanted. Now the pattern of the plot, the pattern of the plan, let us talk of the plan, the overall plan which had a whole series of facets, was of course never followed out as far as one can see in any consecutive way. For instance, a whole series of things was supposed to happen when Dr Banda was arrested but they did not. A whole series of things was supposed to happen when they had reached the stage when they could get what they called the 'massacre plan' into operation but of course they never got there. As I see it they took it into their heads that they could disrupt government here. Now how were they going to do it? They strung together a whole variety of things: disorders everywhere; release of prisoners; disruption of communications ... and as part of that pattern the murder of a variety of people. I just regard that plan to murder as part of an overall plan ... I regard the murder part of this as part of a phase in a plan which they never got to

– they were never allowed to get there. They were not allowed to get to
a variety of other things ... I doubt if you would find any evidence in
this country that there was a greater or a lesser degree of emphasis
attached to the murder part of the plan than I have given you.[216]

Having been in the country only four days and having heard only one
other witness – who did not mention it – Wyn-Harris seems to have
believed that the Governor's allegations of the existence of a 'murder
plot' might be sufficiently doubtful as to merit reappraisal. Even so,
the invitation to reappraise enabled Armitage to set out quite clearly
his view of the part which murder played in the multifaceted Congress
plan, and to put it into perspective.

The following day Ingham gave evidence[217] and was questioned
almost exclusively on the publicity the government had deployed in
telling the population about the emergency and the reasons for
declaring it. The commissioners thought it possible that the crowds
gathering on 3 March had done so simply to inquire about the reasons
for the arrests, and if the district commissioners had been able to tell
them Congress had planned murders this might have convinced them
and they might not then have created further disturbances. Devlin,
with this in mind, asked whether it would not have been better for
government to have publicised their belief in a murder plot at that
time. Ingham, who said that 'the fact of the murder plot ... is not
generally believed', thought publicising it would not have calmed the
crowds. The commission was not impressed by Ingham. Nor were
they impressed by Footman, Finney and King.[218]

Another early witness was Kettlewell, who recalled:

> The attitude was hostile from the start. Devlin – and only Devlin –
> asked questions. His first, based on his understanding that I drafted
> operation orders was 'What right had I to order a "punitive expedition"
> (which was to take place in part of the Southern Province)?' The ques-
> tion and its hostile tone took me aback; but with great help from Denys
> [Roberts], we asserted that in circumstances of serious local disturbance
> punishment was justified. And in any case the final instructions emanated
> from the Governor ... my very strong recollection is of Devlin's personal
> hostility. I reported accordingly to [Armitage] afterwards and got the
> impression that he found the atmosphere the same ... Devlin's hostile
> attitude during my interview with the Commissioners could be in-
> terpreted as 'disdainful'.[219]

Kettlewell was closely questioned on the instructions issued by the
Operations Committee and especially on troops being allowed to open
fire at road-blocks. He was also questioned about agricultural legislation
and enforcement.[220] Williams later recalled that Kettlewell was one of

only three Nyasaland civil servants who favourably impressed the
commission. The other two were Haskard and Brock.[221] Devlin and
Williams also thought Roberts was 'very good'.[222]

Armitage knew little of who else gave evidence but 'gathered' a lot
of people did. He was privately contemptuous of the evidence which
the Church of Scotland had probably given – 'I am sure they have had
a long and tortuous story from a lot of members of the Church of
Scotland missions.' Indeed, at that stage he knew very little of what
was happening with the commission: 'We do not hear much about its
thoughts, they keep those to themselves!'[223] He did later pick up a few
anecdotes about the commission's visit to Livingstonia Mission: they
felt they needed to take alcohol with them but Primrose said he dare
not take it in the car with him – Williams took the whisky instead;[224]
and Devlin 'was not very appreciative' of having to sing psalms in
church before breakfast; but, as the Governor wrote, '... we have no
authentic news!'[225] What he did not know was that not all the commissioners kept their thoughts to themselves, because Primrose revealed
a number of things to Livingstonia missionaries which 'let [them] in
fairly deeply on the conclusions that the Commission were likely to
reach'.[226]

In the early days of the commission's work the government did not
try systematically to discover what they were doing and what their
thinking might be: Mullin did not ask his police officers who had
given evidence about their reception by the commission nor, from his
point of view, 'did they have any occasion to comment'.[227]

When the commission was in the central and northern provinces
their documents were locked in a safe carried on the back of a lorry.
Members of the entourage struck up friendly relations with the
government African drivers who transported them and who at the end
of their work in Nyasaland wrote to them saying:

> We drivers still give more and more congratulations for the hard jobs
> which you have done here in Nyasaland. You travelled in very difficult
> places without [getting] tired and this job will never never be forgotten
> [by] us and the people of Nyasaland.[228]

Devlin and Williams normally travelled together and Wyn-Harris
travelled in another car with Primrose. After the major questioning
Devlin sometimes travelled on to the next venue, leaving his colleagues
to do the 'mopping up' questioning.[229] In these cases, the questioning
of ordinary African witnesses, Wyn-Harris was usually the chairman
and he routinely introduced the commission as 'elders' sent out from
Britain to inquire into the disturbances. It is likely that although he
intended the word 'elder' to mean 'elderly wise men' as in 'tribal

elders', he was taken by Africans listening to him to mean 'senior members of a church congregation' as in 'church elders'. Given the important role of the Scottish Church in Nyasaland – in which the term 'church elder' was common – and the well known fact that Banda (and the lesser known fact that Primrose also) was an elder of the Church of Scotland, Wyn-Harris's use of the term 'elder' may have been misleading. It was in any case unneccessary and unwise.

Members of the commission were deeply impressed by the evidence of Brock, district commissioner of Nkata Bay where 'by far the gravest of any' incident occurred in the emergency, when 48 people were shot, 20 of them fatally. A legend had quickly grown in Nkata Bay that Brock had tricked the people by leading them 'down the jetty with the promise that their leaders would be released and that then he led them into the arms of the soldiers who shot them'.[230] At the close of his evidence, just before he left,

> John Brock said something to the effect that he hoped the Commission did not imagine he had led his people to the dock and therefore was responsible for some of them being slain. And Patrick [Devlin] replied that nobody who had heard John's evidence that day would have any doubt about his devotion and integrity.[231]

Thirty-four years later, Williams recalled this as 'the most moving memory of our tour'.[232] Even so, in his report Devlin said of the legend only that: 'The facts show that there is no foundation for this.'[233] In his draft for the report Devlin included the words, 'If the tragedy was greater than it need have been, it was perhaps because his humanity was too deep'[234] but in the final report, in dealing with the legend, he omitted these charitable words and made no reference to the devotion and integrity which had impressed him at the time of receiving the evidence although he did say that Brock was 'not a man lacking in courage' nor in humanity.

Quite the opposite impression was created in the commissioners' minds by the principal special branch witness. Thomas Andrew Karua, who had been at college with Jomo Kenyatta, was a Tanganyikan and had been in charge of the Congress cine-camera, for example during the 20 January Zomba riot and the bush meeting five days later. He was examined a number of times in great secrecy, on one occasion at night in a house near Zomba. The meeting was arranged by Finney and Richardson, and implemented by Fairclough. Roberts brought Karua in and stayed throughout the meeting. Williams 'was landed with the questioning and it soon became apparent he [Karua] was lying because he contradicted himself and Denys [Roberts] realised this'. Armitage also learned of Karua's unreliability.[235]

On 21 May, two days before the commission left Nyasaland, Armitage spent two hours with them,[236] accompanied by Ingham and Roberts. The purpose of the meeting was for the commission to put to him various criticisms which they had received.[237] First, Devlin dealt with a number of paragraphs in the 18 March despatch which, it was alleged, were incorrect; and in most cases the commission simply made the point and noted Armitage's reply: they did not inquire into the reply or seek further elucidation. They pressed him on whether knowledge of the murder plot affected the actions of pick-up parties on 3 March. They spent a good deal of time on the allegations of illegal action, including excessive force in making arrests, meting out punishment for uncooperative attitudes, burning houses and confiscating weapons including agricultural implements from whole villages. On this last point Armitage said:

> It would be a sheer waste of time for a [district commissioner] to go and search a village that had never given any trouble just for the sake of taking away its weapons. If it was a village which was well known to be troublesome and from which any particular crowds had been known to have emerged, then I should have thought that he was fully justified in removing the weapons.

Devlin said that it must depend on whether the district commissioner had legal authority, and the Governor replied that even if legal powers had not been given, 'on the practical issue I should say that he was acting administratively correctly'.

> In other words, if you have got a situation where you think that you can take certain administrative action to save something worse happening you take it.

Devlin then said that he was very anxious to get the Governor's point of view on this and he bluntly put the other side:

> The objective of this whole exercise as stated over and over again is to initiate respect for the law. Should that be achieved by the commission of lawless acts even though they may be administratively correct?

But without waiting for an answer to this deeply important question, and indeed scarcely waiting to draw his breath, Devlin – notwithstanding his anxiety to get Armitage's view – moved immediately and peremptorily to the next issue: the murder plot. The Governor's view, stated many years later, was:

> Devlin ... did not pay any attention to the fact that in a state of emergency, when lives were being threatened, property is being destroyed,

tempers are being raised, my administrative officers had to deal with each situation as it arose in the way that they could best handle it to protect lives and property. Now you can't approach an incident of this sort having regard entirely to the legalistic and judicial aspect of what you are doing. [Devlin] took no account whatever of the administrative side of the situation and in my mind the whole emergency was an administrative episode requiring administrative action.[238]

By late February 1959 the security situation in Nyasaland had so deteriorated that Armitage, as Devlin found, had no choice – save to abdicate[239] – but to declare a state of emergency because with the forces at his disposal, including reinforcements, the ordinary law was not sufficient to enable him to cope with the problems. To do this he needed extra powers – powers which, because they were far more wide-sweeping and severe, were only temporarily conferred upon him by emergency regulations: it would be too harsh and oppressive for them to be permanently available. The law makers recognised that, having set a general standard of government powers to cope with normal events, there might be occasions when circumstances arose which rendered those powers insufficient for the government to fulfil its prime duty of maintaining law, order and the security of the state and its peoples. For such occasions, emergency, additional and temporary powers were made available. Since law makers are not omniscient it is conceivable, indeed likely, that occasions might arise when even the extra powers are insufficient to enable the government to fulfil its prime responsibilities. On such occasions the government, it could be argued, still has to act or to abdicate and such action would, under these circumstances, not be authorised by law. Basically, the Governor's argument was that unlawful administrative action might be justified if it prevented far more damaging breaches of the law, and injury to life and property.

The Governor's view of this second meeting with Devlin was that they all sat glum except the judge, who did all the talking. He was sure they were all 'pretty fed up with the whole thing'. Williams's recollection was that they were not fed up with the inquiry but were getting fed up with the sorry story that was emerging.[240]

Devlin recognised that 'his relationship to the Governor was essentially awkward' but told Perth his purpose was to assist Armitage rather than inquire into him.[241] His own impression of Armitage was:

He was not impressive as a witness but he was of course in a very difficult position – a Governor in the days when Governors expected to be treated as royalty summoned to give evidence in his own bailiwick.[242]

Devlin's impression of the Governor was shared by Williams:

'Armitage was an ineffectual witness and seemed quite unprepared for a Devlin-style cross-examination.' Devlin's impression seems also to have been shared by Primrose: when two missionaries at Livingstonia 'tried to put in a good word for the Governor, Sir John only grunted'.[243] A senior civil servant who observed Devlin at close quarters said that he 'obviously was satisfied that he was a most superior person and did not attempt to disguise his disdain for the Government of Nyasaland'.[244] It is probable that Devlin and Williams were over-sensitive to what they saw as Armitage's regard for status. Williams recalled:

> Armitage seemed to have been embarrassed by the Commission. When he came to give evidence they met him on the bottom step of the Legislative Council building so that there would be no question of hierarchy in their or his positioning. As he stepped out of the car he suddenly found that he had his hat in his hand and didn't know what to do with it so he threw it into the back of the car.[245]

Even the Queen's personal representative might be forgiven for not wanting to take his hat into an interview with one of Her Majesty's judges! Other examples of a similar over-sensitivity are provided in respect of General Long and Dingle Foot. Williams had known Long, a Rhodesian, during the war in North Africa and both had become brigadiers; and he had to caution Long when giving evidence against taking a 'sort of old boy and men of the world attitude' when he discussed incidents of soldiers 'roughing-up' Africans. When Foot first appeared before the commission he was wearing a Balliol tie which Williams felt was stupid; and he told Foot it would do him no good and, in any case, he (Williams) was a Merton man although a fellow of Balliol. Williams never forgot Wyn-Harris saying that members of the colonial service were one and a half ranks above what they would have been had they stayed in Britain in the civil service.[246]

Immediately following his second appearance before the commission, the Governor made two points in his private correspondence: there would be 'some interesting comments [on the] murder part of the plan' and there was certain to be criticism that in the arrests and later in the searches more force was used than at times was necessary. Of the former he said he did not emphasise it in his early announcements because he did not want to put ideas into people's heads and he hoped to forestall murders – 'which', as he said, 'we did'. Of the latter he simply said, 'you can't have an emergency without things happening that should not'.[247]

A number of government officers giving evidence felt they had undergone a 'gruelling'. The commissioners frequently used the word 'interrogation' of their questioning,[248] but it was the chairman who was thought to be particularly severe. Officers who felt that they had nothing to be ashamed of were none the less unsettled and put on the defensive by Devlin's aggressive questioning.[249] It was not only government officers who came in for a gruelling since the commission, Devlin in particular but also Williams, were severe in their questioning of the few informers special branch felt able to present before them. A special branch officer recalled:

> I made elaborate arrangements for a regular, reliable informant to meet Devlin in a safe house in Blantyre under the strictest secrecy and Devlin gave him a dreadful time. Devlin tried and tried to make the source say that he gave information, anything at all, to get money. Devlin pounced with delight when the source said that he had occasionally been given expenses. The source came out from the meeting absolutely livid, told me about it ... and asked why and what had he done wrong. He was not a source who relied on money payments or 'worked' for financial gain. I had quite a time placating him later.[250]

Primrose told two of the missionaries at Livingstonia:

> Some of the white security men had had a terrible time in front of Sir Patrick Devlin. The evidence against some of these men was appalling, and the judge had lashed them mercilessly with his tongue.[251]

When Perth discussed this manner of questioning with him, Devlin said it was inevitable, with no counsel, that he had had to do the job that they would normally do in the courts. He added that he had to do all the talking because he alone had experience of cross-examination 'and the rest of the commission were in a sense the judge and jury to the replies'.[252] This argument may have explained the questioning but it did not excuse the manner. Devlin, the overwhelmingly dominant member of the commission, in this way became cross-examiner as well as judge and jury. He thought the Africans probably felt as badly about their questioning as did the European civil servants.[253] No one had suggested the contrary, although Livingstonia missionaries 'heard repeatedly from African people how pleased they were with their treatment' by the commission.[254] Certainly Devlin's cross-examinations of Chipembere and of Yatuta Chisiza were vigorous, relentless and gruelling.[255] Devlin must have felt sensitive about this matter because he later referred to it in the published report:

> A searching inquiry into disputed facts cannot be conducted without some form of cross-examination, such as is ordinarily forthcoming from opposing counsel. Under the conditions in which we were conducting this inquiry that task fell upon us. A witness whose knowledge of what

we were doing could only be derived from our reception of his own evidence, may have felt at the time that he was being singled out for criticism. We regret this, and can only say that in this respect we endeavoured to treat all witnesses alike.[256]

The transcripts of evidence – especially a comparison of the cross-examination of Banda on the one hand and Chipembere, Yatuta Chisiza and a number of government officers on the other – show the extent to which they failed in this endeavour.

In both his reply to Perth and his report, Devlin refers to cross-examination rather than examination-in-chief despite pointing out that in the absence of counsel he had to do the job which they would normally do – presumably for both sides equitably. The overwhelming impression one gets in reading the transcripts of evidence where Devlin does a major part of the questioning is that he sees himself predominantly, and much of the time exclusively, as a cross-examiner – as one trying to disprove or cast grave doubt on what the witness is saying. His recorded questioning often gives an impression of belligerence, of hectoring, of trying to trip up or trap the witness, of putting words into their mouth, of tying them up in verbal knots. These are the marks of a ruthless cross-examiner, quite the opposite of an examiner-in-chief, yet Devlin had said that in the absence of counsel – and Roberts or Foot were not always present – he had had to do their jobs.

Devlin's vast and distinguished experience of the law in action was of the adversarial system of the British trial which, in his own words, in some respects resembles a battle. In a later published work[257] he referred to the 'virtual pugilism which is so characteristic of the British trial' and said that 'it is in cross-examination that the British trial comes closest to fisticuffs'. He referred, too, to 'the inestimable benefit of cross-examining ... leading ... to all that is favourable and challenging ... all that is not'. He recognised that where there is a suspicion of villainy there is 'the temptation to fisticuffs', 'display fighting' which varies in 'bellicosity' and which 'has now become a traditional part of the process'. In this process:

Cross-examination ... is uninhibited. Its object is to challenge and discredit, taking care not to let in incidentally material helpful to the other side. [The cross-examiner] will not seek to improve upon the surprisingly favourable answer lest on reconsideration the witness modify it.

He acknowledged that hostile cross-examination had become a 'distinctive feature of the English trial'. With this experience and these views it is not surprising that in personally adopting the role of cross-examiner Devlin also adopted a belligerent approach. He seemed to believe, without question, that this was a much more effective way of getting at the truth than the use of more varied legitimate techniques, including less aggressive techniques, used by other professionals such as experienced, trained intelligence and police officers for example.

Two specific examples may be given of what police officers could have felt was a harsh approach by Devlin. One incident at Fort Manning in which a man was shot dead by a military captain was the subject of three paragraphs in Devlin's report;[258] in summation of the incident he said they were satisfied that the district commissioner, the captain and the police inspector, all honestly believed that their party was in danger. The parts played by the district commissioner and the captain were examined in the report but not that of the inspector even though he had been attacked and wounded with a panga. Yet Devlin had asked him the entirely hypothetical question – the purpose of which does not appear clear from the transcript nor was it explained – 'Which do you think is ... worse ... that a police officer should get the sort of injuries you have told us about or that a man should be shot dead?' The inspector – who had not done any shooting – was not to be intimidated:

> I was extremely lucky. Had the panga been sharp I would not have had an arm and I think I would immediately answer if I had no arm I think it would be much better that he was shot dead. Obviously, though, with the injuries I did receive it is much better not to shoot him dead.[259]

Devlin made no mention of this attack, which could so easily have amputated the inspector's arm, in his report; indeed he found that there was not much in the evidence which pointed to an intention by the crowd to use force. The other example comes from Rumpi. In his report Devlin said:

> The [district commissioner] then turned his back on the small crowd and proceeded to go towards the road block to walk round it. One man came out of the crowd and walked after him brandishing or pointing a spear. The inspector shouted at him, raised his rifle, fired accidentally before he had his rifle in position with a shot that went over the heads of the crowd and then fired again at the man, killing him ... We are not satisfied that the man was really going to attack the DC. He had ample time in which to throw the spear if he had wanted to; or if he was going to make a jab with it, he would have run at the DC. Moreover ... we are not satisfied that at the time [the inspector] thought the DC to be in imminent danger; if he had, we think that he would have shouted to the DC rather than to the man, and the DC heard no warning.[260]

The inspector did not recall being asked why he had shouted to the assailant rather than to the district commissioner. In questioning him the commissioners were persistent, apparently trying to get him to say the man was not going to throw or jab with the spear and that he did not genuinely believe the district commissioner was in imminent danger. Although, as he had expected, the questioning was persistent, the inspector did not feel that he was unfairly treated under the circumstances. His description of what happened was that the man pranced, or trotted after the district commissioner – the impression of 'walking' after him was not given. Indeed, the inspector's description was quite graphic and conveyed a clear impression – to those familiar with Africans in that area – of a sort of 'war dance' movement in sizing up a victim and preparing to attack him. The intended effect of including the word 'really' in the sentence 'We are not satisfied that the man was really going to attack the district commissioner' is unclear save that it served to play down the seriousness of the incident. Since the district commissioner was walking, probably slowly, away from his potential attacker there are no grounds for believing that the African would have run at him to stab or jab at him – he had plenty of time to implant the spear in the district commissioner's back. That the district commissioner in the middle of a riot heard no warning shout does not mean that no shout was made. Suffice it to say that the man most intimately involved, the district commissioner, was convinced – and remained so – that the inspector had saved his life.[261] In a somewhat similar case, where an African approached an inspector, 'swinging an axe across his body', Devlin again did not think the man was going to attack the inspector; Devlin said of the special constable who fired at and wounded the African, 'if the constable had shouted a warning to the African or to the inspector, it might have turned out that there was no need to shoot'.[262] Why he thought that in one case the inspector should have shouted at the district commissioner who was about to be attacked rather than at his assailant, and in the other case that the constable should have shouted at either the attacker or the victim, is not clear. Of the Rumpi case, no doubt trying to be kind, Devlin said:

> The inspector, a young man, had had a very long and difficult morning – he was concerned in nearly all the incidents we have recorded ... and this was the first time in his life at which he had had to shoot at a man.[263]

In fact the inspector was 27 years of age, had been involved in all, not just most, of the incidents Devlin recorded, and had had in addition 'a hundred and one other things to attend to'. As he later recalled:

I had not been to bed or had any sleep whatsoever since I rose at 6.00 a.m. on the morning of Monday 2 March; these events occurred on the afternoon of Tuesday 3 March, by which time I was in a state of near exhaustion. A long and difficult morning indeed!![264]

A number of officers gained the impression that Devlin and his colleagues were not particularly interested in what they had to say to them. Officers from the far north of the protectorate, presumably aware of the commission's general inexperience of remote rural Africa, tried to be helpful by explaining a background against which they could appreciate more detailed evidence.

I did not feel that this evoked much of a sympathetic response in the Commission members, who were polite but detached and much more concerned to have succinct, factual replies to their questions than to allow me to initiate a description of our situation and working conditions ... the Commission didn't seem particularly interested in what it was like to be responsible 'on the ground' for a remote, backward district ... Devlin seemed only interested in whether I had exceeded my powers in any respect.[265]

A missionary who gave evidence recalled that Primrose 'looked as if he wanted his lunch'.[266] A senior district commissioner also felt at least one of the commissioners of inquiry was not paying close attention to what was being said. He described how after trying other means to disperse a rioting crowd, accompanied by only two police officers, he eventually handed over to the military.

One of the Commissioners, who quite obviously had not been listening very carefully to what I had said at the beginning of my evidence, asked me if I had not considered trying to disperse the crowd with a baton charge rather than handing over to the military. My reply did not please him one little bit – I replied that I should have liked to be in a position to order a baton charge but this was hardly feasible with only two constables at my disposal against a crowd of some 600.[267]

This official 'gained the impression that the Commission was not really interested in what [he] had to say as they had already made up their minds as to where the fault lay'.[268] Devlin's report said the district commissioner 'would have preferred to have dispersed them with a baton charge but the police had no batons'.[269] This was not true: the district commissioner had told them the police did have batons but a charge was impossible as there were only two constables present. Similarly, in his report on the Nkata Bay tragedy Devlin said, 'The [district commissioner] could have sent a message to the ship to leave', but in saying this Devlin ignored what he clearly knew: that the district commissioner was surrounded by a large, noisy and gravely threatening riotous crowd and was by himself – there was no opportunity for him to send a message to the ship.[270]

A reason why some witnesses may have gained the impression that the commission was not really interested in what they had to say could have lain in the procedure adopted, particularly in the relegation of a good deal of the evidence given, with witnesses presenting themselves before what the commissioners called the 'balderdash committee'. Devlin recalled:

> We got a large number of witnesses who really had nothing to say at all except either that they disliked Dr Banda very much and what a wicked man he was, if they were European, or, if they were Africans, to say how much they loathed the idea of federation ... [W]e were under considerable pressure to get to the report as soon as possible and so I started drafting while we were still in Africa ... by means of sitting in an adjoining room while the other three heard the witnesses who were dealing with the pro forma sort of stuff. They would send for me if they wanted because I was only next-door ... I said to the others ... 'We are having the most frightful amount of balderdash and it isn't really necessary that I should hear all of it. It is vital that we should hear any witness who has got anything to say and he might after all say something important but I think we ought to form a balderdash committee, that is all except me and leave me to get on with [writing] the report outside.'[271]

Consequently there were many witnesses who were heard by only one, two or three of the commissioners and who never saw Devlin. Since the chairman was often absent and since, presumably, he or his colleagues had decided in advance of them being heard that what they had to say was likely to be balderdash, it is not surprising that some witnesses felt that the commission was not particularly interested in their oral evidence.

A number of pieces of evidence support the view that the commissioners, or some of them, had already virtually made up their minds on certain points well before hearing all the evidence. For example, we have already seen how quickly Wyn-Harris invited Armitage to reappraise the murder plot. Similarly, after only six days in the country and having heard 15 witnesses, only five of whom were Africans, the chairman tried to dissuade witnesses from giving evidence about federation by saying, 'We have heard a good deal of evidence to show that federation is something that is not wanted by the Africans of this country.'[272] Again, when a number of detainees who were being jointly examined spoke of federation, Wyn-Harris, in declining to hear what they wished to say, told them the commission had received 'hundreds of memoranda and each ... has expressed ... your points of view ... so we have had it and it would be just labouring the point'. Williams added, 'we know you are not very much in favour of federation and that you have many colleagues who have said that'.[273] Also, only three weeks after arriving in the country, Primrose told missionaries at Livingstonia that he was convinced the 'massacre plot' was a fabrication.[274]

In a number of cases where government witnesses did not feel they had been aggressively interviewed, Devlin still did not favourably impress them. In one extremely important case, the translation of a document – possibly the most important original document produced to the commission[275] – covering the points raised at the 25 January meeting, including reference to the cutting of throats and written by a person present at the meeting, the officer translating the document (who had also questioned the person who wrote it) said:

> The Commission left me with the feeling of its veiled hostility and Devlin himself did not impress me. Certainly the impact of the words in English didn't appear to concern him – he was cold about this ... that is the abiding impression I have of that occasion.[276]

In yet another case – in which a police officer did not feel he was particularly aggressively interviewed – the witness sat for rather a long time with his legs crossed and as a result felt a sharp pain of cramp as he rose to leave, causing him to stumble. Embarrassed, he looked at Devlin and believed he saw on the judge's face a look which said, 'Oh, yes. There stumbles a guilty man if ever I saw one!'[277]

On the other hand, a number of officers considered they were civilly and properly received; a district commissioner felt he was 'treated property and correctly';[278] a police mobile force commander recalled, 'I thought that the hearing was polite and respectful, and that I had been given a fair opportunity to give my evidence';[279] and the provincial commissioner of the northern province said:

> Devlin and Williams were the two members ... who asked the most searching questions. I did not think that, given the fact that they were conducting an investigation, and not a whitewash exercise, their questions were unfair or biased.[280]

This view was expressed notwithstanding the fact that Devlin closely questioned the provincial commissioner and asked a number of very probing questions, especially about the murder plot, the handling of detainees and the mopping-up operations.[281] The overwhelming impression, however, which Devlin and his colleagues left in the minds of the government officers they questioned was one of aggression and of having prejudged the issues.

The commissioners seemed intent on playing down damage done, or threats made, to Europeans. The examples from Fort Manning and Rumpi have already been given but probably the best illustration is the case of Bundy, a forest officer in Dowa district, who was not a member of the security forces. On the morning of 4 March he was travelling by car with an African forest ranger on the main north road. Caught between road-blocks he was attacked by a group of 20–30 Africans.

> Mr Bundy found himself with his back to a tree, being hit with sticks and axes and trying to keep his attackers off by using his [shot] gun as a stick. Someone grabbed the barrel and forced the gun to the ground; the gun went off and the remaining cartridge went into the ground. Mr Bundy went down and was struck on the head. For a long time, about an hour, he laid on his face, covering his head with his hands and was beaten all over the back. As he lay there they came up and struck him from time to time.[282]

The doctor who attended Bundy told the commission of the injuries: a wound to the head one to one and a half inches long which was stitched; a three-quarters of an inch fracture to the skull, the result of 'considerable force'; a deep penetrating, rough-edged wound of the deltoid muscle about two inches deep by a sharp pointed instrument, the spike of a hoe or an axe; abrasions on his arms, and 'bruises all over his back, the lower part of his back and over his buttocks – really big bad bruises'; a black eye and bruises down one thigh. He was 'very shocked indeed. Every time he stood up or tried to walk he grew pale and cold and sweaty and had to lie down. He was very close to fainting every time he got up ... He was very shocked indeed.' When he left hospital two or three days later, 'He was still very shaky, very shaky and having lots of pain. He was very stiff from bruises and had a bad headache.' He had been concussed 'for quite a long time' and the result was unpredictable: 'the patient could be left with epilepsy and all sorts of things like that'.[283]

In giving his evidence to the commission,[284] Bundy said that he left hospital after three days of his own accord because he was bored in hospital and went back to work.

> *Sir John Primrose*: It is true to say this then, that they could really have killed you if they had wanted?
> *Answer*: Oh quite easily, yes. I was waiting for it.
> *Question*: You do not know why they did not kill you?
> *Answer*: I have no idea.

Yet all that Devlin said of Bundy's injuries in his report was:

> Mr Bundy's skull had been very slightly fractured; although severely

shocked, he was able to leave hospital after two or three days. He had, as
well, a wound on the arm and very severe bruising all over his back.[285]

A Congress leader was even more brief but encapsulated the seriousness of the attack when he said that had the security forces not arrived
the 'great injuries ... would have sent him back to his ancestors'.[286]

Devlin could more fairly and objectively have made it clear that
Bundy had discharged himself from hospital rather than giving the
impression that he was fit after two or three days; he could have given
the doctor's diagnosis more fully; and he could have said that the
wound in the arm was two inches deep and that the very slight fracture
of the skull was none the less a serious injury, being three-quarters of
an inch long and the result of considerable force. Perhaps he felt, as
Primrose seems to have, that the salient point was that Bundy was
'lucky to be alive' and that consequently little else was of importance.

Banda appeared before the four commissioners, with Foot, Kellock
and Mills-Odoi present, at Bulawayo on Saturday 16 May.[287] A crowd
of about five hundred Africans waited outside the building where
evidence was given; there were no incidents and the police kept 'a firm
but good natured control' over them. Banda, smiling, gave the Congress
salute and shouted 'Kwacha!' to which the crowd responded with
clapping and cries of 'Freedom!' Despite the intervention of Welensky,
Whitehead and the mayor of Bulawayo, no hotel would accommodate
the Ghanaian barrister Mills-Odoi, who consequently stayed with a
local Indian trader.[288] The interview with Devlin was a long one and
the typed transcript covers 79 pages of foolscap. Foot led the examination and took Banda through his early personal history, emphasising
his Western education, his professional training and his membership
of the Church of Scotland of which he was an elder. He then moved
to Banda's reasons for returning to Nyasaland and, briefly, to the
history of the Federation and the personalities in the country's politics.
Next he dealt with Banda's representations on constitutional advance
and his meetings with Armitage and senior officials; his public
speeches, strongly refuting the allegations made by the Governor about
encouraging racial friction, disobedience to agricultural laws, hatred of
the police and expatriate civil servants; and the reasons behind appointing the various members of the Congress central executive in order to
achieve a balanced and representative group. Foot was attempting to
present Banda as a reasonable, patient, restrained, highly moral,
tolerant person, and to counter the various criticisms of him which
had appeared in Armitage's 18 March despatch. He spent a good deal
of time on the Congress emergency conference, about which Banda
said that he knew very little. Most of his questions were quite briefly

answered, often with a simple 'Yes' or 'No' response; the information conveyed was thus couched in Foot's words and with Foot's emphasis rather than Banda's, although from time to time the doctor launched into a longer, more wide-embracing, answer. Foot concluded by establishing Banda's long and close friendship with the Reverend Fergus Macpherson and told him that it was alleged that he, the doctor, was a party to a plot to massacre Europeans including missionaries, which gave Banda the opportunity to end on a note of high dudgeon:

> What, my own Macpherson! What a defamation. I had a plot to kill Macpherson! That is an insult! Even the Bishop of Nyasaland, whom I know personally? Could I have planned that? That is defamation!

It was then the time for the commission to question Banda and this was done almost exclusively by Devlin himself. He took Banda back no further than his return to Nyasaland, 6 July 1958, and directed his questions mainly to the same issues Foot had covered, particularly his selection of executive committee colleagues, his views on having dealings with Europeans, non-cooperation, civil disobedience, law breaking and violence, the effect of his speech-making, his knowledge of what happened at the emergency conference, and his opinion of Chipembere, especially in relation to violence which he dealt with at length. Although Devlin covered all the important points, at no time did he press Banda hard; he was much more gentle and accepted Banda's answers significantly more readily than was the case with any other major witness, including the Governor and many of the government officers questioned. With Banda he did not give the impression that he was cross-examining. His whole tone was quite different and contrasted very markedly with his cross-examinations of Chipembere and Yatuta Chisiza in particular.

After a few more questions by Foot, Banda finished his evidence in impressive style:

> Now if I may say something else – I must stand up to do this – I want to thank the Commission very much, but there are one or two other points, I want to express to the Commission, that I am rather disappointed. The Governor's despatch would seem to be personally bitter against me. I cannot understand that. As I said before, when I was in Ghana I discussed the Governor and I was given to understand that he was a very good man and when I saw him in London I got the impression he was a very very good man. As I said before, I also got the same impression about Mr Youens. So while we may have differed politically I was very much looking forward to the time when these two men, His Excellency the Governor at Government House, and Mr Youens at the Secretariat, between the three of us we could do something [when] the

Constitutional proposal, or whatever it was, a White Paper, came out, a compromise somewhere after all. But when the Governor shows bitterness like that I begin to wonder whether I have the wrong impression. I hope I have not. But if you ever see His Excellency I want you to convey this to him, that even now when I am speaking to you I have nothing against him, against any of the Government Officers at all, and I am sincere. I would like you to convey that ... [m]y fight is political and straightforwardly honest. I hide nothing. I will speak bluntly to anybody but I have nothing to harbour in my heart. That is all I wanted to say.

It was a performance almost certainly well rehearsed and planned. No wonder the commission was impressed by the doctor's 'charm'. Banda himself felt that Devlin had treated him 'very fairly'.[289]

Shortly after Devlin submitted his report, Mr Justice Beadle submitted the report of a tribunal which he headed in Southern Rhodesia.[290] Beadle and his colleagues formed a very different impression of Banda whom they also interviewed. They discovered a number of 'obvious conflicts between his evidence and the proven fact' – he was lying – but they were also not impressed with his demeanour: the final impression which he made on them as a witness 'was a bad one'. Indeed, they found him 'a wholly unreliable witness' and 'unworthy of credit'. Banda was asked questions by the Beadle tribunal and he was then cross-examined and re-examined in a much more rigorous and penetrating process than that to which Devlin had seen fit to subject him.

In evidence-in-chief Dr Banda did not make an unfavourable impression on the Tribunal; but after he had been cross-examined and re-examined the Tribunal took a different view of him as a witness. Considering his evidence as a whole, each member of the Tribunal came independently to the conclusion that from the manner in which he had given his evidence he could not be regarded as reliable.

When, shortly, Devlin read Beadle's Report he wrote to Perth and said it was quite clear Banda had been caught lying and wondered whether if he and his commission colleagues had known of Banda's evidence to Beadle it would have affected their conclusions about him. As he said, 'Interesting but now academic!'[291] He also told Beadle that he did not see how the tribunal could have come to any other conclusion about Banda's evidence. He again wondered what effect it would have had on his mind if Beadle's Report had appeared first and they had known of Banda's evidence: 'That is an interesting – but now fortunately academic – question.'[292]

It may be that Devlin deliberately handled Banda gently, feeling that if he were provoked into one of his well-publicised rages, it might not be possible to get any worthwhile evidence out of him.[293] More likely, Devlin was trying to differentiate clearly between Banda and his more extreme colleagues, and have him portrayed as a reasonable, non-violent leader with whom the government could deal and upon whom they could pin their hopes for peaceful political progress in Nyasaland. In a private letter written at the end of July 1959 Devlin said the reason he went so deeply into the murder plot and attempted to see how far the facts which he found supported Armitage's claims in his 18 March despatch, was:

> If there was a plan to assassinate the Governor and all his officers and massacre the European population, most people would probably feel that Congress was an organisation which like Mau Mau must ruthlessly be broken up. If on the other hand, there was no such plan, but a lot of reprehensible talk of killing among the wilder element, then people might feel there was a case for more lenient treatment of Congress and that an attempt might be made to restore goodwill.[294]

Presumably he also felt that future peaceful progress would be much more securely assured – or at least would become possible – if Banda were not portrayed in the same light as the much more extremist Chipembere and Chisiza. The *Guardian* had pointed out in March the danger of Devlin finding that there was no murder plot – it would render political reconciliation beyond hope – and the same could be said if it was found Banda was implicated in the plot or otherwise a violent extremist. Although publicly they found him a charming man, privately at least Williams was 'dismayed by Dr Banda's monumental conceit'.[295]

Two former presidents-general of Congress were less deferentially treated than was Banda: Phiri and Chinyama. Devlin did not himself attend when they appeared before the commission and Chinyama, at least, found this a discourtesy. By failing to be present when these two particular Congress leaders gave evidence, Devlin deprived himself of the opportunity personally to learn more of the events leading up to the emergency before Banda's return to Nyasaland; but then he probably did not know they had been presidents-general and he had in any case already decided that Banda's return was to be the starting point of his narrative. Wyn-Harris, who chaired these two sessions, certainly did not know Phiri had been president-general or that he had immediately preceded Banda in this office, and he did not know Chinyama had also been president-general for a long period that included the 1953 disturbances. In both cases Wyn-Harris at the outset put pressure on the witnesses to keep their evidence short, although, because of their persistence, they both in fact spoke at some length.[296]

On the same day as Banda, Chipembere also gave evidence.[297] All four commissioners were again present as were Foot, Kellock and Mills-Odoi. Foot's questions were largely of the type that require a single word answer, and in very many cases the answer sought was indicated by the question ending with 'did you not?' or 'were you not?' One of Foot's first questions was to show that Chipembere's father was an Anglican priest. This – as with many of Foot's questions – was a courtroom tactic to create a favourable impression of his client and had little, and probably no, relevance. The large number of points made by the government against Chipembere were now put to him systematically by Foot and he denied them all; it is clear that Foot had discussed them in advance with Chipembere.[298] The commission left the questioning almost exclusively to Foot on this day but two days later, when the sitting resumed, Devlin took over and closely cross-examined Chipembere, trying to trap him, switching quickly from one topic to another and back again, cutting off his partly completed answers, seizing on any loose reply and all the while attempting to discover his attitude towards violence.[299] Chipembere said he had changed his mind on violence since Banda's return to Nyasaland and now utterly rejected it. Despite Devlin's persistent and probing questioning, Chipembere stuck to his claim to reject all violence and his belief in non-cooperation if negotiation failed. The difference between the ways in which Devlin questioned Banda and Chipembere was very marked, the probing being very much more persistent and aggressive in the case of Chipembere. This difference probably stemmed from the evidence of a few district commissioners who had known both Banda and Chipembere personally and who had been asked by Devlin about their attitudes to violence. One said of Banda soon after his return to Nyasaland that he joined them for dinner and 'was very friendly, very charming' although shortly he changed and shunned European social contact. He also said of Chipembere, who was his district assistant: 'He was an extreme fanatic, especially over his relations with Europeans.' Chipembere told this district commissioner that ever since he had once been caned at school by a European 'as far as he was concerned all Europeans were dogs'. Devlin found this evidence 'most valuable and helpful'.[300] Another district commissioner who knew Chipembere personally said of him that he accepted Europeans 'as a rather unpleasant form of life ... he just had nothing to do with us'.[301] Youens later recalled how Chipembere spoke of not liking white men ever since he had got his ears boxed for not taking off his hat to his housemaster at school.[302] The commission did not form a good opinion of Chipembere; and seven years later, when he had attempted to overthrow the Banda government by armed force and had had to leave

the country, Wyn-Harris, in his Christmas letter to Devlin from Rara-
tonga in the Pacific, suggested that the commission should meet to
'celebrate the downfall of "Chips"'.[303]

Dunduzu Chisiza gave evidence in Bulawayo on 18 May, also in
front of the four commissioners with the three lawyers present. Again
Devlin asked a number of questions but, although he was fairly aggressive, he did not give him the persistent, penetrating gruelling which
Chipembere had received earlier in the day. As with Chipembere,
Chisiza was taken through the points alleged against him which had
been submitted by the government and which Foot had discussed with
him in advance.[304] Williams formed the view that Chipembere, Chisiza
and Chiume 'were furious that they had brought Dr Banda back to
Nyasaland and now he was getting "uppity" and running things'.[305]

The following day General Long gave evidence[306] and Devlin, who
once again did most of the questioning, was keen to know what role
the military forces had played and what their instructions had been. It
was clear that Long did not like the army having a police role placed
upon them as a result of the paucity of police officers and because the
loyalty of the African policemen, he suspected, might be questionable.
He was very forthright in his evidence and the tone of what he had to
say may be indicated by his replies to some of the questions asked by
Devlin. When the judge asked about cordoning and searching by his
soldiers the general replied:

> The plan was usually at night they would surround the village and then
> go in at dawn and bring out the people. In so doing, where someone was
> abusive or got in the way, or prevented them doing their task, a slap on
> the face, and occasionally using the rifle butt ... they were undoubtedly
> knocked around a bit, there is no question about it.

When Devlin asked about searching houses, 'Would you accept that
there might have been a certain amount of what I might call unnecessary bullying going on – stand up, sit down, and all the rest of
it?' Long replied, 'Yes, I am sure it would be part of the treatment. I
think that is the only way you ever achieve your aim with these sort of
people.' Again, when asked if in the areas called 'bad spots' the
intention was that the troops should make themselves unpleasant, he
replied, 'Exactly. In my view it was the job of the Army to be
unpleasant and not the police.' General Long must have created an
extremely unfavourable impression on the commission – Primrose was
'rather appalled'[307] – and must have done the government's case inestimable harm.

Yatuta Chisiza also gave evidence on 19 May and Kellock asked

1. Sir Robert Armitage

2. Sir Patrick Devlin

3. Dr Hastings Kamuzu Banda

4. Assistant Commissioner Philip Finney

5. Leading Congress detainees, and Counsel (H.B.M. Chipembere, D. Chisiza, F.W.K. Nyasulu, G. Mills-Odoi, D. Foot, Dr H.K. Banda, T.O. Kellock)

6. The British South Africa Police 'Yellow Scarves'

him questions about a speech he had made in the second week of February 1959. He denied all the many violent passages in the transcript of the speech. Devlin then took him through the transcript and he again denied all the violent passages. Chisiza did not know that the commission had a tape-recording of the speech and when Devlin then asked him if he would like to hear the recording, he said 'Yes'. At the end Devlin asked, 'Mr Chisiza, do you want to alter any of the answers you gave a short while ago?' and received the reply 'No'. The chairman concluded that it was 'not worth asking him any further questions'.[308]

While Devlin was busy gathering material and forming opinions upon which to write his report, the Governor was much exercised with the problem of how to end the emergency as quickly as possible yet have legal powers to retain some people in detention. Deeply anxious about lack of progress towards passing a detention bill, he was 'distressed' that Lennox-Boyd had not yet 'been able to clear the principles' of such a bill.[309] He had no doubt they would not be able to hold constitutional discussions and make any constitutional advance

> until we can make it plain that there is detention legislation under which Banda and his main confederates can be kept out of the way for several years ... [N]o new African leaders are going to risk emerging unless they ... are assured of being free from intimidation and the consequences of having not gone in with Dr Banda. So the Detention Bill is the most vital matter that we have at present.[310]

Lennox-Boyd recognised how worried Armitage was about the absence of permanent detention legislation and admitted that they were in 'something of a dilemma' over this:

> If we now authorise you to introduce permanent legislation enabling you to detain people without trial, there will certainly be a big row here and there is a considerable likelihood that the Labour Party will make a public statement to the effect that, if they are returned to power, they will see that any such legislation is repealed. If, on the other hand, we do not authorise you to introduce such legislation now, and ... continue to rely on having a declared state of emergency until after the election there is the danger that, if the Labour Party won the election, they might not themselves feel able to authorise the introduction of permanent legislation even though they might not have found it necessary to repeal it if it were there already.[311]

He confessed that this was 'a very real dilemma' by which he and his colleagues were 'much perplexed'.[312]

5

The Devlin Report

There are one or two redeeming features in it ... Otherwise it is almost uniformly bad – hostile, tendentious and grossly unfair.

There were signs during Devlin's inquiry that the government recognised that the report might not be favourable to them and they might wish to reject parts of it. Maybe, even very early on, they began to wish they had accepted Alport's advice to let the examination of the disturbances 'be mounted locally ... as an administrative inquiry'.[1]

It became very clear after the first, and more senior, government officials had been interviewed that the tone of the report would be adverse.[2]

Only 10 days after Devlin arrived in Nyasaland, Gorell Barnes sent Armitage a copy of the secretary of state's 1950 circular despatch on 'the principles to be followed when a Governor wishes to dissent from the findings or opinions contained in the report of a Commission of Inquiry',[3] and he advised that the way was open for him to proceed along the lines indicated in the despatch if he saw fit.[4] A week later Morgan, following up Gorell Barnes's letter, said:

We should be grateful if you would keep us in touch as closely as possible with the course of your dealings with the Commission to let us know ... whether you are running up against any particular difficulties.[5]

In response Armitage wrote 'a summary of the situation' to Lennox-Boyd, towards the end of May, based on the points which the commission had put to him at their second meeting.[6]

First, he understood the commission was now satisfied that there was a plan for civil disobedience including a variety of disorders and the state of emergency was, therefore, justified, but they seemed 'quite unable to reconcile the massacre plan without any corpses produced'. Second, the commission had concentrated almost exclusively, so far as government witnesses were concerned, on incidents and orders given during the emergency, and neglected the causes of the disorders which led up to it. The large amount of documentation covering the lead-up which he had given the commission may have so satisfied them that they did not need oral testimony, but he had 'the impression that they [were] looking at the immediate circumstances and not being interested in what went some months or years before'. The commission 'cross-examined ceaselessly' witnesses as to the need for using firearms; firing a number of shots; searching and burning houses; and arresting people, how they were arrested and why they were handcuffed.

> The Commission has been very much like a court of law without oaths being taken or evidence led etc. Government officials have certainly come out from the presence feeling that all the Commission was interested in was trying to establish what they had done wrong ... there will be very few Government officials who will not be happy to see the back of the Commission.

Third, he said there were a number of unfortunate incidents where they were bound to be criticised but he hoped these would 'not be too many and not of great material account'. Finally he commented on the activities of the Church of Scotland, members of which had gone to great lengths 'to produce a tremendous weight of evidence against the Government'.

> It is clear that the Commission will not be happy in indicating that the Government's policies and those of the Church were in complete conflict. I am sure that the Commission will say that a Church has the right to hold its own opinion and that a Government should not attack the adherents of a Church merely for disagreeing with government policies. On the other hand, quite a number of disorders were carried out by the adherents of the Church of Scotland, particularly in the North, and I hope that they will carry some weight with the Commission.

In his reply to Gorell Barnes about the 1950 despatch, Armitage had said it would be desirable for him and Lennox-Boyd to 'see and if necessary comment on' the report while still in draft. Again, on 13 June, he told Morgan he had 'been doing some speculation on the possible findings of the Devlin Commission and ... trying to assess the probable local reactions to them'. He thought it 'highly important from an internal security angle' that he should know the gist of the main findings as far in advance of publication as possible.[7]

The Nyasaland government assessed the likely danger of violence when the report was to be published. Specifically, the commissioner of police asked the provincial commissioners, 'What would be likely to happen if by chance the Commission ... brought out a report favourable to Congress and to Dr Banda and against the Government?'[8]

When the provincial commissioners' assessments were received in the Colonial Office, it was felt the permanent secretary and ministers should read them immediately since they raised very serious possibilities.[9] The provincial commissioners' views were broadly the same. First they considered the possibility that the report would exonerate Banda and Congress and conclude that the state of emergency should not have been declared. In such a case they believed there would be an increase in Congress's prestige and support from outside; strong pressure to release Banda and other Congress leaders; a deteriorating security situation; a collapse of civil service morale accompanied by resignations; and chiefs and other Africans would need special protection. The provincial commissioners thought this possibility 'unlikely but just possible' and the Colonial Office saw that it 'would clearly [create] the most serious situation'. Second, they considered the possibility that the report would condemn Congress generally in respect of violence, vindicate the declaration of the state of emergency, but exonerate Banda personally. In this case they felt there would be an 'almost imperative necessity' to release Banda and allow him to return to politics, in which event he would quickly organise a new party indistinguishable from Congress in its aims but non-violent; there would be the need for 'very early concessions in [the] direction of African dominance in Government' and further pressure for secession from the Federation. The provincial commissioners thought – correctly as it transpired – this second possibility was 'exceedingly probable' or there would be 'a variant of it casting doubt on the murder plot'. Third, they considered the possibility that the report would generally vindicate government action without exonerating Banda or Congress, but strongly criticise the handling of the emergency including the use of unnecessary force. They thought this possibility was 'the best to be hoped for'. In this third case, they believed there would be renewed Congress activity and external criticism of the government, the internal security situation would continue to be 'uneasy' and the government would need to govern by force unless secession was conceded.

> It is taken as axiomatic that the report will refer to the universal and deep-seated opposition to Federation and ... this fact alone will increase opposition both inside and outside Nyasaland and make the task of Government difficult ... The possibility of a clean bill for Government's assessments and actions is completely excluded ... we must accept this as certain.[10]

Despite the opinion of some secretariat senior officials that a 'reasonably favourable' report was still possible, in view of their growing suspicion that it would be highly critical and unfavourably received,

Armitage personally and the Colonial Office in general became increasingly anxious about seeing the report before it was published so that they could 'prepare [them]selves against the effects of publication'.[11] Armitage and his Colonial Office colleagues, including ministers, therefore took a close interest in how and when Devlin would submit his report.

Williams, Primrose and Fairclough arrived back in Britain on 24 May, and by 3 June, Devlin and Wyn-Harris had also arrived.[12] They planned to start taking evidence in Britain on 22 June and before then to have circulated their individual contributions to the report among themselves, anticipating that any further evidence would not lead to much amendment. They expected the report to be published about the middle of July.[13] Fairclough expected to draft the report and was surprised at the time when Devlin said he would do it, although later he said there was no question but that, with this commission, the chairman would draft most of it.[14] Devlin, with a substantial contribution from Fairclough, wrote the historical conspectus – 'an excellent piece of writing' in Williams's view – and Williams 'was saddled with the armed forces and police bit' with which he was 'not displeased' although it lacked 'the intellectual distinction of Patrick's dictation which came out well and was scarcely changed in the revision'.[15] Wyn-Harris produced a draft on the Federation which was not used.[16] Primrose played no part in the drafting.

Devlin received 'a tremendous amount of paper' – sent by air freight in the care of a courier[17] – when he arrived back in Britain and spent time trying to 'accumulate the evidence' in the country at Pewsey, where he was less likely to be interrupted. It was a good summer and he was able to do most of his writing in the garden.[18] Although much of the drafting had been done in Nyasaland, he worked under great pressure from about 9 a.m. until midnight daily.[19] Indeed, he felt he had not worked so hard since his early days at the Bar. Throughout this period, he played his cards very close to his chest. Butler visited him one weekend, and Fairclough, who was present, remembered how they had a delightful 'pas de deux', as it were, the secretary of state deliberately giving Devlin opportunities to reveal something about the content and flavour of his report, the judge politely failing to notice the opportunities being offered – all over strawberries and cream at tea time![20] Devlin recalled:

> I remember Rab Butler, who was a friend of mine, coming down just casually as it were for a social visit ... he didn't ask any questions and I didn't give any answers ... He was one of those people with the extraordinary gift of being able to get answers without asking the questions.[21]

Although the understanding of the Colonial Office was that Devlin would 'render his report in the first instance in confidence to the Secretary of State' before publication,[22] by late May they were deeply uneasy about the possibility – put to them, they thought, by Fairclough (who was not aware that he had given them that impression) – that Devlin would arrange to publish his report without first letting Lennox-Boyd see it.[23] In considering whether they should ask to see the draft before publication Gorell Barnes said:

> If this is going to be done at all it is something that can only be done by the Secretary of State himself; and that, a decision on ... whether or not it should be done, may well depend on the mood Mr Justice Devlin displays on his return.[24]

Shortly after this, Gorell Barnes confessed he was 'a little alarmed' – meaning he was gravely perturbed – by the suggestion that Devlin might publish his report before Lennox-Boyd saw it: 'This would not only put us on the spot [but] it would also be out of order.' Consequently he urged Lennox-Boyd 'to persuade ... Devlin to show [them] a copy of the report in draft before it [was] finished'.[25] Morgan's view was that Lennox-Boyd should seek an early opportunity to tell Devlin he hoped to see the report sufficiently far in advance of publication for him to consider whether the government should issue a statement parallel with it and whether he wished to ask the commission to consider any amendment: a 'tricky operation' on which he realised Lennox-Boyd would probably not wish to decide until he had seen Devlin and 'been able to judge his mood'.[26] Both Gorell Barnes and Morgan were extremely sensitive to Devlin's 'mood'.

On 2 June Fairclough told Morgan the commission intended to 'have their report published about the middle of July to allow time for debate on it before the end of the session'. Nothing was said about making a copy available before publication. So, while it was clear Devlin intended the report to be ready for debate in Parliament, it was unclear whether he intended it to be ready for study by Lennox-Boyd in advance; Morgan pushed the point about dates, saying ideally they would like the report on 10 July but in any case not later than 17 July. Fairclough replied that the former date was too early for the commission but they would probably be able to produce the report by the latter date.[27]

When Wyn-Harris called on Gorell Barnes the next day his personal estimate was that the report would be signed and delivered to the secretary of state about 12 July and, in any case, not later than 14 July. He 'did not know if it was [Devlin's] intention that the Secretary of State should see the report in draft before signature'. Gorell Barnes did not 'pump' him on this point and they agreed it was a matter for Lennox-Boyd to discuss with Devlin.[28] The possibility of publication before Lennox-Boyd saw a copy was still very open and seems to have been entirely in Devlin's hands since Wyn-Harris did not know what the intention was.

During May and June, a number of incidental issues cropped up which added to Armitage's and the Colonial Office's worries. First, on 6 May, the Nyasaland information department published in one of its regular *Bulletins* an article headed 'The Bad Advice of Congress'.[29] In it the government wrote of Congress's false promises, its bad advice and how the people had suffered because of it. It then turned to 'The End of Congress' and said that, whether charged or not, Congress leaders were going to stay in prison for a long time: 'It is the Government's intention to clean the country of Congress now and to keep it clean always.' Finally, the *Bulletin* asked people to report any 'group of Congress members' to the police or district commissioners, if necessary by post without using a postage stamp.

It was an inept article, transparently liable to cause offence, and *The Economist* was quick to exploit it.[30] *The Economist* accused Armitage of announcing his intention to keep Congress leaders in prison indefinitely, and of prejudging their case while Devlin was investigating the issues; he was also accused of 'encouraging systematic peaching', which many people would see as 'an invitation to work off old scores'. In a letter to *The Times* a correspondent voiced her objections strongly: 'This appeal for anonymous denunciation is worthy of any totalitarian State.'[31]

The *Bulletin*, the *Economist* article and the *Times* correspondence inevitably caused a fluttering in the Colonial Office dovecotes, especially since questions were asked about them in the Commons. Gorell Barnes, acknowledging that ministers had no choice but to support the *Bulletin* statement, none the less asked

> whether we ought not to ask Sir Robert Armitage to be a little more careful ... I do ... rather feel that this is a matter on which, in the circumstances, he might have consulted ministers first and I am not sure that it was very wise to include the paragraph about informers in a bulletin of this kind.[32]

Morgan, however, stoutly jumped to Armitage's defence. He pointed out that the Governor was bound to make sure 'no African will be troubled or frightened' by Congress in the future, because Congress had been made an illegal organisation with Lennox-Boyd's approval: 'I do not see how the Secretary of State could remonstrate with the Governor on this point despite the presence of the word "always".'

While he felt that inviting the public to inform against Congress members was 'not a method which has any appeal to people in [Britain] and none to [him] ... there [was] nothing unusual in this in the African situation, especially since the position in Nyasaland had been, and could again be, extremely dangerous'. Regarding long-term detention, ministers had repeatedly said detainees would be held in detention so long as the Governor considered it necessary. And finally:

> I doubt if any of us who know what [the] realities are would think it possible for the Secretary of State to insist on the Governor actually withdrawing the detention orders until he considers it safe to do so; and if the Secretary of State did so insist I should expect Sir Robert Armitage to resign. So on this point at any rate, I do not see how the Secretary of State could possibly object to what the Governor put out in the Bulletin, and if he does not object, there is nothing to take up with the Governor at all.[33]

Morgan's robust minute brought discussion on the *Bulletin* to a close in the Colonial Office.

About the middle of June a second matter intervened to cause Armitage and the British government further worries. Foot asked the government for assistance in securing documents for Karua to travel to London for the 'purpose of giving evidence before [the] Devlin Commission'. He had already appeared a number of times before the commission who, although utterly unimpressed, were none the less prepared, if he came to London, to hear him again.[34] Armitage was puzzled:

> As [Karua] was produced by us ... as [a] Government witness, Dingle Foot's interest [is] not fully understood, and [I] assume Foot is aiming at examining Karua as his own witness which, in view of Karua's unreliability under pressure, might seriously damage our case.[35]

The Governor was keen that Roberts should be present during any further evidence being given by Karua.[36] When Karua left Dar es Salaam, on around 21 June, he carried a sworn affidavit reversing the evidence he had previously given to the commission.[37] It was probably this affidavit, selectively leaked to the press, upon which the *Sunday Express* of 19 July based its article on 'the explosive Devlin Report' – which had not yet been published – claiming:

> Some of the evidence cited in support of the emergency measures was forged. Officials in the Colonial Government may be involved ... Mr Roberts and Mr Finney helped to assemble evidence for the Devlin Commission.[38]

Armitage quickly agreed to the Nyasaland government paying for legal proceedings against the *Sunday Express*; Roberts immediately issued a writ and settlement was made out of court.[39]

A week after this article was published, the *Sunday Empire News* took up the Karua story and reported an interview David Roxan had had with him on 25 July.[40] He claimed Karua had 'slipped quietly' into the country some four weeks earlier and that his presence in Britain was still unknown to many Colonial Office officials. Karua's current story was:

> Now I am in London after telling the Devlin Commission the truth I couldn't tell them when I twice appeared before them back home ... Everything I said was fabrication – but the police and the governor believed me ... It was all lies. I told them because I thought it would give me my only chance of getting out of the country because I was the only Congress Party member with a Tanganyikan passport.

Karua went on to explain how he was employed in Zomba as a police radio mechanic and on 9 May was taken through a rehearsal of his evidence, with Government officials sitting in place of the members of the commission. He said he appeared before Devlin on 12 May at Zomba Police station with an official – presumably Roberts – present all the time.

> I wanted to tell the truth but it seemed to me impossible. They asked me if my story of the massacre was true and I said it was. On May 21 I appeared again, this time in Blantyre ... Two days later I flew to Tanganyika. I left my family there and made arrangements to come to London. On June 23 I appeared before the Devlin Commission. This time I could tell the truth. This time I could speak freely – there was no massacre plot and I had heard no one talking of it. I cannot describe the relief to be able to speak as I wished at last.

A third matter which added to Armitage's worries was the way in which detainees were and should be treated. In May, Pinney submitted his report on 'A System for the Holding, Rehabilitation and Release of Detainees'[41] which was heavily influenced by experience of terrorism in Malaya and Kenya. For example, a crucial element involved confessions of Congress activities as a condition for a detainee to move from one stage of rehabilitation to another. Pinney recommended a hierarchy of camps including a special camp where, from the moment of arrival, the detainee would be faced with such 'efficiency, bustle, vigour and self-assurance that [it] undermines his power to resist and sweeps him into obedience'. He paid special attention to the hard core detainees about whom little could be done other than keeping them safely outside the protectorate, but every effort should be made to reduce their number by trying any [means] to ensure their straightforward progress in the pipeline [because] those who remain will undoubtedly deteriorate to the level of the most dangerous of their number ... It would be desirable for the hard core detainees to work voluntarily but there will certainly be difficulties in the way of this.

Opposite this last point about work by hard core detainees a Colonial Office official wrote the single word 'Hola', in capital letters and with an exclamation mark.

When Pinney's report arrived in the Colonial Office Perth asked Armitage for his reactions and how he intended to handle 'the problem of the detainees'.[42] Perth also gave his own 'very preliminary and tentative thoughts' which were that the techniques of rehabilitation and confession – successful in Kenya – were not applicable in Nyasaland except possibly to 'those detainees ... known to have taken part in conspiring to violence, murder or sabotage'; such detainees, he imagined, were few and 'infinitely less numerous than were the Kenya detainees'. This suggests that while Perth believed some sort of murder plan had existed, he now felt relatively few people were party to it. With the Hola prison camp atrocities in mind, he was particularly anxious about compulsory work by detainees.

A word of warning about compulsory work ... It is necessary ... to be absolutely certain, first, that any plans involving compulsory labour are consistent with the international obligations ... of Nyasaland and, second, that the arrangements made for their execution are such that there is no danger whatsoever of their getting out of control as they did in Hola.

Two days later, on 5 June, Armitage replied[43] that he had already 'given careful consideration' to Pinney's recommendations and had discussed them with his provincial and district commissioners. He readily accepted that Kenyan techniques were not suitable in Nyasaland and assured the minister of state that the release of detainees was kept under constant review; a number even of Operation Sunrise detainees were being released and he was anxious to release those he could as soon as possible.[44] None the less, he felt the situation had not yet returned to normal and there was 'a real danger of premature and numerous releases causing a serious deterioration' which would require 'widespread security operations'. He again stressed the need for early enactment of a detention bill. Finally, he was careful to reassure Perth about compulsory labour:

I had already concluded that it was not feasible to insist on compulsory labour and we have gone no further than to provide opportunity for voluntary work.

The Colonial Office, however, was not reassured by Armitage's correspondence and was worried especially about the handling of detainees in Kanjedza because Perth continued to receive letters alleging they were not being properly treated. At least one camp official admitted to a degree of harsh treatment but defended himself on the grounds that he acted much as a prefect at school would act.[45] Perth thought that, 'as soon as the Hola debate was out of the way' they should send someone out to Nyasaland to advise Armitage on running detention camps.[46] The Colonial Office also proposed an inquiry into conduct at Kanjedza but were anxious that it should be acceptable to, and not cut across the remit of, the Devlin commission because Foot had collected statements from inmates alleging ill-treatment and had sent them to the commission.[47] Consequently, Lennox-Boyd asked Devlin if the proposed inquiry would cover ground within the commission's terms of reference.[48] Devlin replied that their terms did not cover the treatment of detainees after they were handed over to the prison or camp authorities.

> We have, however, received in evidence written statements from some detainees alleged to have been made when the detainees were in detention camps to officers employed by the Government of Nyasaland. Some of these detainees have subsequently appeared before the Commission and declared that the statements attributed to them were fabrications or were obtained under threats or inducement or in the hope of obtaining their release.

This had raised issues on which the commission had heard evidence about conditions at Kanjedza and he might need to deal with them in his report, but he had made no general investigation and would make no general finding on conditions at Kanjedza.[49]

Although these three issues – the *Bulletin*, Karua's visit and the Kanjedza detainees – were worrying matters, it was the question of when and how Devlin's Report was to be published that most concerned the British and Nyasaland governments. Perth had a long talk with Devlin around 22 June[50] and the judge could not be certain but thought the final version might be ready by about 10 July, when he hoped to be able to let the secretary of state have two copies, 'even if it had not got all the i's dotted and the t's crossed', for submission to the printers. Perth explained to him the government's anxiety to have the report so as to debate it in parliament before the recess and to give all parties adequate time to study it before the debate, and also for government and Armitage to be able to examine it before publication in case the Governor needed to take security measures in Nyasaland. In reporting this talk to Lennox-Boyd, Perth spoke of 'the sixty-four dollar question': 'what the report is going to say'.

> I think it is going to find that the main trouble lay in fear and opposition to the Federation ... I did not ask nor was I given any indication of what the Report might contain. I know that once the Report has been submitted Devlin and others of the Commission would very much like to meet us to give their impressions and ideas as to the possible line of future action, but of course that is not something with which they are concerned in their Report.[51]

When, about mid-June, Lennox-Boyd was told Devlin's Report would not be ready until some time between 10 and 17 July and probably nearer the latter date, he asked if the judge was expecting to be invited to come and see him. He had deliberately not seen Devlin himself and had left contact to Perth. He also wanted to know about the submission of the report to him before it was published: he wanted to know the exact date. Lennox-Boyd also wished to consult the prime minister.[52] Gorell Barnes's view was that if the report reached them as late as 17 July they would 'be placed in a quite impossible position unless [they had] seen a copy first in draft'. Even if the debate on the report were to be held on one of the last days in July, the report would have to be laid before the House several days in advance 'which would leave practically no time for copies to be sent out to Nyasaland and for [them] to consult the Governor'. Assuming it was not possible to ask for the report earlier than 17 July, he suggested that plans should be made immediately for Armitage to be available in London for consultation 'as from whatever day the report is likely to be received'.[53]

By 24 June, Lennox-Boyd had firmly decided not to publish the report until he and Armitage had read and consulted about it, 'by means still to be decided'. Devlin agreed with this and Lennox-Boyd told Armitage the 'first step is therefore to get copy (unprinted) report by quickest means possible'.[54]

At the very beginning of July, Devlin said he hoped to complete the first draft of the report by 4 July; it was being sent to the printer piecemeal as it was produced and the commission should be able to consider the galley proofs on 7 July when they met; given two or three days for amendments, it should be ready for signing and submission by 10 July.[55] However, as the days passed the Colonial Office realised the schedule had slipped badly. They had assumed they would receive the report on 10 July and might be able to get it published by 16 July

– the latest date, they felt, for it to be debated before the end of the session. Since, however, Lennox-Boyd was 'quite firm' the final document should not be printed until at least he (if not Armitage) had read it and this might cause further delay, publication could not be expected before 22 or 23 July.

> This means that it is not possible to carry out the programme which was envisaged including warning the Governor of Nyasaland that he might receive the document on 12 July and need [to] be prepared to come home on 15 July ... Unless it is possible to get the report ... considerably earlier than 10 July (and it is very doubtful if this is possible) ... the whole programme [will be thrown] out of gear and we have to consider what to do. Our own first reaction is that ministers might find it best to take the Opposition into their confidence and explain that it is not physically possible for the report to be produced in time for a debate ... before the end of the session ... But we naturally do not know whether such an approach to the Opposition is possible.[56]

So anxious were Colonial Office officials to receive the report that they asked how long it would take to print 'if the Cabinet gave direction that it was to be ready at the first possible moment irrespective of cost'; the answer was, at the very least, 10 days.[57]

To try and hurry things along, Fairclough suggested on about 2 July, that Perth should explain to Devlin how advantageous it would be if they could have the corrected galley proofs on 9 July. At this time 122 pages had been received by the printer from Devlin, about half the number expected eventually.[58] The schedule was still slipping and on 6 July Perth told the chief whip 'the sad news' that the report was likely to be delayed until 15 July, with 21 July as the earliest date for publication. They felt, however, it would be unwise to talk with Devlin 'with the idea of trying to speed him up or slacken him off'.[59] The 'slacken off' reference and the proposal to take the opposition into the government's confidence suggest that the Colonial Office was considering delaying the report, and therefore the debate, until after the recess. Although the advantage of this would be that the session did not end on a sour note, the chief whip's anxiety now was 'not so much the Labour party but being unable to answer the strictures if any in the Devlin Report in a convenient forum in order to satisfy moderate opinion and the party supporters'. Perth thought that if the report were delayed beyond the end of the session 'it would always be possible to issue a statement which would get adequate publicity'. However, an autumn general election was a distinct possibility: they could not risk delaying the report and the debate on it until after the recess and incurring dissent among their own ranks or violent attack from the opposition on the eve of an election. They decided to check the position a week later, about 13 July, and if things were still going wrong they would consider a joint statement by Devlin and Lennox-Boyd explaining the position.

On the evening of 9 July, Primrose having departed for Scotland, Devlin, Wyn-Harris and Williams had a long discussion at Devlin's flat about the report which was all but completed.[60] Both Williams and Wyn-Harris were worried about the closing paragraphs. Wyn-Harris proposed to dissent from the findings of the commission and submit a 'separate expression of his own', and was torn between loyalty to the service of which he had long been a distinguished member and joining in the comments which Devlin proposed to make on the facts as they had found them.[61] Williams's worries were different. He felt the Nyasaland government could be criticised for bad administration as well as for ignoring the law; he also felt they could not 'let themselves loose' on bad administration but that if they did 'let themselves loose' on the law it might give the impression that that was all they thought was significant. The final part of the report as Devlin had drafted it[62] – and the part to which Wyn-Harris took grave exception – was a hard-hitting condemnation of the Nyasaland government for abuse of power. It hinted that a number of the emergency regulations were too broadly drawn and therefore open to wide interpretation and excessive use, and they might be *ultra vires*. Devlin's draft set out his view of 'the British way of thinking [on the principles] which should control the conduct of a government even in times of emergency':

> In an emergency a government is entrusted with sweeping powers of legislation. In ordinary times it is the duty of the lawmakers to find a just balance between the powers that should be granted to government and the freedom that should be left to the individual. The existence of an emergency does not absolve the Government as lawmakers altogether from this duty ... the need for a just balance remains.

He believed that in a country where the executive and the legislature were virtually the same there must inevitably be a temptation to treat emergency regulations 'as if the law creating them was an inexhaustible armoury from which the government can requisition weapons as and when wanted for use in the field', and he added: 'But this is to make the law the servant of government and not its master and that is despotism.' Devlin's second principle was that no matter how the law was made the law makers themselves must be 'most scrupulous' in observing it. This, he felt, was the foundation of the rule of law.

Devlin's draft went on to say that they had found, perhaps under the stress of the emergency, 'an indifference to and misuse of the law' at every level of the administration. By 'misuse' he meant that the emergency regulations were 'treated solely as a source of power to be exploited and added to if necessary' rather than as setting limits to what government could do. He argued that if a particular sweeping regulation was indeed the law, then one might think it was the sort of regulation that could not be justified 'even by the gravest emergency'. If it was not the law, then actions under it 'must be added to the catalogue of admitted illegalities'. He did not claim that the government had no standards by which to regulate its actions but its standards 'were not the standards of the law'.

> The test applied at the highest level was not what was lawful but what was 'administratively correct'.

This was unfair. The unfairness came from Devlin over-generalising and not giving the Governor the opportunity to expand on his point – which he never claimed to use as a 'test' – about 'administrative correctness' or to argue the question further: Armitage's evidence had been suddenly cut off and the chance to explore and contribute to this extremely important question was lost. It also came from Devlin's self-introduced and undiscussed narrowing of his terms of reference from 'inquiring into the recent disturbances', in practice to 'inquiring into the legality of the recent disturbances'.

Devlin claimed that the men arrested under the Governor's order were 'clearly regarded as dangerous criminals and fit only to be treated as such', and the fact that there was no evidence to prosecute them for a crime would 'if it were thought about at all, probably be dismissed as a legal technicality'.

> No one thought of them as innocent men who had to be deprived of their liberty because in exceptional circumstances the security of the state so requires.

This also was unfair and an unwarranted generalisation. Leaving aside the point that the reason for detention was precisely that there was insufficient evidence to prosecute for a crime, to say that 'no one' thought of them in the way Devlin described was untrue. He had spoken with only a small proportion of civil servants and members of the security forces and not all of them – indeed probably very few – held the view which he now attributed to them all. Had he not confined himself to incidents where the use of firearms had resulted in death or grave injury and had he allowed officers to give the evidence they thought important, then he would have known that there was a very large number of people who did not regard the people they arrested as 'dangerous criminals' and who did see them precisely as innocent men who had to be deprived of their liberty in the interests of state security.[63]

By 'indifference' to the law he meant that while some illegal acts were committed in an excess of zeal, in other cases individual officers were given a latitude which allowed them to behave as they liked 'and their illegalities, often recorded in their own reports, went unnoticed or unrebuked'. Some of these illegalities were expressly or impliedly 'authorised from the top':

> If African soldiering is told to be tough in a village, it must be obvious to anyone that what in fact happened is likely to happen ... The Army regarded [the mopping-up or harassment campaign] as a military operation the object of which was to subdue troublesome areas. An aggressive and bullying attitude was part of the treatment and expected from the troops; and lack of submission to it meant hitting and beating.

This was fair. General Long had clearly said that bullying was 'part of the treatment' and 'the only way you ever achieve your aim with these sort of people'. He felt it was the Army's job to be unpleasant in these circumstances.[64] It would, however, have been fairer if by 'the top' Devlin had made it clear he meant Long and not Armitage. Later he defended himself by saying that he had not claimed the Governor had been party to any of the measures: 'Well, we never said he had. It was the army command that we said had done it.' This was only half true: while he did not say the Governor was the person at the 'top' who authorised the illegal acts, he certainly did not say, as he claimed, that the army command 'had done it'; he simply said 'the top', by which many, perhaps most, people would think he meant the Governor.[65]

When Devlin sought opinions on this in Nyasaland 'at every level' the responses varied from those who thought it perfectly proper and desirable down to those who thought it regrettable but inevitable. He 'did not at any time find anyone who disapproved'. That he did not find anyone who disapproved was because he did not seek sufficient opinions; had he, for example, asked the district commissioner of Blantyre and other administrative officers he would readily have found many who disapproved most strongly.[66]

The commission had recorded 'deviations from standards that [they thought] would be universally accepted as applicable in Britain'. Yet Devlin was careful to put the point of view of others: that the standards were not applicable in colonial government and once respect for the government had been lost it had to be restored in a way which would impress the African mind by making it plain that 'force will be met by greater force' and 'the influence of Congress could not be stamped out except by a strong hand'. He felt bound to ask, however:

If it is wrong for Congress to disregard the law, why is it right for the Government to do so?

The only answer to this deeply important question must be that the government has an overriding duty to ensure good order and the security of the state. Not to fulfil this duty is truly to abdicate and if the only way to fulfil it is to take powers not expressly authorised in advance by a less than omniscient legislature, then those powers must be taken. It is such an answer that Armitage may well have had in mind when challenged on his view of 'administrative correctness', but he was not allowed to give it.

With Williams wanting a tough approach, and Wyn-Harris a very much less tough approach, Devlin wrote to Primrose:

> I have come to the conclusion therefore that it would be best to stick strictly to recording facts without saying what could be considered to be comment, however outrageous some of the facts may be. So I have drafted a new ending. This has been passed by all the others and P. Wyn considers that it is not necessary for him to indicate any sort of dissent from it ... We all feel from what you have said that you will probably agree with this.[67]

Wyn-Harris argued in a 'passionate manner' and, although soon after he felt that he had overstated his case, he alleged that the report as originally drafted was unfair. He admitted to being 'very disturbed', and to making a number of 'intemperate remarks'. Williams was able to put Wyn-Harris's views into 'a clearer form' and Wyn-Harris recognised that personally he was 'not any good at putting a case unless [he could] have time to look round a matter and marshal [his] arguments and then if [he was] not to say more than [he] intended [he] like[d] to have headings'.[68]

In later years Williams said it was he, Williams, who 'got P. Wyn to agree to the report which turned his back on his whole career, as he felt';[69] and Devlin wrote to Williams, saying:

> You have in particular one quality which I very much admire – and that is the art of persuasion. It does not consist in repeating crescendo all the arguments that appeal to the persuader, but in finding out what is the trouble in the other man's mind and in addressing yourself to curing it.[70]

Primrose had expected that when his three colleagues 'got down to putting Law and Order in their right places, there would be alterations'. He told Devlin:

> If P. Wyn's honour is satisfied with the new ending then I am delighted,
> it reads well and gives I think the 'kick in the pants' to the proper
> personages.[71]

The result of the evening's discussion and differences of opinion
was that Devlin removed the paragraphs which offended Wyn-Harris
and replaced them with a shorter section which covered, factually, four
matters which 'might be the subject of criticism': burning houses,
confiscating implements, using unnecessary force in arrests and using
force in villages. He retained some of the commission's opinion on
these matters but without expanding on them. He did, however, add:

> The Government has not at any time, either before us or, so far as we
> are aware, to anyone else, expressed any regret for or disapproval of
> what has been done under these heads.[72]

This was an astonishing and untrue allegation because when questioning the Governor, Devlin had asked, 'If ... we find cases where ...
people have been struck, not only with fists but with rifle butts, what
... do we say about it? Do we say the Government approves, or do we
say the Government disapproves and regrets, or what?' Armitage's
reply was immediate and clear: 'I would have to say that there can
only be an answer that the Government disapproves and regrets.'[73]
The Colonial Office had been working on the practicalities of getting the report, in whatever form, to Armitage as soon as possible, and
Morgan contacted 'an old friend' in the Air Ministry who agreed to
'fix it' for Bomber Command to make a special flight to take a parcel
containing the report to Salisbury. He emphasised he would not require
a ministerial order and it would be embarrassing if the Colonial Office
insisted on sending a courier: the pilot would do the job and they
should 'leave it to him'.[74]
As an alternative to this offer, the Colonial Office arranged for a
Nyasaland administrative officer, G.B. Jones, currently on leave in
Britain and who would soon be returning to the protectorate, to take
copies of the report to Armitage.[75] On 10 July Armitage wrote privately
that he expected the report to be 'ready in 10 to 14 days'[76] but on 13
July he noted that the Colonial Office expected to receive copies of the
report on 14 or 15 July and cabled them to say:

> Time is of the essence. If I am to arrive in United Kingdom on 19 or 20
> July, I must leave here day before and have provisionally booked to leave
> here 18th. I clearly must have at least 24 hours to consider report with
> my advisers. It should therefore reach me by afternoon 16 July or at
> latest early on 17 July.[77]

In the event Jones flew from London on 13 July and arrived at Chileka the following day. Many years later Jones, who had been a student of Williams's at Oxford, recalled:

> I hung around waiting for nearly a week. Eventually I was told the document was ready for collection the next day, and my flight was booked for the day after. I collected – I suppose from Great Smith Street – a brown manilla envelope ... secured with red sealing wax; also air tickets. I was to deliver it to Government House in Zomba without delay. I shoved it in my briefcase and toddled off. I don't remember signing for it, or any special instructions from the clerk who handed it over ... My mother expressed the fear that I would forgetfully leave it somewhere, and I reassured her by saying I would strap it to my wrist. But I do not believe I did this.[78]

Although – in splendid district officer fashion – Jones started his journey by shoving the envelope into his briefcase and toddling off, his arrival in Nyasaland was significantly less casual. He was met at the airport by a secretariat officer who had driven from Zomba to collect him. Jones carried in his manilla envelope two copies of page proofs of the report which were not fully amended, so that Armitage and his 'closest advisers only' could study them. The Governor, who was presenting medals at a parade at police headquarters, left abruptly and went to Government House to read the report as soon as he learned of its arrival.[79] A copy of the report was also sent on 13 July from the Colonial Office to Armitage by diplomatic bag, and Welensky and Greenfield received copies:

> Welensky and I were in London when Lennox-Boyd gave us copies hot from the press and asked me as a matter of urgency to give him my views about the report ... I sat late into the night before flying back to Salisbury preparing my comments.[80]

Morgan told Armitage that the *Observer* of 12 July had claimed the report had been submitted to the secretary of state:

> This is not correct and press enquiries are being told that Commission has not yet presented its report. Please arrange accordingly if enquiries made your end until we tell you signed report is in.[81]

To cover the question of whether the secretary of state had seen a copy before it was formally presented, Devlin agreed that Perth should say the commission did submit to him for his observations a final draft of their report, because, having access to a great deal of confidential information, they were concerned lest the report might contain 'some expression of it not essential to their findings which might unwittingly be damaging to the public interest'. They wished also to be sure it did not contain any inessential phrase which, in the secretary of state's view, would cause unnecessary harm. The final draft was therefore shown to Lennox-Boyd on the clear understanding that the responsibility for the contents and phraseology was solely the commission's.[82]

Although Devlin agreed – initially reluctantly[83] – that the secretary of state should see a final draft of the report, it is unclear whether other members of the commission knew this, or whether the secretary of state secured page proofs other than the final draft copy to which Devlin had agreed. The way in which the government obtained copies of the report and the number of copies they obtained, rankled with Devlin and Williams for a very long time. Five years after submitting his report, Devlin wrote:

> I do not think the Colonial Office emerges very creditably ... they were [not] entitled to send a copy to Welensky without at least telling us ... I am sure that if the Commission had been asked if they would consent to it being sent to Welensky, they would not have done so. Secondly, they grabbed many more copies of the Report than they were entitled to and used them for the purpose of preparing their counterblast. It is quite true of course that they could have held up publication of the Report until their counterblast was ready. But that would have put them in a jam politically as they had to get in a debate before the end of the session. So they preferred to do it in this rather underhand way.[84]

Devlin was particularly worried others might claim his actions created a precedent for government having access to draft copies of commission reports and the right to seek amendments before the reports were finalised,[85] but it is also likely he felt the government had been less than entirely open with him. Williams's recollection was quite clear: the commission did not agree to the government having an advance copy of any sort: 'No, certainly not.' He believed an advance copy was acquired surreptitiously:

> The Commission's understanding and intention throughout was that they should complete the report, sign it, print it and hand it over to the Secretary of State. It was disgraceful that ministers and officials should secure copies from the Government Printer and send them out to Armitage and especially to Welensky without the knowledge and consent of Devlin or any other members of the Commission. We were amazed that the proof went to anybody but ourselves and certainly Welensky and Armitage should not have seen it till we'd signed it and handed it all in ... On this issue the Government, in my view, behaved disgracefully especially as they were relying on us to be impartial and they depended on our integrity. About their [own] integrity I leave [others] to judge.[86]

In a formal letter from the secretary of state to Armitage accompanying the copies of the report which Jones delivered to Zomba, he emphasised they were unamended copies and he expected finally amended copies to be available 'in a few days', when they would be flown to Nyasaland. He particularly stressed:

> the Report has yet to be completed and signed by Mr Justice Devlin and the members of the Commission and ... the document in its present form should therefore be treated as secret.[87]

In a personal letter sent with the report, Lennox-Boyd told Armitage, 'I know you expected a bad report and so did I, and I'm afraid it confirms our expectations.'[88]

> There are one or two redeeming features in it, notably the endorsement of the action you took in declaring a state of emergency as being the only possible one you could have taken, and the exoneration of the security forces from some of the charges against them. Otherwise it is almost uniformly bad – hostile, tendentious and grossly unfair.[89]

Having received the report and having had his immediate offer to resign rejected by the prime minister,[90] Lennox-Boyd turned quickly to offer Armitage some comfort and to decide what should now urgently be done. In his personal letter accompanying the copies sent out with Jones he said:

> We are giving urgent consideration to our next moves ... but I hope you will find it possible to come to London ... bringing Roberts with you ... Meanwhile I would like you to know how much I sympathise with you in this further ordeal and how admirably I think you have handled everything. We are all in this together.[91]

As early as 18 June Gorell Barnes had begun to 'lay plans' for Armitage to consult with Lennox-Boyd when the report became available.[92] These plans were frequently changed as estimates of when the report would be ready changed and conflicted with each other, and Armitage provisionally booked to leave Nyasaland on 18 July.[93] He received the report on Tuesday 14 July, and this plunged him and his colleagues 'into a maelstrom of activity'. For three days they worked on the report, analysing in great detail Devlin's account of events, the conclusions he had drawn, his references to evidence given and the ways he had interpreted it. They worked without break for many hours and the end result was 'a very full brief' for him to take to London.[94]

There was also feverish activity at the Colonial Office where security advisers considered possible reactions to the report.[95] In Britain they felt that, apart from reactions on political party lines, there would be 'general and adverse' press and church comment about security force violence and the references made by ministers to a murder plot which the commission found did not exist. In Nyasaland 'there will be the wildest and inaccurate rumours which might well lead to trouble' with the Africans who would believe that Banda had 'won his case' and was to return to Nyasaland and that 'freedom is at hand'. Among the Europeans in Nyasaland, also, there could be trouble and at least minor disturbances. Elsewhere in Central Africa they expected 'a tightening of belts and standing together among the whites and possibly a swing ... away from moderation'. In other parts of Africa and at the United Nations the report would be used to attack the British government.

The British government quickly decided that a very high level working party of ministers and senior civil servants, with Armitage, Roberts and Finney, should spend the coming weekend at Chequers, drafting a despatch from the Governor to accompany the publication of the Devlin Report.[96] The matter was now one of the greatest importance to the Conservative government. They had been badly mauled during the 3 March debate; the Hola prison killings were still an acute embarrassment to them; many of their own supporters were uneasy about the handling of affairs in Africa, especially Central Africa and particularly Nyasaland. The full five years of the current parliament would end in June 1960 and there was talk of an autumn 1959 election.

The composition of the Chequers working party shows the seriousness with which their task was being taken. On the British side were the lord chancellor, the attorney-general, the secretaries of state for the colonies and Commonwealth relations, two Colonial Office ministers of state and the chancellor of the duchy of Lancaster. They were supported by a number of very senior officials, including security advisers. From Nyasaland, Armitage, Roberts and Finney also spent the weekend at Chequers helping with the drafting.[97]

Arriving in London on Saturday 18 July, Armitage went straight to Chequers, taking with him – in addition to his 'very full brief' – a first draft of the despatch providing a 'framework examining the main paragraphs of the Report and commenting on them'. This draft resulted from the Governor asking special branch and other officers to go through the report 'with a fine tooth comb to see where [the commission] had gone wrong, what clear errors they had made, and where there were discrepancies which [they] could later take up'.[98] A draft had also been prepared by the Colonial Office covering the status and functions of the Nyasaland government, the Congress threat and murder plot, and criticism of the security forces.[99] Together they worked on the full draft which was 'considered most carefully and amended'.[100] Armitage later recalled:

> So with deletions, additions, amendments, all accompanied by discussions and argument, the hours went by. Manningham-Buller and Lord Kilmuir shouldered a lot of the work as we had to get the correct judicial approach to many of the accusations. But Julian Amery was unflagging. He produced a draft of the proposed despatch which was of great help. I well remember his arriving at a memorable sentence, when referring to the murder plot, with talk of beating and killing and cold-blooded assassination or massacre, that 'massacre may be a matter of numbers, but murder is murder whether you call it killing or assassination'. The Commission had appeared to seek to differentiate between different types of murder. I was unable to appreciate the distinction.[101]

Armitage was particularly incensed by the allegation in the report that Nyasaland was a 'police state', and this feeling of injustice remained with him throughout his life. There was a great deal of concern in the Colonial Office about the expression 'a police state' which was felt to be 'a most unfortunate and unfair description of affairs and would be politically very difficult to counter'.[102] Many others were also disturbed by the allegation, which they found 'mischievous', 'an over-statement', 'misleading' and 'carelessly glib'.[103]

> The phrase, with its echo of wicked foreign practices, had most unfortunate and inflammatory effects, which perhaps the Commissioners could not have been expected to foresee. Looked at in wider political and international terms it was a gift to the government's enemies. For them it had the advantage of being both pejorative and vague.[104]

According to Williams the commissioners were conscious of the problems which might arise from the expression 'police state' but were determined to get it in. The only question was where in the report it should appear; in fact it appeared on the first page. On reflection Williams thought it would have been better to have prefaced the expression with words which made it clear that in times of violent trouble, when an emergency has been declared, a country inevitably becomes a police state; this was the sense that the commission had intended to convey.[105] Devlin recalled that the phase first cropped up while they were taking African evidence and they found plain clothes police outside who were taking the names of people coming to give evidence. He did not explain how he knew they were plain clothes police officers but said:

> We thought that was intolerable and we put a stop to it and we complained and it was not done further. I think it was in that context the

phase 'a police state' arose. Somebody said 'You know, one really might be in a police state.' That was the start of it.

Devlin subsequently regretted using the phrase and thought it 'an injudicious observation not because it wasn't true but it's frequently injudicious to speak the truth'.[106]

The expression seems first to have been used of Nyasaland by Chiume when, exactly a month before the emergency was declared, he wrote to Lennox-Boyd about the existing 1953 emergency regulations. In these regulations he saw the curtailing of freedom of speech, assembly and organisation, and the intention 'to curb the political growth of Africans in Nyasaland'. He protested against the further, more recent legislation giving additional powers to control meetings, and ended by saying 'I appeal to you to use your influence to halt the drift of Nyasaland into a police state.'[107]

Yet had Perth and his officials been bolder or more vigilant, it is very likely they could successfully have asked Devlin to remove the expression from the final draft of his report, and thereby saved themselves and others a great deal of anguish and misunderstanding. Some two months after submitting his report Devlin wrote to Perth, acknowledged there had 'certainly been a great hub-bub some of which [he had] very much disliked' and added that there was one thing he wanted to write about 'frankly':

> I agree that 'Police State' was an unfortunate phrase to have used. What we meant by it was that the Police were given and were using extremely wide powers against which the individual is denied the ordinary protection of the courts of law, and this is what we sought to justify in the closing paragraphs of the report, but we did not mean that Gestapo methods were being employed. I can quite see that the phrase could have been misquoted for that purpose, and should have been removed, but that is the main reason why we gave you the report in draft. You asked us to alter two things because of the danger of misquotation, and the 'Police State' was not one of them. Did you overlook it yourself or what?[108]

Perth could only reply that they did fear it as an expression but, 'timidly and under the pressure of events', he felt for a while that it would be unwise to press 'too many things' on the commission. When he finally decided to ask Devlin about it, he found that the report had already been printed and all he could have done was to add a corrigendum – which 'by drawing attention might do more harm than good'. Consequently, he allowed the matter to lapse. In later years, Perth privately admitted he had simply overlooked the phrase.[109]

Roberts's recollection was that most of the redrafting at Chequers was done by Manningham-Buller who would 'redraft a section and push it across the table' to him and ask if it was alright. Occasionally Roberts had to say it was not alright, and although Manningham-Buller disliked changing his draft, Kilmuir made him do it on several occasions.[110] Lennox-Boyd had Macmillan's ukase 'to handle the report robustly' and consequently was 'cheerful and expansive'. He and Manningham-Buller were the dominant personalities. Colonial Office officials thought Armitage 'played a rather passive part in the proceedings': he had, of course, put a great deal of work into the draft which he brought from Nyasaland.[111]

So hectic had been the activity that 'constant changes' made it impossible for Armitage to keep Footman informed and seek his views and those of executive council. The Governor regretted they had not enough time to deal with a number of items but hoped they had successfully handled the main ones.[112] In two days they had tried to cover four months of the commission's work. Yet he was 'most heartened' by the British government making 'an all out effort ... to defend [the Nyasaland government] where the Report criticised [them]'.[113] Having been up till the early hours of the weekend, following a long and tiring air flight from Central Africa, Armitage's work was still not completed. On Monday 20 July[114] he spent 11 hours at the Colonial Office, where the despatch was finalised, and a guide to the contents – with cross-referencing to the report – was prepared for issue as a White Paper[115] and the Cabinet approved it.[116] Its preparation was a rehearsal of the government's case in the subsequent Commons debate.

Armitage was still concerned about the security effects of the report, despatch and impending parliamentary debates which he expected to be 'extremely bitter and hostile', and he told Footman that if, instead of staying in London with Finney 'to give fullest assistance', he thought they should return to Nyasaland they would do so. The commissioner of police had already placed the security forces on alert and ensured 'the necessary build-up of reinforcements had taken place', and consequently it was felt Armitage need not return to the protectorate immediately.[117]

In a private letter of 20 July Armitage wrote:

> All the ministers are getting pretty weary ... the opposition is intensifying attacks on everything. The general feeling is that when they adjourn on 29th there will be an Autumn general election. All our affairs are of course being thrown into this intense cauldron of UK politics. One has first to decide what it is right to do and then to accept the least possible amendments due to political considerations.[118]

The Commons debated the Devlin Report during the late afternoon and evening of 28 July on a government motion taking note of the report, thanking the members of the commission and endorsing their conclusions that a policy of violence had been adopted by Congress leaders and the declaration of a state of emergency was fully justified. The motion regretted the loss of life but acknowledged that the Governor's action had prevented a more serious situation. It expressed gratitude to the administration and security forces, and looked forward to normality returning and to continued constitutional and economic progress based on respect for law and order.[119]

Manningham-Buller opened for the government, and set the tone of his speech by 'expressing polite surprise' at, and being 'rather intrigued' by, the commission's methods of interrogating some witnesses in groups – 1300 witnesses, 'they say' – and by pointing out that no government, in appointing a commission, was bound to accept all their conclusions, criticisms or recommendations. He reminded those opposition members who had said there were insufficient grounds for declaring a state of emergency, that Devlin had found the declaration justified. He then turned to the impression some people seemed to have gained that because the commission had found no murder plot, Lennox-Boyd and Amery had put a false case before the House to justify declaring a state of emergency. He attacked the commission's statement that on 3 March references to massacre, murder and plots were being freely made by the secretary of state and minister of state, by stating that Hansard showed neither of them had referred even once to a plot and that Lennox-Boyd and Amery had each only once used the word 'massacre'. The term 'murder plot' did not appear in the White Paper and it was never used by ministers: 'It was ... an expression applied by others to the White Paper. It made a good headline.' Although he did not say so, Devlin had fallen into the same trap: a whole part – one of six – of his report was headed and devoted to 'The Murder Plot', despite holding the view that it was 'rather a loose term'.[120]

The attorney-general found Devlin's choice of the expression 'police state' to describe Nyasaland after the proclamation of a state of emergency 'singularly unfortunate'. He criticised the commission for putting forward the wrong reason for Lennox-Boyd's decision for them to sit in private; they based the decision on the assertion that Nyasaland was a police state whereas the secretary of state's real reasons – as Devlin well knew – were: first to encourage witnesses to testify and second to enable those in government service, presumably primarily special branch officers, to speak with greater freedom than it was desirable they should in public. He regretted the unnecessary force used in a number of arrests but felt that under the circumstances these were not

to be wondered at, especially since they feared arrests would immediately provoke violence and since attempts had been made to release
detainees. He pointed out that only in 10 out of 263 arrests did the
commission find illegal use of force. In any case, he doubted 'whether
the commission's findings in every instance [would] be universally
accepted'.

Manningham-Buller emphasised that the power to make detention
orders was solely the Governor's and although the secretary of state
could make his views known to him 'he could not direct the Governor
to detain or release from detention'. In respect of Banda's knowledge
and approval of a policy of violence, he said the commission's view
that the doctor was ignorant of the policy of violence adopted by his
lieutenants was 'against the weight of evidence they had found
themselves', and the government could not take as favourable a view
of him as that taken by Devlin: 'The Government find it impossible to
acquit Dr Banda of responsibility for the policies of Congress and of
complicity in them.' Finally he said the commission's finding that
Armitage was right to declare a state of emergency was 'its most
important conclusion'.

Callaghan, for the opposition, moved an amendment that the House
should accept the Devlin report *in toto*. He criticised the attorney-
general for his 'lawyer's speech' and the government for rejecting not
conclusions, but 'the firm basis of fact' that Devlin had provided. He
added:

> What the Government had done was to winnow through the report,
> sieving out and dredging up everything that would support their case
> and averting their eyes from anything that might in the slightest degree
> be embarrassing to them.

He highlighted Devlin's findings about unreasonable force, burning
houses and seizing tools and implements as weapons. He also pointed
to the deficiencies and errors Devlin found in the Governor's 18 March
despatch, including the claim that Banda was not prepared to negotiate.
He alleged that Welensky's pressure was the factor finally deciding
Armitage to declare the state of emergency. Turning to the murder
plot, he reminded the House that it was the secretary of state and not
the Governor who first referred to it. He attacked Lennox-Boyd and
defended Banda, and finally rounded on Macmillan saying that he was
'prepared to sacrifice the future of the people of Nyasaland for the
sake of winning the general election' because he would not accept
Lennox-Boyd's offer of resignation, thereby depriving Nyasaland of
the chance of new men and new approaches to solving its problems.

Six major speeches were then made on each side by leading

members specially interested in Africa and in colonial affairs, each supporting the motion proposed by their party's spokesman.

Closing for the government, Lennox-Boyd said it was not only open to a government to reject a commission's findings but its duty to do so where it disagreed with them. He emphasised there was no option but to declare the state of emergency, and he put as favourable a light as possible on the criticisms covering handcuffing and gagging prisoners, burning houses, and confiscating implements and tools, while denying that any of the illegalities was authorised by higher authority. An incomplete and misleading picture had been given by Devlin investigating only incidents where shooting occurred, and he did not believe that 'anyone engaged in practical administration' would have anything but sympathy for the Governor in 'his inability to distinguish between talks of killings and beatings of Europeans and talk of cold-blooded assassination or massacre'. The secretary of state, as Armitage saw it, 'knocked most of the stuffing out of the detailed accounts of criticism in the plan'.[121] Lennox-Boyd concluded:

> The test was – was there a real threat to the lives of Europeans and Africans as a result of the adoption by Congress of a policy of violence? From the Commission's report it was clear that there was.

When the House divided, the opposition amendment was defeated by 317 votes to 254, a government majority of 63; and the government motion was carried by 316 votes to 254, a government majority of 62. Devlin doubted whether this victory could have been obtained 'without the aid of the party whips'. He also thought that Manningham-Buller's speech, when he read it in Hansard, was 'flimsy'.[122] Throughout this Macmillan, as his biographer recalled, 'seemed to be behaving, as he had after Suez, as if nothing had happened: it was the low point of his political morality'.[123]

In the Lords the next day, Perth introduced an identical motion to that moved in the Commons and Lord Alexander an identical amendment to that proposed in the lower house. Although couched in more stately, wide-ranging terms and delivered with greater politeness, the content of the speeches was very similar to that of those in the Commons. When, at the close, the amendment was defeated by 80 votes to 34, the resolution was agreed.[124]

The commission members were naturally distressed by the government's reaction to their report. As Williams put it when writing to Primrose on the day of the Commons debate:

> The Judge is very down. He feels that he is being made a political football and he's obviously very hurt. If you found time just to send him a

friendly wave at this hour, it would be well taken, I fancy. I am not so down as he seems to be but rather I alternate between being downish, philosophical and hopping mad.

Shortly this is it: you have four chaps to get you out of a Parliamentary scrape and you play up their integrity and their freedom from politics. Then, damn it, they come back and though it's impossible to impugn their integrity without imperilling your own, you have to pretend that though they are upright, they are so upright their feet never hit the ground. (P-Wyn, for example, whose behind almost bumps the ground when he walks.) All this one now comes to recognise as Boyd's law or the technique of the discarded Kleenex.[125]

Wyn-Harris confessed to the report having 'an even rougher passage' than he had anticipated, although he felt that 'in a few years' time its beneficial effect on Nyasaland and its real honesty would be recognised'.[126] Devlin's own reactions the day before the Commons debate were revealed in a letter to Williams:

I am very troubled by the present situation. I think it is clear that the Government never intended to accept any hostile findings. I don't mean that they intended a sham inquiry from the beginning. I think that like so many litigants they were confident that they would win and just did not contemplate a situation in which they lost. When it came they found it politically impossible to do otherwise than to stick to their guns. If they were attempting to make any real assessment of the Report and reasonably came to the conclusion that we had made a balls of it, we could not complain. They were simply saying in effect: 'We always believed the Governor's case right and we still do and will go on doing so whatever anybody says.' The consequence is that the findings in the Report are inevitably made into a political issue, and the Devlin Report becomes an election counter. That is very damaging, especially to a judge whose value depends on a complete detachment from party politics.[127]

A week later, Devlin was a little more comforted:

Well, on the whole, I think the Government now emerges as bloody and we as unbowed. I was much comforted this morning by a letter from Arnold McNair (who used to be President of the Hague Court) [who] wrote to say that he deeply resented 'the scurvy and ungrateful treatment that [I] and [my] colleagues have received'.[128]

Others now rallied to his support and provided private comfort. Fox Strangways, formerly secretary for African affairs in Nyasaland, could not understand why the British government was making such a fuss over the report.[129] Perth referred to the 'great importance of your report to us and to one and all'.[130] Sir Lynton Andrews, editor of the *Yorkshire Post*, wrote to say he felt 'ashamed that some of [his] fellow

Conservatives [were] being so unjust to the Devlin Report'.[131] And Primrose was effusive and outspoken:

> I don't think my worst enemy could call me a blasphemous man but since our politicians have to save their own petty little skins, by twisting the Commission's report to suit their own ends, I have blasphemed like a trooper. Long after the guilty men are forgotten the Devlin Report will remind people of the humanity, integrity, sound judgement and experience of an honest man, Sir Patrick Devlin. Please do not be hurt, Sir, by the verbiage of stupid politicians, who would rather sacrifice people than admit to their own mistakes. A Scotsman is the last person to wear his heart on his sleeve, and hates being accused of sentimentality, but as far as I am concerned you are the tops, and come hell or high water the Devlin Report shines like a beacon, and I am sure stands as an example and an encouragement to honest men in a period when evasion seems the accepted order.[132]

In early August Devlin was still finding it a 'rather unhappy time' and was 'so depressed' that he was beginning to think he might have led his fellow commissioners 'into a mess'. His depression stemmed, he said, from a realisation of 'the harm that must have been done all over Africa' by the government being so 'un-British' as to say that 'the umpire was right every time he said No Ball to the opposition and wrong every time he gave a batsman out'; this, to Devlin, 'destroyed the essence of what we stand for in the colonies'. Even so, he was able to be at least mildly amused: his sons' school reports had just arrived and they told their father that since they were Devlin reports they could accept only what was favourable and must reject all the rest.[133] As the weeks and months passed he became more settled and philosophical. By September he was able to say he was not at all sick with the political situation in Central Africa but, rather, was 'still immensely fascinated' by it,[134] and his view of the government's rebuttal was:

> I can only suppose that the British Government thought that the opposition would try to make political capital out of it just before the election so decided to get in first.[135]

Devlin, who thought the government's rebuttal of his report was a 'deplorable' way of handling it, consulted his fellow judges 'but not with any success':

> My view was that we should be very much more careful about taking part in these sort of inquiries but they didn't think so ... In general they took the view that judges ought to take part in [them] and must expect, what is the phrase, about the kitchen, it's no use complaining about the heat. That was their general view and they didn't feel that it did any harm to the judiciary.[136]

It is natural that Devlin should be offended by, and feel a deep sense of resentment and impotence resulting from, being so massively challenged. He was proud of his report, telling Perth that it would be 'voluminous, containing a great quantity of fact', he had secured unanimity among the commissioners, and he had been looking forward to meeting ministers to give them his impressions and 'ideas as to possible lines of future action'.[137] As a judge he was not used to having his findings of fact challenged and even his findings on law could be overruled only by his few judicial superiors; he certainly did not see the Governor or ministers as his superiors. Devlin had worked under the sure assumption that the evidence he had heard would never be known to anyone other than the commissioners and their staff. If no one else would ever know the evidence, how could anyone ever challenge his conclusions based on that evidence? In addition the government had had so little time between the submission of his report and the debates on it that it was not reasonably conceivable that, even if they wished, they would have time to prepare an effective rebuttal. Yet he now found himself not unassailable and not unchallengeable. Since he had subjected Armitage's March despatch to detailed dissection, he could scarcely complain in principle to the same being done to his report.

If his report was to have its full potential value, it was important – whether or not his findings were palatable to them – that it should be accepted by the government. To achieve this he needed to ensure that his conclusions were unanimous, that his arguments and findings were proof against reasonable and logical attack, and that any advice he had to give the government was clearly given. The proof against attack required him, first, to adopt procedures which would achieve a balanced, two-sided view of the disturbances and the events leading up to them; second, to avoid an overly legalistic approach to the evidence and findings; and third, to allow time in which to write his report and present it in a form that the government would accept.

Achieving unanimity may not have been easy. By drafting the final part of the report in the hard-hitting terms in which he initially did so, Devlin risked incurring Wyn-Harris's dissention. Since Wyn-Harris was the most relevantly experienced commissioner in the sense that he alone had experience of colonial administration and African affairs, this was a considerable risk and indeed Devlin had to climb down to a significant extent. On the other hand, Devlin's own dominant role on the commission and his close working relationship with Williams contributed to their agreeing on all major and most minor issues; Primrose did not seem to mind what was in the report provided it was anti-federation and along Church of Scotland lines; and Wyn-Harris recognised that he was no intellectual match for Devlin and Williams, who eventually talked him out of submitting a minority report.

Devlin could have adopted procedures more likely to ensure a non-one-sided view of affairs in Nyasaland, but he failed to discuss with professional, experienced intelligence officers questions such as the circumstances under which the evidence of informers might be accurate, and when evidence might be accepted in the absence of oral examination of primary witnesses and scrutiny of original documents. Consequently, he dismissed – in the sense of not even taking it into his consideration – a good deal of evidence which others, including those whom some would argue were in a better position than he to judge, accepted. He seemed to believe that cross-examination by lawyers was not only the best but indeed the only way to arrive at the truth, even though much interrogation by intelligence officers is less aggressive and hectoring and, therefore, less likely to be alienating. Devlin's ignoring of evidence other than that of primary witnesses and original documents, together with the massive mobilisation of anti-government witnesses by the Church of Scotland at least at Livingstonia, his belief that his most important qualification for undertaking the inquiry was a judge's 'traditional ignorance' and having 'no particular qualification for dealing with the African scene',[138] and his deep reluctance to listen to the evidence that experienced administrative officers felt should interest him regarding the background to the events into which he was inquiring, all added to the risk of a one-sided, unbalanced report being produced.

There were other aspects of his procedures which ran the risk of his report's arguments and findings being rejected. In consigning a good deal of evidence to 'the balderdash committee' and in relying too much on the only person with African experience directly available to him – Wyn-Harris – Devlin was in danger of failing to arrive at the truth in a number of matters, particularly the murder plot. Potentially one of the most important sources of information about what happened at the 25 January 1959 bush meeting was the evidence of detainees in Khami prison because a high proportion of them had attended the meeting. Some, also, made statements which convinced the interrogators that the murder plot was true. Since, however, the statements were withdrawn by the time Devlin questioned these detainees, he rejected them all:

> we did not investigate any of them in detail; we did not place sufficient weight on any of the statements ... to make it worth our while to do so. They lacked weight first, because of the fact that they were withdrawn, and secondly because of the circumstances under which they were made

[which] were such as to offer a strong temptation to anyone to say what he thought his interrogators wanted to hear if he thought that it would be likely to secure his release.[139]

Had Devlin decided to investigate these statements in detail – to cross-examine as he believed a searching inquiry required – he might readily have discovered what was later revealed by one of the 'second eleven'. Soon after they learned of the Devlin commission's appointment, Yatuta Chisiza, Harry Bwanausi, Augustine Bwanausi and Orton Chirwa got together in Khami,

> and Augustine said, 'Well, I think I have an idea. We will have a school where we will teach the people what to say to the Devlin Commission ... we will teach the people civics [and] simple arithmetic ... ' So we decided to have the school and we mooted the idea to the [Prison] Superintendent. He said, 'Well, I'll think about it'. After some time he said, 'I think you can have your school provided my warders attend'. So we said, 'Alright they can be educated as well because we know they haven't been to school'. So the school went on for about a week and the warders got fed up and did not attend. At this point Orton decided to teach the people what to say to the Devlin Commission.[140]

In the event those who had made statements to the police interrogators withdrew their statements and they, and all others from Khami prison appearing before the commission, gave remarkably similar – often identical – accounts of the bush meeting proceedings, denying that violence had been planned. Twenty of those, including some of the 'second eleven', jointly gave evidence to Wyn-Harris in the absence of all the other commissioners, at Bulawayo.

The risks involved in an over-legalistic approach were clear: it might be considered so unworldly and theoretical that the conclusions would not be accepted as being of practical value. Devlin peremptorily avoided discussing the question of whether administrative correctness ever justified breaches of the law, despite the argument that it is at least conceivable that action outside the law can prevent much greater and more damaging breaches of the law.[141] He seems to have been much less concerned that 20 people should be shot and killed lawfully, as at Nkata Bay, than that a number of temporary grass huts containing looted property should be burned unlawfully without any personal injuries being inflicted, as at Mlanje. Again he seems not to have been worried that a man should be shot and killed by an unlawful act provided, as at Rumpi, the killing was made lawful by another act. Also, where a district commissioner took what many would see as the wise precaution of bringing in the firearms owned by people in his already disturbed district just before the emergency was declared,

Devlin was much concerned with the district commissioner's legal authority for doing so and little – if at all – concerned with the reasons for, and clear precautionary benefits of, doing so.[142]

Yet the biggest risk to rejection of his report lay not in a lack of unanimity, in procedures resulting in an unbalanced view, or in an over-legalistic approach, but in not giving sufficient time to writing the report. Although no direct pressure was put on him to submit the report in time for a Commons debate before the summer recess, a good deal of indirect pressure was applied and he was fully aware of the government's anxiety for an early submission. In his efforts to be accommodating Devlin worked extremely long hours and did nearly all the drafting himself, possibly to avoid being delayed by less fast-working and clear-thinking colleagues. He may have become over-tired – he sought and received from the Lord Chancellor permission to take a holiday immediately after completing the report[143] – but more likely he just did not allow himself sufficient time. The result was that, although they knew very little of the evidence on which the report was based, the Chequers working party was quickly able to point to numerous inconsistencies and illogicalities in the report itself. Other inconsistencies also remained. Hurried proofreading led to a number of printing errors remaining in the published report, and to the naming of a number of government officers involved in incidents rather than preserving their anonymity.[144] Failure to devote sufficient time to resolving the differences of opinion between himself and Wyn-Harris over the final paragraphs led to the ending of the published version being somewhat abrupt and unhelpful: it was not well rounded-off. Furthermore, by his manner and methods, he had so extensively – virtually universally – alienated officials at all levels in Nyasaland that their advice to the Governor and the secretary of state was unlikely to be sympathetic to Devlin and his findings. These risks which Devlin took resulted in the government rejecting a great many of his findings, and this seriously diminished the report's value.

Had he not been so rushed in writing it he could have devoted more time to making it acceptable to the government by, for example, being more accurate and careful about such matters as the Governor never expressing regret, and by removing or explaining the points which were so readily seized upon and turned against him at Chequers. He could have called upon the professional skills and experience of the commission's secretary, Fairclough, who had considerable and intimate knowledge of the way government worked, of the political sensitivities of ministers and of parliament. He was also skilled in the drafting of documents with a keen eye to their effect on their readers and their repercussions wider afield, and was experienced in the presentation of words and ideas to ministers and other politicians. It may well be that Fairclough, if asked, could have helped to make the report – its wording and presentation, rather than its content – more acceptable to the government, and thereby have made it of greater practical value. But Devlin was indifferent to the government's reaction; when Wyn-Harris, early in July, said to him that he supposed he realised the report would make him very unpopular with the government, Devlin said, 'I didn't think he was right about that ... I didn't attach great importance to the matter':

> It was purely a judicial job, almost entirely a judicial job, finding out what had happened and reporting and delivering a judgment, and I no more thought how the government would react than I thought how a plaintif and a defendant were going to react. You've given your judgment and you've done your job and that's the end of it.[145]

Perhaps the most tragic of all the risks Devlin took was not to make clear the advice he wished to give to the government. He had hoped he and his colleagues would discuss their experience and findings with ministers and be of assistance in working out a way forward in Nyasaland, but it was unwise to rely on this as a means of communicating his advice. In the event, the government's massive rejection of most of his report, together with the preparations for a general election, made such discussions virtually impossible. The only other way would have been to include the advice in the report itself but in this he was hampered by his terms of reference not including the making of recommendations. In fairness, he did give a hint of the advice in his report:

> our duty is to find the facts about the activities of Congress so that you can consider how it should be dealt with ... we have not found any detailed plan for massacre and assassination.[146]

But only a very careful reading of these words, and a realisation that by saying 'should be' instead of 'should have been' Devlin was indicating future policy rather than referring to past policy, could have uncovered the advice. Perhaps it was pressure of time or perhaps having to redraft and truncate the ending of the report to placate Wyn-Harris which caused Devlin not to make his advice clear, or indeed make clear that he had advice to give. Perhaps, too, he suffered from the defect which renders some highly intelligent people unaware that others, lacking their acute intellect and sharp perception, are unable to see as quickly or as clearly that which is abundantly obvious to themselves. In his report Devlin deliberately, perceptively and courageously distinguished between Banda on the one hand and his more violent lieutenants on the other, thereby opening the door for the government to deal with the doctor and develop a way forward. Had he found that there was a murder plot and that Banda was implicated in it, it would have been very much more difficult for the government to deal with the doctor openly, amicably and constructively, and at as early a date as turned out to be the case. At the time, however, this was not clear to the government who believed that Banda was implicated in a plan that, in certain circumstances, included murder – and as a consequence they were unable to see that the judge was trying to give them a message. Some years later, when Devlin reread his report, he commented on the impact which rereading it had on him:

> Very little consideration was given to the last part of the report. It seems to me to be the most important part ... the report was saying clearly enough to anybody who looked behind the words, though it wasn't one of the necessary findings, that either the government must come to terms with Dr Banda or it could only govern Nyasaland by the methods which we had described, judiciously or injudiciously, as the methods of a police state. That was the choice with which I felt the government was confronted.[147]

Although the government's demolition of the Devlin Report had been very thorough and its success in the Commons debate had been both substantial and gratifying, Macmillan realised how very considerable the danger to the cabinet had been.

> Lennox-Boyd had once more asked to resign, and with him in all probability would have gone two other Colonial ministers ... plus the Governor of Nyasaland. Nothing could have been more embarrassing to a Tory government in the run-up to a general election, with the wounds of Suez only recently cauterised. Macmillan put the issues squarely to the Cabinet, calling upon each member in turn to give his unprejudiced view, before giving his own. Thus drawn, the Cabinet to a man backed Armitage and Lennox-Boyd. Gratified, Macmillan recorded ... 'had it gone otherwise, I should have not continued as Prime Minister' ... Nevertheless, the despised Devlin seems to have sown the first strong seeds of doubt in Macmillan's mind as to whether the Federation had any future at all.[148]

It was not only worries about the Nyasaland commission of inquiry which had been troubling Macmillan because he also had difficulties over the federal review preparatory commission.[149] Both the Labour and the Liberal parties had 'refused to be associated with the commission, or even to give it a reasonable measure of support'. Welensky still had very grave reservations but after 'two days' high-pressure negotiations' with Macmillan in London on 6–8 July he accepted, subject to Whitehead's agreement, the terms of reference and the composition of the commission. Welensky agreed

> eventually and very reluctantly ... only in deference to [Macmillan's] urgent request and [his] hopes that by this means the affairs of the Federation would be taken out of the election arena and also in the longer term out of British party politics.[150]

Lord Monckton, a close friend of Macmillan, was asked to be chairman and accepted.[151] Other appointments had to await the general election.

After the Commons debate, which Armitage attended in the gallery,[152] he spent a further day in London and discussed with Footman, by telephone, the arrangements for his arrival back in Nyasaland. Footman proposed a formal airport reception with a guard of honour, executive council and 'other dignitaries', and a press conference. Armitage did not like the proposed publicity and feared his reception might be 'described as an ovation by whites and a boycott by blacks'. Consequently there should be no official reception unless his arrival was non-racial. As things turned out his arrival at Chileka in the afternoon of 31 July was accompanied by a guard of honour and 'close on 1000 people who had gathered spontaneously to ... give a rousing reception'. Those present were indeed from all races and a number of chiefs joined the official reception party. Two aircraft from a local flying club flew overheard in a close formation salute. So much for an absence of publicity![153]

Armitage found the cheering and waving and the dozens of congratulatory letters[154] which he received 'staggering and bewildering'. He was both pleased and embarrassed by his welcome at Chileka.[155] He used the press conference 'to bring together in one comprehensive statement some decisions of importance that [had] been taken ... during [his] absence'.[156] His first point was a reminder that Devlin had found the declaration of the emergency justified, and he added there was no intention to lift it at present although its application could be relaxed, and detainees would continue in detention although he would review their cases from time to time. His second point was to announce a very limited constitutional advance: in the absence of holding elections under existing conditions he proposed to increase the number of African members of the legislature by nomination – matching them with an increase in official members – and appoint two Africans from the legislature to executive council. He hoped that by these means – which privately he described as 'rather meagre'[157] – African members of the legislature would feel more intimately associated with the formation of government policy; but some, including Livingstonia missionaries, thought the government was 'making a mere empty gesture to improve their image overseas after the Devlin Report', and others believed that it was a 'useless gesture' to postpone more permanent and far-reaching changes.[158] His third point was to announce that the advisory commission preparatory to the 1960 federal review would comprise 26 members, of whom 13 would come from the United Kingdom or the Commonwealth, and 13 from the Federation, including three from Nyasaland of whom two would be Africans. He thought it very important to announce this proposal at this stage, even before details had been worked out. In his fourth point he said that during the discussion on the limited constitutional advance,

> the Prime Minister made the position of HMG very clear as regards their responsibility for Nyasaland. He said that the British Government would not withdraw its protection from Nyasaland in the short run, and in the long run the object is to advance the territory to fully responsible government. When there was fully responsible government Nyasaland will be able to dispense with HMG's protection and stand entirely on its own feet as a component of Federation. The same applies to Northern Rhodesia. When all the units are in a position to agree and are agreed that British protection is no longer needed, then and only then can the whole Federation go forward to full independence and full Commonwealth membership. This would all be discussed at the 1960 review.

Next Armitage announced his government's decision to postpone federalising non-African agriculture, and he gave a 'categorical denial' to those who saw in this a government desire to work for Nyasaland's secession or to belittle its part in the Federation. Finally he spoke of the 'many things to keep us busy', including forming a local, non-racial, civil service and increasing the number of Nyasalanders in responsible positions in the service.

The enthusiasm with which the Governor had been greeted by Europeans at Chileka was repeated shortly after when he attended a function at the Zomba Gymkhana Club, where he was 'cheered to the rafters', and in Limbe where a performance of 'HMS Pinafore', which he had missed while in London, was specially laid on for him to attend on his return.[159] It was also evident in Southern Rhodesia where he was embarrassed by many Europeans telling him he 'had saved them by his firm stand' against Devlin: they had begun to think they would have to leave their homes.[160]

Now the work of the Devlin commission was completed, a decision had to be made as to what should happen to the large quantity of papers which they had amassed. This decision fell to Devlin as chairman. Five copies of the papers submitted by the Nyasaland government had been made and four of these were destroyed; the remaining copy was placed with the other papers, including a copy of all memoranda received and transcripts of oral evidence, in Devlin's rooms at the law courts in London. Initially the commission had intended to destroy all the papers about a year after the report was submitted but this was not done, principally because Devlin wanted to retain them lest any significant question or challenge was ever raised. Also he might want to write about the commission's experience one day and would need the records. Williams, who did not propose to write about this, 'felt that if an honourable man was asking [him] anything about it [he] should do [his] best, as an historian, to answer as well as [he] could', and consequently agreed to retaining the papers in order that he should be able to do this.[161]

This is where matters rested until September 1963 when, with Nyasaland approaching independence, officials asked Fairclough to confirm that all copies of Nyasaland government documents made available to the commission had been destroyed. Fairclough suggested to Devlin that they could now safely be destroyed, but Devlin regarded their future as being in his discretion:

> Whatever action is now taken would have to be considered in the light of events since the matter was last discussed. The then Governor of Nyasaland ... saw fit to treat the Commission which he had appointed as a hostile body. He was furnished with an advance copy of the report on the plea ... that he might have to guard against disturbances after publication and he made use of the privilege to prepare a tendentious document attacking the findings of the Commission which was published at the same time as the report. Thereby he started a controversy. None of us thought it right at the time to take part in the controversy. But that is not to say that we might not wish to do so in the future if the controversy was revived or if some other occasion arose which made it desirable to justify the findings he attacked. For that purpose we might wish to refer again to our working papers. I do not therefore myself think that the time has come for the wholesale destruction of all the available documents.[162]

When Devlin moved to the House of Lords he transferred all the documents to his house at Pewsey. He thought, however, that the papers and the few files that Fairclough still held ought at some stage to be brought together and possibly lodged in Rhodes House, Oxford. Devlin's papers were sent there in August 1969, and Fairclough's files joined them in May 1971. At that time, Fairclough suggested they should tell the Foreign and Commonwealth Office where the papers were lodged, that they were available only to members of the commission and that they would open them up, in line with the government's own 30-year-rule in 1989, although a few years earlier Williams had suggested that they place 'a stopper' on access to them 'until Kingdom come'. Devlin agreed with Fairclough but said that they should tell the Foreign and Commonwealth Office only if they asked and not otherwise.[163]

When Devlin first decided to keep the papers one of his reasons was that he might wish to write about the commission's work. Many years later he did indeed write about his experiences with the commission, but only to a limited extent and indirectly, when in 1985 he published *Easing the Passing: the trial of Dr John Bodkin Adams*.[164] Adams, a general practitioner in Eastbourne, was tried in 1957 on a charge of murdering one of his elderly patients who had bequeathed to him a number of legacies. There were thought to be other murders committed by him for the same purpose. At the trial, two years before the emergency in Nyasaland, Devlin was the judge and Manningham-Buller led for the prosecution.

Towards the end of the book Devlin devotes four pages to the Nyasaland commission of inquiry. Throughout it, however, he is highly critical of Manningham-Buller and his presentation of the prosecution case. The explanation of this criticism, this scarcely veiled animosity, may lie in two apparently irrelevant digressions from the account given by Devlin of Adams's trial. The first concerns the succession to the lord chief justiceship of England when the then incumbent, Goddard, retired; and the second was the reference to the Nyasaland inquiry. It is not only the latter of these which is important to an understanding of Devlin's attitude towards Nyasaland affairs in 1959 but so also may be the former, because both Devlin and Manningham-Buller were contenders for the chief justiceship. They were ranged against each other both in the Adams trial in 1957 when clearly the judge, Devlin, held the whip hand, and also during the Commons debate on the Devlin Report in 1959 when Manningham-Buller held the whip hand, since Devlin could not be present and had decided to keep quiet in public.

It is clear from numerous passages in his 1985 book that Devlin considered Manningham-Buller to be a not very gifted or even particularly competent lawyer, and one, presumably, unfitted for the chief justiceship – views which since he expressed them in 1985 in referring to events of 1957 he must also have held in 1959: the passage of time is more likely to mellow at least the expression, if not the holding, of unfavourable opinions than it is to strengthen them.

If Devlin and Manningham-Buller were at that time the front runners for the chief justiceship and if Devlin held such a poor opinion of his rival, he must have felt fairly confident of the outcome. In any case, he knew that Goddard wanted him, Devlin, to succeed him as chief justice. Manningham-Buller's last realistic chance of being made chief justice was the prospect of Goddard retiring in 1957 when he was 80 years of age. At that time the Adams trial was about to begin and 'the trumpet sounded for Reggie [Manningham-Buller] to make his claim'. 'The fortune-tellers at the Bar were eager to see how he would perform in a spectacular criminal trial.' But the trial was also Devlin's chance – how would he perform? His summing up was in favour of the defence and an acquittal, and Manningham-Buller complained that it was one of Devlin's rulings which lost him the case. In the event, Parker was appointed chief justice in 1958, but there is no reason to suppose that their rivalry had in any way diminished by 1959. It is conceivable that when Manningham-Buller helped to draft Armitage's despatch and addressed the Commons, rejecting many of Devlin's findings, he was in effect retaliating. Certainly Devlin saw it somewhat in this light, saying that the attorney-general 'prosecuted' Banda after he had been 'acquitted' by the commission and that he 'appealed' against that 'acquittal'.

In writing, in *Easing the Passing*, of Manningham-Buller's speech in the Commons when the report was debated, Devlin said:

> In July [1959] when the sitting Parliament was at its last gasp, there occurred an incident with curious echoes of the past. Reggie undertook the 'prosecution' of another doctor for murder, a doctor who had been 'acquitted' by a Commission over which I had presided, and found himself able, as he had not been in the Adams case, to 'appeal' from the acquittal ... The doctor concerned was a Dr Banda ... who was arrested on 3 March 1959, the most serious charge against him being complicity in an unsuccessful plot to assassinate the Governor, the Chief Secretary and all the top brass downwards in strict order of precedence, finishing up with the massacre of all Europeans, children to be mutilated ... The Commission found that, though violence of a sporadic sort was contemplated, the plot was an emanation of the overheated imagination which seems so easily to infect informers to the Special Branch ... Reggie was put up in the House to demolish the Commission's Report. Treating the House, as he said, as a court of appeal, Reggie submitted that the acquittal was so far against the weight of the evidence as set out by the Commission itself as to override the Commission's disbelief of the police informers and their acceptance of Dr Banda's denials. The appeal succeeded. It was a remarkable result, even though it would not perhaps have been obtained without the aid of the party whips.

So, a quarter of a century after his commission had reported, Devlin's account of the Adams trial reveals a deep animosity towards Manningham-Buller and a rivalry that may help to explain the thoroughness with which the latter rejected the former's findings and conclusions. It may also be that Devlin, unconsciously nursing a feeling of resentment against those ministers of the government which had declined to make him chief justice on Goddard's retirement in 1958, was not unhappy to reach conclusions which publicly placed that government, and those ministers, in an unfavourable light – notwithstanding his friendship with some of them such as Perth and Kilmuir.

Even so long after the event, Devlin's prime concern was still the question of the 'murder plot'. There has been much dispute over the years and there have been many differences of opinion over what happened at that bush meeting on 25 January 1959 but, at the very least, one can accept the Devlin commission's conclusions:

> that violent action was to be adopted as a policy, that breaches of the law were to be committed and that attempts by the Government to enforce it were to be resisted with violence ... further that there was talk of beating and killing Europeans.[165]

What, if one stays within Devlin's findings, might have been intended by Chipembere and his colleagues? It may be that they wished to achieve no more than to instigate a widespread rumour that murder was intended. The step was a narrow one between, on the one hand a decision to break the law and resist attempts to enforce it with violence, and talk of beating and killing, and, on the other hand a belief that murder was envisaged. Such a rumour, even if it had no basis whatsoever, would so alarm the government that a pre-emptive declaration of a state of emergency would inevitably follow and bring the crisis to a head. Only a gravely irresponsible government would for long run the risk that the rumour was without foundation, particularly if violence was seen to be escalating. A simple but widespread rumour might suffice to achieve Congress's aims.

Alternatively, they may have hoped that mere 'talk of beating and killing Europeans', within a policy of violence that had at the same time been agreed, might have been enough to achieve the lieutenants' objectives. Once the policy of Congress was put into effect, and once the fact that beating and killing had been talked about at the meeting became known, it was highly likely that the government would arrest Banda as leader of Congress. Additionally, and if necessary, provided they themselves were not arrested, Chipembere and his colleagues could use his arrest to incite further violence on a wide scale and – if it had not already been done – bring about the declaration of a state of emergency. Even without inciting violence on a wide scale, the lieutenants may have hoped that the talk of beating and killing would stimulate a number of individuals among the more ardent and vicious members of Congress into blood-letting when confrontations occurred in future. This would be enough for special powers to be used to arrest Banda. Mere talk of beating and killing might suffice.

Devlin also found that there was 'not [talk] of cold-blooded assassination or massacre ... [nor] anything that can be called a plot nor, except in a very loose sense of the word, a plan'.[166] The most satisfactory meaning to be attached to these words is that the talk at the 25 January meeting did not extend to carefully calculated killing of officials and other specified individuals – assassination – or carefully calculated but indiscriminate killing of large numbers of people in certain categories – massacre – or that any of this was subjected to the laying down of the detailed steps to be taken. The words 'cold-blooded', 'plot' and 'plan' imply calculation and the advanced detailed working out of what was to be done, by whom, to whom, when and where: what Armitage described to Devlin as 'a coldly calculated staff plan worked out by a high level military organisation' – which the Governor also rejected.[167] Even staying within these findings of Devlin there is scope for the talk of beating and killing to be translated into action as the policy of violence was implemented. That is, as the agreed violence (sabotage, wrecking of communications, etc.) and other breaches of the law, which Devlin found had been agreed, took place they would inevitably be resisted by government officials – whose duty it would be to bring the law breakers to justice and to prevent further breaches and crimes. The bush meeting had agreed, Devlin also found, to resist these actions of government officers with violence – and it would be then that the talk of beating and killing could be translated into murderous action.

Another possibility is that by rejecting a plot and rejecting a plan, Devlin was rejecting an agreement by all or a large number of people present at the meeting. But, the policy of violence having been agreed or accepted by the meeting as a whole or by a majority of those present – as Devlin found – the talk of beating and killing could have been done in quite small groups. This is a much more likely way for it to have happened because, while undefined violence might secure wide support, beatings and killings would be acceptable to only the extremists present – who may have been relatively few as Perth came to believe.[168] It is these extremists with whom Chipembere and Chisiza are most likely to have discussed, and come to some understanding about, beatings and killings. This theory would also account for so many people who were present denying that there had been talk of beatings and killings.[169]

A further possibility, still keeping within Devlin's findings, is that the lieutenants very soon realised Banda was not going to be content to be a mere messianic figurehead and a tool in their hands to secure independence and secession, after the achievement of which they would take over and run the country. They also believed that Britain and the federal government were not going to allow Nyasaland to secede and become independent, and would have to be forced to give way. At the emergency meeting Banda was not present, not simply so that he could say he did not know what was decided but so that, in fact, he did not know. Banda had already encouraged his people to go to gaol in their thousands and now at the bush meeting his lieutenants got the delegates to reinforce this. They agreed there should be illegal non-violent meetings (necessary to win over the doubters against violence) and they should offer themselves for arrest if the opportunity arose (thereby implementing peaceful non-cooperation and demonstrating solidarity). Banda had also said he was prepared to go to gaol himself. The lieutenants decided to take him at his word – to fill the gaols, the doctor included. With so much law breaking and so many people in prison, normal government would become impossible. Also, with so many of his followers in gaol, Banda could ill afford not to be detained himself and suffer with them. Once Banda was arrested and taken away, the lieutenants would say he had been killed – thereby very easily stirring up the masses to extreme violence – and the R-Day decision would be implemented. This would cause a quick and chaotic vacuum: there would be no government and Banda would be out of the way. And into this vacuum would step the lieutenants, taking over the government of the country. One of the guards at Banda's house on the morning he was arrested told Devlin that he and his colleagues were there 'as witnesses that Dr Banda had been arrested and had not been killed'; they waited until he was arrested and driven off un-harmed.[170] This is a significant matter possibly indicating that Banda knew of – or knew something about – a plan by the lieutenants to stir up extreme violence by claiming not only had he been arrested but had also been killed. The special branch report on the murder plot said that the plan for violence, including murder, was to be imple-mented if Banda were arrested or killed.

Beyond this point the lieutenants may not have thought things out very carefully, but Britain would probably not have allowed federal troops to restore order as such a move might have inflamed things further, nor would they have released Banda because this may also have made things worse and the doctor's life might well have been endangered. The lieutenants would be 'pure' because they could say they had not caused the violence but, on the contrary, like responsible citizens, good political leaders and members of the legislature, they had stepped in to restore peace and to run the government of the country. Of course, if Britain or Welensky then tried to remove them, even worse chaos would ensue, so the chances are that, somehow or other, they would be left in charge. In fact a few years later Chipembere and Yatuta Chisiza, separately, did try to overthrow the government – Banda's government – by force, including killings.[171] Of very great significance is the interview that Chipembere gave to David Martin, a journalist, in the late 1960s:

> Chipembere says that Armitage did not over-react and that Armitage was right and Devlin was wrong [about the murder plot]. Chipembere described a somewhat lengthy meeting in the forest outside Blantyre and he named those who attended. He says that the belief then was that Banda was going to be arrested and likely killed. They therefore decided that if this had occurred they would take the government and others.[172]

Chipembere made it clear that 'taking' the government and others meant killing senior officers and non-officials.[173]

There is one other possibility concerning the murder plot that needs to be mentioned. A view was held by a number of police officers including those whose later successful careers were in the international intelligence community – and a view which they held for many years – that the murder plot was a fabrication by government intelligence officers. There are three forms of this theory. The first is that senior Nyasaland intelligence officers felt it essential for Armitage to take action and declare a state of emergency because only in this way would the disorder be brought to an end. But Armitage was reluctant to declare an emergency and call in the necessary reinforcements, partly because Perth was about to arrive and constitutional talks then might ward off further disorders, and partly because of a deep natural disinclination to curtail rights which the normal law provided. Nyasaland intelligence officers, the possibility goes, fabricated the murder plot story in order to force the government into quick and firm action to put down the disorders; they wanted to shock senior secretariat officers into realising how very dangerous the situation was becoming: Mullin and Welensky both thought the chief secretary 'played down' the seriousness of the escalating disturbances. Possibly, too, the Nyasaland intelligence officers wished to be more fully consulted by the Governor and the shock of a murder plot would ensure that this happened: Thomson left earlier than he need have precisely because he felt that he should be more fully consulted. The second version is that federal intelligence officers believed the federal government needed to be able to demonstrate that Britain was making an expensive mess of matters in the northern territories and that it would be better to hand them over to the federal government – which could then readily demonstrate its ability to maintain law and order in a way that, manifestly, the colonial and British governments could not. To make this point, the version goes, federal intelligence officers – with or without the help of Nyasaland intelligence officers – made up the story of the murder plot, deliberately intending it to precipitate the Nyasaland government into a state of emergency from which the federal security forces would emerge as having saved the country from a very dangerous situation. Thereafter it would be relatively easy for the federal government to argue that Britain ought to hand over at least internal security to them. Barrow had long argued for a federal police force; Welensky was very willing to commit large military forces to bringing Nyasaland under control; Whitehead was anxious to let the BSAP control a large area of southern Nyasaland for an extended period; and Benson and Armitage felt that both Welensky and Whitehead were using the emergency to extend their influence in Nyasaland. The third version of this theory is that British intelligence officers believed the conflict between retaining federation and advancing Nyasaland to self-government could not be resolved, and that the possibility of great bloodshed, with endless military and financial commitment, was so great in a clash between the races in Central Africa that only rapid advance to African self-government in Nyasaland and Northern Rhodesia at least – and eventually the whole of eastern, central and southern Africa – could avoid an Armageddon. Thus it was they, British intelligence officers, with or without the help of Nyasaland and federal intelligence officers, who concocted the murder plot story. Very little would need to be done in any of the three versions to start the story rolling, and then various agents would pick it up, possibly embroider it, and pass it on to their controllers. These are unlikely yarns, but possible.

6

The wind of change

The wind of change is blowing through this continent, and, whether we like it or not, this growth of national consciousness is a political fact.

Early in October Armitage wrote a long confidential letter to Lennox-Boyd.[1] He felt it was time to review the political situation and assess trends in Nyasaland, and to bring the departing and a possibly new government up to date with affairs in the protectorate. His general view of conditions in Nyasaland at this time was: 'We are in a state of surface normality, but in many places we find the undercurrent of African opinion is very aloof.'[2]

He wrote first of the continuing need for detention. Five hundred Africans were still detained and he could see 'little likelihood of a flood of releases'. Although there was a steady flow of detainees being released, the Governor remained cautious:

> there remains a hard core of Congress adherents who, given the slightest encouragement, would not hesitate to come out into the open and undo everything we have achieved. We just cannot afford to let this happen.

The Governor dealt at length with Banda whom he saw as 'a major problem'. The influence of Congress was so great and the 'messiah-like concept of its leader' still so alive that the vast majority of Africans, especially potential politicians, continuously saw 'the shadow of Dr Banda over their shoulder', and were consequently reluctant to voice any views not clearly conforming to those of the doctor. He did, however, hold out just a little hope: 'one redeeming feature' albeit 'but a straw in the wind'. They had an interim constitution and had rearranged the machinery of government to prepare, by 'natural evolution', for a form of ministerial government. There were signs too of some Africans appearing prepared to follow political parties with aims very different from those of Congress and to cooperate with Europeans and Asians: 'Dr Banda was never permitted to do this.' He thought it 'possible if not probable', however, that only by eliminating the opposition of the 'most forceful and indeed able' Congress leaders, and the proscription of public meetings, would they have a chance of fostering a non-racial and liberal approach to politics. He concluded with the words, 'We must not give too little too late but if we give too much too soon we could wreck the whole future of the Protectorate.'

The despatch arrived in the Colonial Office just before the general election. Although Lennox-Boyd did not find it as depressing as others did, and thought there were 'chinks of light showing',[3] Perth read it 'with interest and depression' and Macmillan found it a 'pretty depressing picture', although he did say – but no more – that the paragraph on the 'one redeeming feature', the 'straw in the wind', was 'interesting'.[4]

Macmillan, as foreign secretary, had formed a poor impression of Armitage when Governor of Cyprus in 1955, feeling he had failed to grasp sufficiently early the distinct likelihood of severe violence, and he had resented the Governor's insistence on Britain conceding the principle of self-determination as a means of constitutional advance acceptable to Greek Cypriots.[5] Yet despite the unfortunate impression which Macmillan, now prime minister, had formed of Armitage, he had none the less firmly supported him over the declaration of the emergency in Nyasaland and the findings of the Devlin commission. Macmillan's reasons were purely pragmatic: he dare not risk defeat in the Commons, which failure vigorously to defend the Governor's – and consequently his own – actions would have risked. His support was effective, he was not defeated and his government remained in office.

Having weathered these storms, Macmillan called a general election for 20 October 1959, at which the Conservatives were returned to power with an increased majority of 100 with 'the right wing ... less in evidence'.[6]

For some time Macmillan had realised Africa would demand a great deal of his urgent attention. On the basic issues, on the conflict in Nyasaland and the dilemma which it presented, little or nothing had changed: the crisis continued, the governments were no further forward, and Banda – content to bide his time – also was no further forward. An impasse had been reached, indeed had been created by the emergency which, in many ways, had made it more difficult to remove the conflict and resolve the dilemma than before. Neither side – Congress or government – could afford to bend towards the other without losing face and without risking it becoming very obvious that the emergency had been unnecessary: if compromise or collapse were possible and acceptable now, why had they not been possible and acceptable before? Had all the anguish, the loss of life, the destruction of property, the cost of detention and of restoring law and order, the damage to race relations, been for nothing? Neither side could admit that. The crisis had got stuck in a seemingly endless stalemate; someone needed to do something to break it and move towards solving the dilemma.

With the confidence which his more secure position in the Commons brought him, Macmillan now determined to act positively and quickly. The previous year Britain had decided to seek membership of the European Economic Community and, consequently, the Commonwealth and the colonies became relatively less important to her. Outside Africa, India, Pakistan, Burma and Ceylon had become independent and Britain had withdrawn from Palestine – all over a decade earlier – and Cyprus was to follow within a year; inside Africa, Ghana had been independent for two years and Nigeria was to become independent within a year. The air of change in Africa had already begun to move, albeit as a gentle zephyr at this stage. If its passage across the continent from West to Central and Southern Africa were impeded by white settler countries standing in its way and resisting its progress, the resulting turbulence would be deeply damaging and costly to Britain.

The British government was anxious to find acceptable means of being relieved of its responsibilities in colonial Africa without appearing too irresponsible in doing so. The Central Africa Federation presented such a possible means. If a politically and economically stable, non-racial, state – possibly a dominion – could succeed, then Britain could transfer its own responsibilities to that state with a clear conscience. What stood in the way of success was African opposition to the Federation, especially in Nyasaland. This opposition had long been known to Britain although its immense strength had not always been recognised. Armitage had been appointed Governor with only one specific instruction: 'to win the Africans over to federation'.[7] He was working earnestly to fulfil this instruction, but African opposition had become stronger and infinitely better organised since Banda's return to his home country and it rendered the Governor's task of winning African support much more difficult, probably impossible. There was still a chance that in time Nyasaland could make major constitutional advances as a self-governing state within the Federation but Britain had come to the view that constitutional change significantly advancing African representation and participation in government was urgent, and that no progress could be made towards this while Banda remained in detention since he was manifestly the leader of the Nyasaland African population. But:

The Conservatives were in a muddle. The two strands of Tory policy in Africa – the traditional relationship with the white communities in the south and the new support for independent black States in the north – were increasingly in conflict, and caught between them was the Central African Federation.[8]

Shortly after the general election, Macmillan spent a few days at Chequers 'resting and meditating', and on Sunday 1 November – the day after he read Armitage's 'pretty depressing' letter – he wrote a note to Sir Norman Brook, secretary of the cabinet,[9] in which he first reflected on the Commonwealth tour he had undertaken early the previous year which he felt had, on the whole, been successful. He then turned his mind to Africa, 'the biggest problem looming up for us here at home'.

> We just succeeded at the general election in getting by on this but young people of all parties are uneasy and uncertain of our moral basis. Something must be done to lift Africa onto a more national plane as a problem to the solution of which we must all contribute ... by some really imaginative effort. I have been thinking of bringing this into the centre of affairs by undertaking a journey immediately after Christmas.

In effect, casting his mind back to events in recent months in Nyasaland, he was relieved his government's Africa policy had not resulted in his defeat at the general election – although Callaghan was convinced there was 'never the slightest prospect' of his defeat[10] and Welensky was sure Central African Affairs would not influence the election[11] – but he realised how vulnerable that policy had made him and his party. He did not propose to run that risk again and he determined on two things: first, there should be a change in the policy or at least in its application and, second, he would try to 'lift Africa onto a more national plane', by which he meant 'a plane above that of narrow party politics'. To accomplish these things he decided to do what he 'had long determined': to visit Africa. He also decided to appoint a new type of secretary of state for the colonies: Iain Macleod. Macleod had been taking an obvious and increasing interest in African affairs for the past six months and privately hoped, through taking 'a thoroughly radical line in winding up the residue of the imperial system', to be the last colonial secretary.[12]

Macmillan thought the order in which he visited countries in Africa would be important and, with the eye of a historian and politician rather than of a geographer, he suggested the criterion should be the age of the countries as members of the Commonwealth:

> That would be the Union [of South Africa] first, Ghana second and the

Federation [of Rhodesia and Nyasaland] (almost Commonwealth) third. That leaves the question of Nigeria which I would like to go to and East Africa, Kenya, etc., to which I think the Colonial Secretary is paying a visit during the recess.

He asked Brook whether he should 'set about the job' but made it clear that he himself thought it a good idea and might 'just get something moving in what seems another log jam of ideas'.

Brook's response[13] was enthusiastic and he believed people would see the visit as 'an imaginative gesture'. Macmillan's biographer saw the tour as 'the first sign of earnestness' by the new government concerning Africa, and found the sign 'spectacular'.[14] In Brook's view the visit would have the effect of 'turning more serious thought to a problem which has been serious for some time and is now becoming urgent'. While in no way trying to dissuade the prime minister, however, he felt it his duty to warn him:

It will be very difficult ... and you will be saddling yourself with the personal responsibility for making progress towards a solution [but] this is probably a responsibility which you cannot escape.

Brook also had to warn the prime minister about geographical realities – although he expressed it gently; while Macmillan's initial suggestion had been made, as he admitted, 'regardless of geography', Brook said he had been considering it 'with the aid of a map'. The order of seniority in Commonwealth membership was 'attractive' but would involve 'zig-zagging across Africa in a manner which would look highly eccentric'. He thought the 'logical thing' would be to visit Ghana first, then Nigeria, South Africa and the Federation last, but the prime minister ought also to visit Kenya so as to 'have looked at the multi-racial problem in its entirety'. Since, however, this order might upset South Africa he felt that country must be visited first, and consequently he suggested: South Africa, the Federation, Ghana, Nigeria, Kenya. The zig-zagging and eccentricity had been lessened but not eliminated! The suggestion, Brook added, would at least avoid putting the whole of 'white man's Africa' before West Africa: he must, therefore, have been including Kenya within the 'white man's Africa'.

At this stage what was clear was, first, Ghana, South Africa and the Federation (Commonwealth Office responsibilities) were central to the visit while Nigeria and Kenya (Colonial Office responsibilities) were less so; second, racial attitudes were seen as at the heart of Africa's problems; and third, Macmillan and Brook were very sensitive to the reactions of South Africa. Consequently, on 5 November Home sent a top secret cable to the British high commissioner in Pretoria, Sir John

Maud,[15] telling him of the proposed visit. A tour of Africa would underline the importance Britain attached to Africa's problems. He emphasised the crucial role of the visit to South Africa:

> The Prime Minister recognised that Dr Verwoerd may not be specially pleased to welcome him there but the purpose of the tour would be largely frustrated if it did not include a visit to the Union. Indeed, if Dr Verwoerd was unwilling to receive him at all it might be necessary to call the whole thing off.

It was, therefore, essential to settle South Africa's inclusion before further planning could proceed, 'and certainly before any approach is made to the other governments'. Home added that Macmillan thought it politically desirable that South Africa should be visited first and emphasised that very few people at this stage knew of the proposals.

Maud was delighted with the idea of a prime ministerial visit, and spoke with Verwoerd who immediately sent a friendly message welcoming the proposal.[16] Macmillan wrote to Verwoerd on 11 November,[17] by which time, taking into account that the end of January would suit Verwoerd better than the beginning, South Africa was to be 'the culmination of the tour' and this would be made clear when the announcement was made. Macmillan said how much he looked forward to visiting South Africa and meeting Verwoerd:

> Your affairs and ours have been and will continue to be mixed up intimately and even the close liaison we maintain at present is no real substitute for personal discussions.

Now that this crucial South African part of the tour – that upon which the rest depended – and its timing had been agreed, the way was clear to fit in the remainder of the countries to be visited. First, Macmillan sent a personal message to Welensky, on 11 November,[18] stressing the 'extremely secret character of its contents, knowledge of which is at present confined to a very small circle indeed'. Macmillan had told Welensky he hoped to visit the Federation when they had met in July, and he now said he would have time to do so in January and get:

> a first hand opportunity of seeing and hearing about some of the problems which are going to be of such deep concern to us all during the coming months. I need not tell you how especially valuable it would be for me in this rather crucial period to visit you in the Federation and meet your colleagues.

Welensky's response[19] was quick, warm and enthusiastic: he was 'delighted' and was sure everyone in the Federation would be too. He offered his government's hospitality for the whole of the visit, said the visit 'cannot fail to be helpful' and that his stay would enable Macmillan 'to see something of our country'. This last comment gave Macmillan the opportunity to say he wished to visit Northern Rhodesia and Nyasaland, 'even if it means rather a rush', and he asked Welensky to make arrangements for this directly with the Governors.[20]

By 13 November, then, less than a fortnight after Macmillan's minute to Brook raising the suggestion of an Africa tour, the agreement of South Africa and the Federation had been secured. Macmillan then approached Ghana and Nigeria.

In writing to Nkrumah on 14 November,[21] the British prime minister reminded him that he had said, when he saw him in August, that he hoped to visit Ghana early in 1960, and he now felt he had time to do so. In reply Nkrumah briefly thanked him for the message, said he was pleased he was planning a visit and added – almost as if the invitation were to afternoon tea – 'Any time between 5 and 10 January will be convenient to me.'[22]

On 18 November a Downing Street press release announced that the prime ministers of South Africa, Ghana, the Federation and Nigeria had 'extended an invitation' to Macmillan to visit their countries, and *The Times* the following day said:

> Mr Macmillan is known to be keenly conscious of the importance of Africa in the general pattern of Commonwealth development and he recognises that African problems are likely to be dominant for the British Government during the next few years.[23]

The January–February 1960 Africa tour by Macmillan came to be known as the 'Wind of Change' tour – although Macmillan was later to use this phrase as the title of the volume of his autobiography covering the much earlier years of 1916–1939 – both because he used this expression in speeches made during the tour and because the tour seemed to mark a change in at least the application of British colonial policy.

Macmillan first used the expression during an after-dinner speech in Accra on 9 January 1960 at the very beginning of his tour. This 'apparently impromptu reference ... went unnoticed by the attendant press' and he used it again when addressing the joint houses of parliament in Cape Town on 3 February at the very end of his tour.[24] Horne traces the phrase to Stanley Baldwin in 1934: 'There is a wind of nationalism and freedom blowing round the world.'[25] Yet, although Baldwin used the word 'wind' he did not use the expression 'wind of change'.

Similarly, Colby got very close to the sentiments lying behind the expression during his very early days as Governor of Nyasaland. In July 1948, he said:

> It is inevitable that the very considerable development and awakening that has taken place in East and West Africa will take place in Nyasaland. We ... must be ready to receive the impact that is sweeping Africa.
>
> The political awakening of Africa is something irresistible which arises deep in human nature and no government can arrest it.[26]

But close as he got to the ideas behind the phrase, he did not use the words 'wind of change'. Midway in time between Colby's expressions, the 'political awakening of Africa' and 'the impact sweeping Africa', and Macmillan's expression, the 'wind of change' in Africa, John Masters published his *Bhowani Junction*. In writing of the Anglo-Indian Victoria Jones and the rapid political changes in India just after the Second World War, Masters used precisely the phrase later used by Macmillan:

> Then the great changes swept across India and the world, and she had searched, not by deliberate plan but because the wind of change blew through her too, for ways of escape from a life that had come to seem small and doomed.[27]

How, then, did 'the wind of change' – which was to blow especially rapidly and fiercely in Nyasaland after Macmillan's tour – come to enter the British prime minister's speeches?

One of the Commonwealth Relations Office officials closely involved in the preparations for the tour, and who was a member of the tour party, was David Hunt, who has published his account of the prime minister's speeches and his own part in them:

> The major speeches involved a great deal of careful preparation. The High Commissioners involved were always consulted and made valuable suggestions. Sir John Maud, for instance, contributed a felicitous passage ... about the extent to which the maxim 'mind your own business' applied to relations between South Africa and Britain. The Colonial Office had something to suggest for the Lagos speech. Generally speaking, however, I put together the speeches for the tour and the Prime Minister was content to take my advice on wording.[28]

In referring to the use of the phrase 'wind of change' in the Accra speech, Hunt said his intention in including it was to assure the Ghanaians that Britain was well aware that numerous changes were taking place in Africa and that, far from opposing them, they intended to foster and 'direct them towards useful purposes'. Just before the prime minister reached his peroration he inadvertently turned over two pages of his speech script together, and Hunt knew this because he had written it. Turning to the Cape Town speech, he said:

> As nobody had paid any attention to the phrase in Accra I thought I might as well use it again and had put it in with only minor variations.[29]

Hunt, then, played a leading role in the composition of Macmillan's speeches but, as Horne points out, 'at least half a dozen other people' claimed to have had a hand in it including Maud, Brook, Home and Amery;[30] and Johnston, Maud's deputy, says that 'many hands ... made their contributions to the speech'.[31] Another official helping in the preparations for the tour and who accompanied Macmillan on it, was James Robertson, a Principal in the Colonial Office and the son of the Governor-General of Nigeria. The main purpose of involving Robertson was to 'help in the drafting of speeches'.[32]

Preparations for the tour – including speeches – did indeed involve many people, and they were made in a remarkably short period of time. Macmillan's minute to Brook initiating action was written on 1 November 1959, the agreement of the governments of the countries to be visited was secured by 14 November, and the tour party left Heathrow on 5 January 1960.

The Cape Town speech was intended to be the most important of the four major speeches of the tour and on 23 November Macmillan and Home decided to ask Maud to fly to London and to seek his advice, since he had the reputation for having 'achieved the art of making quite important speeches in the Union which [did] not actually give offence to the locals'.[33] On 14 December, Macmillan and Home met with Maud to discuss in rather more detail the speeches to be made in South Africa. Maud thought three major speeches would be necessary. In the after-dinner speech it would not be necessary to deal with any difficult problems, and the broadcast speech could simply review the Africa tour as a whole. 'The address to the Houses of Parliament would be altogether more difficult':

> Sir John Maud thought that the safest plan would be to try to get the South Africans to look at themselves against the background of the world as a whole. They were very ostrich-like and self-contained and should be made to realise what they did was of compelling interest all over Africa and whatever happened in Africa was of interest to everyone in the world.[34]

The following day Macmillan and Maud discussed 'possible topics and themes' for speeches in South Africa. They agreed that Maud should prepare the speech for delivery to parliament in Cape Town, and have this ready for a further meeting two days later.[35] Maud quickly sent a telegram to his deputy in South Africa asking for suggestions. In reply, Johnston recalled,

> I sent him back a long telegram ... setting out the ground I thought the speech should cover, on the general theme of the awakening of national consciousness across the world, first in India and Pakistan, and now in Africa, and the need to recognise the irresistible nature of this historic movement, and to come to terms with it.[36]

Thereafter, as Johnston continued, many hands made contributions to the speech and it was being polished and refined until just before it was delivered, but the central proposition outlined by Johnston survived as the main burden of the speech. Following a further meeting on 17 December, the revised draft speech was sent to Maud, now back in South Africa, on 23 December, seeking his comments. Maud replied that what was missing was an 'authoritative discussion of current major international problems which flatters [the] audience and underlines [the] Prime Minister's position as [a] world statesman'.[37] On points of detail he suggested revisions which later were incorporated almost word for word in the speech that Macmillan actually delivered.

Maud's input to the Cape Town speech – with Johnston's help – was thus very substantial and involved at least three personal meetings with Macmillan. His contribution seems to go far beyond 'a felicitous passage ... about the extent to which the maxim "mind your own business" applied to relations between South Africa and Britain'.

At a meeting called by Brook on 8 December the Colonial Office was asked to prepare two draft passages, one on 'Race relations and partnership' and another on 'The importance of Africa today with particular reference to the British connection'; and the Commonwealth Relations Office was asked to prepare three drafts on 'The Commonwealth', 'Parliamentary democracy' and 'Education'. The Commonwealth Relations Office felt it would be too difficult to draft a general speech which the prime minister could use everywhere, and it would be better to produce 'passages of general application which could be woven into speeches directed to particular audiences'.[38] Poynton from the Colonial Office made it clear that:

> these drafts are not intended to serve exactly as they stand ... They have been drafted rather with the aim of setting out certain ideas of which use might be made in one place or another with omissions or emphasis as appropriate.[39]

Hunt produced the three Commonwealth Relations Office draft passages,[40] and Robertson produced the two from the Colonial Office. In Robertson's draft on 'The importance of Africa today', sent to

the prime minister's office on 15 December – the day after Maud's
first meeting with Macmillan and almost certainly before a reply could
have been received from Johnston – he wrote:[41]

> Far reaching changes of tremendous importance are taking place in
> Africa today. Ghana, a colonial territory only three years ago, is today
> one of the most important countries in Africa. Nigeria, the largest
> country (so far as population is concerned) in Africa and the fourth
> largest in the Commonwealth, will become independent in October.
> Important decisions affecting the future of the Federation of Rhodesia
> and Nyasaland fall to be taken in 1960.
>
> Rapid change is taking place simultaneously in many other parts of
> Africa. The Sudan, Libya, Morocco, Tunisia, Guinea, and last of all the
> Republic of the Cameroons (ie French Cameroons) have all recently or
> fairly recently become independent countries; the evolution of the
> French Community in its present form is of very recent origin; in 1960
> Togoland and Somalia become independent, and so we believe does Mali;
> the wind of change is blowing through British East Africa and the
> Belgian Congo.
>
> It is this rapid emergence of the countries of Africa which gives the
> continent tremendous importance as a new force in the world. A hundred
> years ago, in spite of the existence of ancient cultures in certain regions,
> the continent as a whole played no part in world affairs. Today Africans
> all over the continent are helping to shape the destiny of the world.

It was in this draft written by Robertson between 8 and 15 December
that the expression 'the wind of change' first appeared in the material
being prepared for incorporation in the prime minister's speeches.

In Hunt's draft on 'The Commonwealth' he also dealt with change
but nowhere did he use the phrase 'the wind of change' although it
was in this passage, if it were to have been used at all, that it was most
likely to have appeared. It did not.

> It is plain for everyone to see that the Commonwealth is in a perpetual
> state of change and development. In the last ten years this process has
> been going ahead markedly and although much of this development has
> been quite unexpected the result has been to strengthen it as a com-
> munity of like-minded peoples.[42]

On 18 December Hunt sent to the Colonial Office a draft for the
prime minister's Accra speech prepared by Snelling, high commissioner
in Ghana, and suggested that some of the material in the Colonial
Office draft on 'The importance of Africa today' should be added to
it. Poynton, who thought the draft speech was 'broadly on the right
lines', could 'see no objection' to the material on 'The importance of
Africa today' being included in the Accra speech although he thought

it 'might need some working up to be suitable for a Ghana audience'.[43] This was almost certainly the way in which the Colonial Office passages on the 'importance of Africa today', including the phrase 'wind of change' drafted by Robertson, were incorporated by Hunt into the Accra speech drafted by Snelling.

A note in Brook's file on the Africa tour, written in the first five days of January 1960, was attached to the finalised passages 'for use as required in the Prime Minister's speeches during his Africa tour'.[44] The note explains how, up to 31 December 1959, the various passages had been used in each of the four main draft speeches. At this time, the 'importance of Africa today' material, in which the phrase 'wind of change' was to be found, was used only in the Ghana draft speech and not any other speech, including that to be made in Cape Town. The Cape Town speech, at that time, used passages from 'The Commonwealth' and 'The United Kingdom's role as a world power' only. The 'importance of Africa today' draft was identical to that which Robertson had drafted in mid-December, save that the words 'and so we believe does Mali' had been deleted.

On 5 January 1960, the prime minister and his party set off for Africa, with 'about a ton of baggage and equipment including a large number of despatch boxes' and the drafts for his speeches.[45] This was Macmillan's first visit to sub-Saharan Africa, a continent he regarded as secondary to Asia and isolated from the rest of the world; and his view of African affairs, conveyed to Brook shortly before starting his tour, was 'Africans are not the problem of Africa, it is the Europeans'.[46]

In West Africa, he visited Ghana which had been independent for two years, and Nigeria which was about to become independent. In Accra on 9 January he made the speech in which he said:

> The wind of change is blowing right through Africa. This rapid emergence of the countries of Africa gives the continent a new importance in the world.[47]

Sampson, Macmillan's biographer, claimed that Home had used the phrase 'months before', and he felt the Ghana visit 'was not exactly a success' because although Nkrumah was ebullient in public, he spent only a short time alone with Macmillan and during the visit 'gave a noisy anti-colonialist tirade'.[48] Snelling thought the first evening 'an utter failure to communicate'; at least 20 people did not turn up at the formal banquet.[49] It will be recalled also that Nkrumah's agreement to the visit was almost casual in its brief wording. The Ghanaians treated the British prime minister with a degree of indifference or contempt. However, at Nkrumah's request, Macmillan did discuss Banda with him:

I said that I hoped we would be able to make fairly rapid progress with liberating all except the hard core of Nyasaland detainees. I did not think he need worry too much about Dr Banda's position. He accepted this.[50]

In Nigeria he had discussions with the Governor-General, whose 'very sensible' advice was that granting early, possibly immediate, independence to African countries was wise – essentially to avoid 'violence, bitterness and hatred' and the waste of time in which it would otherwise result rather than in its profitable use in 'learning administration [and] getting experience'.[51] This advice was diametrically contrary to that given to Macmillan by Home only two weeks earlier[52] but coincided with Macleod's view that although it would be 'nice and tidy if recruitment and training of African officials could have been in step with constitutional advance', if one waited for the former, the latter – and the political momentum – would be lost.[53]

From Nigeria the prime minister flew to Salisbury, arriving early on 18 January. Macmillan's published itinerary suggests he was not intended to meet any Africans in Southern Rhodesia.[54] During talks with the federal and Southern Rhodesia prime ministers he said the main objective in Nyasaland must be to end the emergency and make a start with constitutional progress.[55] Welensky expressed his displeasure over not being consulted, as he had hoped to be, about Banda's release which, he said, had apparently already been decided by Britain: 'If this were true, [he] warned Macmillan, an early release would simply increase the risk to Nyasaland's security.' He also warned that 'the result would be bloodshed for which the British Government had to accept responsibility'.[56] As a consequence of this, Macmillan agreed to discuss Banda's release and the general security situation with the Nyasaland Governor, and 'undertook to consult further' with Welensky after his visit to Nyasaland.[57] In writing to Armitage on 20 January, Welensky did not conceal 'his deep concern for the consequences of an imminent release', since his security reports on Nyasaland were 'most disturbing' and he believed Banda's release, with other detainees, would be 'the catalyst for disturbances'.[58] A month earlier Macleod had formed the view, based on Nyasaland intelligence reports, that the emergency was no longer defensible.[59] The federal intelligence reports were different – or were interpreted differently – and caused Welensky graver doubts. Footman's tendency to play down worrying aspects may have contributed to this difference.

At a separate meeting held by Macmillan with the federal cabinet, Barrow took the leading part.[60] He described the situation in Nyasaland as 'extremely delicate' and said the political vacuum created by the emergency was being filled, with Armitage's encouragement, by the Malawi Congress Party which – despite its protestations – did not eschew violence. A situation was building up similar to that before the emergency. An accelerated release of detainees would 'reinforce the Malawi party with militant leadership'. Even if Banda were released to Britain the position would be the same.

> If the United Kingdom government were a party to the release of Dr Banda, bloodshed could ensue in Nyasaland for which they would have to take responsibility.[61]

Macmillan repeated that he would discuss detainee releases with Armitage and consult with Welensky when he returned from Nyasaland. He also told Home of this agreement and hoped the delay would not inconvenience Macleod. In any case, he said, it was 'more seemly' for him to talk with Armitage 'before bringing it to a final issue' with Welensky.[62]

In Northern Rhodesia Macmillan met Hone – Benson's successor as Governor – with whom he was much impressed, and executive council including two African ministers and Glyn Jones, minister for African affairs. The weekend was spent privately at the Victoria Falls and early on Monday 25 January he and his party left for Nyasaland, arrived at Chileka, were met by the Governor, drove the 50 miles to Government House in Zomba, and lunched with members of executive council and their wives.[63]

For an hour after luncheon, he met with executive council and the financial secretary, Phillips, gave an account of Nyasaland's benefits from federation, for which 'exposition' the prime minister thanked him 'quite warmly'. They then discussed 'the position of expatriate civil servants and money for education and development generally', but executive council did not find the meeting helpful and Armitage was hurt by the prime minister's 'cold indifference'. There then followed three half-hour meetings with African political party delegations: the Malawi Congress Party, the Congress Liberation Party and the Central African Party. These meetings were 'highly amicable but they all objected to Federation and wanted Banda released'.[64]

Early that morning, before leaving Livingstone, Macmillan had received a cable in which Macleod clearly and firmly set out his views in advance of the prime minister's discussions with Armitage:

> It seems to me impossible to contemplate continuance of the emergency for 6 to 8 months longer and be prepared if necessary to keep Banda in detention for that length of time. We were, after all, contemplating his release in a few days. I also consider it quite impracticable to contemplate

constitutional talks in London which would last more than two or three weeks ... I've also never been convinced of practicability of release to United Kingdom as now suggested. The proposal would at once give Banda a chance to horse-trade; if we were not ready to do that we should have to keep him locked up and even if we got him here I have never seen how we could keep him from returning to the Federation of which he is a belonger. In short, I still consider real choice lies between release on 25 February, which the Governor prefers, and 15 February which still has my preference. I can, of course, come out in early March as originally proposed.[65]

Macmillan, consequently, was well aware of the firm stance his colonial secretary was taking and of his current thinking.

The agreed programme[66] for the Nyasaland visit included a period from 4.30 p.m. to 7.30 p.m. for 'United Kingdom business' and it had been made clear that the 'Prime Minister must have three hours a day ... to deal with London business'.[67] Although the timing of the period to be given to this business varied, and often depended on telephone calls and telegrams from London and the arrival of diplomatic bags, the time would be devoted to other purposes only if a local problem was more pressing than any United Kingdom problems awaiting attention.[68] In the present case Macmillan had agreed with Welensky that he would discuss Banda's release with the Governor (indeed Evans described the visit as 'the Nyasaland–Banda visit'),[69] and the period after 4.30 p.m. was in fact devoted to a discussion between Macmillan and Armitage – with Brook, Hunt, Robertson, Footman, Ingham, King and, intermittently, the Governor's private secretaries, Rowan and Maxwell-Lawford, present – in the Governor's study. So important was the discussion that, after a break from 7 p.m. to 10.50 p.m. – when they changed for dinner which was taken in the study, and attended a reception – they resumed talking until half-past midnight. Macmillan then retired but Armitage continued discussions with his officials, including Finney and Lodge, acting commissioner of police, until 2 a.m.[70]

Macmillan's officials had prepared a note setting out a number of points for his discussion with Armitage.[71] So far as the timing of Banda's release was concerned, there was a number of fixed points: 27 January, Macmillan to leave the Federation; 6 February, Monckton to arrive in the Federation; in the first fortnight of March, Macleod to visit Nyasaland; mid-March, Monckton to visit Nyasaland. A number of steps had been agreed between Armitage and Macleod: before Banda was released his fellow detainees would be moved from Gwelo to Marandellas; on the day of Banda's release – which would not be announced in advance – a statement would be made about introducing Kenya-type security legislation; the end of the emergency would coincide with Macleod's visit. The note also gave Macleod's and Armitage's views. The secretary of state felt there would be 'considerable advantages' in Banda being released by 15 February, soon after Monckton arrived in the Federation, and further delay would 'make things difficult in parliament'. Armitage, however, was unwilling to agree to Banda's release before 25 February. In the first place it would be difficult to let Banda be at large for more than ten days before Macleod's arrival; secondly, security planning could not begin until the prime minister left the Federation; thereafter Footman would have to visit Banda and subsequent coordination of announcements with the colonial secretary would be needed. He felt these arrangements could not be completed before 25 February.

Of the remaining differences between the British and Nyasaland governments, one was a matter of opinion: the likelihood, scale and severity of violence following Banda's release. In any case the Nyasaland government felt – depending on the timing – that they could handle this, and the commissioner of police 'was not unduly worried [because] the security forces ... held a commanding position'.[72] Another difference had not yet reared its head in a clear and immediately important way: that concerning the length of time to elapse between self-government and full independence in Nyasaland. The single, crucial, difference between the two governments was as to Banda's release, particularly the timing and, even more important, the place to which he would go: Nyasaland, as Macleod wished – so as to place no restraints on him – or the United Kingdom as Armitage wished – mainly to reduce the likelihood, scale and severity of violence. The dilemma had been seen by *The Economist* six months earlier:

> Again the key position is held by Dr Banda. If he were now returned to Nyasaland, it would become almost intolerable for the Government and certainly for the Governor; if he were brought to Britain and freed, so that he might be declared a prohibited immigrant, everyone would feel that it was a dirty trick.[73]

In June 1959 the matter – 'the problem of disposal' – had been discussed in the Colonial Office:

> We might accept Banda and one or two others in the U.K. but we do not want an irredentist colony of Nyasas in London – nor perhaps in Ghana which might welcome them. Even, therefore, if we could get Banda and a few others out of [Nyasaland] we may have to face continued detention of a largish block of 'hard core'.[74]

The question of deporting Banda or declaring him a prohibited immigrant in the Federation had again been raised by Lennox-Boyd early

in September 1959 when he asked for a note on the federal legal
powers which might be used to effect such exclusion. Barrow thought
it was not possible to exclude Banda from the Federation, even during
the emergency, because he was a 'belonger'. This view surprised the
secretary of state who thought that just as it had been possible to get
Makarios out of Cyprus – by exiling him to the Seychelles – and then
forbid his return, so it ought to be possible to do the same with
Banda. He also asked 'what legislation would then be necessary in
order to keep out Banda' once the emergency was over.[75] Although his
officials advised that there was currently no legal provision to exclude
Banda from the protectorate,[76] it is clear that in September 1959
Lennox-Boyd was seriously contemplating this action and the law
needed to effect it.

A number of accounts of the evening discussions at Zomba on 25
January exist, five by Nyasaland officials – Armitage, Rowan, Maxwell-
Lawford, Ingham and King – and three by those from Britain: Hunt,
Robertson and Macmillan. There is sufficient common ground in these
eight accounts of the ten people present, for a reasonably clear picture
of the meeting to be drawn.[77]

Of the two parts of the meeting, that following the reception was
the more acrimonious and controversial. No conclusion was reached
during the earlier part, although Macmillan agreed about the possible
dangers that might follow from Banda's release before concrete constitutional plans had been approved by the British government. The
prime minister changed his mind on this during the break in the
meeting, almost certainly as a result of conversations during the
reception. Almost all the talking was done by Macmillan and Armitage;
few others contributed and none significantly. The only points argued,
and strongly so, were the date of Banda's release and the place to
which he should go when released.

As to the date of Banda's release, the British cabinet had already
decided on a number of early dates and had currently fixed on 3
March; although Armitage was reluctantly prepared to release him
before then, he was not prepared to do so on that date. A decision of
the British cabinet was an immensely difficult obstacle to move but
Armitage was prepared to defy Macmillan, saying he, the Governor,
was responsible for law and order and Banda would not be released on
that date. Macmillan must have felt cornered by this response – because
his ministers had made great play in parliament that the Governor was
exclusively responsible for ordering detention and release from detention – and he started to leave the room. Whether this was a theatrical
gesture, he was persuaded to return or he changed his mind is unsure;
in any event he did not leave.

As to the place to which Banda should be released, the differences between the two men were even more pronounced. Armitage was trying to do a deal: release at an early date, if necessary before – but not on – 3 March, in exchange for exile to Britain. Macmillan wanted both release on 3 March and return to Nyasaland. Both dug their heels in deeply and neither gave way. Both were tired and stressed, and, especially following the reception, not in the best mood for polite conversation and compromise. The Nyasaland officials found Macmillan's behaviour 'rude and gross' while the British officials found Armitage 'deliberately offensive' and 'stubborn to the point of insubordination'. At one point Armitage accused Macmillan of being prepared to risk lives in the colonies for the sake of votes in Britain. 'Governor, that was a most offensive remark,' objected Macmillan. 'Prime Minister, it was intended to be,' retorted Armitage.

When Macleod heard from the prime minister, by cable the following day, of the 'unsatisfactory and inconclusive' discussions with Armitage[78] he immediately cabled back, as if to counter any wavering by Macmillan and to strengthen his resolve:

> I am so sorry that you have had difficulties about Armitage's new plan which seems the more impossible the more I look at it. I am sure that if we go on with this emergency, which as you know rests on the shakiest of grounds, political conditions are bound to worsen and the only hope of a change is to get Banda back into Nyasaland and then for me to have constitutional talks with him as soon as possible which we will try and implement before the review, which cannot now be before the spring of 1961, takes place.[79]

The discussions at Government House on the evening of 25 January were neither happy nor – with one possible exception from Macmillan's viewpoint – fruitful. The exception concerned Banda's lawyer, Foot, who had had long conversations with Banda, Chipembere and Chisiza in prison on 23 and 24 January;[80] unbeknown to Foot and the federal authorities, the BSAP had tape-recorded the conversations.[81] Two days later Welensky received a copy of the tape. Foot had had discussions with Chiume, Macleod[82] and Monckton in Britain before he left and he now told Banda that Monckton did not intend to be restricted by his commission's terms of reference, and that Monckton and Macleod were 'extremely anxious' to release Banda. He also asked the doctor's opinion of being exiled to Britain where he could renew his medical practice, but Banda asked who would negotiate a new constitution in his absence. Foot advised that exile should be accepted only if Banda had freedom of speech, and pointed out that exile had not done Makarios any harm. Foot and Banda drafted a memorandum which

they showed to Chipembere and Chisiza, who agreed with its contents.[83] In it Banda said he had carefully considered Footman's
suggestion that he should give evidence to Monckton but had rejected
it because he would be giving evidence on behalf of his followers
whom he would not have been able to consult. He believed, too, that
Monckton could not conduct a full inquiry while over four hundred
people were still in detention and while the emergency still existed.
He would, however, be prepared to give evidence provided a number
of conditions were met. For example, the emergency should be ended
and all detainees released and none of them, or any other witnesses,
should be further detained on account of their evidence; all evidence
should be absolutely privileged in both civil and criminal courts; and
witnesses should have the right to decide whether to give evidence in
public or privately, and be free to comment on government policies
including advocating secession and alternatives to the present Federation. They agreed that a copy of the memorandum should be shown
to Monckton, Macmillan, Macleod and Astor, editor of the *Observer*.

Foot immediately got in touch with the British prime minister in
Nyasaland and asked for an interview in Blantyre on 26 January.
Macmillan – advised by Brook – felt his schedule did not allow him
space to see Foot then but he arranged for him to be invited to the
evening reception at Government House on 25 January.[84] It may well
be that the prime minister wished to be in possession of any information which Foot had to pass on to him on 25 January, before
concluding his discussions with the Governor, rather than wait until
the following day when any such information would be significantly
less useful to him and when he might have committed himself the
previous evening. When Macmillan first saw Foot at the reception he
said, fairly loudly, 'What the devil are you doing here, Foot? You know
damned well that as a Member of Parliament you are not supposed to
travel overseas without my knowledge.'[85] This was purely theatrical
because not only did Macmillan know Foot was in the Federation but
he had himself invited him to the reception. He must have been
deliberately attempting to mislead others within earshot in order to
avoid any suspicion that Foot's presence was engineered and not co-
incidental. Shortly afterwards he took Foot to one side for half an
hour and was handed Banda's memorandum.[86] Foot also made a number of points and said Banda would 'never under any circumstances'
change his opposition to federation.

> If he were released from detention at this stage he would be prepared to
> give evidence before the Monckton Commission and would advise his
> followers to do the same. As his influence in Nyasaland was almost
> unlimited his advice would be accepted.

Banda would not agree to be released from detention unless his friends were also released or a definite early date fixed for their release. Foot also said Banda would be pleased to join in discussions on Nyasaland's constitutional future, could be trusted to keep his word, was opposed to violence, would be 'very susceptible to a personal approach at a high level', and would want to be released to Nyasaland and not anywhere else. To a remarkable degree Foot was providing Banda's responses to precisely those questions to which Macmillan needed up-to-date answers. Foot had guessed with extraordinary accuracy – or had been told – what those questions were. When Macmillan asked if Banda would be prepared to take a responsible view and be ready to cooperate in good faith to try and find an acceptable solution to the problems confronting them, Foot replied that Banda would be ready to cooperate and do this only if his points were met. Later, when Welensky tackled Home about the memorandum, the federal prime minister was incensed that Macmillan had not even mentioned its existence to him when they re-met in Salisbury. Home, having checked with Downing Street, said that Foot thought Macmillan might like to see a copy for his personal information and the prime minister had not thought it worthwhile to mention it to Welensky in the short time they had available together.[87] Macmillan was, therefore, briefed – almost up to the minute – not only on Macleod's position before his discussions with Armitage but, even more importantly, on the stance being adopted by Banda during those discussions. Armitage also knew at least the broad outline of what Foot had said to Macmillan.[88]

The next day the prime minister told the Governor that Banda would not be sent to Britain and the date of his release would be fixed with Macleod.[89] Macmillan left Zomba at 10 a.m. and was seen, by roadside spectators, in the back of the Governor's Rolls-Royce languidly moving his hand from a semi-stifled fulsome yawn to wave to them on his way to Blantyre[90] – little wonder that he remarked to Lady Armitage, 'When I wake up in the morning I don't know which country I'm in.'[91] At Blantyre he met delegations of the United Federal Party and the Asian community at the home of the acting provincial commissioner to whom he

> made it clear that though most of the detainees ought to be let out shortly, Banda and two or three of the principal Congress leaders (such as Chuime and Chipembere) would continue under some sort of restraint for a considerable time: there was no question of independence for Nyasaland or the Federation being dissolved.[92]

Macmillan then attended a civic luncheon at Ryalls Hotel during the course of which a demonstration took place outside. This demonstration, mild and small in scale as it was, was seized upon by a hungry press who had found little else of great interest to report during the Africa tour, and they gave it high prominence in Britain, as a result of which the Southworth commission of inquiry was set up.[93] They were 'heard in the press plane that took them to Salisbury that same afternoon encouraging each other to give the affair a sensational turn'.[94] When the prime minister left Ryalls Hotel he drove to Chileka airport and flew to Salisbury. The following day, he flew to Johannesburg.

The South Africa visit, once it was clear it could not be the grand opening of the Africa tour, had been billed as its culmination and the climax was the speech Macmillan made to parliament at 10.30 a.m. on Wednesday 3 February. It was a speech into which a great deal of thought and effort, by numerous people, had been put over the last two to three months, 'and it was being titivated and amended here and there by the Prime Minister and the Cabinet Secretary [right up to] the night before it was delivered'.[95] It included the 'wind of change' passage.

> In the twentieth century, and especially since the end of the war, the process which gave birth to the nation states of Europe has been repeated all over the world ... Fifteen years ago the movement spread through Asia ... Today the same thing is happening in Africa ... In different places it takes different forms, but it is happening everywhere. The wind of change is blowing through this continent, and, whether we like it or not, this growth of national consciousness is a political fact. We must all accept it as a fact, and our national policies must take account of it.[96]

Before leaving South Africa, Macmillan exchanged many telegrams with the colonial and Commonwealth secretaries 'on the questions of constitutional advance in Nyasaland and above all on the release of Dr Banda':

> The Colonial Secretary was determined, and I thought rightly, to let out Banda as soon as possible ... it would be almost a farce to discuss constitutional reforms of Nyasaland without Banda. But the Federal Government was opposed to this, and the Governors of Northern Rhodesia and Nyasaland were also for delay ... There was a real clash of opinion over Banda. The Commonwealth Office, not unnaturally, felt there was strong reason for accepting the views of the Federal Cabinet, who were bitterly distrustful and adamantly opposed to his release, at least while the Commission was in Nyasaland. But this view was argued against with equal vehemence by Macleod.[97]

Armitage had gravely offended Macmillan by defying him and standing firm on what he saw as his duty to preserve law and order.

Macmillan's response – his retribution – was swift. Initially the prime minister's officials thought Armitage would be dismissed at a very early date: the prime minister 'thought very poorly of Armitage, rejected his views and was determined to replace him'.[98] Armitage himself thought he might be sacked or induced to resign.[99]

On 29 January Macmillan cabled Macleod and said he agreed there were only two alternatives: unconditional early release for Banda or indefinite detention, and the first was preferable;[100] this view was the opposite of what Macmillan had himself told the acting provincial commissioner in Blantyre only three days earlier. He made it plain to Macleod, however, that in taking this course they would be acting contrary to the view of the security position taken by the Governor, Welensky and Hone. He was, therefore, 'somewhat concerned' about the way in which the Nyasaland administration might deal with any disturbances following Banda's release.

> To be frank I was not favourably impressed with the administration there. Even now they seem very quick to take represssive measures against demonstrators etc. The recent incident [outside Ryalls Hotel] during my visit to Blantyre is significant. If they are now ordered to take a course which they believe will lead to disorder they may well be predisposed to take a somewhat exaggerated view of such troubles as arise and to react to them too strongly. In other words I think we must be prepared for a repetition of what Devlin thought they did last time.[101]

These considerations, Macmillan felt, should not deflect them from what they believed to be the right course but he would feel very much happier if Macleod were able to take immediate steps to strengthen the administration in Nyasaland.

> I understand for example that Footman is due to retire in a few months time. Could you not send a good man there to replace him now? You may think that this would not be enough. If you would prefer to find a new Governor you could count on my full support.[102]

Perhaps the prime minister recalled Callaghan's jibe six months earlier that by failing to demand Lennox-Boyd's resignation he had been unable to dismiss the Governor and had thereby deprived Nyasaland of the chance of new men and new approaches to solving its problems. Macmillan believed Macleod's recommended course was right but he doubted very much whether Nyasaland had the men to carry it through. In a letter to the Queen written on the last day of January, while still in South Africa, Macmillan said:

> I am particularly anxious about the situation in Nyasaland. There the

white population is small and anxious, and the Administration struck
me as tired – from the Governor downwards. To govern a modern
Colonial territory while looking over your shoulder every morning and
evening at Questions in the House of Commons must be an almost
impossible burden upon our officials. It takes a very great man to overcome these difficulties.[103]

Macmillan did not view Armitage as a very great man capable of
overcoming Nyasaland's difficulties, but to dispose of a Governor so
quickly – when he had been stoutly defended and supported over the
state of emergency and the Devlin Report, when many pressing political and security issues needed to be settled in the coming months,
when Welensky's grave wrath would be incurred, when many of his
own party would be dangerously offended and when there was already
the imminent risk of one or other of the colonial and Commonwealth
secretaries resigning – was not a task to be undertaken lightly. Nor,
provided new blood and new thinking could be injected into the higher
levels of the Nyasaland government, was it absolutely necessary to
dispose of the Governor – at least not yet. Fortunately, as Macmillan
suggested, there was an obvious alternative candidate available for
removal, the chief secretary. On 2 February, eight days after the Government House row, and the day before the prime minister delivered
his speech to the South African parliament, Armitage received a cable
from Macleod:[104]

> We are entering a new phase in constitutional and other developments in
> Nyasaland and there will be great advantage in having continuity from
> now on for some time in the higher posts in the Nyasaland Adminis-
> tration. I have, therefore, come to the conclusion after consulting with
> the Prime Minister that Jones [minister for African affairs in Northern
> Rhodesia] must take Footman's place at a much earlier date than we had
> in mind when we discussed in Dar es Salaam. I hope that Hone will be
> able to agree that Jones can take over immediately.[105]

Macleod said the decision had been made by Macmillan, Home and
himself after 'the most careful thought' and after a personal appreciation of the situation by the prime minister, and 'he was certain it was
by far the quickest way to dispose of this small affair'. He admitted
this was 'a drastic step' and one which 'only the interest of the Service'
would induce him to take.[106] Armitage 'thought back to Macmillan's
visit and what Footman could have said or done to bring about the
early change' in the date of the chief secretary's departure. He thought
it was Brook who took a dislike to Footman.[107] In fact, of course,
although the blow struck Footman, the damage was aimed at Armitage.
He pointed out the potential damage that might result from removing

Footman – who was in charge of organising security planning – when they were faced with the risks of Banda's imminent release, but there was nothing he could do about the decision. Footman was devastated.[108]

On 19 February Footman was seconded to 'special duties' for two months, Jones was transferred from Northern Rhodesia and assumed the duties of chief secretary of Nyasaland.[109] A week later Devlin wrote to Fairclough:

> I am following African affairs with great interest and cannot help feeling that, consciously or unconsciously, attention is being paid by the powers that be to the conclusions that we arrived at in our report.[110]

7

Resolving the crisis

There may be something to be said for going too fast rather than too slow in Nyasaland.

While the preparations were being made for Macmillan's Africa tour, Armitage's principal dealings continued to be with the Colonial Office, now headed by Macleod. Very soon after taking office the new secretary of state asked the Governor to fly to London for consultations and this Armitage did.[1]

Just before leaving Nyasaland Armitage had a meeting with the office bearers of the recently formed Malawi Congress Party:[2] Orton Chirwa – released from detention in August – president-general; Aleke Banda, secretary-general; and Kamwendo, treasurer. They were able to communicate with Banda in Gwelo and the doctor approved of what they proposed – a new political party to replace the Nyasaland African Congress[3] – and the Malawi Congress Party was launched on 30 September.[4] Within a month membership exceeded 8000 and after a further month 15,000;[5] within six months there were a quarter of a million members.[6]

At their meeting on 6 November Chirwa told Armitage the interim constitution was causing great uncertainty and a statement of the government's intentions would help to clarify the situation. He repeated Congress's earlier demands for elected African majorities in both legislative and executive councils on a universal or very broad franchise. The Governor replied that the present arrangements were temporary and more permanent arrangements would follow the deliberations of the Monckton commission and the federal review. When Chirwa emphasised that his party 'were absolutely in favour of secession' the attorney-general said the terms of reference did not preclude the commission from 'considering a blue print for an alternative federation, if that were to be submitted'. Chirwa would not commit himself as to whether his party would give evidence to Monckton. He felt that with normality having largely been restored, there was no justification for continuing the emergency. He had been at pains to ensure that his party caused no breach of the peace but he was handicapped from representing the views of the people because many were still in detention.

Almost immediately after this interview Armitage flew to London. At the first meeting at the Colonial Office on 9 November,[7] Macleod opened by welcoming the Governor and 'expressing his admiration for the handling of the emergency ... and gratitude for his coming to London at short notice and some personal inconvenience'. He then asked him to survey developments in Nyasaland since the general election: in effect, since his despatch of 6 October.

Armitage said the election had had a 'sobering effect' on the Nyasa-land Africans who were disappointed by the result. Whereas earlier they had been reconciled to Banda staying in detention until March 1960, they now had the impression it would last much longer. Although Orton Chirwa was giving the impression that the Malawi Congress Party had Banda's support, he doubted this because he did not think Chirwa had been in contact with Banda; in addition, Chiume had written to some chiefs instructing them not to join the party, which the Governor saw as possibly opening up splits.

Armitage spent some time discussing Banda, in Gwelo gaol with the 'four main extremists'. He did not think the relationship was 'altogether happy'. The doctor was working hard, reading and writing, but was 'doubtless being worked on by the other four'.

> The question was at what stage we might use him. The time could not possibly be right until after the Advisory Commission since if Dr Banda were released earlier, that would inhibit *all* other Africans from ex-pressing their views before the Commission. On the other hand, once other politicians got going strongly enough, his release would need to be considered. The idea of release was anathema to the Federal Gov-ernment. Much would depend upon the ability to keep the core of extremists in detention with arrangements short of a state of emergency. It was quite essential to be able to assure both the Africans who were co-operating with Government, and other Africans, that the situation could still be controlled if the state of emergency was lifted.

He felt 'the first essential' was to discover how Banda himself was thinking, particularly whether he would dissociate himself from his colleagues. He was already considering whether Banda could be re-moved from Gwelo and thought, if the advisory commission had gone reasonably well, it would be 'timely' to consider his release after the federal review conference, but if he were released at the current time 'the situation would clearly become very serious'. He did not accept the view that Banda was the only person with whom he could treat. In fact, he had the gravest doubts whether one could ever negotiate with Banda as a man who would keep his side of a bargain.

> On his arrival in Nyasaland he had fallen immediately into the hands of his associates and might well do so again. However, if he could be kept reasonably under control, [the government] might be able to use him. Admittedly, although he certainly could not be let loose in Nyasaland again – for then there would be meetings, illegal meetings, and possibly a challenge to the authority of the Government – alternatives might be considered, but it was essential to make certain that the Advisory Commission could do its work, and then see what came of the 1960 Review before letting him out. On the other hand, because time alone would show how far [the government] could build-up [W.M.] Chirwa, how far [they] could enlarge the police force, etc., [Armitage] did not wish to be categoric now that [they] would have to keep Banda in detention until the Monckton Commission had reported; there could be a reappraisal after the Commission had finished their work in Nyasaland.

Armitage agreed there was a chance that if Banda were released out of Nyasaland 'he would not go back to thoughts of violence' but he was not himself yet ready to analyse African feelings.

Macleod's views on Banda were that they would need to decide whether he should be distinguished from his colleagues, separated from them and given 'weekend amenities'. They had to face the necessity of keeping him in detention until the advisory commission left Africa and, conceivably, until it reported. They needed also to think about whether other political organisations would be strengthened or weakened by his release to Britain or 'somewhere else outside the Federation'.

This question of possibly releasing Banda to a place other than Nyasaland – as a means of securing agreement on release before Monckton left Nyasaland or the Federation – was fairly new. Two days after the Commons debate on the Devlin Report, Callaghan had asked the secretary of state if he would release Banda to live in London until other arrangements could be made and so that he could 'start the constitutional talks which will be necessary sooner or later in order that the next stage may begin'. Lennox-Boyd was not to be drawn, but the point did not go unattended and a few weeks later Monson wrote to Armitage saying that ministers wished to know whether

> it might be possible to 'approach' Dr Banda with a view to obtaining from him a firm renunciation of violence, as a condition of his release; whether such a renunciation could be regarded as in any sense reliable; and even if it were made and Dr Banda were released whether it would be possible to allow him to return to Nyasaland, i.e. whether he could only be released to return to the United Kingdom.[8]

In considering Banda's future they agreed his conditions in detention ought to be improved and it was important to isolate him from
the influence of the extremists detained with him. They were concerned the federal government would be suspicious of any action which
appeared to improve Banda's conditions. Consequently, they had to
proceed very carefully – especially in how they presented the matter.
Macleod wanted to see a distinction made between Banda on the one
hand and Chipembere and Chisiza on the other – as had Devlin whom
he consulted just after taking office[9] – and hoped they could make it
clear that, whatever Banda's future, the extremists 'were likely to be
out of circulation for a very long time'. Macleod concluded by saying
he planned to visit Nyasaland after the advisory commission had left
but before they made their report: about July or August 1960.

Armitage's first impressions of Macleod were favourable:

> I found him reasonable and considered [him] to hold a practical view of
> things ... We had [a number of] quite satisfactory meetings and I do not
> go away disappointed ... My new Minister appears very reasonable and
> I did not have to give anything away.[10]

Macleod took an early opportunity also to see Orton Chirwa, and
he did this on 18 November at the Colonial Office. Although Chirwa
produced a memorandum,[11] he preferred 'an informal meeting in which
he could develop freely the various points he had to make'.[12] He
repeated what he had said to Armitage about ending the state of
emergency, the need for urgent constitutional progress, the difficulties
of giving evidence to Monckton, and that he was particularly worried
about the commission's membership. They had another meeting, on 1
December, with Perth present. Chirwa said that if the emergency were
lifted and Banda released it was very much more likely that Africans
would give evidence to Monckton: at present they feared victimisation
for expressing anti-federal views. He said, in confidence, that through
his personal and professional relationship with Banda he was able to
influence him and, having provided an instrument for non-violent
political activity – in the Malawi Congress Party – he felt he could
keep Banda on a constitutional path. In writing about this meeting to
Armitage, Monson said:

> The question is to what extent he could be used as a steadying influence
> on other leaders. Though nobody mentioned the 'Cs' we all assumed
> that Chirwa's suggestion that Banda should be released to become leader
> of a constitutional party carried the implication that he would be separ-
> ated from the 'Cs' and brought under the influence of Chirwa.[13]

Macleod and Perth both told Chirwa of their willingness to see him again even though, like Monson and Armitage, they were convinced 'he ... [was] certainly not a political leader' – not that this mattered because Chirwa was 'perfectly ready to admit that the party had been specially created as a vehicle for Banda'.[14]

It is clear that as early as November, Armitage felt he might need to treat Banda specially, in order to distinguish him from the extremists and thereby be able to release him and use him in the advancement of the country, but he was very unsure of how to do this in his quest for constitutional advance within the Federation. The Governor's attitude towards the release of detainees generally at this time was:

> there were a number of hard core detainees who could not be released in the foreseeable future. We even considered moving such persons to a variety of prisons in Southern Rhodesia so as to break them up and out of the groups they now formed. There was a controlled and steady release of persons and we saw no possibility of accelerating this. But we aimed at ending the state of emergency.[15]

On his return to Nyasaland, Armitage called a meeting of executive council with the African members, Mtawali and Chinkondenji, present and explained what had happened in London: 'no new policies or plans', which provoked 'no particular comments'.[16] He and his colleagues were not anticipating any particular or swift changes from the new secretary of state. Armitage was much concerned with what was still the basic problem – introducing a new constitution for Nyasaland – and he had already worked out his 'own plan for the future':[17] a legislature with 16 members elected in general constituencies, six seats reserved for non-Africans and three ex-officio members – the chief secretary, attorney-general and financial secretary; and an executive council comprising the Governor as president, the three ex-officio members, two non-Africans as ministers without portfolio, and five African ministers – a leader of government business and ministers controlling education, social services and labour, natural resources and local government. But the British government's view was that, despite the security dangers, no constitutional advance could be made while Banda was still detained; from Britain's point of view, therefore, releasing him as soon as possible became an urgent necessity.

The differences between what Armitage was now prepared to recommend in a new constitution compared with his proposals 10 months earlier were considerable. No longer was he hampered by the conflicting and unrealistic demands of numerous political parties and sectional interests, and the emergency had introduced a significant air of realism and progress into his thinking. His legislature of 29 members would now be reduced to 25, of whom only three would be ex-officio as against 15 ex-officio and nominees earlier; the non-African non-officials remained at six; and definite African non-officials would in effect increase from 8 to 16. His executive council would increase from 10 to 11, including himself as president; his official members decreased from five to three; non-Africans remained at two; and Africans increased from two to five. Whereas no non-officials would have been ministers, now the five Africans would all be ministers. There would be a clear African majority in legislative council and, excluding the president, parity – of a sort – in executive council, the number of African ministers matching the combined total of official and non-African members. Yet the air of realism and progress which the emergency had introduced still fell short of envisaging Banda playing a part in the proposals the Governor was prepared to recommend: for this the air needed to be stirred into something more like a wind – maybe a gale.

Among the matters the new secretary of state discussed with Armitage at their London meeting were the possibilities of proscribing the Malawi Congress Party, releasing Banda and accelerating the rate of release of other detainees. On his return to Nyasaland the Governor corresponded with Monson about these.[18] He felt that in the absence of direct evidence against the Malawi Congress Party he could not proscribe it, a view with which the Colonial Office agreed. In respect of Banda's release he told Monson:

> I have discussed with Hone what the reactions would be if Dr Banda were released or brought back to [Nyasaland]. Hone is quite clear that if this were to happen his own internal security position would be aggravated. For my part, I am equally clear that with the inflammable situation which we have we should run an unjustifiable risk of a recrudescence of disorders and violence.

He went on to say Senn, the International Red Cross representative, had recently seen Banda and asked him what he thought his future was. The doctor's prompt reply was either he stayed where he was, in detention, or he returned unconditionally to Nyasaland. Armitage could not 'regard this as very promising' and therefore felt that 'Dr Banda must be treated as any other detainee': if Banda insisted on unconditional release there was no point in treating him specially. Turning to an accelerated rate of release of detainees generally, the Governor pointed out that already 'the tempo is quickening'. He hoped that once they enacted a permanent detention bill he could accelerate the rate still further, as indeed was his object, but he refused to quote figures and said he could not reasonably assess the position until he had experience of working the new arrangements. With the Labour

Party refusing to cooperate with the advisory commission he was at a loss to see why Monson was suggesting so strongly that detainees should be released at a 'very accelerated' rate. He was soon to learn.

Early in December Macleod wrote a note to Macmillan – who shortly discussed it with him, Brook, Perth and Monson[19] – setting out his thinking on Nyasaland: 'probably the most difficult single problem' they had in the field of colonial policy.[20] There were then 470 men still in detention, 90 of them in Southern Rhodesia. The early 'fairly swift' release of detainees had recently slowed down and, to Macleod's disappointment, the numbers had started slowly to rise again. He was convinced they had to achieve a 'substantial reduction very swiftly' and soon bring the emergency to an end. He also wanted to treat Banda differently from the other detainees, improve his conditions, and then, at an appropriate moment, order his release. Indeed, Macleod 'was really determined to release him from the moment [he] became colonial secretary'.[21]

> I aim, therefore, to move as swiftly as possible towards a reduction ... to the true hard core, which might number perhaps 50. If this can be achieved before Monckton arrives in February it would transform the situation and give him a real chance to operate ... I have no doubt at all that some time we will have to deal with Banda. It will make it all the more easy to deal with him if we can separate him from the 'Cs' ... I am convinced, although this may sound paradoxical, that Banda is the most likely African Nyasa leader to keep Nyasaland within the Federation.

Macleod believed the best chance lay in a swift reduction of detainees to the hard core before Monckton arrived; the receiving, in due course, of 'imaginative proposals' from Monckton which would allay African fears; the promise of early constitutional advance for Nyasaland; and a period of stability after the 1960 federal review 'during which we must try by every means in our power to see that federation works'. There were risks in this policy but he was certain it represented 'the most hopeful possibility of advance'. He had not discussed the rapid reduction of detainees with the Governor. He proposed to ask Armitage to meet him in Dar es Salaam during his imminent visit, to discuss this. Home was not present at Macmillan's meeting but he told the prime minister he agreed that the faster the release of ordinary detainees the better the political prospects would be, but he was very doubtful about an early release for Banda: he would need 'much more information' before he felt justified in supporting it.

> The main test here must be the effect which his release will have on the Africans in Nyasaland. It might easily tip the balance in favour of

violence and make matters worse. I cannot answer whether that would be so. Nor do I think that anyone can other than those who like the District Officers are living among the Africans or like the Governor who has access to intelligence officers who are working among Africans.[22]

Home felt that they would need a very careful and up-to-date assessment before a decision could be taken. This was an early sign of Home not viewing things in the same light as Macleod – a dangerous situation for a prime minister who had divided cabinet responsibilities for Central Africa between two ministers.

On 18 December the Governor flew with Theunissen to Dar es Salaam; there he had a number of interviews with Macleod during which he quickly learned his original impression of 'no new policies or plans' was gravely mistaken. The meetings were somewhat 'stiff and rigid' and had to be fitted in between Macleod's scheduled meetings on Tanganyikan affairs.[23] The secretary of state opened by saying that the Nyasaland Intelligence Committee reports no longer justified a state of emergency and he could not defend it before the Human Rights Committee. He expressed his strong view that they should have a very rapid rundown of all detainees and deal with Banda separately. Armitage, in response, 'was staggered by the approach', 'fought him all the way', and 'argued vehemently' that there was a serious security risk in Macleod's proposals and they would need to call in federal troops. He felt strongly that to release the detainees quickly in the absence of any indication of future policy, would be to release them into a vacuum which would result in further and worse disturbances, necessitating the calling in of federal troops. Furthermore, he argued, Banda's release 'might well jeopardise the whole tour of the Monckton commission'.[24] The Governor insisted he would 'run-down detainees in order so as not to have troubles in [the] districts'. They then adjourned for a time while Theunissen worked on some detailed figures for Macleod to consider,[25] and eventually they agreed to an accelerated release of detainees with Banda being treated as any other detainee. Macleod undertook to take this proposition to the cabinet. It was a compromise, Armitage giving way as to the pace of release, Macleod giving way over treating Banda as a special case. They agreed that when the advisory commission left Nyasaland, Macleod would visit the protectorate, by which time they hoped only the extremists would remain in detention. They could then lift the emergency and have detention legislation ready to control the hard core.

Armitage privately commented, 'I do not know whether Macleod was being deliberately provocative, but Monson was no help to me.'[26] The following day, after a great deal of arguing and straight talk about the rate of release of detainees and progress towards ending the emergency, they agreed that releases could be accelerated: 100 in January, 80 in February, 70 in March, 41 in April, 38 in May and 38 in June, leaving only 49 detainees in July. Macleod was adopting a mechanical approach to release numbers; Armitage decided each case on its merits at the specific time. Perhaps in order to get Armitage moving more quickly he was setting him a target: 'Release 100. I don't mind who they are, it's up to you, but release 100.' They thought it should be possible to judge in March whether the releases had caused a serious security deterioration and whether the remainder of the programme could be followed. Of the 49 remaining in detention after July, whom the Governor considered to be hard core, 'it would be impossible to say when they could be released' although Macleod had said he intended to visit Nyasaland about July when it might be possible to make further decisions about the numbers involved. The secretary of state thought he could then announce the end of the emergency, 'provision having previously been made on the Kenya lines for continued detention of the hard core by name'. They were agreed that Banda could not be released until after the advisory commission had left Nyasaland. Macleod was anxious to announce the accelerated programme of releases – without giving actual figures – before the prime minister arrived in the country. Of their meetings Macleod wrote to Armitage:

> Personally, I found our talks worthwhile in every way, and I hope that you feel also the effort of coming up from Zomba was not wasted. I think I should now be much better able to put all our problems to my colleagues in London than I should have been able to do on the basis of correspondence alone.[27]

The Governor replied[28] that he also was certain their talks were worthwhile, and privately he said: 'I returned quite satisfied with my interviews with Macleod; we seem to have more or less reached agreement to do nothing, but he makes a statement in January and comes out in June, [and we are] to get our detainees out as soon as possible.'[29] Presumably both thought they had made some progress against the other's arguments.

While Macleod was in Tanganyika, Home continued to ponder Macleod's note to Macmillan.[30] He was concerned about its implications for 'the future of the Federation and [Britain's] general interests in Africa'. It was clear to him that the future would bring African majorities onto the voters' roll in Nyasaland 'and probably in the long run in Northern Rhodesia', and the withdrawal of British protection at the Africans' request would be not more than 10 to 15 years away.

Rather than name a final date for self-government, he believed that constitutional advance should be in two or three stages so that Africans could gain experience in administration and government. As for releasing Banda, he said:

> The familiar sequence [of] violence-detention-release-parley has done us great damage in Africa. One individual after another has held us to ransom and got away with it and our prestige and that of the white man has been severely damaged. If we wish to retain any semblance of control (and we must for the sake of the Europeans in the Federation) we need a plan and the determination to stick to it. I am inclined therefore to think that the Colonial Secretary is right in proposing to release Dr Banda but that he must be absolutely clear on the terms of his release and we must be clear on how we mean to manage matters thereafter.

Their object should be to use Banda to further their constitutional plans 'and ruthlessly to destroy his apparatus of violence'. This meant Banda should be released on the 'absolute understanding' that if he acted unconstitutionally or in ways which would lead to violence, 'he would be banished for life'. It meant also the continued imprisonment of Chipembere and the other lieutenants for as long as necessary: 'we should certainly contemplate ten years or even more'; or they should be banished if this was possible. The police needed strengthening to deal quickly with lawlessness. He believed this plan would give the best chance of a settled period of 10 or 15 years and, thus, the best chance for Nyasaland continuing in the Federation. Home trusted neither Banda nor Orton Chirwa and felt at best they wished to make the white man the servant of the black, although they might decide to cooperate on a definite plan for the foreseeable future. 'They would know that this was their last chance, that if they forfeited it they would be off the stage and that direct rule would continue until others more reasonably minded came along to take a hand.' He concluded:

> I am therefore in general agreement with the Colonial Secretary but at present we are on the run and the rot must be stopped and that can best be done by a definite programme of constitutional advance, by firm administration, by absolute insistence on political action within the law and following the Monckton Commission's report by an all out and sustained effort (especially by the Federal Government and the three Territorial governments) to make Federation work and to make it acceptable to Africans and Europeans alike.

In making these comments he had three thoughts 'very much in mind'. First was the need to be just towards African legitimate political aspirations. Second, they must be certain not to make the position of

Europeans in Africa unbearable because that would 'deal a deadly blow at British interests and at the security and influence of the free world'. Third, to retain any sort of authority, they had to have a definite plan and stick to it: if it were seen to be reasonable they could sustain it.

Although the agreement which Armitage and Macleod had reached in Dar es Salaam was submitted as an outline cabinet paper, the secretary of state asked Perth to accompany it with a covering note when it went to the cabinet on 4 January:[31]

> Attached paper on Nyasaland is the result of discussions with Armitage at Dar es Salaam and represents the highest common factors of agreement. Firstly, I feel that programme is too slow, although release rate represents twice the rate Armitage first suggested. There are no rehabilitation problems in the Kenya sense and rate of release is simply judgement of security risk and can be increased or decreased as the situation requires.

No serious problems had so far arisen following releases and intelligence reports were not alarming. He hoped, therefore, to step up the February and March releases and reach the hard core position by about the end of April when the state of emergency might be ended.

> Secondly, I feel that 50 hard core is much too high and doubt if we could justify more than about 20, if that. Thirdly ... Armitage now agrees that we must discuss, some time, constitutional matters with Banda. If Banda can be freed as soon as the Monckton Commission leaves Nyasaland I could see him during the week's visit I contemplate to the Northern Territories in June. Again I would prefer to consider his release earlier but suggested timing may be convenient. Chief Secretary Nyasaland is going to see and sound Banda this week and I will report orally to the Cabinet.

In another note to the cabinet dated 24 December, Macleod said he was anxious to ensure that the emergency in Nyasaland was brought to an end as soon as possible; meanwhile the release of detainees should be accelerated and the conditions of Banda's detention relaxed. Armitage was not told about either of Macleod's notes to the cabinet, even though they significantly altered the agreement reached with him; the Governor later expressed the view that Macleod 'was utterly ruthless so that he just bulldozed his way through any views ... which were put up to him'.[32]

Just before Macleod's paper went to the cabinet, Bligh made two important points to Macmillan:

> The paper seems to take as accepted the policy that Dr. Banda should not be freed until *after* the Monckton Commission leave Nyasaland. This

may be right but you may think the point worth exploring ... There may be something to be said for going too fast rather than too slow in Nyasaland.[33]

The prime minister agreed with these points and asked to see Macleod before the cabinet meeting.

On his return to Zomba, Armitage consulted Dixon, Blackwood and Finney on how they might best spend the six-month period before Macleod came out to Nyasaland so as 'to make things better for the eventual rapprochement with the African nationalists'.[34] He recognised Banda's crucial role and arranged for Footman to visit the detainees in Southern Rhodesia and meet with the doctor there. The Governor's dilemma was to decide just what role Banda should play. The question was not so much releasing him but using him to secure constitutional advance and, given Senn's report, release was essential if he was to be used.

Armitage also had a long meeting with his provincial commissioners, the chief secretary and other senior advisers, on 29 December.[35] They believed the programme agreed with Macleod for releasing detainees – which they accepted – was not likely to be a security risk for a few months. If Banda were released to Nyasaland, whether under a Governor's detention order or as a free man, this would be 'the beginning of the end': the chiefs and others would all follow him. Consequently, on release he should be sent to the United Kingdom, and negotiations with him should be delayed until the advisory commission had reported and the federal review had taken place. Thereafter, once the Nyasaland constitution had been arranged, he could return to Nyasaland. All wanted early constitutional development but they did not believe this was possible unless the European and Asian political parties liaised with Banda. This belief was a hangover from the view held by Lennox-Boyd that the various communities should get together and try to agree on a new constitution. If the Nyasaland government itself initiated change at this stage they would antagonise the federal and Rhodesian governments and local Europeans. A political solution was essential, whether or not it involved Banda, and such a solution was unlikely to happen quickly enough. They concluded:

> [Our] only course seems to be to hold on to what we have and keep the lid on. All three Provincial Commissioners think we can do this if we switch troops and police rapidly and can suppress or nip in the bud any disorder.[36]

They felt a dangerous security situation might develop but it could be contained. In later years Armitage recalled how nervous they were that conditions would deteriorate into another emergency, and in retrospect he felt they placed too much weight on this fear; at the time they 'were too close to the emergency to recognise that it was by providing a chance for further constitutional change that [they] would enable the hard core element to come back into political life'.

At the close of 1959, Armitage was feeling somewhat helpless in a fast-developing situation:

> I find life most depressing and see myself with no room to manoeuvre, only sit on a boiling pot getting more steam!

> I am not sorry to see the end of 1959, but 1960 opens with the prospect of being much worse.[37]

At the same time, Banda wrote from Gwelo gaol to the Registrar-General, who was looking after his property in Nyasaland:

> I hope you will have a very Merry Christmas and a very Happy New Year. I am already having a very good one here. A number of parcels from Britain, to say nothing of cards from just everywhere, and from people I do not know and have never heard of.[38]

At about this time Orton Chirwa was making it known Macleod had told him Nyasaland would soon get its freedom and the country's constitution was to be reformed in February.[39] When, at the suggestion of Pretorius, chairman of the African affairs board of the federal assembly, Armitage shortly saw him, he formed the impression that Chirwa – whom Pretorius 'found far too self-confident and very changed since his visit to the U.K.'[40] – had plenty of time for politics, since his law practice was not flourishing, and that he was organising the Africans: telling them not to hold meetings – which were legally banned – and not to cause trouble, so that there would be no undue delay in releasing detainees, removing the emergency and starting talks on constitutional change.[41] All this very helpful advice would be consistent with Macleod – without telling Armitage – having taken Chirwa into his confidence as to Nyasaland's future, at least in broad terms.

When Footman visited Gwelo, against a background of polite and personal pleasantries the doctor confirmed he would give evidence to the advisory commission and enter into constitutional discussions only if he were released from detention. Banda advocated boldness in the Nyasaland government; if the Governor were prepared to be bold and take risks, he would meet him halfway. Banda pressed for an early end to the state of emergency and the early release of all detainees – then they could forget the past. He also emphasised that 'it was no use looking for other leaders', as if to warn the Governor against relying on the Chirwas as possible leaders with whom he could deal.[42]

On the day before Macmillan left Britain to start his tour, Armitage received a cable from Macleod saying the cabinet had just agreed, subject to the security situation and Macmillan's discussion with Welensky, that Banda should be released after Macmillan left the Federation on the last day of January, although the Governor might see merit in deferring it a few days. There was to be accelerated release of detainees – at least 120 a month with immediate effect – but there was no question of constitutional talks being held. He asked for fortnightly reports on releases and he did not reveal that his advice to the cabinet on accelerated releases – so as to leave only 50 by the end of March and 12 by the end of April – was at a significantly greater rate than that agreed with Armitage in Dar es Salaam.[43] Armitage was 'absolutely astonished to receive this telegram'.[44] Home told Welensky of the cabinet's decision greatly to accelerate releases and said that Macmillan looked forward to discussing the emergency and Banda's release with him later in the month.[45] Privately, officers of FISB felt it was high time someone prodded the Governor into taking some form of constitutional action even though it might be unpleasant for the federal government.[46]

A few days earlier, in 'a little discussion' with Macmillan and Home, Macleod had 'produced the ideas' about this increased rate of release and said he wished to think more about them before making definite recommendations. Home said Monckton would 'need to be appropriately briefed' so as to assure, as far as they could, that his commission would be 'sound on the subject'. Macleod had outlined a possible programme: an announcement to be made at the time Monckton reached the Federation, in the third week of February, that the emergency would soon end; Banda to be released at normal March review of detention orders; and Kenya-type detention legislation to be made in April. Chipembere, who was 'still regarded as a dangerous man', would stay in detention 'for some years'.[47]

Armitage told executive council on 6 January that in Macleod's view all detainees should be released by April, and, with the permanent detention legislation in place, the state of emergency would then be ended. Council's reaction was that this would be proceeding too fast to gauge the possible effects and, in any event, those who were a threat to security should remain in detention. There were, however, some signs of their recognising the political realities since Blackwood accepted that an end to the emergency was inevitable and territorial constitutional advance might have to precede the federal review.[48]

Two days later the Nyasaland intelligence committee discussed the possible effects of accelerating all but a dozen hard core releases and lifting the emergency by the end of April. The committee believed

Congress had created a protectorate-wide organisation ready for the release of the leaders; they feared widespread violence and disorder before the security forces could be deployed to prevent or deal with it, and that 'the release of large batches of detainees may lead to a security situation developing about March or April'.[49]

On 7 January 1960, Macleod gave a speech at Leeds in which he said constitutional advance in Nyasaland was necessary, he would shortly visit the protectorate, he looked forward to an early end to the emergency and he was happy to announce Armitage felt the release of detainees could be accelerated, although he did not intend to mention any figures. This speech was sufficiently important for the Commonwealth Relations Office immediately to cable its broad contents to all British high commissioners in Commonwealth countries.[50] In Nyasaland, Armitage 'had to answer all sorts of awkward questions put by the press' as a result of the speech.[51]

The Governor met Dixon and Blackwood on 13 January[52] but did not tell them Banda might be released as early as 31 January. Their reaction was extremely hostile when told that Banda was not considered hard core and would, therefore, qualify to be released with other detainees. They were particularly opposed to his release to Nyasaland and resisted the idea that all but hard core detainees would be released by April. As for discussions on constitutional advance and Armitage's view that these had to be with Banda, they said the discussions should take place in prison; Armitage dismissed this because, following Footman's visit, he knew the doctor would refuse discussions while still in prison. In reply to their questions as to what would happen if, being released, Banda refused to negotiate or if he preferred not to be released rather than negotiate on the basis of a self-governing Nyasaland within the Federation, Armitage said they would have to keep him in gaol, release him to Britain or send him back to prison. They finally made two further points: before Banda was released they must have decided on the phased constitutional development over the next 10 years, after which Africans would be in complete control; and all constitutional proposals must be discussed with Welensky – which, of course, was the current practice. Reporting this meeting to the Colonial Office,[53] Armitage said his provincial commissioners were taking a very serious view of the security situation if Banda's release were to be combined with the accelerated release of other detainees, and consequently he advised that releases should be decelerated and the possibility of a large hard core accepted if Banda were released before 1 April. In any case, Banda should not be let out unless Macleod himself visited Nyasaland and unless Banda clearly expressed a willingness to enter discussions on the basis of self-government within the

Federation. He pointed out that release could be to Britain and discussions could take place there; if Banda objected to this, for example because he could not properly consult his people, they 'might just have to send him there'.

The day following his meeting with Dixon and Blackwood, Armitage wrote to Macleod about the security aspects of the accelerated release of detainees, especially Banda. He began by explaining why he preferred not to ask for BSAP personnel. As he had shown 10 months earlier, Whitehead would use such a request to interfere in Nyasaland affairs. Armitage's objections did not apply to federal African troops although there had been criticism of using federal European soldiers. All the advice Armitage was receiving was that if Banda went willingly to Britain the danger of disturbances would be greatly reduced, especially if the doctor could announce that he was discussing matters with the secretary of state. On his present assessment, he felt it unlikely Banda would go to Britain willingly and in any case the doctor never had controlled, or could control, the hooligans among his followers. He told Macleod he would need three companies of RAR, two of 1 KAR, three of 2 KAR, nine PMF platoons, air transport, reconnaissance aircraft and the services of his special constables. During the past year the African police had been increased by 230, with 350 more in training. He concluded, however, 'If situation seriously deteriorates it is anybody's guess' what forces would be required.

Armitage also told Macleod he was now convinced early constitutional talks were desirable, the secretary of state should visit Nyasaland as soon as possible, and talks could only be fruitful if they were with Banda and if he had by then been freed. He also proposed that Banda be separated from his extremist colleagues by removing them from Gwelo to Marandellas; this might be preceded by another visit from Footman 'to prepare the ground'. Banda should then be released on 25 February with an announcement that this would make him available for talks with Macleod early in March, the date Armitage now suggested for his visit,[54] before Monckton arrived. At the same time Kenya type security legislation could be made and the emergency ended. Reporting this to Macmillan on 16 January Macleod suggested the prime minister, in speaking with Armitage, should propose a release date not later than 15 February and that it might ease some of the Governor's anxieties if Macmillan told him he could slow down other releases for two or three weeks after Banda was freed, until they could assess the security risk of his release. Macleod said, '[I]t is obvious that there will be a good deal of elation and some demonstrations and possibly hooliganism may get out of hand' and it was 'certainly conceivable' the situation might deteriorate beyond this. Although he recognised Armitage 'must take what precautions he thinks necessary', he was not prepared then to sanction reinforcement of security forces ahead of Banda's release. He concluded by telling the prime minister he very much welcomed Armitage's 'more forthcoming attitude'.[55]

The Governor disagreed with two of the points made in Macleod's report to Macmillan: he preferred 25 February for Banda's release and Macleod continued to prefer 15 February – to avoid the Opposition in the Commons pressing for release during the Supply Day debate on 18 February; and he wanted reinforcements in place before the release whereas Macleod wanted them on short call outside Nyasaland. The secretary of state asked the prime minister to discuss these differences with the Governor and also whether United Kingdom troops should be sent to Nyasaland – to avoid using federal European troops and BSAP personnel; Macleod thought perhaps Macmillan ought to hint at this possibility with Welensky, as he was bound to object.[56]

Writing to Armitage on 21 January,[57] Monson said Macleod was 'very doubtful' about placing conditions on Banda's release, such as a willingness to participate in talks and be of good behaviour, because to seek specific undertakings before release would be to invite horse-trading in which Banda 'would seek to get [the Colonial Office] to go all the way to meet him before he moved'. He thought a release coinciding with an announcement of Macleod's visit for talks would be the 'bold and imaginative step' Banda advocated and he could be told Macleod looked forward to the doctor joining in those talks. As a free man, also, he could appear before Monckton if he wished. Monson thought Footman should not visit Banda again because this might lead to the horse-trading they wished to avoid. In any case, they were moving so close to a solution which Banda was bound to accept – unconditional release – that there was no point in a further visit.

> This means that risk of Banda proving non-co-operative on release has to be accepted and faced. If his attitude and activities led to renewed threat to security, he would have to be redetained.

The Colonial Office strongly objected to security legislation being the subject of discussion or bargaining with Banda, as Armitage had suggested to get him to accept release and talks while some of his followers remained in detention. No mention of this should be made to Banda before his release; indeed, given a deceleration in other releases from 1 February, security legislation should be delayed until shortly after Macleod's visit and it would then be possible to announce the end of the emergency during April.

The position, then, by the middle of January 1960 may be summarised as follows. In Britain, the government – or at least Macleod and Macmillan but much less so Home and Perth[58] – were intent upon faster progress towards self-determination in Africa generally and Nyasaland in particular. They felt unable to justify continuing the state of emergency – the seven-year emergency in Kenya was ended on 12 January while Macmillan was in Nigeria,[59] and Devlin's barbs about a 'police state' in Nyasaland still smarted. They were anxious to reduce the number of detainees at a fast rate, and were prepared to release even many of the hard core whom they felt could be dealt with by enacting preservation of public order legislation. They recognised Banda as the only real leader of Nyasaland Africans and the person who could most readily – and quite easily – command virtually total African support. To retain the Federation, they envisaged a self-governing Nyasaland within it, but knew that to stand any chance of succeeding in this aim, they needed to act very fast and make substantial and very early advances in the Nyasaland constitution. Such advances could not be made while Banda was in detention: he had to be an active party to them and he ought to be released before Monckton arrived in Nyasaland so that he could give evidence to him and so that other Congress followers would also give evidence. They acknowledged that releasing Banda was a security risk since it might be accompanied by political agitation and violence. They believed Armitage's attitudes were hampering the breaking of a political deadlock, and early and radical changes were essential.

In Nyasaland, Armitage's non-official advisers were much more certain deteriorating security and violence would accompany Banda's release. Blackwood felt his early release would cause Southern and Northern Rhodesia to withdraw from the Federation and then 'there would be no federation to contain Nyasaland'. Dixon believed his release would involve 'the gravest disorders'. Both, unlike the Governor, considered Banda to be one of 250 or so hard core detainees. They advocated he should not be released until the pattern of the Federation had been decided and he should be kept out of Nyasaland for two further years: if he then returned 'the new constitution would be working and he would be deflated'. By then, too, they added, all the governments would be supporting the post-review federation.[60]

Notwithstanding these hard line opinions of the non-official members, Armitage, with his official advisers, had moved towards agreeing with most of the British government's views; no doubt they had recognised the direction in which Macleod was going and his determination not to be thwarted and they were adopting a 'more forthcoming attitude'. They, too, wanted an early end to the emergency, with permanent legislation to cover detention and public order. They, too, wanted to run down the number of non-hard core detainees as

soon as possible although they had in mind a significantly slower rate
of releases than that advocated by the British government. They, too,
recognised Banda as the only real leader of Nyasaland Africans: 'we
could only improve the situation by dealing with him'.[61] This was a
turnaround from their earlier position when they had gravely doubted
whether Banda was the sort of man with whom they could deal because
he might not negotiate, and they had toyed with the idea of supporting
and using the Chirwas and had hoped that by their keeping Banda in
detention other, more moderate, leaders would be encouraged to
emerge. They, too, agreed they could deal with Banda only if he were
released from detention. They, too, aimed at a self-governing Nyasaland
within the Federation and recognised that very early and substantial
territorial constitutional advance was essential if they were to stand a
chance of succeeding in this aim. They, too, believed there was a
security risk in releasing Banda but felt – provided they were allowed
to draw on sufficient reinforcements – they could, at least for a while,
contain any violent trouble.

The Nyasaland government, however, differed from the British
government in two respects. First, and most important, they believed
territorial constitutional discussions and advance could proceed without
Banda being in Nyasaland, and it would be much safer if he were sent
to Britain when released; in effect Armitage wanted to attach conditions
to Banda's release whereas Macleod was convinced it should be unconditional. Second, they placed greater emphasis on the inevitability,
scale and risk of violence accompanying Banda's release to Nyasaland
from detention especially if it coincided with an accelerated general
release of detainees. Armitage wanted to release Banda as soon as
possible but was held back because he had nothing, as yet, to offer him
which he would accept.

> To have let him out without offering some constitutional advance and
> some indication that secession was not entirely ruled out would have
> been catastrophic. Armitage wanted HMG to concede the principle of
> secession but it was not until [much later] that anyone from HMG said
> it was possible.[62]

Both Home and Armitage, separately, proposed plans for Nyasaland's
constitutional future which they felt would provide a clear framework
for negotiations with Banda. Macleod also accepted the need for having
a plan of some sort to put to Banda but his officials were simply
'working on it'.

It was into this scene that the British premier walked when he
visited the Federation as part of his Africa tour.

When Macmillan left Nyasaland on 26 January 1960, he dined with

Welensky, Malvern and Whitehead in Salisbury. According to the federal prime minister, he – Welensky – was especially anxious to discuss Banda's release but every time he attempted to raise the question Macmillan evaded it and talked about something else. The same thing happened at the airport the next morning.[63] According to the British prime minister the evening was a social affair and his hosts 'were not anxious to talk business'.[64] The Governor of Southern Rhodesia was even clearer and told Home 'your Prime Minister when here would not discuss the subject with Welensky at all'.[65] Armitage's understanding was that Macmillan had 'funked it' and had refused to discuss Banda's release with Welensky and Whitehead who were 'most upset' by it.[66] Macmillan had, however, prepared notes[67] for his talk with Welensky in which he said that Armitage and he agreed that constitutional talks must take place as soon as possible and these must be with Banda, but that his release might prejudice Monckton's work. Armitage proposed that Banda should be released, immediately sent to Britain and kept there until the end of the summer. Macmillan's objections to this were that the legal basis was dubious, it would not satisfy demands for his release without restraint, and talks would not be satisfactory – indeed agitation would be whipped up and harm Monckton's inquiry. The choice was between keeping Banda in gaol throughout 1960 or releasing him fairly soon without conditions. They must take the second choice but Macmillan was 'ready to contemplate' constitutional talks in London. Perhaps they could manage a sequence of meetings in London and Nyasaland, and if they could keep Banda on the move for a few months this would reduce the likelihood of his stirring up serious disorder in Nyasaland. He proposed to tell Welensky that these were his tentative thoughts, that his conversations with Armitage were 'inconclusive', and that he had delayed consulting his colleagues in London until he had spoken with Welensky. But Macmillan's plans for handling the question of Banda's release with Welensky had gone awry. He had intended to raise it 'in a fairly non-committal manner' during his first visit to Salisbury and to discuss it again, and presumably more fully, on his return from Nyasaland. Indeed, from the prime minister's office point of view, 'the necessary arrangements for ensuring there [would] be time for these discussions [had] been made'.[68] His meeting with Armitage the previous evening prevented him reaching a clear decision on Banda's release which he could put to Welensky. He was able, however, to tell him he would consider very carefully the Nyasaland security situation and would keep him informed about Banda's future, although he was clear that the doctor could not be held in detention for much longer.[69] As he explained to Home, he was sorry they were 'having all this trouble' through his failure, as he saw it, to deal effectively with the Banda issue when he was with Welensky.

> My difficulty, of course, was not only the time factor but the ambivalent advice which I received from the Governor of Nyasaland and to a lesser extent from the Governor of Northern Rhodesia.[70]

In respect of Armitage's advice, Macmillan had already told Macleod he was 'rather staggered' when he arrived in Nyasaland to find the turn which events had taken and 'the entirely new proposal' to remove Banda to London under restraint. As a result, he said, he had a lot of new ground to cover and he was not able in the available time to bring Armitage to a definite decision.[71] This was unfair because the Governor and the Colonial Office had from time to time over the past six months raised the question of Banda being sent to Britain, and Armitage was not ambivalent; in fact, only 11 days earlier he had made his views on this and related points clear to Monson.[72] If indeed the idea of Banda's release to Britain was to Macmillan an 'entirely new proposal' it could only have been because Macleod had concealed from him both that this had been Armitage's strong view for some time and also that he, Macleod, had discussed the idea with the Governor.

Macmillan suspected Armitage had been persuaded against his better judgement to accept Macleod's plan in Dar es Salaam, and on returning to Zomba had been reproached by his advisers and was now trying to find a course they would accept.

> But however that may be we must take it as a fact that the Governor and his Council now consider it an unacceptable security risk to have Banda at large in Nyasaland when the Monckton Commission is there. And we must take account of Hone's anxieties about the reactions in Northern Rhodesia. If both Northern Rhodesia and Nyasaland explode together we should be in trouble. It looks as though we should then have to bring United Kingdom troops from Kenya.[73]

On the other hand Macmillan could see the obvious risks in 'hanging on without any positive policy', and suggested a 'middle course' by which they would appear to be taking a positive step towards constitutional advance.

> If we could get Banda to London as a free man we should be seen to be making an advance in that direction while at the same time meeting the Governor's fears about the security position in Nyasaland.[74]

On 1 February Armitage received a long telegram in which Macleod restated the area of agreement between them:[75] that constitutional talks should be started as soon as possible and these must be with Banda.

On the other hand, he pointed out, Armitage, his advisers, Welensky, his cabinet and Hone concluded that the security risks in releasing Banda to Nyasaland were not to be underestimated and, therefore, ought not to be accepted. Macleod was convinced that Armitage's alternative proposal of releasing Banda to London was not feasible, even though Macmillan was inclined to consider it.

> It is simply not a practicable proposition to keep Banda in play here for so long a period, however amenable he might be. Further, if he came here under any kind of restraint designed to prevent his return to the Federation (and legal basis for that is dubious), that would neither satisfy agitation for his release nor substantially reduce risk of disturbances in Nyasaland during Monckton's visit; and there would be little or no prospect of constitutional talks getting anywhere in such conditions. If he came here without restraint, there would be no effective means of stopping him from returning short of the threat of re-detention in Nyasaland (which would involve keeping on the emergency much longer than we wish).

Macleod went on to say that, having considered the problem very carefully, he, Macmillan and Home had reached 'agreed and firm conclusions':

> All this boils down to the straight proposition that the only choice lies between releasing Banda unconditionally in Nyasaland as soon as possible, or keeping him in detention and the emergency in force throughout 1960. We have concluded that on every ground the arguments for the first course are overriding. We have reached this decision from the broad standpoint of our responsibility for forwarding a solution of the problems of Central Africa, to which the political pressures in the United Kingdom are incidental.

This meant accepting, with their eyes open, the security risks as assessed by Armitage, Welensky and Hone. There was no means of avoiding them, but there might be ways of reducing them. The crucial period would be that immediately following Banda's release, and if they could get over that period and if Macleod could make some impression on the doctor during his visit, the security danger would lessen. To minimise the risk during this crucial period, they had agreed that the time between the release and Macleod's arrival should be very short so that Banda had 'as little opportunity as possible to strike public attitudes over conditions' before the secretary of state saw him. Alternatively, Banda could be released a day or so after Macleod's arrival. Armitage – as he had suggested – was to be allowed to 'predispose additional security forces within Nyasaland' to contain from the outset any local demonstrations. Macleod agreed that detainee releases should immediately be decelerated – but not below 50 a month – until they could judge the effects of Banda's release and his own visit. The plan was, therefore, to announce Macleod's visit about mid-February, to release Banda on 25 or 26 February, Macleod to arrive in Salisbury on 27 and in Zomba on 29 February, and in the meantime Armitage was to arrange reinforcements in consultation with Hone and Welensky. Macleod then added, in response to the Governor's repeated urging that they have something fairly clear to offer Banda:

> I should hope to come out with some pretty firm ideas in mind about lines on which constitutional progress might be made, and we are working on this. If preliminary talks with Banda went well and appeared to establish a basis for further discussions, it might at that point be useful to pursue the idea of a conference in London, to be timed after Monckton's visit to Nyasaland. This would help to keep Banda in play, and [induce] him to co-operate with Monckton Commission in interval, and meanwhile to keep his followers in order.

Although nothing had yet been said to Welensky, the British government were considering bringing in British troops if the situation so deteriorated that 'reinforcements from within the Federation which would be acceptable to [Britain were] soon ... exhausted'.[76] This reference to reinforcements acceptable to Britain related to Armitage's and Macleod's objections to the use of white federal troops and the BSAP. Not only was the constitutional responsibility for bringing in British troops ambiguous, but it was likely to be heavily criticised in Britain by the 'left wing and Church of Scotland' and to revive Devlin's criticisms of army actions in the early part of the emergency.[77]

Macleod concluded by assuring Armitage they had reached their decisions after 'the most anxious thought' and in full recognition of Armitage's own views on 'the difficult dilemma' which they faced, and of the 'heavy responsibility' which it placed upon the Governor. They were sure it was the 'proper, logical and courageous course'.

The contents of Macleod's cable followed very closely those of one Macmillan had sent him four days earlier from South Africa.[78] In his cable the prime minister said Macleod should consider calling a conference in London very soon after Banda's release which would then replace Macleod's proposed visit to Nyasaland.

On 2 February Home cabled Welensky to say that Macleod would arrive in Zomba on 29 February and Banda would be released just before or just after this.[79] Welensky's and Whitehead's reaction was 'very sharp';[80] they felt Banda's release meant taking uncalculated risks and insisted that Home visit Central Africa or they would go to

London.[81] The federal prime minister immediately cabled Macmillan, still in Cape Town, and said the British premier would not be surprised to learn that the message about Banda 'gravely perturbed' him.

> I know that the decision you have taken is wrong. I would have liked to believe that you did not appreciate the seriousness of it but I can not. The unanimous advice of all governments in the Federation has been against Banda's early release. The fact that your government has decided to ignore all this advice compels me to draw the conclusion – and you can imagine how reluctantly I do this – that extreme African nationalism in Nyasaland is to be appeased.[82]

Banda's release at this point, he continued, would jeopardise Monckton's work and put paid to any chance there might be of reaching a solution for keeping the Federation intact. It could only lead to the Federation's early disintegration, with all the dire consequences of which Macmillan was aware. So strongly did Welensky feel that, through holding an election on the basis of severing ties with Britain and keeping Banda away permanently, he hoped to expose publicly how the British government was acting against the strong advice of all four governments in Central Africa. Belligerently, he said that the Monckton Commission 'could go' as far as he was concerned. To Armitage, this threat amounted to Welensky 'proposing to commit suicide',[83] and – despite the 'firm conclusions' of very senior members of the British cabinet – he himself had not yet given up hope that Banda would not be returned to Nyasaland:

> I still do not think the release of Dr. Banda to U.K. has been finally thought out. He can't be the security risk there that he could be here and we should get a better chance to assess the risks.[84]

The British high commissioner in Salisbury warned the prime minister that Welensky had the support of his whole cabinet in putting forward his views and a little later, having talked with Tredgold, confirmed Whitehead's view that a referendum in Southern Rhodesia would result in a large majority in favour of secession: 'The break-up of the Federation may well start in Southern Rhodesia.'[85]

The Governor-General, too, warned of the very serious developments taking place.[86] Welensky saw him and formally said that if Banda were released his government would resign, and he would go to the country on the general theme of freedom from British control and the Banda issue in particular. If returned to power, Welensky would boycott the Monckton Commission. Dalhousie added that Whitehead had told him Banda's release would probably result in the defeat of his government and a swing towards the Dominion Party: 'In all events, if Banda is released now Southern Rhodesia could wish to secede from the Federation.'

Home advised the prime minister that the language used by Welensky and Whitehead 'must be taken seriously'[87] and a little later he told Monckton that when British intentions in Nyasaland were mentioned to them 'the roof blew off':

> A political crisis arose which, if it had broken, would have put paid not only to the work of the Monckton Commissioners but to all the progress towards a multi-racial society which we have achieved since the British came to this part of Africa.[88]

On 3 February Macleod told Armitage to make a public statement 12 days later that Banda was shortly to be released and that he, Macleod, would arrive in Salisbury on 27 February and in Nyasaland two days later. He made it quite clear he wanted Banda released and in Nyasaland before his own arrival.[89] He told Home there was 'little give in the present plan' except perhaps to postpone Banda's release for a week or two. He could not contemplate keeping him in detention until after Monckton left Nyasaland in mid-April.[90] Also:

> The Minister of Defence [Welensky] and the G.O.C. [Long] arrived in Zomba on 4 February for discussions with the Governor and other senior officials ... Immediate orders were despatched by the G.O.C. to Bulawayo for Colonel Bob Prentice to proceed to Nyasaland the following day ... to take over command of the Nyasaland area. At the same time the R.A.R. were stood to in preparation for orders to proceed to Nyasaland.[91]

The grave seriousness with which Dalhousie viewed the stance adopted by Welensky and Whitehead is illustrated by the fact that on 5 February he also flew to Nyasaland and met Armitage, to whom he confirmed this stance and with whom he discussed Home's and Macleod's visits. In telling Macleod this, the Governor stressed that it was now more important than ever for him to come to the Federation – despite Macmillan's view that this might not be necessary.[92]

The Nyasaland intelligence committee also met to consider the likely security position if Banda were released in February. They believed news of the release would produce 'overwhelming emotional reactions followed by mass demonstrations, disorderly and large illegal meetings and processions' likely to cause breaches of the peace and riots.

> African, European and Asian reactions will be that Banda and his Congress have defeated the Government. Provocative insolence, racial incidents, stone throwing, disregard of authority, coupled with flouting of laws and control orders by detainees may also be expected. Loyal

chiefs and Government servants will be dejected and will feel betrayed and discredited. There will be danger of further deterioration of police morale and possibly of some of clerical staff of KAR. Hooligan elements, possibly led by ex-detainees, will start to take action against suspected informers, 'stooges' and loyal Africans. An intensification of intimidation and physical attacks on Government installations and possibly isolated Europeans. Dislocation of communications, particularly postal and tele-graphic services should not be discounted.[93]

The committee felt that the extent to which they could confine the security reactions would depend on Banda's conduct, particularly how much he chose or was able – which they gravely doubted – to control his followers, and the firm use of security forces in sufficient strength. They hoped any initial unfavourable reactions would of their own accord die down in a week or two but they emphasised the importance of an announcement about constitutional talks being made either before or just after Banda's release since without this and unless they were satisfactory to him, 'much deeper and more serious' disturbances would occur. Alternatively, his release to Britain, rather than Nyasaland, for talks would ease the security pressure. They feared Banda's reactions were 'completely unpredictable'. Based on this assessment, the com-mittee advised that the Malawi Youth League should be proscribed and its leaders detained in order to check hooliganism and reassure the public.[94]

Having received this assessment and advice, Armitage told Macleod it was extremely important for the government to decide what its maximum concessions to Banda would be, beyond which they would not be prepared to go, and to embody these in a clear plan for con-stitutional advance.

> Until such agreement is reached, and until we have a firm basis on which to negotiate with a free Banda, any discussions on precise timing of Banda's release must necessarily be premature. I can think of nothing more disastrous than to free Banda and keep him kicking his heels while HMG, Federal Government and ourselves debate framework of a pro-gramme for constitutional advance ... The most helpful suggestion I can make is for a decision to be taken on the future territorial constitutional programme as early as possible with view to discussing with Banda in April.[95]

Macleod, however, wanted to keep his options open and give himself room to manoeuvre in response to Banda's reactions – whatever they might be – so he told Armitage he did not think it necessary before Banda was released to have 'a firm and final plan', agreed in advance with Welensky, for how far Britain was prepared to go on constitutional advance. He would, of course, have to have 'some pretty firm ideas' of the limits within which they might be able to operate, and 'enough of a political carrot' to secure Banda's cooperation. He thought it sufficient for the immediate purpose if he were to give the doctor a general indication of the kind of political progress which might now be made, together with a clear indication that – whether or not a new constitution were actually implemented before the federal review – he and some of his colleagues could expect, subject to good behaviour in the meantime, to be part of the Nyasaland representation at the review conference. He hoped this would be enough to keep Banda 'in play' and out of serious mischief at least until they could hold further discussions in London, perhaps in May or June.[96] Home was far more cautious and sceptical and told Macleod it was anyone's guess what Banda would do when released, but his own view was that:

> Banda will do a sit-down-strike until his gang are out, and refuse to co-operate in any constitutional advance. If he did that, could you dictate your own plans and get any Africans to co-operate? Probably not unless Banda was banished ... It is very difficult to see through this tangle.[97]

At the same time Macmillan cabled Home from sea on his way back from South Africa, saying that they must keep the question confined to its simple points, namely, 'Can Banda be kept indefinitely in prison?' and 'If not and he is let out can we avoid reviving the constitutional discussions which Lord Perth was about to initiate last year when the troubles broke out?'[98] Macleod had already answered both questions – which were probably rhetorical.

Armitage felt strongly that the Monckton Commission should come first and Banda be released only after they had left Nyasaland and possibly the Federation.[99] Such a course would, naturally, mean Banda would not give evidence to Monckton and nor, very likely, would any of his followers, but it would also mean Monckton's work would be less likely to be influenced by intimidation and Armitage's security problems would be lessened.

Although Home told Welensky on 12 February that no final decision to release Banda had been reached[100] and although Macmillan seemed still to be undecided, Macleod cabled Armitage the following day to say he was sticking to the plan to release him but in March when he, Macleod, would be in Nyasaland; he added that they must accept the risk of disturbances although he hoped to get Banda 'to see reason'.[101] Home assured Welensky that if Banda's release were accompanied – as the federal cabinet believed – by 'the greatest turbulence' he would be willing to return him to prison.[102] Armitage suspected Macleod had hinted that Banda would be released in the middle of February, when he spoke with a number of leading Africans, because on 14 February 'many hundreds' of people went to Chileka in the hope of welcoming the doctor back to the protectorate.[103]

Welensky's insistence on seeing Home resulted in his being invited to London on 17 February, which meant postponing the announcement (to have been made two days earlier) that Macleod would visit Nyasaland at the end of February. Even so, arrangements went ahead for organising the military dispositions required for the second half of February.[104]

The British government were much concerned by Welensky's firm line and Home asked him not to seek a postponement of the Monckton Commission until he had been to London and talked matters over with Macmillan: 'To call off the Monckton Commission now would be a very serious blow to the Tory Government.'[105] Armitage felt Welensky had, temporarily at any rate, outmanoeuvred the British government. He himself had given them all the advice and hints he could since November 1959 on the need to consult the federal government and on the importance of 'keeping in' with them.[106]

Macmillan's view, expressed to Evans on 15 February while flying from Las Palmas to London after the Africa tour, was that Banda could not be released until there was confidence in the Nyasaland administration's ability to handle the security situation.[107] This probably related as much to Jones's arrival as chief secretary as it did to having adequate security forces available. On 20 February Home told Welensky that Macleod would leave London on 28 February and arrive in Zomba, via Salisbury and Lusaka, on 6 March; Banda would be released two days later.[108]

At this time Macleod was being advised by George Loft, an American Quaker who had paid a number of visits to Gwelo gaol and had lengthy discussions with Banda, with Welensky's concurrence. For example, following earlier meetings with the doctor and correspondence with Macleod, Loft saw Banda on 25 February and on the secretary of state's behalf impressed upon him the importance of keeping Nyasaland peaceful so that constitutional talks could be held. Banda replied 'quite vigorously':

> Mr Macleod can depend on me to hold absolute peace. I can control my people. I can promise him that. Mr Macleod's people in Zomba do not believe me. If they would allow me to do what I think is necessary, there would [be] no trouble.

Banda was reluctant to accept Loft's request that he draft a suitable statement for use on his release and consider how this might best be disseminated, saying, 'I cannot issue a statement from Gwelo. Once I am out, yes, but not from Gwelo.' Loft concluded a letter to Macleod, written the day after this visit:

> It seems to me that an effort should be made to work out with Dr Banda such essentials as what he will say on release, and the basic mechanisms of his return to Nyasaland, timetabling and so forth. It may well be that Zomba is working on this. I must say, however, that while I did not probe Dr Banda on this point, I had the impression that there was nothing in the way of sustained consultation between him and Zomba on these matters.[109]

Armitage was aware of these discussions and this correspondence and knew of the several visits to Banda, but he felt that Loft's influence on the doctor might have waned since he, apparently, had given information to the press after one of his visits, much to Banda's anger.[110]

Macleod hoped to persuade Welensky to agree to Banda's release on 10 March and to start talks on a new constitution; he also hoped to persuade Banda to accept official majorities on both legislative and executive councils.[111] Armitage could not see Banda even starting discussions on that basis. The Governor was taking some comfort from the fact that 'the date of the release of Banda was being set back a little' – now from 8 to 10 March – but still he 'was obsessed with the plan to get Banda to the U.K. somehow'.[112] In discussing the release with Dixon and Blackwood he said it would have to take place at the latest in June but he would prefer it to be to Britain and 'that had not been fully explored in [his] opinion'.[113]

Instead of Welensky going to London, Home decided that the problems were so great and important that he should go to the Federation himself.[114] This was on the advice of Macmillan who had changed his mind, probably because he preferred not to face the federal and Southern Rhodesian premiers personally. Home had been strongly urged by Gibb, Governor of Southern Rhodesia, to go to Salisbury:

> We seem to be heading for a serious bust-up, and I feel it is absolutely imperative that you come out here and tell our people exactly what is in your mind.[115]

Gibb wrote this because Macmillan had left in the Southern Rhodesian government's mind the 'strongest feeling' that the British government would welcome the break up of the Federation. All the hopes they had had of the good which Macmillan's visit would do had been 'completely shattered' and there was 'a total loss of confidence' in the British government. It was vital that Home should visit Southern Rhodesia to verify these things for himself. The Governor-General also urged Home to visit Salisbury to see for himself 'the high temper of feeling out here', but Dalhousie's focus of blame was Macleod rather than Macmillan. Macleod had given the impression in Central Africa that, 'You can do anything provided your face is black.' The antagonism against Macleod was 'already considerable' and he was in danger of 'seriously jeopardis[ing] any future dealings he might have' in the Federation. Dalhousie urged that they should 'get Iain's stock a bit higher before he comes out' to the Federation.[116] Maybe it was Macleod's low stock which induced Macmillan to suggest the colonial secretary might not need to visit Central Africa.

At a cabinet meeting the day Home left for Salisbury, Macmillan told his colleagues about the main points he felt should guide the talks with Welensky and Whitehead. The note to which he spoke[117] had been prepared by Home because he was not particularly keen to go to Salisbury and he needed 'the most careful instructions [and] the authority of the cabinet as to the limits to any plan [he] might put forward'.[118] First, the prime minister said the cabinet had decided Banda should be released as soon as possible in order to be able to give evidence to Monckton and 'create the right conditions in Nyasaland for the Commission's work', and to be able to discuss constitutional advance for Nyasaland. There was, he added, difficulty in justifying Banda's continued detention. Second, he believed the security risk was as great if Banda were kept in detention as it would be were he freed. Indeed, he thought early release, talks with Macleod and evidence to Monckton would have 'a calming effect on African opinion'. If trouble erupted, Banda would be detained again. Further, the Federation's chances of securing sufficient African confidence for its survival would be greatly reduced if some early progress were not made in Nyasaland. He proposed therefore that Home should try to secure a timetable in which Macleod would go to Salisbury on 29 February, Banda would be released on 10 March, Monckton would arrive in Nyasaland on 21 March, and constitutional talks start in London on 1 June. He recognised that:

> in order to reach agreement on Dr Banda's release the Commonwealth Secretary will have to [offer] the removal of [Britain's] remaining restrictions on the Southern Rhodesian Constitution provided they were replaced by adequate constitutional safeguards [for the Africans].

This offer would be conditional on Whitehead agreeing to Banda's release early in March and to Nyasaland's constitutional advance being parallel with that of Southern Rhodesia. Slightly earlier the prime minister had told Home that he did 'not feel at all happy' about the plan to make constitutional concessions to Southern Rhodesia part of a bargain.[119] The idea of relieving Southern Rhodesia of the reserve powers had been mooted for some time: Whitehead had gone to London for this purpose in November 1959[120] and, in a guarded telephone conversation with Home on 9 February, Welensky had suggested a deal over constitutional concessions.[121] The prime minister concluded:

> It is clear that if we fail to secure agreement in Salisbury to Dr Banda's release, we shall face a most serious situation. We might then have to decide whether to release him nevertheless, and risk Southern Rhodesia breaking away from the Federation; or to agree to keep him in detention, at any rate until the Monckton Commission leaves Nyasaland, in which case the Commission's work will have been seriously affected, a grave security situation may develop, and it will be widely assumed that we have given way to pressure from the Federation and Southern Rhodesia.

In telling Armitage about the cabinet's decision Macleod said Home would have two objectives: to persuade Welensky to acquiesce in Banda's release and to agree to the holding of initial talks with him in Nyasaland. To secure these objectives two concessions would be offered: no constitutional change in Nyasaland would be implemented until after the federal review conference and constraints on the Southern Rhodesia constitution would be removed.[122]

Armitage was fearful that since the British government intended to adhere to release on 10 March, 'this may bust the Monckton Commission because of disorders'.[123] He pointed out that Banda might – as he had indicated would be the case in the absence of the release of all detainees – decline to give evidence to the commission, and he was convinced it was vitally important 'to get the Monckton Commission in the bag', and Banda could give evidence in the United Kingdom later if he could be persuaded to do so.

> It is a toss up whether a longer or shorter gap between Banda's release and the Monckton Commission's arrival in Nyasaland will lead to lesser or greater disorders. Macleod thinks he can get Banda to agree to limited constitutional advance and give evidence before the Monckton Commission. How can I disabuse him of his firmly held views? If not, can one let him come and see what happens? We have made all the representations we can. If he overrides us on timing, it is his affair. Welensky will do all he can to stop it, no doubt, but it looks as if the die has been cast in London and they will listen to no one.[124]

The press at this time reported rumours that Armitage had threatened to resign if Banda were released,[125] and when he inquired into this Macmillan was told: 'the Colonial Office … feel quite certain that there have been no public utterances by Sir Robert Armitage on these lines'.[126] Against this minute Macmillan wrote, 'I am not so sure!'[127] It is more likely that Armitage was beginning to accept the problems with a degree of resignation, and of Macleod he wrote:

> As he is doing all the driving from the back seat, one wonders if it is not time to let him come out and try his hand on the steering wheel. He obviously fancies that he is a good negotiator and if he can establish confidence with Banda well and good. But I pity Home having to sell this to Welensky and Whitehead.[128]

In any event, the resignation rumours died down fairly quickly.

Since the federal government refused to alter the dates of Monckton's arrival in Nyasaland to take place after Banda's release, the British cabinet agreed that as long as he was released in March it could be on the last day, and the visit would be planned accordingly. Armitage wanted to avoid the doctor's release while the commission was in Northern Rhodesia because, if that happened, he would not be able to call on security reinforcements since they would be needed there at the same time.[129]

There was grave disagreement in the British government over Banda's release. The Commonwealth Relations Office, under Home, supported the federal government 'who were bitterly distrustful and adamantly opposed to his release, at least while the Commission was in Nyasaland'. Macleod and the Colonial Office argued vehemently against this view, very much preferring earlier release so that Banda could give evidence as a free man, but partly for parliamentary reasons as well. Macmillan feared no reconciliation was possible and that one or other of the secretaries of state would resign; indeed, it appears he had on his table the resignation of both of them at one stage.[130]

Home spent from 19 to 26 February in Salisbury trying to resolve Banda's release.[131] Both Welensky and Whitehead reacted very strongly to the plan for release early in March. Home found the federal ministers 'uneasy and resentful', and the Europeans profoundly suspicious of Britain and 'fear[ful] that [they were] prepared to sacrifice the interests of Europeans in order to appease extreme African nationalism or for reasons of political expediency at home': the very point with which Armitage had so upset Macmillan three weeks earlier. Home reported:

> As regards Dr Banda ... they regard our hopes of dealing with him on any reasonable basis as quite illusionary. They think he is not 'negotiable' and that if released he will relentlessly crusade against Federation and in favour of secession, and that even if he does not actively foment agitation, his presence in Nyasaland will inevitably create a grave security risk. They also expect that his release will encourage the intimidation of potential 'moderate' witnesses before the Monckton Commission. They

believe that he himself, if he gave evidence ... would only put forward
violent anti-Federation views which it would be quite outside the Commission's competence to receive.

Home recognised that the 'fundamental difficulty' was the federal
ministers seeing Banda 'as a man who has no redeeming features and
who is dedicated to breaking Federation and [to] nothing else'.[132] They
did not believe he would be sidetracked by limited talks on Nyasaland
from pursuing his main aim of breaking federation. Welensky's principal worry was there might be a long period between Banda's release
and the federal review during which he could create a serious security
problem, 'which will be aggravated by feeling on both African and
European sides that we have demonstrated in our approach to Banda
that extremism pays'.[133] The federal ministers preferred Banda not to
be released to Nyasaland but 'either kept permanently in detention or
banished to the UK or elsewhere'. If this were not practicable, he
certainly should not be released before Monckton left the Federation.
They made it clear that if Banda were released before then they would
denounce Britain's actions, they might demand the commission's withdrawal from the Federation, and Welensky might resign and go to the
country on a platform of independence from Britain. Home countered
that if Banda were not released to take part in constitutional talks as
a free man it might well be that after the constitutional review the
British parliament would find it impossible to continue federation in
the face of implacable Nyasaland African hostility. Mainly by using
this point and 'every device of patience and argument',[134] he was able
to secure agreement that Banda should be released on 6 April: several
days after Monckton arrived, so that moderate African opinion could
be put, but several days before they left, so that Banda could give
evidence as a free man.

The federal government's acquiescence, Home reported, was 'utterly
against all their feelings which are deeply, however wrongly, held'.[135]
In agreeing to this Welensky asked if Macleod's arrival in Zomba
could follow, rather than precede, the release so that it might not
appear that the two were directly connected.[136] Macleod firmly rejected
this request:[137] he would arrive in Nyasaland towards the end of March.
Home believed Welensky accepted the compromise because he realised
he was 'on the brink of a political abyss'. In exchange, Home agreed
that the Nyasaland constitution would not go beyond that already
agreed for Northern Rhodesia, the new constitution would not be put
into operation until after the federal review, and constraints on the
Southern Rhodesia constitution would be almost entirely removed.
Although the cabinet, including Macleod, agreed on 23 February to

Banda's release after Monckton left Nyasaland – a course which they believed to be 'inescapable'[138] – Macleod had told his colleagues that while it might be necessary to delay Banda's release this would 'greatly increase his [own] difficulties' in discharging his responsibilities as secretary of state for the colonies and he would 'have to consider the implication of such a decision on the conduct of colonial policy in Africa'.[139] Macmillan, thus threatened with Macleod's resignation, anxiously cabled Home on 23 February:

> For your private (repeat private) information we are having serious difficulties here ... we are going to have great trouble in persuading our friend that he can personally, honourably continue in view of his known attitudes and public statements. It is vital – for obvious reasons – that you should keep this point entirely to yourself.[140]

Macleod and Macmillan were much relieved by Home's success in achieving the compromise with Welensky and Whitehead. This 'Macleod felt would save his face sufficiently' and he wrote to Home, saying, 'Many congratulations on your success. I am sure you understand how much it means to me personally and to us all in government' and he told Macmillan he was 'content and deeply happy with the arrangement'.[141]

In order to impress on his cabinet colleagues the seriousness of the difficulties, Home emphasised the general conclusions which he had drawn:

> The reports of the jittery state of mind of the Europeans in the Federation are in no way exaggerated. They see and fear the advance of extreme African nationalism on their northern border, and if Nyasaland is to 'become a Ghana' there are very many Europeans in Southern Rhodesia who would rather go it alone or even throw their lot in with the Union [of South Africa].[142]

He also said that they were 'now at the crunch' and he impressed upon Macmillan that his advice – on an early April release – was 'decisive':

> Either we accept this situation and present and play this hand as best we can or Federation breaks now and we lose for good all our white friends in this part of Africa. That would, on this issue of a few weeks, never be forgiven.[143]

To Home it was increasingly evident that Britain's 'critical problem' in maintaining the Federation was that any advance in Nyasaland and Northern Rhodesia which came anywhere near satisfying the Africans that their political aspirations were not being frustrated by the mere

fact of being in the Federation, might well scare Southern Rhodesia
out of the Federation: 'We must hope that the Monckton Commission
will find some way for us to steer our policy through this dilemma.'[144]

Home had secured a major advance because when he arrived
Welensky presented him with a full written statement of the federal
government's reasons for not releasing Banda, which 'revealed an
absolute gulf between us', so much so that he feared he might as well
go straight back to Britain.[145] He also succeeded with Whitehead, whom
he said they were right to have anticipated as being 'the main
obstacle'.[146] When Home told him what the British government wished
to do in Nyasaland the Southern Rhodesia prime minister promptly
retorted:

> I tell you straight, that if you release Banda in Nyasaland, Southern
> Rhodesia will blow up and I shan't be able to stop them.[147]

Only two of his supporters had to cross the floor to put the Dominion
Party in power and Britain then, by their own act, would have achieved
not only the secession of Southern Rhodesia but also union with South
Africa. At this point Home asked if European confidence could be
restored if, as part of a comprehensive plan, restraints on the Southern
Rhodesia constitution were removed. Whitehead's response was very
positive: 'That would make all the difference in the world, but it must
be done quickly and completely.' A little later he told Home that so
far as the Southern Rhodesia electorate was concerned, what Britain
was proposing to do in Nyasaland by releasing Banda early in April
'may prove to be the last straw', but if they could remove the remaining
restrictions on the constitution it might help to restore public confidence and make it easier 'to dissuade the electorate from doing
anything hasty before the Federation Conference'.[148]

As Armitage recorded:

> This could have been arranged long ago ... if we had not been faced by
> Macleod saying that the Cabinet decision on 4 January had been to
> release Banda on 29 January. The new date nearly reaches my first day
> of compromise, mid-April ... I can't imagine I can get any further
> advance on this except that I would like to release him on a Monday, i.e.
> 4 April.[149]

He felt crowds were less likely to gather on a working day, Monday,
than at a weekend; also he was concerned that release this particular
weekend, following the end of month pay-day for labour, 'would inevitably increase one hundred fold [the] risk of disorders accompanied
by drunkenness'.[150] Even at this late stage the Governor pressed that
release should be to London:

As you know we have always advocated release to the United Kingdom. Is this finally and irrevocably out of the question? We are still strongly in favour of it as opposed to release here.[151]

It is not clear that it was finally and irrevocably out of the question because during March the Colonial Office legal advisers were asked whether Banda could be deported from the Federation and, if so, could he also be prevented from returning there? They advised that there was no existing legislation permitting either of these.[152] Lennox-Boyd had, of course, sought advice precisely on these questions nine months earlier.

Armitage was aware at the time that if the compromise had not been reached, either Macleod or Home would have resigned, resulting in a cabinet split:

All of [this] is so unnecessary. Macleod had agreed with me in Dar es Salaam to put the accelerated release of detainees only, and Banda not treated differently to the others, to the Cabinet. He obviously got the Cabinet on 4 January, on the eve of Macmillan's departure, to agree to extra accelerated release of detainees and Banda out at the end of January, all without consulting Welensky, a thing Leslie Monson and he would not think of doing in Dar es Salaam.[153]

Contemplating these affairs, Armitage wrote in his diary, 'What a worrying life!' and looking back over what had happened since early January:

I find it clear how determined Macleod was to get his way, bullying his Cabinet and trying to ride roughshod over Welensky and Whitehead. This course of action provoked Welensky into making the extravagant claims of breaking with Her Majesty's Government and going it alone with the Federal Government. This perturbed me and made me wonder whether he would not try to take possession of Nyasaland. A lot of other people got very agitated with all these ideas flying about.[154]

At the beginning of March the Governor wrote: 'So we start the great move to see whether we can contain the Monckton Commission, Macleod's visit and Banda's release all at the same time! The Federal Government reckon we can't and I suspect Her Majesty's Government feel we shall fall down on all this.'[155] He was right: as we have seen, Macmillan was 'somewhat concerned' about the way the Nyasaland administration might handle disturbances following Banda's release. The prime minister feared a repetition of what Devlin thought they had done a year earlier and of what he, Macmillan, thought – or pretended to think – they had done outside Ryalls Hotel a month earlier.

Throughout March, much of Armitage's time and thought were devoted to considering Banda's release, when and how it was to be done and the security implications of doing it. He had already told Monson he wished to keep the release secret because prior notification would enable Congress to stage demonstrations that might be widespread and so disperse the security forces. He realised this would deprive Congress of the opportunity to warn their supporters to behave themselves and secrecy over this matter might cause some resentment. 'We feel, however, that jubilation at his return will inevitably overshadow any possible feeling of resentment.'[156] Macleod was less inclined to keep arrangements of the release completely secret because he told Home he would like to tell Foot of them[157] – and this notwithstanding that he did not regard Foot as trustworthy. Home and Alport were 'rather uneasy' about Macleod's wish and advised against it, especially since they had been 'badly shaken' by Foot's misrepresentation of an interview he had had with Monckton, 'as well as other indiscretions'.[158] Macleod also considered, towards the end of March, whether he should tell the 'press inner circle' in London about the release, but decided not to although he did ask Perth to let Oliver Woods personally 'into the picture' on the morning of the release[159] 'in order to get Times [sic] comment right' the following day. Woods, in fact, personally regarded Banda as 'a very dangerous if not evil man'.[160]

On 2 March Macleod announced he would visit the Federation from 13 March to 9 April, and made it clear to Armitage he expected to meet Banda soon after his release. The Governor wondered if there might be demonstrations on 3 March, the anniversary of the declaration of a state of emergency – as Finney had warned – but these were now unlikely, he thought, because the prospect of Banda's release on that day had 'retreated' in the public's mind. Even so he had his police ready for trouble but warned them 'to be cautious in the use of force': he had been criticised previously for police over-zealousness. Finney attributed the absence of demonstrations to Congress having an 'inkling of what might happen' while the secretary of state was in the protectorate: Banda's release. Alternatively, he thought Orton Chirwa was very confident, after what Macleod had told him in London in December, that even if Banda were not released in February, as they had expected, he was bound to be released before Monckton arrived on 21 March. Far from an increase in tension, there was a decrease and the intelligence committee attributed this to the recent announcement of Macleod's intended visit and the people's confidence in Banda's release before Monckton arrived.[161]

Details of how the release and Banda's return to Nyasaland were to be effected were now being worked out, and Armitage assumed he would be delivered to Government House, meet Macleod and then go to Limbe for the weekend. It was clear that a 'very elaborate programme [would] have to be organised', and detailed work on this began after the secretary of state's plans on his arrival were telegraphed to Armitage on 9 March.[162] Jones was sent to Southern Rhodesia on the same day 'to see Banda and find out what he is now thinking'. He saw him 'and all the others' for three and a quarter hours, but discovered nothing more about Banda's position and thinking than Footman had done earlier.[163] Macleod thought that if Banda met him and the Governor at Government House this 'would give him too much kudos' but Armitage did not think so.[164] It may be that the secretary of state felt meeting at Government House would also give the Governor too much kudos. Macleod proposed as an alternative the chief secretary's office but Armitage again disagreed, pointing to its exposed position and the large number of people working there who would immediately recognise the doctor, and excited crowds would quickly gather 'which would be unlikely to make for profitable and balanced discussion'; demonstrations and noise would 'mar the effect of [the] talks'.[165] When the Governor strongly advised against the secretariat, Macleod accepted his arguments and then suggested police headquarters.[166] Once more Armitage disagreed and argued that since Banda must be a free man when he met the secretary of state, to do so at police headquarters would be 'psychologically wrong', as this would suggest some sort of continued restraint. Furthermore, Banda might blame any failure of subsequent talks on the venue of the initial meeting. Armitage told Macleod:

> The point as we see it is that kudos accruing to Banda will stem from the fact of his coming straight from prison to meet with you and the Governor. I feel that his being summoned to meet with you and me at Government House will be accepted by Banda in the right spirit and be accepted by all as being the proper line to take. A meeting anywhere else might in fact confer additional kudos upon him in that it will be interpreted as the mountain going to Mohammed.[167]

Finney's prediction that there would be no demonstrations when the Monckton Commission arrived in Nyasaland on 21 March was accurate, although there was an isolated incident at Mlanje and a number of worries about security in Fort Manning.[168] Armitage had a talk with Monckton giving him 'a general background on affairs, some ideas on the problems and why we had them, and also on some solutions'.

Monckton is very annoyed and so are his commissioners, that Macleod should come out and discuss Nyasaland affairs and that Southern Rhodesian affairs should also be discussed before the Monckton Commission has reported. They don't want to have anything to do with Macleod here ... [Monckton] knows of Banda's release and is horrified and wonders what his commissioners will say when they hear. He obviously wants to meet him but appreciates he is unlikely to be prepared to give evidence in Nyasaland, but might indicate willing[ness] to do so in U.K.[169]

On 23 March Armitage met the official members of executive council and spoke of the recently resolved crisis in the cabinet 'caused by Macleod's desires on Banda' and added that they could not now hope to alter the compromise reached, since Macleod would have to resign in order for this to happen.

Most of us, I think, recognised that we ought to keep Banda away for a year or so, until we had the new constitutional pattern accepted and he could come back in this framework. As that appeared impossible, it was a question of time. We would like to keep him away until June and give less time to play with him before the Federal Review. But that would compromise the Queen Mother's visit. So it really came down to April ... We agreed that we should approach Banda in the spirit of forget the past and let us work together for the future. But we recognised we had no constitutional pattern which we could attract him with, so how could we hold him? ... He may go early to the U.K. and U.S.A. That would keep him away, but what would his followers do? So we go round in the circle of not being able to reach any final agreement which we think likely to contain him.[170]

He concluded this diary entry with the words: 'How could we plan when we might be out of the Federation in a short time?'

A 'constitutional pattern' was sent by Macleod to Armitage on 26 March[171] in which he gave his views on changes for discussion with Welensky and Whitehead and then Banda: the retention of an official majority and reduction of non-Africans to three in the legislature. This seemed to Armitage to suit neither Welensky nor Banda, and he was worried that Banda would be freed and would reject all changes of this sort and thereby leave Macleod with no room to manoeuvre. He concluded: 'One can do little except build on Banda's honesty and capability.'[172]

The Monckton Commission arrived in Nyasaland on 21 and Macleod on 29 March.[173] When the secretary of state met Welensky in Salisbury on his way to Nyasaland he said his approach was to get Banda back into circulation and immediately involved in constitutional talks 'to keep him occupied'. He was not starry-eyed about Banda nor optimistic that he would prove a satisfactory leader, but banished or detained he would always be a threat to the Federation and that way there would be no chance of political contentment in Nyasaland. If Banda proved intransigent he would have to be restrained again. On the other hand there was a prospect that if, through this move, a middle way could be found 'between European fears and African aspirations' the economic advantages of federation for Nyasaland 'might begin to exert some attraction on the African mind'.[174] In a meeting with Whitehead, Macleod tried repeatedly to discuss Banda's release and its timing but the Southern Rhodesian prime minister avoided the issue, preferring to talk about 'his social and economic problems and the excellence of his police force'. Macleod got the impression Whitehead was intent on wringing the maximum political advantage out of their difficulties.[175]

The scene was now fully set for Banda's release. Armitage had pushed the date as far back as he could and had moved it from late January until mid-February, then late March and now 1 April. He was still much concerned about the possibility of violence, and his non-official advisers and Welensky were convinced there would be bloodshed. Blackwood later said: 'The risk of violence being renewed was considerable but ... the Federal Forces could have controlled it easily enough.' The Governor's official advisers were much less sure.[176] The combination of the Monckton commission's presence, the arrival of the secretary of state for constitutional talks, and Banda's release, could have been an explosive mixture, difficult to control, and Armitage was pleased Northern Rhodesia had agreed to let him have police reinforcements.[177] Irrespective of the fears of others, Macleod was determined to take the risks involved and try to persuade Banda to keep the African population peaceful.

The federal government cooperated fully in the mechanics of the release although Welensky made it clear his government dissociated itself from the decision to release Banda and accepted no responsibility for it. Theunissen twice flew to Southern Rhodesia to undertake the detailed planning with the head of FISB and the director of the prison service.[178]

On 30 March the Governor and the secretary of state held a meeting at Government House, attended by the provincial commissioners and the most senior provincial police officers. For at least one of these officers it was:

a disagreeable experience ... Macleod was gratuitously offensive to the Governor in front of the six of us. Macleod also criticised [the provincial commissioner of the Central Province] about some incident and was not

prepared to listen to [his] reply. [Another provincial commissioner] ...
was not personally an object of Macleod's venom but ... took a strong
dislike to him ... I do not forgive Macleod's treatment of the Governor
on that occasion nor his treatment of [the provincial commissioner].
Macleod looked evil – an unfair statement I dare say – but I took a great
dislike to him ... as an individual, not because of the policy he advocated.[179]

The following day, Macleod, Armitage and probably Jones had a
meeting with Dixon and Blackwood at Government House. Codrington, whose function was to take notes of the meeting, recalled Armitage
said very little, as did Dixon who simply followed the line being taken
by Blackwood. Macleod's attitude towards Blackwood and Dixon
throughout was aggressive and boorish. Halfway through the meeting
Blackwood said something to the effect that things would be better in
Nyasaland if the Conservative Party in the United Kingdom were not
divided on the policy to adopt. This remark touched Macleod on a
raw nerve and he lost control of himself, shouting at Blackwood, 'What
the blazes are you talking about, Blackwood? You mind your own
bloody business.' There was a long silence while he cooled down.
Blackwood did not respond – just turned a bit pink. Armitage looked
embarrassed but did not speak.[180] As with Macmillan two months
earlier, Armitage was hurt by Macleod's 'cold indifference'.[181] Kettlewell also recalled Macleod's attitude:

> I met him ... at an evening meeting with official members of Executive
> Council ... after dinner at Government House the day Macleod arrived.
> He surprised and antagonised us all – on this his first visit to Nyasaland
> – by virtually ignoring his audience. He asked no questions and sought
> no opinions from those present, but simply announced what he was
> going to do regarding the release of detainees.[182]

Just before retiring for the night Macleod sent a cable to Macmillan
in which he brought the prime minister up to date with his activities
and he hoped, if all went well, to meet Banda early the following
morning. He was quite convinced the course being adopted was the
right one although 'on this, as indeed every other single subject, every
member of every deputation [he had] met expressed diametrically
opposed views'. He added: 'I dare say if I lived here for long I would
change my mind every few minutes.'[183]

The task of bringing Banda back to Nyasaland fell to Youens. His
instructions were that Banda was to be removed from Gwelo and
produced in Zomba without anybody, particularly the press, getting at
him first; to this end there was 'a very complicated exercise' mounted
with the Royal Rhodesian Air Force.[184] No flight plan was lodged for

the flight back to Nyasaland; air traffic control were simply told that an aircraft giving a single call sign would enter the control zone at the Tete beacon and must be given priority. The area had to be kept clear until the RRAF Dakota had landed.[185]

> I went down under an assumed name [Ian Young of the Federal Power Board] to Gwelo and Hawkins, who subsequently became Marshal of the RRAF produced a plane in which he was going to fly Banda and me from the Gwelo airport at dawn. We had to get him out of the gaol first, I remember, and we did this – there were all sorts of reporters all round the gaol because they believed that something was going to happen, so we carried out the old hoary trick of putting someone the same age as Banda with this Anthony Eden hat and [dark] spectacles into a staff car and driving that out of the prison. Inevitably, of course, the Press dashed after the car, and Banda was removed in a [laundry] van and he was produced [by the prison authority] at Gwelo airport at dawn. I went up to him – I'd always been very friendly with him and of course we had always got on very well together when I'd known him before he was put in gaol, but I admit when I went up to greet him on that dark morning of 1 April, I had certain feelings of, not apprehension, but slightly uncomfortable. I said, 'Good morning Dr Banda, do you remember me?' And then he peered at me and burst out laughing. He said, 'Of course I do! You did the greatest possible kindness to me that any man has ever done when you put me in gaol. I shall never forget you and I shall always remember you and I shall always be thankful to you.' And he burst into roars of laughter and we had really a very cheerful trip back.

Youens told Banda on the plane that he was being flown to Zomba to be released there although the doctor seemed already to have worked this out for himself. Youens's account was complemented by another officer who had helped to plan the release:[186]

> On 31 March 1960 Youens flew to Salisbury by regular flight and, if asked, was to say that he was going to a routine meeting. At Salisbury he was met by an RRAF officer who [flew] him that evening to [Thornhill airfield near] Gwelo. During the night Youens [and Donovan, federal secretary for law] went to Gwelo prison and [the next morning met Banda. They then flew from Gwelo to Salisbury]. From the non-public side of Salisbury airport – the military side – they flew in a [military] Dakota to Chileka arriving at 8.00 a.m.: Banda, Youens and a prison officer. Captain Florence of Central African Airways had been asked to have a charter [Beaver] ready to fly to Lilongwe.

This small plane was positioned with a private car next to the threshold of the runway. The very few people who were able to observe these happenings believed that those getting off the Dakota were transferred to the car and departed via an emergency exit in the perimeter fence.

In fact, Banda, Youens and the prison officer boarded the Beaver at a secluded place and flew, not to Lilongwe, but to Zomba. At Zomba airfield, which was the turf club, two cars were waiting: one with Leonard, district commissioner of Zomba, driving it and the other driven by Theunissen.

> Banda, Youens and the prison officer got into Theunissen's Chevrolet and the aircraft went to the far side of the airfield and revved furiously so that young boys who were watching would look at the plane and not at Banda et al. They drove, followed by Leonard in his 'back-up' car, into Zomba and stopped outside Theunissen's house where he handed Banda's release warrant, previously signed by the Governor, to the prison officer who left the car and went into the house. Banda was effectively a free man from that moment. The aircraft flew on to Lilongwe and then back to Chileka. Theunissen, Youens and Banda drove to Government House, arriving at 09.03 on 1 April 1960. Banda thus arrived at Government House a free man. When someone in the car joked about the date being All Fools' Day Banda said it was All Freedom Day.

What happened on the day of Banda's release was also recorded in Armitage's private diary for 1 April 1960:[187]

> We got through this morning with no [public] hint of Banda's release. A bright morning and so no danger to the aircraft, which landed at Zomba ... Banda was brought to Government House by Youens and Theunissen. Youens went with him to [the private secretary's] flat where he had a bath and shaved and had breakfast. Then shortly after 10 a.m. he came down to see Macleod and me in my office. We exchanged a lot of pleasantries and then broached the subject of constitutional talks, etc., with a later meeting with the Malawi Congress Party. Banda seemed to bear no resentment against any of us and said he had been well treated in Gwelo, was pleased that Youens met him. Just after 11 a.m. he went back to [the private secretary's] flat and at 11.15 a.m. Orton Chirwa and Aleke Banda were brought by Jones ... to meet him. They had been asked to come over to see the Chief Secretary and had no idea of what was in store. They all came down and then [Macleod] asked Banda whether he would like to broadcast a message of peace, which he had stressed throughout. This he agreed to do ... after Orton Chirwa had introduced him.

Banda's message, which he was 'persuaded' to record before he left at 11.45 a.m. for broadcasting later,[188] was short and helpful. Armitage was 'surprised' that the doctor agreed to make this message.[189]

> I'm back. His Excellency the Governor and the Secretary of State brought me back from Gwelo today and I have had a very, very friendly discussion with them here this morning. Tomorrow at their invitation

I'll be back at Government House to begin preliminary discussions on our Constitution and they have assured me that, if everything is calm in the country, we will have a round table conference. And so I want to add: peace.

Codrington, who was again present as a note-taker when Banda arrived at Government House from Gwelo, recalled that Armitage was amicable, relaxed and again said little. Banda, polite and happy, also said very little. The contrast in Macleod's demeanour between the previous day and now was very marked. The day before he had been dominant, rude and angry. Now he was sickeningly and effusively friendly, deferring to Banda and greeting him with an artificial and exaggerated handshake with both hands.[190] On the other hand Macleod told his colleagues on 4 April that Banda was 'immensely vain and very ignorant' and would show up very badly if he were questioned critically in public.[191] Youens gained the distinct impression that Jones, 'if not disgruntled was certainly not gruntled' not to be involved in Banda's release except to be asked to go to Government House during the late morning.[192] Jones would have known of, and possibly regretted, Armitage's rejection of the suggestion that Banda meet the Governor and the colonial secretary in his, Jones's, office in the secretariat.

Armitage was relieved the release had been accomplished easily and smoothly and 'things were going well'. The first statement of Banda's release was made by the Nyasaland information department at 10.30 a.m.[193] The statement had already been prepared and by a previously arranged signal authority to release it was given by Theunissen to the chief information officer.[194] When Armitage tried to listen to the one o'clock news on the radio he found that 'sunspots had blanketed all radio communications South of the Sahara' and he felt divine providence had undoubtedly helped him because it was several hours before the news reached outsiders. The evening radio news reported that all was quiet and he was appreciative of the effectiveness of Banda's 'slow infiltration into circulation'.[195] Macleod was 'very obviously relieved when it became clear that the release had not led to widespread disorder – he was unusually flushed and talkative at dinner that night',[196] and he told Macmillan that it was 'a great relief now to have the little man out of gaol'.[197] The secretary of state's private secretary had 'a clear memory of Macleod being in a high state of what might be called relieved tension on the evening of the release when it became clear that there would not be any ... major disturbance'.[198] They finished the day noisily at Government House with Macleod 'hurling cushions across the room in the style of a rugby scrum-half' with the Governor – less enthusiastically – retrieving them.[199]

In releasing Banda, Armitage took the first and most important step in breaking the impasse which declaring the state of emergency and proscribing Congress had created. Macleod spent the next few days in a fast succession of visits. On 5 April Orton Chirwa handed over the president-generalship of the Malawi Congress Party to Banda and the next day the doctor, on his own initiative – although Armitage had for a while thought it likely – flew from Chileka to visit London and the United States.[200] At the airport before leaving, Banda bade the people of Nyasaland to 'behave like ladies and gentlemen' adding, 'If you do as I tell you [Macleod] will be able to help us, because I trust him.'[201] Macleod felt there was good reason to hope Banda's lieutenants would obey his instructions to keep the country quiet in his absence.[202] The lieutenants in question were Orton Chirwa and Aleke Banda because Chipembere and the Chisizas were still in gaol and Chiume still in Britain.

Banda was away from Nyasaland for a month and during this time, on 29 April, the ban on public meetings, imposed when the emergency was declared, was lifted.[203] On 10 May the attorney-general introduced into legislative council bills which enabled the Governor to end the emergency but to continue the detention of certain people already detained.[204] The way was now clear for Armitage to end the state of emergency, and this he did on 16 June.[205] The previous day he had brought the new legislation into force[206] and this enabled him to continue to detain the 20 remaining people who were still in detention.[207] These included Chipembere and the two Chisizas whose release, both Macmillan and Macleod agreed, 'would again endanger the safety of the country'.[208]

> They are men whose record, including their behaviour in detention, shows no sign of readiness to abide by constitutional methods. Their release at this moment would allow them to exercise malign influence over Banda and in consequence lead to disruption of [the] present peaceful state of affairs in Nyasaland.[209]

As a result of his discussions with Banda in the first few days of April, the secretary of state had concluded that there were just sufficient grounds to justify him in holding a constitutional conference during the summer. There were fears by the British, federal and Nyasaland governments that if the London talks broke down there would be an outburst of violence in Nyasaland, and discussions were held to handle this. Welensky's forces would be fully stretched because he needed to arm the Northern Rhodesia border with the Congo, where severe disorders had broken out. Armitage was opposed to any reinforcements by federal troops because it might affect negotiations with Banda. Macmillan offered British military assistance but Welensky objected since they would, it seemed, be answerable to Armitage rather than to the federal prime minister.[210]

The conference opened at Lancaster House on 25 July and its purpose was to advise Macleod on the next stage of constitutional advance. On 4 August it ended with all delegates agreeing to the final report.[211] As Macmillan confessed in congratulating Macleod on the conference's success: 'with all our troubles and difficulties it is rather encouraging when something goes right'.[212] In essence this agreement was that the executive council should be advisory and number ten: three non-official members of the legislature elected on the lower roll – effectively Africans – and two on the higher roll – probably Europeans – and there should be five officials, including the Governor as president. This composition of executive council was precisely that which Macleod sought as his 'opening bid'.[213] All members should have ministerial status. Also, the legislature should have five official members, 20 lower roll and eight upper roll non-officials. This composition of legislative council had rather more African and rather fewer non-African seats than Macleod had in mind, and had no government nominees which he had in mind as his 'opening bid'.[214] There were also agreed safeguards for, or agreements on, the judiciary, fundamental rights, the civil service, local government and the chiefs.[215] All delegates stated their intention to make the new constitution work and their recognition that a reasonable trial period was necessary for stability, a stability upon which economic, social and constitutional progress could be based.[216]

A week after the conference ended Armitage went on leave and Jones took over as Acting Governor.[217] Banda shortly issued a statement in which he said unequivocally, 'I denounce violence and intimidation just as anyone else and all members of my party are aware of my views on this point.'[218] This statement enabled Jones to announce the cancellation of all control orders and the release of all remaining detainees.[219] Although formally the emergency had ended in June, the final releases on 27 September 1960[220] marked in clear terms the practical ending of the emergency. The crisis was resolved.

Notes

1. The seeds of crisis

1. For a compact account of the background to closer association, see J.R.T. Wood, *The Welensky Papers: A History of the Federation of Rhodesia and Nyasaland* (Durban: Graham Publishing, 1983), Chapters 1–3.

2. Colin Baker, *Development Governor, a Biography of Sir Geoffrey Colby* (London: British Academic Press, 1994), Chapter 13.

3. *Nyasaland Times,* 8 March 1951.

4. *Central Africa Territories: Report of a Conference on Closer Association, London, March 1951,* Cmnd. 8233 (London: HMSO, 1951).

5. *Nyasaland Times,* 22 November 1951.

6. Referred to in CO. 1015/2118, Lennox-Boyd to Armitage, 16 June 1958, and in draft brief for Secretary of State for meeting with Nyasaland African Congress delegation on 13 June 1958.

7. *Report of the Nyasaland Commission of Inquiry,* Cmnd. 814 (London: HMSO, 1959), para. 24.

8. M.W.K. Chiume to author, 19 August 1994.

9. Ibid.

10. CO. 1015/1513, Nyasaland Situation Report No. 2, January 1957, IV.X.NA., reporting on Lennox-Boyd's January 1957 visit.

11. A.B. Doig to author, 26 July 1994.

12. Cmnd. 814, para. 26; Wood, op. cit., p. 604.

13. Nyasaland, Federation of Rhodesia and Nyasaland (Constitution) Order in Council, 1953, section 99.

14. T.M. Franck, *Race and Nationalism* (London: George Allen and Unwin, 1960), p. 302.

15. Banda, evidence to Commission of Inquiry (hereafter evidence) 16 May 1959, Devlin Papers (hereafter DP), Box 14, p. 1710 *et seq.*

16. T.D.T. Banda is referred to as such in this book to distinguish him from Dr Hastings Kamuzu Banda who is referred to as Dr Banda, the doctor, or simply Banda. D.K. Chisiza is referred to as such, or Dunduzu Chisiza or simply Chisiza, to distinguish him from his brother, Y. Chisiza, who is referred to as such or as Yatuta Chisiza. Except where the context makes it clear, Wellington Chirwa and Orton Chirwa are referred to by their initials or first names.

17. CO. 1015/2118, Draft Brief for the Secretary of State for Meeting with Nyasaland African Congress Delegation on 13 June, dated 12 June 1958; R. Welensky, *Welensky's 4000 Days* (London: Collins, 1964), p. 96.

18. CO. 1015/1513, Situation Report No. 5, October 1958. See also Armitage Papers (hereafter AP), Armitage Memoirs (hereafter AM 1957), p. 69.

19. Cmnd. 814, paras 29 and 30. Later, Armitage said, 'Again, on the secretary

of state's instructions, I promised new constitutional policies by early 1959': Maxine Baker to author, 30 May 1991.

20. CO. 1015/2118, Note of meeting between Secretary of State and Nyasaland African Congress Delegation, 13 June 1958; CO. 1015/2118, Secretary of State to Officer Administering the Government of Nyasaland, 16 June 1958; Welensky, op. cit., p. 97; Rhodes House Library (hereafter RHL.), Mss. Brit.Emp. s. 527/1, p. 66.

21. AM 1958, p. 51; RHL. Mss. Brit.Emp. s. 527/1, pp. 45–6 and p. 66.

22. H.G. Graham-Jolly to author, 5 December 1994; CO. 1015/1513, Situation Report No. 5, October 1959.

23. Cmnd. 814, para. 46. In this book the spelling of place names follows that used at the relevant time and no attempt has been made to change them to their present form: e.g. Cholo and Mlanje are so spelled, as in colonial days, rather than Thyolo and Mulanje as in their modern form. Similarly the colonial names are used rather than the modern Malawian names: e.g. Fort Hill rather than Chitipa, Port Herald rather than Nsanje and Fort Johnston rather than Mangochi.

24. Welensky, op. cit., p. 98; P. Short, *Banda* (London: Routledge and Kegan Paul, 1974), p. 89. There is some evidence that Welensky wanted to try and prevent Banda's return: Maxine Baker to author, 30 May 1991.

25. E.E. Bailey to author, 23 February 1995.

26. Finney, evidence 12 May 1959, DP, Box 14, p. 1405; PREM. 11/3082, Armitage to Macleod, 6 December 1960.

27. R. Mushet to author, February 1995.

2. The crisis gathers

1. Chisiza, evidence 18 May 1959, DP, Box 12A, pp. 2001–36.

2. Welensky, op. cit., p. 98; Short, op. cit., p. 90; *Despatch from the Governor of Nyasaland*, Cmnd. 815 (London: HMSO, 1959), para. 48.

3. Nicholson, evidence 11 May 1959, DP, Box 14, p. 1319.

4. Welensky, op. cit., p. 98; Cmnd. 814, para. 51; CO. 1015/1513, Situation Report No. 5, October 1958; Chisiza to Armitage, 7 March 1959, Kellock Papers (hereafter KP), Box 2, file 12.

5. Short, op. cit., pp. 91–2; R. Punter to author, 22 January 1996.

6. C.W.H. Sanders to author, 10 October 1994. Crowds of 10,000 and more were not infrequent: H.S. Peters to author, November 1994.

7. AM, 1958, pp. 59–60; AP, Armitage letters (hereafter AL), 5 September 1959; AL, Armitage to Haworth, 8 September 1958; Chisiza to Armitage, 7 March 1959, KP, Box 2, file 12. Except where otherwise stated, all Armitage letters are to his mother.

8. T.R. Wade to B.M. de Quehen, 13 October 1958, privately held.

9. Ibid.

10. Ibid.

11. J.H. Ingham, Note of a discussion between the Secretary for African Affairs and Dr Hastings Banda on 24 October 1958, dated 25 October 1958, DP, Box 5; KP, Box 3, file 20; Short, op. cit., pp. 93–5; Wood, op. cit., p. 631.

12. Banda, evidence 16 May 1959, DP, Box 14, p. 1704.

13. Ingham, Note of a discussion between the Secretary for African Affairs and Dr Hastings Banda on 24 October 1958, dated 25 October 1958, DP, Box 5.

14. Ibid.

15. *Nyasaland Times*, 28 and 31 October 1958.

16. AL, 1 November 1958.

17. B. Jackson, private memoirs (hereafter Jackson), p. 49; Short, op. cit., pp. 96–7.

18. Wood, op. cit., p. 630.

19. AL, Armitage to Haworth, 26 October 1958.

20. J.E. Clements to author, March 1995.

21. J. Cotton to author, 18 February 1995.

22. Graham-Jolly to author, 15 December 1994 and Punter to author, 22 January 1996.

23. Chiume, memorandum to the Colonial Secretary, 3 February 1959, KP, Box 2, file 13; AL, 20 October 1958; L.M. Llewelyn to author, 21 November 1994; Llewelyn to author, 8 November 1994; *Nyasaland Times*, 28 October 1958.

24. Mrs N. Finney to author, 2 April 1995; *Nyasaland Government Staff Lists*, 1958 and 1959; Finney, evidence 12 May 1959, DP, Box 14, pp. 1385–1411; AM, 1958, p. 30 and 1959, p. 11.

25. Late Question, No. 36, Preparation of Sunrise Lists, response prepared by Finney, 4 June 1959, DP, Box 24, No. 5.

26. All African People's Conference, Accra, Bulletin Vol. 1, No. 4, issued by conference secretariat, p. 2, para. 10: KP, Box 2, file 18.

27. Chiume to author, 19 August 1994.

28. Wade to author, 6 January 1995.

29. E.S. Munger, *President Kamuzu Banda of Malawi* (American Universities Field Staff Report, Central and Southern Africa Series, Vol. 7, No. 4, 1959), p. 14, cited in C. McMaster, *Malawi: Foreign Policy and Development* (London: Julian Friedmann, 1974), p. 28.

30. Wood, op. cit., p. 633.

31. Finney, evidence 12 May 1959, DP, Box 14, pp. 1403–4.

32. Short, op. cit., p. 104.

33. Cmnd. 814, para. 84; see also unreferenced, unsigned and undated note in KP, Box 2, file 12.

34. Cmnd. 814, para. 84. For text of speech, see KP, Box 3, file 20.

35. Cmnd. 814, para. 84.

36. *State of Emergency*, Cmnd. 707 (London: HMSO, 1959), para. 21.

37. Chiume to author, 19 August 1994.

38. AM, 1958, p. 106; AL, 2 January 1959; AL, Armitage to Haworth, 1 December 1958.

39. Late question, No. 64, Facilities for Detainees, DP, Box 7, folio 4.

40. Report by D.C. Cameron and E.J. Theunissen, Provision of Emergency Prison and Detention Accomodation, n.d., probably late January 1959, DP, Box 16.

41. Ibid; see also KP, Box 2, file 17; Theunissen, interview with author, 26 June 1994; Late question, No. 64, Facilities for Detainees, DP, Box 7, folio 4.

42. Youens to Armitage, 5 January 1959, DP, Box 5, pp. 71 *et seq.*

43. Armitage was clear that in practice this could not work and his ability to use the veto would be very shortlived: Armitage, evidence 21 May 1959, DP, Box 14, p. 1603.

44. Youens to Armitage, 5 January 1959, DP, Box 5, pp. 71 *et seq.*

45. Chisiza to Armitage, 7 March 1959, KP, Box 2, file 12; Chisiza, evidence 18 May 1959, DP, Box 12A, pp. 2001–36.

46. Oxford Development Records Project (hereafter ODRP), Youens, interview with Kettlewell, 19 February 1985; Youens, interview with Bradley, 26 November 1970, ODRP. Details in the remainder of this paragraph are from these sources.

47. AL, 9 January 1959.

48. Cmnd. 707, para. 15. See also AL, 13 February 1959.

49. Cmnd. 707, para. 23.

50. AP, Armitage Diary (hereafter AD), 31 January 1959.

51. AM, 1959, p. 3.

52. Referred to in CO. 1017/1977, Secretary of State to Armitage, 28 January 1959.

53. CO. 1015/1977, Secretary of State to Armitage, 28 January 1959; Commonwealth Relations Office (hereafter CRO), to High Commissioner Salisbury, 29 January 1959: Foreign and Commonwealth Office, Research and Analysis Department (hereafter FCO).

54. CO. 1015/1977, Armitage to Secretary of State, 29 and 31 January 1959.

55. CO. 1015/1977, Secretary of State to Armitage, 2 February 1959.

56. CO. 1015/1977, Armitage to Secretary of State, 2 February 1959.

57. CO. 1015/1977, Lennox-Boyd to Prime Minister, 4 February 1959.

58. CO. 1015/1977, Macmillan to Perth, 10 February 1959.

59. CO. 1015/1977, Armitage to Gorell Barnes, n.d., probably early February 1959; High Commissioner Salisbury to C.R.O., 12 and 18 February 1959; Armitage to Secretary of State, 13 February 1959; Secretary of State to Armitage, 15 and 16 February 1959; Armitage to Morgan, 17 February 1959.

60. AM, 1959, pp. 4–5; AL, 22 January 1959; RHL. Mss. Brit.Emp. s. 527/1, p. 70; Armitage, evidence 21 May 1959, DP, Box 14.

61. Banda, evidence 16 May 1959, DP, Box 14, pp. 1737 and 1742. Details in the remainder of this paragraph are from this source.

62. AL, 22 January 1959.

63. AD, 20 January 1959; Finney, evidence 12 May 1959, DP, Box 14, p. 1406; Welensky, op. cit., pp. 114–5; Llewelyn to author, 8 November 1994; A.M. Davidson, *The Real Paradise* (Edinburgh: Pentland, 1993), p. 392.

64. CO. 1015/1519, Armitage to Gorell Barnes, 20 January 1959. Details in the rest of this paragraph, except where otherwise stated, are from this source.

65. Provision for declaring unlawful societies existed under s. 70(ii) of the Penal Code, Cap. 23, Laws of Nyasaland, 1957.

66. Provision for restriction existed under the Restriction and Public Security Orders Ordinance, Cap. 49, Laws of Nyasaland, 1957.

67. Provision for deportation existed under the British Central Africa Order in Council, 1902, Articles 25 to 27.

68. AD, 31 January and 1 February 1959; AL, 30 January 1959.

69. AM, 1959, p. 6; AD, 23, 24, 26 and 28 January 1959.

70. Sir Cosmo Haskard to author, 27 February 1994.

71. N. Harvey to author, 10 October 1994. See also R.H. Martin to author, 21 January 1995.

72. Jackson, p. 52.

73. W. Lamborn to author, 7 July 1995.

74. Hansard, Lords, 29 July 1959, col. 787.

75. R. Kettlewell to author, 24 March 1994.

76. J. Mullin to author, 3 July 1994.

77. Mullin to author, 15 April 1994.

78. Welensky also commented on the way in which senior Nyasaland officials, in committee as well as in public, 'did their best to play down the danger': Welensky, op. cit., p. 117.

79. Peters to author, November 1994.

80. AM, 1959, p. 7.

81. Chisiza, evidence 18 May 1959, DP, Box 12A, pp. 2001–36.

82. AD, 24 January 1959.

83. AD, 25 January 1959.

84. Chipembere, evidence 16 May 1959, DP, Box 12A, p. 1945; statement by Nyirenda, undated, KP, Box 2, file 12; statement by Augustine Larry, KP, Box 1, file 9; Cmnd. 707, para. 24; Cmnd. 814, para. 98; Jonas Kaunda, evidence 22 May 1959, DP, Box 15, transcripts file, Vol. 2; AM, 1959, p. 9.

85. H.M. Rowland, evidence 30 April 1959, DP, Box 13, pp. 812–19.

86. Welensky, op. cit., p. 117.

87. Finney to Mullin, 18 February 1959, attached to Mullin to Footman, 18 January 1959, DP, Box 1, also Box 9.

88. Mullin to Footman, 18 January 1959, DP, Box 1, also Box 9.

89. Mullin to Footman, 18 February 1959, DP, Box 1, also Box 9. Details in the remainder of this paragraph are from this source.

90. Sir Richard Posnett to author, 14 September 1993 and 15 March 1994.

91. Ibid.

92. T.P.J. Lewis to author, 12 December 1994 and 20 March 1995; Wood, op. cit., p. 639.

93. AL, 7 February 1959.

94. AL, 7 February 1959.

95. CO. 1015/1976, Summary of Proposals made on Revision of Nyasaland Constitution, February 1959; Chiume, memorandum to the Colonial Secretary, 3 February 1959, KP, Box 2, file 13.

96. Indian High Commissioner Salisbury to Foot, 13 May 1959, DP, Box 16; AL, 24 October 1958.

97. CO. 1015/1976, Summary of Proposals made on Revision of Nyasaland Constitution, February 1959.

98. *Manchester Guardian*, 30 January 1959.

99. Armitage, evidence 21 May 1959, DP, Box 14, p. 1609.

100. Banda, evidence 16 May 1959, DP, Box 14, p. 1727.

101. AL, 7 February 1959; Ingham to Crossley et al., 6 February 1959, privately held.

102. CO. 1015/1976, Summary of Proposals made on Revision of Nyasaland Constitution, February 1959.

103. RHL. Mss. Brit.Emp. s. 527/1, pp. 66–7.

104. FCO to High Commissioner Salisbury, 30 January 1959: FCO.

105. Ibid.

106. Chisiza, evidence 18 May 1959, DP, Box 12A, p. 2006, pp. 2011–12. Congress would have accepted parity on executive council instead of the majority they had demanded.

107. AL, 7 February 1959 and 13 February 1959; Cmnd. 707, para. 26.

108. Llewelyn to author, 8 November 1994.

109. G.J.T. Landreth to author, 11 November 1994.

110. Chisiza, evidence 18 May 1959, DP, Box 12A, p. 2020; Chisiza denied this.

111. Armitage, evidence 15 April 1959, DP, Box (NYC) 15, p. 2.

112. Armitage, evidence 15 April 1959, DP, Box (NYC) 15, p. 4.

113. Chisiza to Armitage, 7 March 1959, KP, Box 2, file 12.

114. Ibid.

115. AD, 17 February 1959.

116. AM, 1959, p. 14.

117. Youens, interview with Kettlewell, 19 February 1985: ODRP; Sir Peter Youens, interview with author, 4 January 1995.

118. CO. 1015/1518, Armitage to Gorell Barnes, 20 January 1959; Armitage to Colonial Office, 16 February 1959. Details in the remainder of this paragraph, except where otherwise stated, are from these sources.

119. CO. 1015/1515 and CO. 1015/1518, Morgan to Armitage, 19 February 1959.

120. CO. 1015/1518, Armitage to Colonial Office, 16 February 1959.

121. AM, 1959, p. 14; AD, 19 February 1959.

122. AD, 20 February 1959; Welensky, op. cit., p. 120; RHL. Mss. Brit.Emp. s. 527/1, p. 71; CO. 1015/1515, Armitage to Secretary of State, 24 February 1959.

123. Lord Dalhousie to author, 24 December 1991.

124. CO. 1015/1515 and CO. 1015/1518, Armitage to Morgan, 19 February 1959.

125. CO. 1015/1516, Benson to Gorell Barnes, 2 March 1959. Details in the remainder of this paragraph, except where otherwise stated, are from this source.

126. Armitage, evidence 15 April 1959, DP, Box (NYC) 15, p. 6.

127. Ibid., p. 7.

128. Cmnd. 707, para. 33; RHL. Mss. Brit.Emp. s. 527/1, pp. 70–1.

129. Armitage, evidence 15 April 1959, DP, Box (NYC) 15, p. 7.

130. CO. 1015/1515, Armitage to Morgan, 24 February 1959. Details in the remainder of this paragraph, unless otherwise stated, are from this source.

131. CO. 1015/1515, Holdershaw to Howard-Drake, 24 February 1959; Perth to Luce, 25 January 1959.

132. CO. 1015/1517, Armitage to Welensky, 26 February 1959; Armitage, evidence 15 April 1959, DP, Box (NYC) 15, p. 8 and p. 9; RHL. Mss. Brit.Emp. s. 527/1, p. 72.

133. CO. 1015/1517, Armitage to Welensky, 26 February 1959.

134. Mrs S. Bevan to author, 1 February 1995; Llewelyn to author, 21 October 1994; Cotton to author, 18 February 1995; Mrs N. Finney to author, 23 October 1994.

135. Armitage, evidence 15 April 1959, DP, Box (NYC) 15, p. 9.

136. Dalhousie to author, 18 June 1991.

137. R.R. Putterill to author, 15 March 1995; M.J. Swart to author, 14 August 1995.

138. CO. 1015/1517, Armitage to Welensky, 26 February 1959; Armitage, evidence 15 April 1959, DP, Box (NYC) 15, p. 9.

139. Putterill to author, 15 March 1995; Swart to author, 14 August 1995; B. Franklin to author, 30 January 1995.

140. Cmnd. 814, para. 135.

141. J. Caine to author, 6–10 April 1995.

142. Ibid.

143. Theunissen, interview with author, 26 June 1994. Not all soldiers were immune from prosecution since two members of the RAR were prosecuted for manslaughter in Lilongwe: R.E.N. Smith to author, 24 August 1995.

144. M. Sabbatini to author, 15 January 1995; D.T. McLinden to author, 1 June 1995.

145. B.L. Walker to author, 6 June 1995.
146. Ibid.
147. Ibid.; Wood, op. cit., p. 642; L.J. Foster to author, 28 July 1995; K. Aspinall to author, 13 July 1995; J.H.E. Watson to author, 13 December 1993; A. Schwarz to author, 23 April 1996.
148. AL, 27 February 1959; AL, Armitage to Haworth, 23 February 1959; see also P. Burkinshaw, *Alarms and Excursions* (Leominster, Davis Brothers, 1991), p. 124, and Davidson, *The Real Paradise*, p. 396.
149. *Rhodesia Herald*, Salisbury, 21 February 1959.
150. Cited in AM, 1959, p. 18.
151. AL, 27 February 1959.
152. *Daily Express*, 24 February 1959.
153. *Guardian*, 26 February 1959.
154. Hansard, Commons, 25 February 1959, col. 1126.
155. D. Cowderoy and R.C. Nesbit, *War in the Air: Rhodesian Air Force, 1935–1980* (Alberton, R.S.A.: Galago, 1987), p. 29; A.M. Bentley to author, 5 September 1995; Swart to author, 30 May 1995; R. Edwards to author, 1 September 1995; J. Wells-West to author, 11 September 1995; R. Wilson to author, 20 June 1995.
156. *Observer*, 22 February 1959.
157. AL, Armitage to Haworth, 23 February 1959.
158. Welensky, op. cit., p. 122; Banda to Armitage, 21 February 1959, KP, Box 2, file 12, and Box 3, file 20.
159. AD, 20 February 1959.
160. AM, 1959, p. 23.
161. CO. 1015/1515, Armitage to Secretary of State, 26 February 1959.
162. Ibid.; see also report on the Congress plan of violence, prepared by Special Branch, DP, Box 6.
163. J. Stonehouse, *Prohibited Immigrant* (London: The Bodley Head, 1960); Cmnd. 814, paras 125–6; M.D. Ashwin to author, 5 October 1994; McLinden to author, 1 June 1995; CO. 1015/1515, Butler to Perth, 24 February 1959 and Holdershaw to Howard-Drake, 24 February 1959.
164. CO. 1015/1515, Secretary of State to Armitage, 25 February 1959.
165. CO. 1015/1977, Welensky to Home, 25 February 1959.
166. CO. 1015/1535, Perth to Manningham-Buller, 15 May 1959.
167. CO. 1015/1538, Armitage to Secretary of State, 25 February 1959, received at Colonial Office at 17.55 hours on 25 February 1959. See also AL, Armitage to Haworth, 23 February 1959.
168. CO. 1015/1535, Perth to Manningham-Buller, 15 May 1959.
169. CO. 1015/1977, Perth to Lennox-Boyd (in Aden), 25 February 1959, 20.10 hours.
170. CO. 1015/1977, Lennox-Boyd to Perth, 26 February 1959, 21.20 hours.
171. CO. 1015/1977, Extract from Conclusions of a Meeting of the Cabinet held at Downing Street on 26 February 1959.
172. Hansard, Commons, 27 February 1959.
173. CO. 1015/1515, Armitage to Secretary of State, 26 February 1959; CO. 1015/1515, Minister of State, Colonial Office to Governor Nyasaland, 27 February 1959; CO. 1015/1515, Secretary of State to Armitage, 1 March 1959.
174. CO. 1015/1518, Armitage to Morgan, 27 February 1959.
175. Wood, op. cit., p. 643; Welensky, op. cit., p. 123.
176. CO. 1015/1839, Armitage to Lennox-Boyd, 6 October 1959, para. 5.

177. Cmnd. 814, paras 133–6.

178. J. Strouts to author, 28 December 1994.

179. Franklin to author, 30 January 1995; D.M. Scott to author, 5 October 1995; AM, 1959, p. 32; CO. 1015/1515, Armitage to Secretary of State, 26 February 1959.

180. *Observer*, 1 March 1959.

181. W.A. Brent, *Rhodesian Air Force: a brief history, 1947–1980* (Kwambona, R.S.A.: Freeworld Press, 1987), p. 8; V. Flintman to author, 2 August 1995; Franklin to author, 30 January 1995 and March 1995.

182. Edwards to author, 1 September 1995.

183. *Evening Standard*, Salisbury, 3 March 1959, p. 1.

184. Scott to author, 5 October 1995.

185. Franklin to author, 30 January 1995.

186. Wood, op. cit., pp. 644–5.

187. R.A. Massey-Shaw to author, 7 September 1995.

188. Caine to author, 6 April 1995.

189. D.C. Waddon to author, 1 May 1995; R. Mason to author, 10 February 1995; R. Finnigan to author, 10 May 1995; *Outpost* (Journal of the BSAP Association), April 1959, pp. 5–12 and May 1974, pp. 15–16; statement to Special Branch by G.P. Jhale, 10 May 1959, DP, Box 7.

190. O.E.C. Chirwa to Margaret Gardner, 2 March 1959, privately held.

191. Davidson, *The Real Paradise*, p. 396.

192. CO. 1015/1515, Transcription of a shorthand note on a press conference by His Excellency the Governor to members of the press at 2.45 p.m. on Monday 2 March 1959; AM, 1959, pp. 27–30 and 35–6. Details of the conference in the remainder of this paragraph are from these sources.

193. *Time Magazine*, 16 March 1959, Vol. LXXIII, No. 11; Macpherson et al. to Haskard, 4 March 1959, DP, Box 5.

194. CO. 1015/1515, Armitage to Lennox-Boyd, 2 March 1959.

195. CO. 1015/1515, Armitage to Secretary of State, 2 March 1959. Details in the remainder of this paragraph, except where otherwise stated, are from this source.

196. M. Harper to author, 22 November 1994. See also Wood, op. cit., p. 643.

197. CO. 1015/1515, Armitage to Lennox-Boyd, 2 March 1959.

3. The crisis breaks

1. *Nyasaland Times*, Emergency Issue, No. 1, 3 March 1959 and No. 2, 4 March 1959; *Evening Standard*, Salisbury, 3 March 1959; AM, 1959, p. 25, p. 27 and p. 42; J.W. Robins to author, 6 October 1994 and 24 October 1994; G. Richards to author, 17 July 1995; *Manchester Guardian*, 7 March 1959; M. Abel to author, 9 August 1995; S.F. Bedford to author, 21 November 1994; Bevan to author, 1 February 1995; M. Pegg to author, 17 July 1995.

2. J.E. Clements to author, March 1995.

3. Details in this paragraph, except where otherwise stated, are from Haskard to Footman, 27 May 1959 and 29 May 1959; Nance to Footman, 28 May 1959; Nicholson to Footman, n.d., probably 28 May 1959 – all DP, Box 26.

4. J.C.A. Hammond to author, 1 October 1994. 'Boma' is the district headquarters.

5. J.M.G. Crossley to author, 25 June 1995.

6. Franklin to author, 30 January 1995; Caine to author, 6 April 1995.

7. Cmnd. 814, para. 229.

8. J. Brock to author, 17 May 1995.

9. Bevan to Long, 31 March 1959, DP, Box 9. The unreferenced material in the following paragraphs on Banda's arrest is from this source.

10. M. Bowery to author, 30 November 1994; Cotton to author, 18 February 1995.

11. Cotton to author, 18 February 1995.

12. Bowery to author, 30 November 1994.

13. Cotton to author, 18 February 1995. Details in the remainder of this and the following paragraph, except where otherwise stated, are from this source.

14. *Manchester Guardian*, 7 March 1959.

15. Caine to author, 6 April 1995; P. Wallace-Jones to author, 18 March 1996.

16. Davis, Report on arrest of Dr Banda, 18 March 1959, DP, Box 9; M. Davis to author, 8 November 1995. Details in the remainder of this paragraph are from these sources, except the Banda quotation, which is from Banda to Dowson, 4 October 1959, privately held. Banda's only complaint about his arrest was that he was not allowed to get dressed: RHL. Mss. Brit.Emp. s. 527/1, p. 102.

17. Bowery to author, 30 November 1994 and 24 January 1995; Bowery, Report on arrest of Dr Banda, 10 March 1959, DP, Box 9; Laja, Wemusi, Banda and Evans, Reports on arrest of Dr Banda, all n.d., almost certainly mid-March 1959, DP, Box 9. Unreferenced details in the remainder of this paragraph are from these sources.

18. Bowery to author, 30 November 1994.

19. Swart to author, 14 August 1995; G.P. Shergold to author, 8 September 1995.

20. Humphrys, Report on arrest of Dr Banda, 16 March 1959, DP, Box 9; Cotton to author, 18 February 1995.

21. O.C. Police, Southern Division to Provincial Operations Committee, 4 March 1959, DP, Box 9.

22. Chipembere, evidence 16 May 1959, DP, Box 12A, pp. 1949–50.

23. Banda, evidence 16 May 1959, DP, Box 14, p. 1746.

24. Banda to Dowson, 10 April 1959, privately held; McAdam, evidence 20 April 1959, DP, Box (NYC) 15, pp. 222 *et seq.*

25. George Clay, 'Dr Banda speaks' in *Colonial Times*, 12 March 1959: copy in KP, Box 3, file 25.

26. Saunders, evidence, n.d., probably 21 April 1959, DP, Box 15, transcripts file Vol. 2. Chipembere was told at 8 p.m. by taxi drivers that Banda was likely to be arrested: Chipembere, evidence 18 May 1959, DP, Box 12A, pp. 1974–5. The message conveyed to Msonthi on 2 March 1959 – see below – is evidence that a number of leading Congress members knew that Banda was about to be arrested.

27. Magogo, evidence 25 April 1959, DP, Box 15, transcripts file Vol. 2. The message, received at 8 p.m., probably resulted from the information which Chipembere had received from taxi drivers at about the same time.

28. Banda to Brockway, 23 February 1959, DP, Box 16.

29. DP, Box 9.

30. Foster to author, 28 July 1995.

31. Mushet to author February 1995; P.C. Dowson to author, 5 July 1995 and Chisiza, evidence 18 May 1959, DP, Box 12A, p. 2004.

32. The Congress plan of violence, DP, Box 6, p. 89; Griff Jones to Williams, 2 August 1959, Williams Papers.

33. Vespers, 3 March 1959, DP, Box 5.

34. Clements to author March 1995; Bailey to author, 12 July 1994; *Nyasaland Times*, Emergency Issue No. 1, 3 March 1959.

35. N. Harvey to author, 10 October 1994; J. Sheriff to author, December 1994.

36. *Nyasaland Times*, Emergency Issue No. 2, 4 March 1959; AM, 1959, p. 27.

37. D. Bolt to author, 3 March 1995; D.L. Baxter to author, 23 December 1994; *Evening Standard*, Salisbury, 3 March 1959, p. 2.

38. D.L. Baxter to author, 23 December 1994; *Evening Standard*, Salisbury, 3 March 1959, p. 2.

39. Davidson, *The Real Paradise*, pp. 395–6; *Nyasaland Times*, Emergency Issue No. 2, 4 March 1959.

40. Daniel Mkandawire to author, 8 July 1995.

41. Bedford to author, 4 November 1994.

42. Bedford to author, 21 November 1994. Orton Chirwa was also with Chipembere and Lubani when they were arrested, and although he was not himself to be arrested he none the less accompanied them to Chileka and then returned to Blantyre in the police vehicle: statement by W.S. Geraughty, DP, Box 9.

43. CO. 1015/1518, Armitage to Secretary of State, 2 May 1959.

44. Ibid.

45. Another version has the words 'Get the hell out of here or I'll stick a bullet in your guts': *Manchester Guardian*, 6 March 1959.

46. CO. 1015/1518, Armitage to Secretary of State, 2 May 1959.

47. Mushet to author, February 1995 and telephone conversation with author, 31 October 1994.

48. CO. 1015/1515, Armitage to Secretary of State, 09.25 hours 3 March 1959; Armitage to Secretary of State, 15.15 hours and 21.10 hours 3 March 1959; Armitage to Secretary of State, 5 March 1959; Devlin Commission, Late Question, No. 36, Preparation of Sunrise lists, response prepared by Finney, 4 June 1959, DP, Box 24, No. 5A.

49. Chisiza to Armitage, 7 March 1959, KP, Box 2, file 12.

50. CO. 1015/1515, Armitage to Secretary of State, 3 March 1959.

51. Nyasaland Operations Committee, Operations Order No. 1/59, 'Operation Sunrise', 27 February 1959, DP, Box 1.

52. DO. 35/7476, Governor to Secretary of State, 9 June 1959.

53. CO. 1015/1515, Armitage to Secretary of State, 3 March 1959.

54. See, for example, F. Seaton, 'One Man's Emergency', *Outpost*, May 1959, pp. 19–22: well over forty people from Fort Manning surrendered voluntarily. See also statement by J.E. Banda, KP, Box 1, file 9.

55. There was an exception to this. A BSAP officer who travelled with detainees from Lilongwe to Bulawayo on 3 March 1959 in a military aircraft recalled: 'I had been warned that the pilot intended to give the prisoners the "ride of their lives", and soon after we left Lilongwe it started to bounce all over the sky ... the rest of the trip was noisy, messy and not one to be remembered': M. May to author, 17 August 1995.

56. Harvey to author, 10 October 1994; similar sentiments are expressed in Lavery to author, 10 November 1994.

57. P.K. O'Riordan to author, 8 December 1994; H.W. Foot to author, 10 September 1995.

58. The other death was at Fort Manning. The Nkata Bay tragedy is dealt with in Cmnd. 814, paras 226–39; Brock, evidence, 7 April 1959, DP, Box 13, pp. 1161–

85; Van Oppen, evidence 20 May 1959, DP, Box 13, pp. 1827–39; Nhlane, Munthali and Chunga, evidence, 2 May 1959, DP, Box 13, pp. 976–83; inquest proceedings, DP, Box 17; RHL. Mss. Brit.Emp. s. 527/1, pp. 149 *et seq.*

59. *Manchester Guardian*, 15 June 1959, letter from Hilda Selwyn-Clarke, Secretary to the Fabian Commonwealth Bureau. The Congress branch chairman at Livingstonia, who was also the Headmaster of the primary school there, later said, 'At Nkhata Bay in the morning, villagers went to the steamer to attempt to rescue the prisoners': Y.R. Chibambo to author, 13 June 1995.

60. The distinction between innocent and culpable encouragement might be difficult for non-Chinyanja speakers to detect: the words *nanga bwanji*, for example, can mean either 'what's happening?' or 'what the hell's going on?': Sheriff to author, 3 September 1995 and A. Mell, telephone conversation with author, 20 November 1995.

61. RHL. Mss. Brit.Emp. s. 527/1, p. 150.

62. Finney, evidence 12 May 1959, DP, Box 14, p. 1399; Hodder, Report on interrogations at Khami Prison, Bulawayo, from 4 to 9 March 1959, DP, Box 9, pp. 336–40; Hodder, evidence, 21 May 1959, DP, Box 12A, pp. 2132–7. Hodder had 35 years' police experience, most of it involving interrogation in criminal and intelligence work.

63. AM, 1959, p. 27.

64. Statement by J.C.C.R. Stokes, 8 June 1959, DP, Box 16.

65. Finney, evidence 12 May 1959, DP, Box 14, p. 1401.

66. Hodder, Report on interrogations at Khami Prison, Bulawayo, from 4 to 9 March 1959, DP, Box 9, pp. 336–40. Later, when these very important witnesses, who were present at the 25 January 1959 meeting, were examined by Devlin, their interviews were very brief indeed and Devlin's questioning was almost exclusively concerned with why they made the statements and not with testing the truth of the statements they made: O. Kayamba and J.W. Chikwita, evidence, 13 May 1959, DP, Box 14, p. 1532 and pp. 1534–5.

67. Finney, evidence 12 May 1959, DP, Box 14, p. 1400.

68. Statement by D.S. Johnston, 9 May 1959, KP, Box 1, file 1.

69. Meldrum, evidence 30 April 1959, DP.

70. Sheriff to author, December 1994.

71. D.S. Johnston to author, 30 October 1994.

72. Sanders to author, 19 October 1994. Other officers, however, found the Northern Rhodesian Police very disciplined and well behaved: Peters to author, November 1994.

73. R. Chasemore, interview with author, 19 July 1995.

74. AL, 5 March 1959; AL, Lady Armitage to Mrs Armitage, 5 March 1959. See also RHL. Mss. Brit.Emp. s. 527/1, p. 75.

75. AM, 1959, p. 34.

76. Mullin to author, 15 April and 3 July 1994.

77. Kettlewell to author, 24 March 1994.

78. Theunissen to author, 7 May 1994.

79. Lord Amery to author, 3 January 1992.

80. A.H.M. Kirk-Greene (ed.), *Africa in the Colonial Period, The Transfer of Power: the Colonial Administration in the Age of Decolonialisation* (Oxford: University of Oxford, 1979), p. 3.

81. Hansard, Commons, 28 July 1959, col. 436.

82. Kirk-Greene, op. cit., p. 3.

83. Hansard, Commons, 28 July 1959, col. 436.

84. Hansard, Commons, 3 March 1959, cols 216–23.

85. Hansard, Commons, 3 March 1959, cols 279–342. Details of the debate are from this source.

86. Lord Callaghan to author, 18 November 1993.

87. Posnett to author, 15 March 1994; Lapping, op. cit., p. 563; RHL. Mss. Brit.Emp. s. 527/1, p. 73.

88. CO. 1015/1522, Secretary of State to Armitage, 5 March 1959.

89. CO. 1015/1517, Minute by Secretary of State, 9 March 1959.

90. CO. 1015/1516, Secretary of State to Armitage, 6 March 1959.

91. Ibid.

92. CO. 1015/1516, Armitage to Secretary of State, 5 March 1959.

93. Cowderoy and Nesbit, op. cit., p. 29; Landreth to author, 11 November 1994; Jackson, p. 62.

94. CO. 1015/1522, Armitage to Secretary of State, 4 March 1959.

95. Putterill to author, 1 May 1995.

96. CO. 1015/1522, Secretary of State to Armitage, 5 March 1959.

97. CO. 1015/1522, Armitage to Secretary of State, 5 March 1959.

98. CO. 1015/1522, Colonial Office to Armitage, 6 March 1959.

99. CO. 1015/1522, Lennox-Boyd to Prime Minister, 6 March 1959.

100. CO. 1015/1522, Secretary of State to Armitage, 6 and 8 March 1959.

101. DO. 35/7478, Minutes of a meeting of the interdepartmental Central Africa Committee, 6 March 1959.

102. CO. 1015/1522, Macmillan to Lennox-Boyd, 7 March 1959; repeated in CO. 1015/1522, Secretary of State to Armitage, 8 March 1959.

103. CO. 1015/1522, Sabattini to Moreton, 6 March 1959.

104. DO. 35/7478, Minutes of meetings of the interdepartmental Central Africa Committee, 6 and 10 March 1959.

105. Clements to author, March 1995; K. Sargent to author, 14 August 1995; T.C. Gardner to author, 15 February 1994.

106. CO. 1015/1516, Armitage to Secretary of State, 7 March 1959.

107. CO. 1015/1516, Secretary of State to Armitage, 6 March 1959; DP, Box 9.

108. R.W.F. Kitchin to author, 17 August 1995.

109. Statement by Gaskell, DP, Box 9; Jane Symonds to Butler (London solicitor), 6 April 1959, KP, Box 2, file 12.

110. CO. 1015/1516, Secretary of State to Armitage, 9 March 1959.

111. CO. 1015/1516, Armitage to Secretary of State, 9 March 1959.

112. Author, participant observation.

113. Msonthi, evidence 19 May 1959, DP, Box 15, transcripts file, Vol. 2.

114. Statement of W.M. Mtiyesa, 26 March 1959, made to J.S. Sheriff and M.J. Ryans, copy enclosed with Sheriff to author, 27 February 1995. Statement by Karua, DP, Box 6, Congress plans of violence, p. 96. Msonthi, however, 10 days earlier had made a statement to Kellock denying that he received any such letters: KP, Box 1, file 9, statement by John Dunstan Msonthi, 9 May 1959. Tennyson Limbe also denied knowledge of the letter: KP, Box 1, file 9.

115. AL, Armitage to Haworth, 12 March 1959. For a description of what was happening in the north, see AL, 13 March 1959; Jackson, p. 68; Cmnd. 814, para. 258; Putterill to author, 15 March and 1 May 1995; Caine to author, 6 April 1995; Kettlewell to author, 24 March 1994.

116. Jackson, pp. 59–61.

117. CO. 1015/1517, Armitage to Secretary of State, 21 March 1959.
118. Jackson, p. 54 and p. 57.
119. Jackson, p. 59. See also J. Kaunda, evidence 22 May 1959, DP, Box 14, p. 1893.
120. Jackson, p. 60.
121. Cmnd. 814, para. 266 *et seq.*
122. AM, 1959, p. 41.
123. AL, 14 March 1959; Armitage, evidence 15 April 1959, DP, Box (NYC) 15, p. 9; *Manchester Guardian*, 9 March 1959; CO. 1015/1516, Armitage to Morgan, 9 March 1959.
124. CO. 1015/1516, Armitage to Secretary of State, 10 March 1959.
125. CO. 1015/1516, Armitage to Morgan, 9 March 1959.
126. CO. 1015/1517, CRO to High Commissioner Salisbury, 18 March 1959. The view that either Welensky or Whitehead, or both, were keen to put a stop to Congress activities and extend their own influence in Nyasaland, may not have been new. In July 1956 Armitage said, 'I have little doubt that the opportunity to use extreme physical force to crush violence in Nyasaland would be very welcome in certain quarters': AP, Armitage to Lennox-Boyd, 4 July 1956.
127. CO. 1015/1517, Armitage to Secretary of State, 18 March 1959.
128. Finnigan to author, 10 May 1995.
129. CO. 1015/1517, Armitage to Secretary of State, 18 March 1959.
130. Ibid.
131. AM, 1959, p. 41; Cmnd. 814, para. 258.
132. DP, Box 9.
133. AM, 1959, p. 33.
134. Cmnd. 814, para. 258.
135. DO. 35/7476, Governor to Secretary of State, 21 March 1959.
136. General Long, evidence 19 May 1959, DP, Box 12A, pp. 2084–98.
137. Jackson, p. 70.
138. AM, 1959, p. 41.
139. B. Walker to author, 6 June 1995; E.L.T. Richardson to author, 17 July 1995.
140. Memorandum by John Mossman n.d., DP, Box 20.
141. Walker to author, 6 June 1995.
142. Jackson, p. 91.
143. Jackson, pp. 68 *et seq.*
144. Graham-Jolly to author, 5 December 1994.
145. S.J. France to author, 9 November 1994.
146. Punter to author, 22 January 1996.
147. Llewelyn to author, 8 November 1994.
148. Franklin to author, March 1995; Wells-West to author, 11 September 1995.
149. Kitchin to author, 17 August 1995.
150. D. Howarth, *The Shadow of the Dam* (London: Collins, 1961), Chapter XII.
151. Cmnd. 814, para. 275.
152. DP, Box 7, folio 17; *Nyasaland Protectorate Annual Report, 1960* (Zomba: Government Printer, 1961), p. 120.
153. CO. 1015/1517, Armitage to Welensky, 14 March 1959.
154. *Manchester Guardian*, 7 March 1959.
155. Memorandum by John Mossman, n.d., DP, Box 20.
156. CO. 1015/1517, Armitage to Welensky, 14 March 1959. Details in the remainder of this paragraph are from this source.

157. CO. 1015/1517, Federal Prime Minister to Governors of Northern Rhodesia and Nyasaland, 13 March 1959.

158. DO. 35/7478, Meeting of interdepartmental Central Africa Committee, 10 March 1959.

159. *Observer*, 8 March 1959; *Daily Mail*, 13 March 1959.

160. Cmnd. 707. Details in the remainder of this paragraph are from this source. See also *Manchester Guardian*, 23 March 1959; *The Times*, 24 March 1959; *Sunday Times*, 29 March 1959.

161. AL, 27 March 1959.

162. Armitage to Lennox-Boyd, 18 March 1959, DP, Box 5.

163. Cmnd. 814, paras 63–71.

164. Banda, evidence 16 May 1959, DP, Box 14, p. 1733.

165. DO. 35/7476, Armitage to Secretary of State, 23 March 1959.

166. Ibid.

167. Landreth to author, 11 November 1994.

168. AL, 20 March 1959.

169. CO. 1015/1517, Armitage to Lennox-Boyd, 23 March 1959. See also Welensky, op. cit., p. 130.

170. CO. 1015/1517, Armitage to Lennox-Boyd, 23 March 1959.

171. CO. 1015/1839, Armitage to Morgan, 18 April and 15 May 1959.

172. *Outpost*, May 1959.

173. Armitage to Kettlewell, 20 April 1959, privately held.

174. AL, 1 May 1959.

175. DO. 35/7476, Governor's Deputy to Secretary of State, 27 July 1959.

176. CO. 1015/1526, draft cable, Secretary of State to Armitage, n.d., probably end April 1959.

177. Dalhousie to author, 24 December 1991.

178. CO. 1015/1515, Transcript of a shorthand note on a Press Conference given by His Excellency the Governor to members of the press at 2.45 p.m. on Monday 2 March 1959.

179. CO. 1015/1517, Minute by the Secretary of State, 9 March 1959.

180. Ibid; see also CO. 1015/1977, C.R.O. to High Commissioner Salisbury, 11 March 1959.

181. CO. 1015/1517, Minute by Lennox-Boyd, 9 March 1959.

182. Lord Perth, interview with author, 27 October 1993.

183. CO. 1015/1516, Secretary of State to Perth, 10 March 1959.

184. CO. 1015/1517, Minute by Lennox-Boyd, 9 March 1959.

185. Perth, interview with author, 27 October 1993.

186. CO. 1015/1522, Armitage to Lennox-Boyd, 12 March 1959.

187. Perth, interview with author, 27 October 1959.

188. J.E.F. Codrington, interview with author, 19 January 1994.

189. Perth, interview with author, 27 October 1993.

190. CO. 1015/1977, Report by the Minister of State for Colonial Affairs on a visit to the Territories of the Federation of Rhodesia and Nyasaland from 12 to 21 March 1959; CO. 1015/1976, Notes of Nyasaland visit, 12 to 17 March 1959.

191. Wood, op. cit., pp. 653–5.

192. CO. 1015/1977, Report by the Minister of State for Colonial Affairs on a visit to the Territories of the Federation of Rhodesia and Nyasaland from 12 to 21 March 1959.

193. CO. 1015/1839, Morgan to Gorell Barnes, 27 April 1959.

194. Ibid.

195. CO. 1015/1839, Minute from Perth, 28 April 1959.

196. CO. 1015/1977, Report by the Minister of State for Colonial Affairs on a visit to the Territories of the Federation of Rhodesia and Nyasaland from 12 to 21 March 1959; CO. 1015/1976, Notes on Nyasaland visit, 12 to 17 March 1959. Details in the following paragraphs to the end of this chapter are from this source.

197. For Perth's visit see *The Times*, 18 March 1959.

4. The Devlin Inquiry

1. A. Horne, *Macmillan, 1957–1986, Vol. II of the official biography* (London: Macmillan, 1988), p. 179.

2. CO. 1015/1535, Secretary of State to High Commissioner Salisbury, 20 March 1959.

3. DO. 35/7478, Meeting of interdepartmental Central Africa committee, 12 March 1959.

4. CO. 1015/1516, Secretary of State to Armitage, 6 March 1959. See also Wood, op. cit., p. 649.

5. CO. 1015/1535, Secretary of State to Armitage, n.d., probably 19 March 1959.

6. *The Times*, 12 March 1959.

7. CO. 1015/1517, Minute by the Secretary of State, 9 March 1959.

8. DO. 35/7478, Meeting of interdepartmental Central Africa committee, 20 March 1959.

9. B. Lapping, *End of Empire* (London: Paladin Grafton, 1989), p. 564.

10. Welensky, op. cit., pp. 138–44. Details in the remainder of this paragraph are from this source.

11. CO. 1015/1536, Lord Privy Seal to Welensky, n.d., probably 23 March 1959.

12. Welensky, op. cit., pp. 140–3; Wood, op. cit., pp. 660–62.

13. Welensky, op. cit., p. 144; Wood, op. cit., p. 663.

14. CO. 1015/1536, Lord Privy Seal to Welensky, n.d., probably 23 March 1959.

15. Ibid.

16. DO. 35/7478, Meetings of interdepartmental Central Africa committee, 17 and 20 March 1959.

17. CO. 1015/1544, Morgan to Macpherson, 6 July 1959.

18. CO. 1015/1535, Armitage to Secretary of State, 20 and 22 March 1959.

19. CO. 1015/1535, Benson to Secretary of State, 21 March 1959.

20. CO. 1015/1535, Lennox-Boyd to Baring, 16 March 1959.

21. CO. 1015/1535, unsigned note, n.d., probably mid-March 1959.

22. CO. 1015/1535, Lennox-Boyd to Armitage, 17 March 1959.

23. Ibid.

24. Viscount Boyd in Kirk-Greene, op. cit., p. 3.

25. CO. 1015/1535, Lennox-Boyd to Armitage, 17 March 1959; *Who's Who*, 1995.

26. Sir Edgar Williams, interview with author, 8 October 1993.

27. Jackson, p. 104.

28. CO. 1015/1535, Lennox-Boyd to Baring, 16 March 1959.

29. CO. 1015/1535, Baring to Secretary of State, n.d., but 17 or 18 March 1959.

30. Tim Satchell, '7 Days', *Hello Magazine*, February 1992. See also *Who's Who*, 1991; *New York Times*, 25 July 1959.

31. *New York Times*, 25 July 1959; RHL. Mss. Brit.Emp. s. 527/2, p. 118.

32. A. Fairclough, interview with author, 26 November 1993.

33. CO. 1015/1537, Secretary of State to Armitage, 27 March 1959.

34. Perth, interview with author, 27 October 1993.

35. DP, Box 20.

36. Lapping, op. cit., p. 481; Perth, interview with author, 27 October 1993.

37. Horne, op. cit., p. 181.

38. CO. 1015/1535, Secretary of State to Chief Whip, 20 March 1959.

39. Kilmuir also implied that it was a matter of public duty that Devlin should accept: RHL. Mss. Brit.Emp. s. 527/2, p. 66, p. 69; Lapping, op. cit., p. 564.

40. CO. 1015/1535, Secretary of State to Chief Whip, 20 March 1959.

41. Williams to author, 28 November 1993; Devlin explained Wyn-Harris' appointment by the need to 'have someone who was experienced in dealing with African witnesses' and 'someone who had experience in deciding whether the African witness was telling the truth': RHL. Mss. Brit.Emp. s. 527/2, p. 70, p. 72.

42. Lord Chandos, *The Memoirs of Lord Chandos* (London: Bodley Head, 1962), p. 387.

43. H.S. Peters, Dzonzi evidence 30 April 1959, DP, Box 13, pp. 838–43; J.S. Sheriff, Chaloledwa's document, 12 May 1959, DP, Box 14; O.E.C. Chirwa, Makata's evidence 18 May 1959, DP, Box 14.

44. CO. 1015/1535, Secretary of State to Baring, 21 March 1959.

45. CO. 1015/1535, Wyn-Harris to Macpherson, 22 March 1959.

46. *Who's Who*, 1979.

47. CO. 1015/1535, Macpherson to Gorell Barnes, 23 March 1959.

48. Williams, interview with author, 8 October 1993.

49. Wyn-Harris to Devlin, 5 April 1959, DP, Box 16.

50. Ibid.

51. CO. 1015/1535, Secretary of State to Armitage, 19 March 1959.

52. CO. 1015/1535, Secretary of State to Armitage, 24 March 1959. Kilmuir told Devlin at a very early stage that 'they wanted to have a Scot because of the importance of the Scottish missions': RHL. Mss. Brit.Emp. s. 527/2, p. 70.

53. *Who's Who*, 1974; *Perthshire Advertiser*, 16 January 1974.

54. Williams, interview with author, 8 October 1993.

55. Fairclough, interview with author, 26 November 1993.

56. CO. 1015/1535, Secretary of State to Armitage, 24 March 1959.

57. Musk to author, 19 September 1995; Jackson, p. 104.

58. Macpherson to Primrose and Hill to Primrose, DP, Box 4.

59. Jackson, p. 106.

60. Williams, interview with author, 8 October 1993.

61. Jackson, p. 104. Williams was not in fact Welsh: Williams, interview with author, 8 October 1993.

62. *Spectator*, 31 July 1959; see also Lapping, op. cit., p. 339 and p. 563.

63. Williams, interview with author, 8 October 1993.

64. Nyasaland Government Gazette, 1959, General Notices No. 199 of 24 March, p. 109 and No. 275 of 8 May, p. 149.

65. Cmnd. 814, para. 1.

66. Devlin to Fairclough, 31 March 1959, DP, Box 1.

67. CO. 1015/1539, Note of Meeting between Secretary of State and Members of the Nyasaland Commission of Inquiry, 2 April 1959.

68. Ibid.

69. RHL. Mss. Brit.Emp. s. 527/2, p. 71. Devlin's recollection was that Lennox-Boyd had no reservations about the commission inquiring into the causes, including federation.

70. Jackson, pp. 105–6, p. 108; F. Macpherson, paper delivered to the Livingstonia Centenary Conference, Edinburgh, 15 October 1994, mimeo.

71. *Daily Telegraph*, 20 March 1959.

72. *Manchester Guardian*, 23 March 1959.

73. *The Times*, 24 March 1959.

74. *Sunday Times*, 29 March 1959.

75. AL, 27 March 1959; CO. 1015/1535, Secretary of State to Armitage, 26 March 1959.

76. Fairclough, interview with author, 26 November 1993.

77. CO. 1015/1536, Macpherson to Devlin, 1 April 1959.

78. RHL. Mss. Brit.Emp. s. 527/2, p. 66, p. 68, p. 114.

79. CO. 1015/1535, Roberts-Wray to Gorell Barnes, 17 March 1959.

80. CO. 1015/1535, Minute (unsigned) to Gorell Barnes, 20 March 1959.

81. Cmnd. 814, para. 5.

82. P. Devlin, *The Judge* (London: OUP, 1979), Chapter 3.

83. CO. 1015/1536, Armitage to Secretary of State, 1 April 1959.

84. CO. 1015/1536, Secretary of State to Armitage, 2 April 1959.

85. CO. 1015/1539, Secretary of State to Armitage, 25 March 1959.

86. AL, 27.3.59. The Commission also asked Armitage a number of 'late questions' on points which had not previously been fully covered; there were at least 64 such 'late questions': DP, Box 7.

87. CO. 1015/1539, Secretary of State, to Armitage, 28 March 1959.

88. CO. 1015/1539, Armitage to Secretary of State, 26 March 1959; Lennox-Boyd to Kilmuir, 3 April 1959.

89. RHL. Mss. Brit.Emp. s. 527/2, p. 76.

90. CO. 1015/1539, Note of Meeting between Secretary of State and Members of the Nyasaland Commission of Inquiry, 2 April 1959; CO. 1015/1539, Gorell Barnes to Devlin, 6 April 1959.

91. CO. 1015/1539, Lennox-Boyd to Kilmuir, 3 April 1959.

92. CO. 1015/1539, Note of Meeting between Secretary of State and Members of the Nyasaland Commission of Inquiry, 2 April 1959.

93. CO. 1015/1539, Gorell Barnes to Devlin, 6 April 1959; CO. 1015/1539, Secretary of State to Armitage, 8 April 1959.

94. King to Kellock, 14 May 1959; the person so arrested was Nyama: KP, Box 2, file 12.

95. Cmnd. 814, para. 2.

96. CO. 1015/1536, Secretary of State to Armitage, 2 April 1959.

97. M. Harris to author, 25 March 1995; RHL. Mss. Brit.Emp. s. 527/2, p. 102; the witness was Thomas Karua.

98. Cmnd. 814, e.g. paras 114, 115, 197, 210, 217–8, 226–8, 237–8, 253.

99. CO. 1015/1537, Secretary of State to Armitage, 7 April 1959.

100. CO. 1015/1539, Note of Meeting between Secretary of State and Members of the Nyasaland Commission of Inquiry, 2 April 1959.

101. Macpherson to author, 15 October 1994.
102. CO. 1015/1539, Note of Meeting between Secretary of State and Members of the Nyasaland Commission of Inquiry, 2 April 1959.
103. CO. 1015/1535, Secretary of State to Armitage, 26 March 1959.
104. Ibid.
105. Armitage to Lennox-Boyd, 31 March 1959, DP, Box 1, p. 25.
106. CO. 1015/1538 and CO. 1015/1537, Secretary of State to Armitage, 2 April 1959; CO. 1015/1538, Note by Shannon, 3 April 1959.
107. CO. 1015/1538 and CO. 1015/1537, Secretary of State to Armitage, 2 April 1959.
108. CO. 1015/1537, Secretary of State to Armitage, 2 April 1959.
109. CO. 1015/1539, Secretary of State to Armitage, 25 March 1959.
110. CO. 1015/1537, Benson to Armitage, 30 March 1959; CO. 1015/1536, Benson to Secretary of State, 2 April 1959.
111. CO. 1015/1536, Armitage to Secretary of State, 30 March 1959; CO. 1015/1537, Benson to Secretary of State, 30 March 1959.
112. CO. 1015/1537, Benson to Armitage, 30 March 1959; CO. 1015/1537, Benson to Secretary of State, 30 March 1959.
113. CO. 1015/1536, Roberts-Wray to Hone, 31 March 1959; Secretary of State to High Commissioner Salisbury, 31 March 1959; Secretary of State to Armitage, 4 April 1959; Gorell Barnes to Secretary of State, 3 April 1959; CO. 1015/1538, R. Hone to Gorell Barnes, 6 April 1959; CO. 1015/1539, Secretary of State to Armitage, 25 March 1959; Southern Rhodesia Act, No. 33 of 1959.
114. CO. 1015/1536, Roberts-Wray to Hone, 4 April 1959.
115. DP, Boxes 12A and 14.
116. Hone to Home, 4 April 1959, DP, Box 1, p. 48.
117. Ibid.
118. Devlin to Williams, 12 August 1964, DP, Box 16.
119. Armitage to Lennox-Boyd, n.d., late March 1959, DP, Box 7.
120. Armitage to Lennox-Boyd, 31 March 1959, DP, Box 1, p. 25.
121. CO. 1015/1536, Secretary of State to Armitage, 2 April 1959.
122. DO. 35/7479, Dixon to Lintott, 3 April 1959; CO. 1015/1538, Note by Shannon, 3 April 1959.
123. CO. 1015/1536, Secretary of State to Armitage, 3 April 1959.
124. DO. 35/7479, Lintott to Shannon, 5 April 1959; CO. 1015/1538, Shannon to Gorell Barnes, 6 April 1959.
125. DO. 35/7564, Shannon to Lintott, 6 April 1959; Home to Lintott, 8 April 1959; CO. 1015/1538, Gorell Barnes to Macpherson and Secretary of State, 8 April 1959; Note from Macpherson, 8 April 1959.
126. DO. 35/7564, Hone to Shannon, 9 April 1959.
127. CO. 1015/1538, Gorell Barnes to Secretary of State, 9 April 1959.
128. CO. 1015/1538, Shannon to Gorell Barnes, 6 April 1959.
129. CO. 1015/1538, Secretary of State to Armitage, 10 April 1959.
130. Ibid.
131. CO. 1015/1538, Armitage to Secretary of State, 13 April 1959.
132. CO. 1015/1538, Armitage to Secretary of State, n.d., probably 20 April 1959. Details in the remainder of this paragraph are from this source. See also Armitage to Devlin, 15 April 1959, AP; Devlin to Armitage, 18 April 1959, AP.
133. CO. 1015/1538, Devlin to Armitage, 10 May 1959.
134. Welensky to Devlin, 5 May 1959, referred to in CO. 1015/1538, Devlin to

Armitage, 10 May 1959.

135. CO. 1015/1538, Devlin to Armitage, 10 May 1959.

136. CO. 1015/1538, Armitage to Devlin, 14 May 1959.

137. It is possible but extremely unlikely that Welensky sent a later and additional telegram to Armitage on the same day. There is no evidence that this happened and a great deal to indicate that it did not.

138. CO. 1015/1535, Perth to Manningham-Buller, 15 May 1959.

139. CO. 1015/1535 and CO. 1015/1542, Manningham-Buller to Perth, 25 May 1959.

140. CO. 1015/1538, Minute by Scott, 2 June 1959.

141. CO. 1015/1538, Morgan to Moreton, n.d.

142. CO. 1015/1538, Perth to Devlin, 23 June 1959.

143. Ibid; Devlin thought that the matter was not very important from his point of view although he could see that from a party political point of view it could be very important: RHL. Mss. Brit.Emp. s. 527/2, p. 88.

144. CO. 1015/1538, Perth to Devlin, 23 June 1959.

145. CO. 1015/1538, Devlin to Perth, 25 June 1959.

146. Cmnd. 814, para. 159. Later Devlin said that the commission was not sufficiently sure that the Governor took instructions from Welensky so they gave him the benefit of the doubt and found that he had not. Similarly, in exchange as it were, since they were not sufficiently sure that Banda had been at the 25 January 1959 bush meeting, they gave him the benefit of the doubt and found that he had not. RHL. Mss. Brit.Emp. s. 527/2, p. 87.

147. Cmnd. 814, para. 160.

148. Devlin, *The Judge*, Chapter 3. The descriptions of the two systems, and the quotations in the remainder of this paragraph, except where otherwise stated, are from this source.

149. Mr Justice Beadle who also examined Banda was clear that 'a finding based largely on the demeanour of a witness in the witness-box may often be faulty': *Review Tribunal (Preventive Detention Temporary Provisions) Act, 1959, General Report* (Salisbury: Government Printer, 1959), Appendix A, para. 2.

150. CO. 1015/1535, Secretary of State to Armitage, 26 March 1959, in which arrangements for arrival are given.

151. AM, 1959, p. 56.

152. AL, 12 April 1959; AM, 1959, p. 56.

153. Fairclough to Richardson, 28 April 1959, DP, NYC/39, p. 71. Fairclough himself lunched with Armitage on arrival and stayed with the Chief Secretary: DP, Box 1; Williams, interview with author, 8 October 1993.

154. Armitage to Lennox-Boyd, 25 March 1959, DP, Box 7.

155. Wilks to Armitage, 26 March 1959, DP, Box 7; CO. 1015/1539, Note of Meeting between Secretary of State and Members of the Nyasaland Commission of Inquiry, 2 April 1959; RHL Mss. Brit.Emp. s. 527/1, p. 75.

156. Governor, Zomba to Governor, Dar es Salaam, 14 April 1959, DP, Box 7.

157. Governor's Deputy, Dar es Salaam to Governor, Zomba, 15 April 1959, DP, Box 7.

158. Fairclough to Mumford, 9 April 1959 and Mumford to Fairclough, 10 April 1959, DP, Box 4. The commission stayed with the Governor of Southern Rhodesia when they took evidence there: Williams, interview with author, 8 October 1993.

159. Jackson, p. 104.

160. Macpherson to author, 15 October 1994.

161. Jackson, p. 104.
162. Williams, interview with author, 8 October 1993.
163. RHL. Mss. Brit.Emp. s. 527/2, p. 73, p. 74, p. 93.
164. Mrs Southworth to Devlin, 16 April 1959, DP, Box 26.
165. Devlin to Mrs Southworth, 18 April 1959, DP, Box 26.
166. A. Macdonald to author, 20 June 1995.
167. DP, Box 1; CO. 1015/1535, Secretary of State to Armitage, 25 March 1959. Armitage pointed out that the allowances to be paid to the commissioners were 'far in excess' of any paid in Nyasaland even for the Chief Justice: CO. 1015/1535, Armitage to Secretary of State, 26 and 28 March 1959. The Nyasaland Government met all expenses of the Commission: CO. 1015/1535, Secretary of State to Armitage, 26 March 1959.
168. Williams, interview with author, 8 October 1993; D. Pearson to author, 16 December 1993.
169. Landreth to author, 11 November 1994.
170. R.B.S. Purdy to author, 6 August 1995.
171. CO. 1015/1542, Footman to Morgan, 15 May 1959.
172. Haskard to author, 27 February 1994.
173. Cmnd. 814, para. 1.
174. Jackson, p. 105.
175. CO. 1015/1538, Index of Collected Papers submitted to the Commission of Inquiry by the Chief Secretary, n.d.
176. Cmnd. 814, para. 2.
177. DP, Boxes 2 and 3.
178. CO. 1015/1535, Secretary of State to Armitage, 26 March 1959.
179. Cmnd. 814, para. 6.
180. Macpherson to author, 31 January 1995.
181. F. Macpherson, paper delivered to Livingstonia Centenary Conference, Edinburgh, 15 October 1994, mimeo.
182. Harris to author, 31 March 1995. There was a widespread belief among Africans that the Devlin commission was inquiring into federation, rather than simply the disturbances, and their general stance of boycotting things federal may account for Mwase's behaviour on this occasion.
183. Williams, interview with author, 8 October 1993. Fairclough believed the District was Cholo: interview with author, 27 February 1996.
184. Jackson, p. 108.
185. Landreth to author, 21 July 1995.
186. Fairclough, note of discussion between Devlin, King and Roberts, 12 April 1959, DP, Box 20. Details in the remainder of this paragraph, except where otherwise stated, are from this source.
187. For example, A.101, evidence 12 May 1959, DP: Box 14, pp. 1464A–G.
188. CO. 1015/1539, Note of Meeting between Secretary of State and Members of the Nyasaland Commission of Inquiry, 2 April 1959.
189. Armitage, evidence 15 April 1959 and 21 May 1959, DP, Box 14, pp. 1601–23 and Box 15, pp. 1–12.
190. Richardson to Fairclough, 14 May 1959, DP, Box 23.
191. Youens, interview with author, 4 January 1995.
192. Fairclough, interview with author, 26 November 1993.
193. Ibid; CO. 1015/1866, Monthly Intelligence Report, April 1959.
194. DP, Box 4.

195. Wyn-Harris to Devlin, 23 April 1960, DP, Box 13, transcript file, Vol. 3, folio 495.

196. Hepburn, Doig, Sangaya, Chintali, Mkwaila, evidence 20 April 1959, DP, Box 15, transcript file, Vol. 2; Jackson, pp. 104–5.

197. W. Mbekeani et al., evidence 19 May 1959, DP, Box 15.

198. DP, Box 4.

199. Ibid.

200. CO. 1015/1542, Footman to Morgan, 15 May 1959.

201. *London Gazette*, 7 April 1959, p. 2268; CO. 1015/1536, unsigned file note for Secretary of State, 2 April 1959.

202. Banda to Armitage, 6 April 1959, DP, Box 16.

203. Chiume to author, 19 August 1994. Chiume also provided lists of Congress detainees to be 'briefed' by Kellock: Chiume to Kellock, 9 April 1959, KP, Box 2, file 12.

204. Cmnd. 814, para. 5.

205. Banda, evidence 16 May 1959, DP, Box 14, pp. 1704–83; Chipembere, evidence 16 May 1959, DP, Box 12A, pp. 1934–2000.

206. Cmnd. 814, para. 3. The important witnesses whom Devlin did not see included two former presidents-general of Congress and five members of the 'second eleven'.

207. For numerous examples of the commission saying that they would carefully study memoranda later, see DP, Box 15 and Chijozi evidence 29 April 1959, DP, Box 13. For examples of statements made to Kellock being 'filtered', see KP, Box 1, files 3 and 9. For an example of a document addressed to the commission being handed over to Congress counsel, see F.R. Munthali to Secretary, Commission of Inquiry, 10 May 1959, KP, Box 2, file 12.

208. Chiumia, evidence 19 May 1959, DP, Box 154, transcripts file, Vol. 2, pp. 1359 *et seq.*

209. *Nyasaland Government Staff List*, 1959.

210. Caine to author, 6 October 1994.

211. Lewis to author, 12 December 1994.

212. Armitage, evidence 15 April 1959, DP, Box (NYC) 15, pp. 1–12. Details in the remainder of this paragraph, except where otherwise stated, are from this source.

213. AL, 12 April 1958 (*sic*, must be 1959).

214. Armitage to Devlin, 15 April 1959, DP, Box 16.

215. M.Q.Y. Chibambo, interview with R.E.N. Smith, 1961, cited in Smith to author, 24 August 1995.

216. Armitage, evidence 15 April 1959, DP, Box (NYC) 15, pp. 1–12. See also RHL. Mss. Brit.Emp. s. 527/1, pp. 78–9 where Armitage describes the murder plan as 'a very minor part of the whole exercise' mounted by Congress.

217. Ingham, evidence 16 April 1959, DP, Box (NYC) 15, pp. 85–96.

218. Williams, interview with author, 8 October 1993.

219. Kettlewell to author, 24 March 1994.

220. CO. 1015/1518, Situation Report from Milia Salisbury to War Office Force, Nairobi, 19 May 1959; Kettlewell, evidence 12 May 1959, DP, Box 14, pp. 1412–17. See also Kettlewell's memorandum on Agriculture: Kettlewell to Fairclough, 13 May 1959, DP, Box 7.

221. Williams, interview with author, 8 October 1993: Williams admired Haskard because he was 'both honest and loyal and drew a line beyond which he would not go', and Kettlewell because he was 'honest, efficient and made no attempt to conceal

or be defensive'; CO. 1015/1540, Notes on Lord Perth's talk with Devlin, 23 June 1959; Devlin to Legum, 19 October 1959, DP, Box 26.

222. CO. 1015/1540, Notes on Lord Perth's talk with Devlin, 23 June 1959; Williams, interview with author, 8 October 1993.

223. AL, 24 April 1959.

224. Jackson, p. 106.

225. AL, 15 May 1959.

226. Jackson, p. 105.

227. Mullin to author, 10 January 1994.

228. Garnett Massingah et al., 23 May 1959, in Williams's papers.

229. Williams, interview with author, 8 October 1993.

230. Cmnd. 814, paras 226–39.

231. Williams, interview with author, 8 October 1993.

232. Ibid.

233. Cmnd. 814, para. 239.

234. Galley proof, para. 239, DP, Box 7.

235. Karua, evidence 12 May 1959, 21 May 1959, 23 June 1959, DP, Box 14, pp. 1464C–G, 1903–1908, 2263–94. The Zomba meeting may, at Armitage's suggestion, have been at the Governor's cottage on Zomba Mountain: Fairclough to Youens, 7 April 1959, DP, Box 4; Williams, interview with author, 8 October 1993; CO. 1015/1542, Armitage to Secretary of State, 19 June 1959.

236. Armitage, evidence 21 May 1959, DP, Box 14, pp. 1601–23. Details in the remainder of this paragraph, except where otherwise stated, are from this source.

237. Points for consideration by the Nyasaland Government, 27 May 1959, DP, Box 16.

238. RHL. Mss. Brit.Emp. s. 527/1, p. 44 and p. 82.

239. Cmnd. 814, para. 149.

240. AL, 22 May 1959; Williams, interview with author, 8 October 1993.

241. CO. 1015/1540, Notes on Lord Perth's talk with Devlin, 23 June 1959.

242. Lord Devlin to author, 3 January 1992. Devlin also thought that 'by any standards Nyasaland was a little place of no great significance in the world': RHL. Mss. Brit.Emp. s. 527/2, p. 92.

243. Sir John Moreton to author, 28 September 1993; Jackson, p. 105.

244. J.H.E. Watson to author, 20 January 1994.

245. Williams, interview with author, 8 October 1993. See also RHL. Mss. Brit. Emp. s. 527/2, p. 92.

246. Williams, interview with author, 8 October 1993. See also Long, evidence 9 May 1959, DP, Box 12A, pp. 2084–98. The commissioners were not always opposed to recognising status: they travelled out to Nyasaland first class while their verbatim reporters were booked to travel on the same plane tourist class: B.O.A.C. to Colonial Office, 26 March 1959, DP, Box 26.

247. AL, 22 May 1959.

248. For example, Williams, interview with author, 8 October 1993; Williams to author, 30 July 1993.

249. Landreth to author, 11 November 1994.

250. Mushet to author, February 1995.

251. Jackson, p. 105.

252. CO. 1015/1540, Notes on Lord Perth's talk with Devlin, 23 June 1959.

253. Ibid.

254. Musk to author, 19 September 1995.

255. Chipembere, evidence 16 May 1959, DP, Box 12A, pp. 1934–2000; Y. Chisiza, evidence, 19 May 1959, DP, Box 14, transcripts file, No. 8.

256. Cmnd. 814, para. 3.

257. Devlin, *The Judge*. Quotations in this paragraph are from this source.

258. Cmnd. 814, paras 187–9.

259. O'Neil, evidence 28 April 1959, DP, Box 13, transcripts file, Vol. 3.

260. Cmnd. 814, paras 249–50. See also RHL. Mss. Brit.Emp. s. 527/2, p. 101.

261. Punter, evidence 4 May 1959, DP, Box 13, pp. 1092 *et seq.*; Mrs J.A.G. Corrie to author, 11 December 1994 and 19 January 1995; Punter to author, 22 January 1996. Details in the remainder of this paragraph, except where otherwise stated, are from these sources.

262. Cmnd. 814, para. 205.

263. Cmnd. 814, para. 250.

264. Punter to author, 22 January 1996.

265. Harvey to author, 10 October 1994; Purdy to author, 6 August 1995.

266. Musk to author, 19 September 1995.

267. Graham-Jolly to author, 5 December 1994.

268. Ibid.

269. Cmnd. 814, para. 136.

270. J. Brock to author, 17 May 1995; Cmnd. 814, para. 234.

271. RHL. Mss. Brit.Emp. s. 527/2, pp. 79–81; Williams to author, 27 October 1993. After the Devlin Commission completed its work, the other three commissioners and their wives gave a dinner for Madeleine and Patrick Devlin and presented to the judge a silver cigarette box inscribed 'From the Balderdash Committee'.

272. N.G. Mkandawire, evidence 17 April 1959, DP, Box 15 transcripts file, Vol. 1.

273. Unnamed witness, evidence 13 May 1959, DP, Box 15.

274. Jackson, p. 105.

275. Cmnd. 814, Appendix II.

276. Sheriff to author, December 1994.

277. B.E. Graves, conversation with author, 1960.

278. O'Riordan to author, 29 October 1994.

279. Llewelyn to author, 8 November 1994.

280. Haskard to author, 27 February 1994.

281. Haskard, evidence 3 May 1959, DP, Box 13, pp. 984–1016.

282. Cmnd. 814, para. 217.

283. Dr Muriel Harris, evidence 1 May 1959, DP, Box 13, pp. 898–900.

284. C.T. Bundy, evidence 30 April 1959, DP, Box 13, pp. 887–97.

285. Cmnd. 814, para. 218.

286. Ibid.

287. Banda, evidence 16 May 1959, DP, Box 14, pp. 1704–83. Details in this and the following two paragraphs, except where otherwise stated, are from this source.

288. *The Chronicle*, Bulawayo, 19 May 1959, p. 1. and *The Sunday Mail*, Rhodesia, 17 May 1959.

289. Cmnd. 814, para. 20; RHL. Mss. Brit.Emp. s. 527/1, p. 105.

290. *Review Tribunal (Preventative Detention Temporary Provisions) Act, 1959, General Report* (Salisbury: Government Printer, 1959), para. 48, para. 48n and Appendix A, paras 1–9.

291. Devlin to Perth, 21 September 1959, DP, Box 26.

292. Devlin to Beadle, 17 September 1959, DP, Box 26.

293. For example, on 18 April 1959 the Commission listened to the recordings of an interview which Ian Miller, a Southern Rhodesian journalist, had with Banda on 23 December 1958 in which the doctor screams and becomes incoherent: transcript in DP, Box 7; see also *Johannesburg Sunday Mail*, 1 March 1959, cited in Wood, op. cit., p. 645. Williams recalled that Devlin 'handled Dr. Banda very well: kindly and carefully': Williams, interview with author, 8 October 1993.

294. Devlin to A.E. Smith, 29 July 1959, DP, Box 26.

295. Williams, interview with author, 8 October 1993.

296. B.M.W. Phiri, evidence 26 April 1959, DP, Box 13; J.R.N. Chinyama, evidence 27 April 1959, DP, Box 13; Cmnd. 814, para. 31.

297. Chipembere, evidence 16 May 1959, DP, Box 12A, pp. 1934–2000.

298. Ibid. For the 36 points covering 9 pages of foolscap put to Chipembere see KP, Box 2, file 12.

299. Chipembere, evidence 16 May 1959, DP, Box 12A, pp. 1965 *et seq.*

300. M. Harris, evidence 1 May 1959, DP, Box 13, pp. 901 *et seq.* If, as is likely, Devlin was keen to distinguish clearly between Banda and Chipembere, Harris's evidence would indeed have been 'most valuable and helpful'.

301. R.B.S. Purdy, evidence 2 May 1959, DP, Box 13, pp. 920–31.

302. Youens, interview with Bradley, 26 November 1970, p. 7, ODRP.

303. Wyn-Harris to Devlin, 21 October 1966, DP, Box 16.

304. D.K. Chisiza, evidence 18 May 1959, DP, Box 120, pp. 2001–36.

305. Williams, interview with author, 8 October 1993.

306. R. Long, evidence 19 May 1959, DP, Box 12A, pp. 2084–98.

307. R. Long, evidence 19 May 1959, DP, Box 12A, p. 2096.

308. Y. Chisiza, evidence 19 May 1959, DP, Box 16, transcripts file, Vol. 8. This was the only case where a major Congressman was not examined by Foot himself.

309. AP, Armitage to Lennox-Boyd, 28 April 1959.

310. Ibid.

311. AP, Lennox-Boyd to Armitage, 23 June 1959.

312. Ibid.

5. The Devlin Report

1. DO. 35/7478, Meeting of interdepartmental Central Africa Committee, 17 March 1959.

2. Kettlewell to author, 24 March 1994.

3. CO. 1015/1535, Confidential Circular Dispatch from Secretary of State James Griffiths to Officer Administering the Government of Nyasaland, 12 August 1950.

4. CO. 1015/1535, Gorell Barnes to Armitage, 21 April 1959.

5. CO. 1015/1535, Morgan to Armitage, 28 April 1959.

6. Armitage to Lennox-Boyd, n.d., but late May 1959, reproduced in AM, 1959, pp. 61–3. Details in the following three paragraphs are from this source.

7. CO. 1015/1535, Armitage to Gorell Barnes, 30 April 1959; CO. 1015/1540, Armitage to Morgan, 13 June 1959.

8. Mullin to Provincial Commissioners, referred to in CO. 1015/1544, Haskard to Mullin, 29 May 1959.

9. CO. 1015/1544, Morgan to Macpherson, 6 July 1959; Probable Consequences in Nyasaland of Publication of the Devlin Commission Report, appreciation of Nyasaland Government, 15 July 1959.

10. CO. 1015/1544, Morgan to Macpherson, 6 July 1959.

11. Ingham, minute to Footman, 29 June 1959 and Footman to Armitage, 29 June 1959: AP.

12. CO. 1015/1535 and CO. 1015/1538, Minute by Morgan, 26 May 1959.

13. CO. 1015/1538, Morgan to Secretary of State, 2 June 1959.

14. Fairclough, interview with author, 26 November 1993.

15. Williams, interview with author, 8 October 1993; Williams to Fairclough, 1 July 1959, DP, Box 20.

16. Devlin to Wyn-Harris, 20 January 1960, DP, Box 26.

17. Fairclough to Civil Commissioner, Bulawayo, 14 May 1959, DP, Box 20.

18. CO. 1015/1535, Perth to Gorell Barnes, 9 June 1959; RHL. Mss. Brit.Emp. s. 527/2, p. 112.

19. CO. 1015/1540, Wilkes to Morgan, n.d., probably mid-June 1959; RHL. Mss. Brit.Emp. s. 527/2, p. 79.

20. Fairclough, interview with author, 26 November 1993.

21. RHL Mss. Brit.Emp. s. 527/2, p. 112.

22. CO. 1015/1540, Gorell Barnes to Shannon, 5 May 1959.

23. Fairclough, interview with author, 26 November 1993; CO. 1015/1535, Submission by Morgan, 2 June 1959.

24. CO. 1015/1535, Gorell Barnes to Morgan, 22 May 1959.

25. CO. 1015/1535, Gorell Barnes to Minister of State, 28 May 1959.

26. CO. 1015/1535, Morgan to Secretary of State, 2 June 1959.

27. Ibid.; CO. 1015/1538, Morgan to Moreton, n.d., probably 2 June 1959.

28. CO. 1015/1535, Gorell Barnes to Moreton, 3 June 1959.

29. Nyasaland Government Information Department, *Bulletin No. 13* of 6 May 1959.

30. *The Economist*, 23 May 1959.

31. *The Times*, 16 June 1959, letter from Violet Bonham Carter to Editor.

32. CO. 1014/1543, Gorell Barnes to Morgan, 4 June 1959.

33. CO. 1015/1543, Morgan to Gorell Barnes, 5 June 1959.

34. Karua to Foot, n.d., probably late May; Rattansey to Foot, 31 May; Deputy Governor, Tanganyika to Secretary of State for the Colonies, 19 June; Fairclough to Foot, 10 June, DP, Box 16; Fairclough to Devlin, 5 June: all 1959 and all DP, Box 16; CO. 1015/1542, Secretary of State to Turnbull, 18 June 1959.

35. CO. 1015/1542, Armitage to Secretary of State, 19 June 1959.

36. Ibid.

37. CO. 1015/1542, Deputy Governor, Tanganyika to Secretary of State n.d., probably between 19 and 24 June 1959. Copy of affidavit is in DP, Box 16.

38. *Sunday Express*, 19 July 1959.

39. CO. 1015/1543, Secretary of State to Officer Administering the Government, Nyasaland, 30 July 1959; CO. 1015/1543, Chief Secretary, Nyasaland to Secretary of State, 7 August 1959; Sir Denys Roberts, interview with author, 1 July 1993.

40. *Sunday Empire News*, 26 July 1959, p. 1 and p. 9. See also Karua's statements to Kellock, KP, Box 1, file 4.

41. CO. 1015/1905, Report on System for the Holding, Rehabilitation and Release of Detainees, n.d., but considered in Colonial Office on 28 May 1959. Details in the remainder of this paragraph, unless otherwise stated, are from this source.

42. CO. 1015/1905, Minister of State to Armitage, 3 June 1959.

43. CO. 1015/1905, Armitage to Secretary of State, 5 June 1959.

44. CO. 1015/1905, Armitage to Morgan, 9 June 1959.

45. CO. 1015/1905, Gorell Barnes to Morgan, 15 June 1959; statement by Charles Evans, 5 May 1959, KP, Box 2, file 10.

46. CO. 1015/1905, Gorell Barnes to Morgan, 15 June 1959.

47. CO. 1015/1905, Armitage to Secretary of State, 16 June 1959.

48. CO. 1015/1905, Lennox-Boyd to Devlin, 23 June 1959.

49. CO. 1015/1905, Devlin to Lennox-Boyd, 24 June 1959.

50. CO. 1015/1540, Notes on Lord Perth's talk with Devlin, 23 June 1959.

51. Ibid.

52. CO. 1015/1540, Secretary of State to Gorell Barnes, 17 June 1959.

53. CO. 1015/1538, Gorell Barnes to Moreton, 18 June 1959.

54. CO. 1015/1540, Secretary of State to Armitage, 24 June 1959; and Morgan to Gorell Barnes, 24 June 1959.

55. CO. 1015/1540, Wilks to Morgan, 1 July 1959; and Note, unsigned, to Morgan, 2 July 1959.

56. CO. 1015/1540, Morgan to Gorell Barnes, 24 June 1959.

57. CO. 1015/1540, Gorell Barnes to Minister of State, 25 June 1959.

58. CO. 1015/1540, Note, unsigned, to Morgan, 2 July 1959.

59. CO. 1015/1540, Perth to Secretary of State, 6 July 1959. Details in the remainder of this paragraph are from this source.

60. Information on the meeting comes from Wyn-Harris to Devlin, 12 July 1959, DP, Box 26; Devlin to Primrose, 10 July 1959, DP, Box 20, p. 48.

61. Williams, interview with author, 8 October 1993.

62. Proof of paras 288–98 of draft report, DP, Box 18. Details in the remainder of this paragraph and the next five paragraphs, except where otherwise stated, are from this source.

63. This assertion is based on the correspondence of a large number of officials with author in the course of research for this book.

64. R. Long, evidence 19 May 1959, DP, Box 12A, pp. 2084–98.

65. Cmnd. 814, para. 285 (4); RHL. Mss. Brit.Emp. s. 527/2, p. 107.

66. This assertion is based on the correspondence of a large number of officials with author in the course of research for this book; Graham-Jolly to author, 5 December 1994.

67. Devlin to Primrose, 10 July 1959, DP, Box 20, p. 48.

68. Wyn-Harris to Devlin, 12 July 1959, DP, Box 26.

69. Williams to author, 29 October 1993.

70. Devlin to Williams, 27 July 1959.

71. Primrose to Devlin, 12 July 1959, DP, Box 26.

72. Cmnd. 814, para. 286.

73. Armitage, evidence 21 May 1959, DP, Box 14, p. 1615. It is probable that the verbatim reporter recorded 'an answer', instead of 'one answer'. Roberts says that in giving evidence 'other witnesses, District Commissioners said how sorry they were that deaths and injury resulted from the necessity for them to maintain and restore law and order': Roberts, interview with author, 1 July 1993.

74. CO. 1015/1540, Morgan to Gorell Barnes, 2 July 1959, and Morgan to Macpherson, 7 July 1959.

75. CO. 1015/1540, Secretary of State to Armitage, 24 June 1959, and Wilks to Morgan, n.d., probably early July 1959.

76. AL, 10 July 1959.

77. CO. 1015/1540, Armitage to Secretary of State, 13 July 1959. On 14 July,

Devlin wrote to Perth saying that he hoped to deliver to the printers early the next morning 'the finally revised draft': Devlin to Perth, 14 July 1959, DP, Box 20.

78. G. Jones to author, 19 November 1993; CO. 1015/1540, Secretary of State to Armitage, 13 July 1959.

79. AL, 20 July 1959; author, participant observation.

80. J.M. Greenfield, *Testimony of a Rhodesian Federal* (Bulawayo: Books of Rhodesia, 1978), p. 169.

81. CO. 1015/1540, Morgan to Armitage, 13 July 1959.

82. CO. 1015/1540, Morgan, 22 September 1959, Draft of possible questions and answers about whether the Secretary of State received advance copies of the report.

83. RHL. Mss. Brit.Emp. s. 527/2, p. 111.

84. Devlin to Williams, 12 August 1964, Williams papers, and DP, Box 16.

85. Devlin to Radcliffe, 21 August 1964, DP, Box 16.

86. Williams, interview with author, 8 October 1993.

87. CO. 1015/1540, Secretary of State to Armitage, 13 July 1959.

88. Lennox-Boyd to Armitage, 13 July 1959, cited in AM, 1959, p. 78.

89. Ibid.

90. Posnett to author, 15 March 1994; N. Fisher, *Iain Macleod* (London: André Deutsch, 1973), p. 143.

91. Lennox-Boyd to Armitage, 13 July 1959, cited in AM, 1959, p. 78.

92. CO. 1015/1538, Gorell Barnes to Moreton, 18 June 1959.

93. CO. 1015/1540, Armitage to Lennox-Boyd, 13 July 1959.

94. AM, 1959, p. 79.

95. CO. 1015/1544, Minute by Posnett, 16 July 1959, and Probable Consequences in Nyasaland of Publication of the Devlin Commission Report, 15 July 1959.

96. CO. 1015/1540, Morgan to Macpherson, 14 July 1959.

97. AL, 20 July 1959; Posnett to author, 15 March 1994.

98. AM, 1959, p. 81. For details of the meeting see also RHL. Mss. Brit.Emp. s. 527/1, p. 44 and p. 80.

99. CO. 1015/1540, Minute by Morgan, 16 July 1959.

100. AM, 1959, p. 81.

101. AM, 1959, p. 81–2; RHL. Mss. Brit.Emp. s. 527/1, p. 81, in which Armitage describes Amery's sentence as his 'chief memory of those two days of non-stop work'.

102. Howard-Drake to author, 27 November 1993.

103. AM, 1959, p. 82; Watson to author, 13 December 1993; Sir John Moreton, interview with author, 27 August 1993; Welensky, op. cit., p. 131.

104. Pearson to author, 16 December 1993.

105. Williams, interview with author, 8 October 1993.

106. RHL. Mss. Brit.Emp. s. 527/2, p. 95, p. 99.

107. Chiume, memorandum to the Colonial Secretary, 3 February 1959, KP, Box 2, file 13.

108. Devlin to Perth, 21 September 1959, DP, Box 26.

109. Perth to Devlin, 28 September 1959, DP, Box 26; Perth, interview with author, 27 October 1993.

110. Roberts, interview with author, 1 July 1993.

111. Posnett to author, 15 March 1994.

112. CO. 1015/1540, Armitage to Footman, 21 July 1959.

113. AL, 20 July 1959.

114. Ibid.

115. CO. 1015/1537, Guide to contents of despatch from Governor of Nyasaland, n.d.; *Nyasaland Despatch by the Governor relating to the Report of the Nyasaland Commission of Inquiry*, Cmnd. 815 (London: HMSO, 1959). See also Wood, op. cit., pp. 682–5 for a summary account of the despatch.

116. CO. 1015/1540, Armitage to Footman, 19 July 1959.

117. CO. 1015/1540, Footman to Armitage, 21 July 1959; Mullin to author, January 1994.

118. AL, 20 July 1959.

119. Hansard, Commons, 28 July 1959, cols 317–454. Details of the debate are from this source. See also *The Times*, 29 July 1959 and RHL. Mss. Brit.Emp. s. 527/1, pp. 44–5.

120. Cmnd. 814, Part IV, Sections 1–4; Armitage, evidence 21 May 1959, DP, Box 14, p. 1617; RHL. Mss. Brit.Emp. s. 527/1, p. 35 and p. 84.

121. AL, 29 July 1959.

122. Devlin, *Easing the Passing* (London: Bodley Head, 1985), p. 189.

123. A. Sampson, *Macmillan: A Study in Ambiguity* (London: Macmillan, 1967), p. 182.

124. Hansard, 29 July 1959, Lords, cols 757–896.

125. Williams to Primrose, 28 July 1959, Williams papers.

126. Wyn-Harris to Williams, 30 July 1959, Williams papers.

127. Devlin to Williams, 27 July 1959, Williams papers.

128. Devlin to Williams, 7 August 1959, Williams papers.

129. Fox Strangways to Fairclough, 28 July 1959, DP, Box 20.

130. Perth to Devlin, n.d., probably August 1959, DP, Box 26.

131. Andrews to Devlin, 30 July 1959, DP, Box 26.

132. Primrose to Devlin, 30 July 1959, DP, Box 26.

133. Devlin to Primrose, 7 August 1959, DP, Box 26.

134. Devlin to Beadle, 17 September, 1959, Williams papers.

135. Devlin to Fox Strangways, 17 September 1959, DP, Box 26.

136. RHL. Mss. Brit.Emp. s. 527/2, pp. 116–8.

137. CO. 1015/1540, Perth, Notes on talk with Devlin, 23 June 1959; Devlin to Fox Strangways, 17 September 1959, DP, Box 26.

138. RHL. Mss. Brit.Emp. s. 527/2, p. 71.

139. Cmnd. 814, para. 161.

140. RHL. Mss. Brit.Emp. s. 527/1, pp. 168–9.

141. Armitage, evidence 21 May 1959, DP, Box 14, p. 1616.

142. Cmnd. 814, paras 226–39, 245–50, 277–8; Purdy to author, 6 August 1995.

143. Kilmuir to Devlin, 21 July 1959, DP, Box 26.

144. Cmnd. 814. For inconsistencies see para. 27, '6 July 1957 ... Dr. Banda had not heard before the name of Mr. D.K. Chisiza' compared with para. 29, 'In January 1957 he [Banda] had a letter from Mr. Chisiza'; para. 229, 'there were the sergeant and eleven men of the RRR ... Four of these were sent to guard the Boma and two to the post office ... This left the sergeant with four men.' For printing errors see p. 14 line 4; p. 19 line 14; p. 19 line 36; p. 77 line 2; para. 198, 'One of the four was a Presbyterian minister and the other [*sic*] a village headman.' For lack of anonymity see paras. 114, 115, 197, 210, 217–8 (the officer's name is mentioned eighteen times in these two paragraphs), 226–8, 237–8, 253.

145. RHL. Mss. Brit.Emp. s. 527/2, pp. 216–17.
146. Cmnd. 814, para. 149.
147. RHL. Mss. Brit.Emp. s. 527/2, p. 123.
148. Horne, op. cit., p. 182.
149. H. Macmillan, *Pointing the Way, 1959–1961* (London: Macmillan, 1972), pp. 135–8.
150. Welensky, op. cit., p. 147 and p. 154. See also Wood, op. cit., pp. 673–4.
151. Wood, op. cit., p. 692.
152. AL, 29 July 1959; Chiume, op. cit., p. 126.
153. AM, 1959, p. 98.
154. AP, letters from Kettlewell, 23 July 1959; John Wallace, 26 July 1959; Donald Brook, 27 and 29 July 1959; Derrick Gunston, 27 July 1959; Gribble, 29 July 1959; G. Conforzi, 27 August 1959.
155. AL, 4 August 1959.
156. AP, Statement by Armitage, 30 July 1959. Details in the remainder of this paragraph, except where otherwise stated, are from this source.
157. AL, 27 August 1959.
158. Jackson, p. 127; *Contact*, Vol.2, No. 17, 22 August 1959, p. 5.
159. Pegg to author, 17 July 1995; Mrs M. Muir to author, 5 January 1996.
160. AL, Lady Armitage to Haworth, 8 September 1959.
161. Fairclough to Devlin, 10 September and 2 October 1963, privately held; Williams, interview with author, 8 October 1993.
162. Devlin to Fairclough, 17 September 1963, privately held.
163. Devlin to Fairclough, 10 October 1963 and 7 June 1971, privately held; Fairclough to Williams, 21 May 1971, privately held; Williams to Devlin, 20 August 1964, Williams papers and DP, Box 7.
164. Devlin, *Easing the Passing*. The following details of the trial and of the book, including quotations, are from this source.
165. Cmnd. 814, para. 168.
166. Ibid.
167. Armitage, evidence 21 May 1959, DP, Box 14, p. 1618; see also CO. 1015/1839, Armitage to Lennox-Boyd, 6 October 1959, para. 3.
168. CO. 1015/1905, Minister of State to Armitage, 3 June 1959.
169. DP, transcript files, especially Box 14.
170. Magogo, evidence 25 April 1959, DP, Box 15, transcripts files, Vol. 2.
171. Short, op. cit., pp. 227–8 and p. 303.
172. R.H. Martin to author, 27 June 1992.
173. Ibid.

6. The wind of change

1. CO. 1015/1839, Armitage to Lennox-Boyd, 6 October 1959. Details in the following paragraph, except where otherwise stated, are from this source.
2. AL, 9 October 1959.
3. CO. 1015/1838, Minute by Lennox-Boyd, 14 October 1959.
4. CO. 1015/1839, Minute by Perth, 13 October 1959; de Zulueta to Howard-Drake, 2 November 1959.
5. In reciprocation, Armitage was not impressed with Macmillan after Cyprus. In February 1956 he said, 'I only hope he makes a better Chancellor of the

Exchequer than he did Foreign Minister; he did not impress me': AL, Armitage to Haworth, 11 February 1956.

6. Sampson, op. cit., p. 183.

7. AM, 1956, p. 2.

8. Sampson, op. cit., p. 181.

9. CAB. 21/3155, Macmillan to Brook, 1 November 1959. Details in the remainder of this and the following paragraph, except where otherwise stated, are from this source.

10. Lord Callaghan to author, 18 November 1993.

11. K. Young, *Sir Alec Douglas-Home* (London: Dent, 1970), p. 113. However, Welensky recalled that at his meeting with Macmillan on 7 July 1959 he found him more harassed than he had ever seen him and worried about the effects of Central African affairs on his election prospects: Welensky, op. cit., p. 146 and Wood, op. cit., p. 673.

12. R. Shepherd, *Iain Macleod: A Biography* (London: Hutchinson, 1994), pp. 151–61.

13. CAB. 21/3155, Brook to Macmillan, 2 November 1959. Details in the remainder of this paragraph, except where otherwise stated, are from this source.

14. Sampson, op. cit., p. 183.

15. CAB. 21/3155, Secretary of State for Commonwealth Relations to High Commissioner Pretoria, 5 November 1959.

16. CAB. 21/3155, High Commissioner Pretoria to Secretary of State for Commonwealth Relations, 6 November 1959.

17. CAB. 21/3155, Macmillan to Verwoerd, 11 November 1959.

18. CAB. 21/3155, C.R.O. to High Commissioner Salisbury, 11 November 1959.

19. CAB. 21/3155, High Commissioner Salisbury to C.R.O., 13 November 1959.

20. CAB. 21/3155, C.R.O. to High Commissioner Salisbury, n.d., probably 14 November 1959.

21. CAB. 21/3155, C.R.O. to High Commissioner Accra, 14 November 1959.

22. CAB. 21/3155, Nkrumah to Macmillan, n.d., probably 15 November 1959.

23. *The Times*, 19 November 1959.

24. D. Hunt, *On the Spot: An Ambassador Remembers* (London: Peter Davies, 1975), p. 102 and p. 116.

25. Horne, op. cit., p. 195.

26. Colin Baker, *Development Governor, a biography of Sir Geoffrey Colby* (London: British Academic Press, 1994), pp. 250–1.

27. J. Masters, *Bhowani Junction* (London: Michael Joseph, 1954), Penguin edition, 1960, p. 359.

28. Hunt, op. cit., p. 102.

29. Ibid., p. 116.

30. Horne, op. cit., p. 194.

31. Johnston to author, 6 December 1993.

32. CAB. 21/3155, Stephen to Bligh, 30 November 1959; J. Robertson to author, 4 January 1994.

33. CAB. 21/3157, Bligh to Brook, 23 November 1959.

34. CAB. 21/3157, Note for the Record, Bligh, 14 December 1959.

35. CAB. 21/3157, Note for the Record, Bligh, 15 December 1959.

36. Johnston to author, 6 December 1993.

37. CAB. 21/3155, High Commissioner Pretoria to C.R.O., 29 December 1959.

38. CAB. 21/3157, Hunt to Brook, 14 December 1959.

39. CAB. 21/3157, Brimblecombe to Stephen, 15 December 1959.

40. CAB. 21/3157, Hunt to Brook, 14 December 1959.

41. CAB. 21/3157, Brimblecombe to Stephen, 15 December 1959, and Brook's file, Africa Tour, Themes for Speeches, n.d., probably 4 January 1960.

42. CAB. 21/3157, Hunt to Brook, 14 December 1959.

43. CAB. 21/3155, Hunt to Stephen, 18 December 1959; CAB. 21/3157, Brimblecombe to Stephen, 22 December 1959.

44. CAB. 21/3157, Brook's file, Africa Tour, Themes for Speeches, n.d., probably 4 January 1960.

45. Horne, op. cit., p. 186; Hunt, op. cit., p. 100.

46. Horne, op. cit., pp. 187–8.

47. Hunt, op. cit., p. 102. Twenty-five of Macmillan's 26 words are taken directly from Robertson's draft.

48. Sampson, op. cit., p. 183 and p. 184; Horne, op. cit., p. 189.

49. H. Evans, *Downing Street Diary: the Macmillan Years, 1957–1963* (London: Hodder and Stoughton, 1981), p. 90.

50. CAB. 21/3157, Macmillan to Brook, 7 January 1960.

51. Macmillan, *Pointing the Way*, pp. 118–19.

52. DO. 35/7564, Home to Macmillan, 21 December 1959.

53. Shepherd, op cit., p. 163.

54. AP, *The Federation of Rhodesia and Nyasaland: Mr. Macmillan's Visit, January 1960, Official Programme.*

55. PREM. 11/3075, Note of meeting of ministers held at Salisbury on 19 January 1960. For Welensky's account of the meeting, see Welensky, op. cit., pp. 171 *et seq.*; see also Wood, op. cit., pp. 731–4.

56. Wood, op. cit., p. 731 and p. 736.

57. PREM. 11/3075, Note of meeting of ministers held at Salisbury on 19 January 1960; Welensky, op. cit., p. 173.

58. Wood, op. cit., p. 736.

59. CO. 1015/1518, Macleod to Perth, 20 December 1959.

60. For Welensky's account of the meeting, see Welensky, op. cit., pp. 173 *et seq.*; see also Wood, op. cit., pp. 733–4.

61. Welensky, op. cit., p. 174.

62. PREM. 11/3075, Macmillan to Home, 20 January 1960.

63. AD, 25 January 1960.

64. Sir Henry Phillips, interview with author, 12 January 1995; Wood, op. cit., p. 739; Sir David Hunt to author, 26 December 1991.

65. DO. 35/7476, Macleod to Macmillan, 24 January 1960.

66. AP, *Official Programme*, op. cit.

67. CAB. 21/3155, C.R.O. to High Commissioners Pretoria, Accra, Salisbury, 24 November 1959.

68. Mrs A. Finchett (neé Barker) to author, 24 January 1994.

69. Evans, op. cit., p. 100.

70. See note 77 below.

71. PREM. 11/3075, Note, Nyasaland, points for discussion with the Governor, 24 January 1960.

72. Mullin to author, 10 January 1994.

73. *The Economist*, 1 August 1959, p. 267.

74. CO. 1015/1905, Unsigned and undated note, probably June 1959.

75. CO. 1015/1518, Minute by Secretary of State, 11 September 1959.

76. CO. 1015/1518, Minute by Neale, 15 September 1959.

77. The following account is drawn from AD, 25–26 January 1960; AM, 1959, pp. 12–13; RHL. Mss. Brit.Emp. s. 527/1, p. 85; R. Rowan to author, 5 July 1993; N. Maxwell-Lawford to author, 26 May 1994; Maxwell-Lawford, interview with author, 26 April 1994; Ingham to author, 19 November 1991; R.M.M. King to author, 6 and 27 November 1991; Hunt, op. cit., pp. 107–8; Hunt to author, October 1991 and 26 December 1991; Robertson to author, 11 March 1992 and 7 October 1992; Macmillan, *Pointing the Way*, pp. 148–9; Wade to author, 6 January 1995.

78. DO. 35/7477, Macmillan to Macleod, 26 January 1960.

79. DO. 35/7477, Macleod to Macmillan, 27 January 1960.

80. DO. 35/7477, Macmillan to Macleod, 26 January 1960; Welensky, op. cit., pp. 175–8.

81. Wood, op. cit., pp. 737–8; Sampson, op. cit., p. 185. Details in the remainder of this paragraph, except where otherwise stated, are from these sources.

82. N. Fisher, *Iain Macleod* (London: André Deutsch 1973), p. 158.

83. DO. 35/7564, Banda, memorandum, 24 January 1960. The original of the memorandum is in PREM. 11/3075.

84. CAB. 21/3157, Minute, Brook to Macmillan, 24 January 1960; PREM. 11/3075, Note, Brook to Macmillan, 24 January 1960, and Bligh to Macmillan, 26 January 1960; AD, 25 January 1960.

85. Maxwell-Lawford, interview with author, 26 April 1994.

86. PREM. 11/3075, Note of meeting between Macmillan and Foot at Government House, Zomba, 25 January 1960. The following details of the meeting are from this source.

87. DO. 35/7564, Home to Bligh, 22 February 1960, and Bligh to Home, 23 February 1960.

88. AD, 25 January 1960.

89. AD, 26 January 1960. Armitage none the less thought that his representations to Macmillan were the cause of Banda's release being somewhat delayed: RHL. Mss. Brit.Emp. s. 527/1, p. 86.

90. Author, participant observation.

91. Mrs B. Leeds to author, 13 April 1995.

92. Watson to author, 20 January, 1994.

93. *The Southworth Commission Report* (Zomba: The Government Printer, 1960).

94. Hunt to author, 26 December 1991; see also AD, 15 March 1960 and AM, 1960, p. 16.

95. Johnston to author, 23 December 1993; see also Sampson, op. cit., p. 186.

96. Macmillan, *Pointing the Way*, p. 475.

97. Ibid.; see also Evans, op. cit., pp. 107–8.

98. Hunt to author, 26 December 1991.

99. AD, 29 January 1960.

100. DO. 35/7564, Macmillan to Macleod, 29 January 1960.

101. Ibid.

102. Ibid.

103. Macmillan to Queen Elizabeth, 30 January 1960; Macmillan, *Pointing the Way*, p. 485.

104. AD, 2 February 1960.

105. Ibid.

106. DO. 35/7564, Macleod to Armitage, 4 February 1960. See also AM, 1960, p. 25.

107. AM, 1960, p. 26.

108. Phillips, interview with author, 12 January 1995.

109. *Nyasaland Government Gazette*, 20 February 1960, p. 55.

110. Devlin to Fairclough, 25 February 1960, DP, Box 16.

7. Resolving the crisis

1. AD, 7 November 1959; AM, 1959, p. 137.

2. CO. 1015/2119, Record of interview by Armitage with delegation from Malawi Congress Party, 6 November 1959; see also AL, 12 November 1959. Details in the remainder of this and the following paragraph, except where otherwise stated, are from these sources.

3. R.I. Rotberg, *The Rise of Nationalism in Central Africa: The Making of Malawi and Zambia 1873–1964* (London: Oxford University Press, 1965), pp. 308–10; Short, op. cit., pp. 126–7.

4. CO. 1015/1518, Nyasaland Intelligence Report for November 1959.

5. Rotberg, op. cit., p. 309.

6. *Malawi News*, 24 September 1960, cited in Short, op. cit., p. 126.

7. CO. 1015/1984, Notes of meetings in the Secretary of State's room, 8 (*sic* must be 9), 10 and 11 November 1959. Details in the remainder of this and the following five paragraphs, except where otherwise stated, are from these sources.

8. DO. 35/7564, Monson to Armitage, n.d., probably August 1959.

9. Shepherd, op. cit., p. 187.

10. AM, 1959, p. 137; see also AL, 10 and 12 November 1959 and AL, Armitage to Haworth, 29 November 1959.

11. CO. 1015/2119, Memorandum to Secretary of State, the Rt. Hon. Iain Macleod by Mr Orton Chirwa, 18 November 1959.

12. CO. 1015/2119, Record of a meeting between the Secretary of State for the Colonies and Mr. Orton Chirwa at the Colonial Office on 18 November 1959. Details in the remainder of this paragraph, except where otherwise stated, are from this source.

13. CO. 1015/2119, Monson to Armitage, 3 December 1959. The 'Cs' were Chipembere and the Chisiza brothers.

14. Ibid.

15. AM, 1959, p. 135.

16. AD, 16 November 1959.

17. AM, 1959, p. 136.

18. CO. 1015/1518, Armitage to Monson, 8 December 1959. Details in the remainder of this paragraph are from this source.

19. DO. 35/7564, Note, unsigned, for the record, 7 December 1959.

20. PREM. 11/3075 and DO. 35/7564, Macleod to Macmillan, 3 December 1959. Details in the remainder of this paragraph, except where otherwise stated, are from this source. See also Shepherd, op. cit., p. 188.

21. Shepherd, op. cit., p. 188; Young, op. cit., pp. 113–14.

22. DO. 35/7564, Home to Macmillan, 7 December 1959.

23. Theunissen, interview with author, 26 June 1994. Details in this and the following paragraph, except where otherwise stated, are from AD, 18 and 19 December 1959 and CO. 1015/1518, Macleod to Perth, 20 December 1959. See also RHL. Mss. Brit.Emp. s. 527/1, p. 84.

24. Theunissen, interview with author, 26 June 1994; RHL. Mss. Brit.Emp. s. 527/1, p. 84.

25. AL, 24 December 1959.

26. AM, 1959, p. 144.

27. AP, Macleod to Armitage, 22 December 1959.

28. AP, Armitage to Macleod, 31 December 1959.

29. AD, 19 December 1959; AM, 1959, p. 144.

30. DO. 35/7564, Home to Macmillan, 21 December 1959. Details in the remainder of this paragraph are from this source.

31. CO. 1015/1518, Macleod to Perth, 20 December 1959, and Note by Secretary of State on Nyasaland Emergency, 24 December 1959. Details in the remainder of this paragraph, unless otherwise stated, are from these sources.

32. DO. 35/7476, Minute, unsigned, dated 24 December 1959, and Minute by Shannon, 29 December 1959; RHL. Mss. Brit.Emp. s. 527/1, p. 36.

33. PREM. 11/3075, Bligh to Macmillan, 29 December 1959.

34. AD, 23 and 28 December 1959.

35. Ibid.

36. AD, 29 December 1959.

37. AD, 28 December 1959; AL, 31 December 1959. The New Year's Honours List, recommended by Armitage, included Haskard, CMG; Mullin, CBE; Roberts, OBE; Long, QPM; Bevan, Finney, Humphreys, Kirkham and Lomax, CPM. It also included, recommended by Welensky, Van Oppen, the Sergeant in charge of the RRR contingent at Nkata Bay on 3 March 1959, BEM. *Nyasaland Government Gazette*, 1 January 1960, p. 1, and *London Gazette*, Supplement, 1 January 1960. Devlin and Williams considered it a 'vindictive omission' that Fairclough's name had not appeared in the 1960 New Year's Honours List. Devlin asked Perth if he could 'do something for [him] about Fairclough': Devlin to Perth, 21 September 1959, DP, Box 26; Williams to Fairclough, 1 February 1960, DP, Box 16; Devlin to Wyn-Harris, 20 January 1960, DP, Box 26. Thirty years later, in 1990, Fairclough was awarded the CMG: *Who's Who*, 1995.

38. Banda to Registrar General, Nyasaland, 22 December 1959, privately held.

39. AD, 14 December 1959.

40. AD, 30 December 1959.

41. AD, 5 January 1960.

42. AM, 1959, pp. 151–5. On his return to Nyasaland on 9 January, Footman called clandestinely at the Malawi Congress Party Office during the evening, accompanied by Downs, Foot's representative in Nyasaland, and he had a further secret meeting there during the third week of January. It is not known what was discussed or who else was present: Wade to author, 6 January 1995.

43. DO. 35/7476, Macleod to Armitage, 4 January 1960.

44. RHL. Mss. Brit.Emp. s. 527/1, p. 85.

45. DO. 35/7476, C.R.O. to Welensky, 5 January 1960.

46. Wade to author, 6 January 1995.

47. PREM. 11/3075, Note for the Record by Bligh, 1 January 1960 and Wyndham to Macmillan, 1 January 1960.

48. AD, 6 January 1960.

49. Wade to author, 6 January 1995.

50. DO. 35/7476, C.R.O. to High Commissioners Ottawa, Canberra, Wellington, Pretoria, Delhi, Karachi, Columbo, Kuala Lumpur, repeated Salisbury, 8 January

1960; see also PREM. 11/3081 for full text of Macleod's Leeds speech on 7 January 1960.

51. AD, 8 January 1960.

52. AD, 13 January 1960; DO. 35/7564, Armitage to Macleod, 14 January 1960.

53. DO. 35/7564 and PREM. 11/3075, Armitage to Macleod, 14 January 1960. Details in the remainder of this and the following three paragraphs, except where otherwise stated, are from this source.

54. Shepherd, op. cit., p. 191.

55. DO. 35/7564, Macleod to Macmillan, 16 January 1960.

56. DO. 35/7564, Macleod to Macmillan, 20 January 1960.

57. DO. 35/7564, Monson to Armitage, 21 January 1960. Details in the remainder of this paragraph are from this source.

58. Shepherd, op. cit., p. 161.

59. Shepherd, op. cit., p. 169; Macmillan, *At the End of the Day*, p. 288.

60. AM, 1960, pp. 5–6.

61. AM, 1960, p. 6.

62. Theunissen, interview with author, 26 June 1994.

63. Welensky, op. cit., p. 179.

64. DO. 35/4564, Macmillan to Home and Macleod, 28 February 1960; Macmillan, *Pointing the Way*, p. 149.

65. PREM. 11/3085, Gibb to Home, 6 February 1960.

66. AM, 1960, p. 21.

67. CAB. 21/3157, Undated and unsigned note, probably 26 January 1960, Nyasaland, for talks with Welensky.

68. PREM. 11/3075, Bligh, note for file, 8 January 1960.

69. DO. 35/4564, Macmillan to Home and Macleod, 28 February 1960.

70. DO. 35/7566, Macmillan to Home, 10 February 1960.

71. DO. 35/7564, Macmillan to Macleod, 28 January 1960.

72. DO. 35/7564 and PREM. 11/3075, Armitage to Monson, 14 January 1960.

73. DO. 35/7564, Macmillan to Home, 28 January 1960.

74. Ibid.

75. DO. 35/7477 and DO. 35/7574, Macleod to Armitage, 1 February, 1960. Details in this and the following paragraphs, except where otherwise stated, are from this source. See also AD, 2 February 1960.

76. DO. 35/7564, Home to Macmillan, 20 January 1960 and Macleod to Armitage, 1 February 1960.

77. PREM. 11/3075, Butler to Macmillan, n.d., but 12–17 January 1960.

78. DO. 35/7564, Macmillan to Macleod and for information of Home, 28 January 1960.

79. Welensky, op. cit., pp. 179–81; Wood, op. cit., pp. 743–5.

80. AM, 1960, p. 27.

81. DO. 35/7564, Welensky to Macmillan, 3 February 1960.

82. Ibid.

83. AD, 13 and 14 February 1960; AM, 1960, pp. 29–30.

84. AD, 2 February 1960.

85. PREM. 35/7564, Metcalf to Macmillan, 4 and 12 February, 1960.

86. PREM. 11/7564, Dalhousie to Home, 4 February 1960.

87. PREM. 11/3075, Home to Macmillan, 4 Febuary 1960.

88. PREM. 11/3076, Home to Monckton, n.d., probably March 1960.

89. Wade, Supplement to weekly FISB notes, No. 27, 6 February 1960, privately held.

90. PREM. 11/3075, Home to Macmillan, 4 February 1960.

91. Wade to de Quehen, 6 February 1960, privately held.

92. DO. 35/7564, Armitage to Macleod, 5 February 1960, and Macmillan to Macleod and for information of Home, 28 January 1960; AD, 5 February 1960.

93. DO. 35/7564, Armitage to Macleod, 10 February 1960.

94. Ibid.

95. Ibid.

96. DO. 53/7564, Macleod to Armitage, 12 February 1960.

97. DO. 35/7564, Home to Macleod, 12 February 1960.

98. DO. 35/7564, Macmillan to Home, 10 February 1960.

99. AM, 1960, pp. 27–8.

100. Wood, op. cit., p. 746.

101. Macleod to Armitage, 13 February 1960, referred to in AM, 1960, p. 29.

102. Wood, op. cit., p. 765; see also DO. 35/7564, Monson to Armitage, 21 January 1960.

103. AD, 14 February 1960; AM, 1960, p. 30. A crowd of a thousand also waited for him in Blantyre: Wood, op. cit., p. 746.

104. Macleod to Armitage, 6 February 1960, referred to in AD, 6 February 1960 and AM, 1960, p. 28; DO. 35/7477, Macleod to Armitage, 1 February 1960 and DO. 35/7564, Armitage to Macleod, 10 February 1960.

105. AD, 10 February 1960.

106. Ibid.

107. Evans, op. cit., p. 107.

108. Wood, op. cit., p. 754.

109. DO. 35/7565, Loft to Macleod, 26 February 1960.

110. DO. 35/7565, Armitage to Macleod, 3 March 1960.

111. DO. 35/7564, Macleod to Armitage, 15 February 1960.

112. AM, 1960, pp. 31–2.

113. AD, 17 February 1960.

114. PREM. 11/3075, Brook to Macmillan, 10 February 1960.

115. PREM. 11/3085, Gibb to Home, 6 February 1960.

116. PREM. 11/3085, Dalhousie to Home, 4 February 1960.

117. DO. 35/7564, Note by the Prime Minister, n.d., probably 18 February 1960.

118. DO. 35/7564, Home to Macmillan, 9 February 1960.

119. DO. 35/7565, Draft Cabinet paper on the release of Banda: discussions in Salisbury, memorandum by the Secretary of State for Commonwealth Relations, n.d., probably late February 1960.

120. PREM. 11/3075, Press Announcement from C.R.O., n.d. but November 1959.

121. DO. 35/7564, Note for the Record, 9 February 1960.

122. DO. 35/7564, Macleod to Armitage, 15 February 1960.

123. AM, 1960, p. 32.

124. AD, 22 February 1960; AM, 1960, p. 32.

125. *Daily Express*, 19 February, 1960; *News Chronicle*, 19 February 1960. The previous May, in commenting on the Nyasaland Information *Bulletin*, Morgan said that if the Secretary of State insisted on the Governor withdrawing detention orders before he, the Governor, felt it was safe to do so, he would expect Armitage to resign: CO. 1015/1543, Morgan to Gorell Barnes, 5 June 1959.

126. PREM. 11/3081, Evans to Macmillan, 20 February 1960.
127. PREM. 11/3081, Macmillan note, 21 February 1960.
128. AD, 16 February 1960; AM, 1960, p. 31.
129. AD, 23 and 24 February 1960; AM, 1960, p. 33.
130. AD, 27 February and 22 March 1960; AM, 1960, pp. 34–43; Lapping, op. cit., p. 569.
131. DO. 35/7565, Draft Cabinet paper on the release of Banda: discussions in Salisbury, memorandum by Secretary of State for Commonwealth Relations, n.d., probably late February 1960. Details in the remainder of this and the next paragraph, except where otherwise stated, are from this source. For Welensky's account of Home's visit, see Welensky, op. cit., pp. 183 et seq.; Wood, op. cit., pp. 751 et seq.
132. DO. 35/7565, Home to Macmillan, 20 February 1960.
133. Ibid.
134. PREM. 11/3076, Home to Macmillan, 22 February 1960.
135. Ibid.
136. DO. 35/7564, Home to Macleod, 25 February 1960.
137. DO. 35/7564, Macleod to Home, 25 February 1960.
138. PREM. 11/3081, Macmillan to Home, 23 February 1960.
139. Shepherd, op. cit., p. 198, citing PRO, CAB, 128 34 cc (60). See also Evans, op. cit., p. 108.
140. PREM. 11/3081, Macmillan to Home, 23 February 1960.
141. PREM. 11/3081, Macleod to Home, 25 February 1960, and Macleod to Macmillan, 26 February 1960. See also Evans, op. cit., p. 108.
142. DO. 35/7565, Draft Cabinet paper on the release of Banda: discussions in Salisbury, memorandum by Secretary of State for Commonwealth Relations, n.d., probably late February 1960.
143. PREM. 11/3076, Home to Macmillan, 22 February 1960.
144. DO. 35/7565, Draft Cabinet paper on the release of Banda: discussions in Salisbury, memorandum by Secretary of State for Commonwealth Relations, n.d., probably late February 1960.
145. DO. 35/7565, Home to Macmillan, 20 February 1960.
146. DO. 35/7564, Home to Macmillan, 21 February 1960.
147. Ibid.
148. PREM. 11/3076, Whitehead to Home, 16 March 1960.
149. AD, 26 February 1960; AM, 1960, p. 33.
150. DO. 35/7564, Armitage to Macleod, 27 February 1960.
151. Ibid.
152. DO. 35/7566, Note attached to Secretary of State for the Colonies visit to Central Africa, Brief, dated March 1960.
153. AD, 27 February 1960; AM, 1960, p. 34.
154. AM, 1960, p. 35.
155. AD, 2 March 1960; AM, 1960, p. 36.
156. DO. 35/7564, Armitage to Monson, 25 February 1960.
157. DO. 35/7564, Macleod to Home, 4 March 1960.
158. DO. 35/7564, Alport to Macleod, 8 March 1960.
159. DO. 35/7566, Macleod to Perth, 28 March 1960.
160. DO. 35/7566, Perth to Macleod, 30 March 1960.
161. AM, 1960, p. 37; AD, 3, 5 and 8 March 1960.
162. AD, 5, 7 and 9 March 1960.

163. For details of Jones's visit, see Wood, op. cit., pp. 765–6; AD, 9 and 14 March 1960.

164. DO. 35/7564, Macleod to Armitage, 9 March 1960; AD, 14 March 1960.

165. DO. 35/7564, C.R.O. to High Commissioner Salisbury, n.d., probably 9 or 10 March 1960.

166. DO. 35/7566, Macleod to Armitage, 12 March 1960.

167. DO. 35/7566, Armitage to Macleod, 14 March 1960.

168. AD, 22, 25 and 26 March 1960; AM, 1960, pp. 41–2 and p. 58.

169. AD, 22 March 1960.

170. AD, 23 March 1960. The Queen Mother visited Nyasaland 23–29 May 1960.

171. DO. 35/7566, Macleod to Home, 26 March 1960; AD, 24 March 1960.

172. AD, 24 March 1960.

173. *Nyasaland, Report for the Year 1960* (London: HMSO, 1961), p. 3.

174. DO. 35/7566, Macleod to Home, 26 March 1960.

175. Ibid.

176. M. Blackwood to author, 25 November 1993; AD, 28 March 1960.

177. AD, 27 March 1960.

178. Theunissen, interview with author, 26 June 1994.

179. Haskard to author, 27 February 1994.

180. Codrington to author, 12 February 1994.

181. Armitage, interview with Wood, cited in Wood, op. cit., pp. 738–9.

182. Kettlewell to author, 24 March 1994.

183. DO. 35/7566, Macleod to Macmillan, 31 March 1960.

184. Youens, interview with Bradley, 26 November 1970, ODRP, p. 19; interview with author, 4 January 1995. Details in this paragraph, except where otherwise stated, are from these sources.

185. Jackson to author, 3 August and 4 November 1995.

186. Theunissen, interview with author, 26 June 1994. Details in this paragraph, including quotations, except where otherwise stated, are from this source. Entries in brackets are from Jackson to author, 4 November 1995 and DO. 35/7566, Nyasaland Information Department to Secretary of State, 1 April 1960.

187. AD, 1 April 1960.

188. DO. 35/7566, Watson to Morris, 1 April 1960.

189. AD, 1 April 1960; AM, 1960, pp. 44–5.

190. Codrington, interview with author, 19 January 1994.

191. DO. 35/7566, Macleod to Home and Perth, 4 April 1960. Macleod told Dixon that he considered Banda 'a vain little man': Wood, op. cit., p. 777.

192. Youens, interview with author, 4 January 1995.

193. DO. 35/7566, Nyasaland Information Department to Secretary of State for the Colonies, 1 April 1960.

194. B. Jones-Walters, interview with author, 2 May 1996.

195. AM, 160, p. 45.

196. Howard-Drake to author, 1 February 1994; see also Fisher, op. cit., p. 160.

197. PREM. 11/3070, Macleod to Macmillan, 3 April 1960.

198. Howard-Drake to author, 7 October 1993.

199. Shepherd, op. cit., p. 204, citing Monson.

200. DO. 35/7566, Macleod to Dalhousie, 4 April 1960; Short, op. cit., p. 131.

201. Welensky, op. cit., p. 192.

202. DO. 35/7566, Macleod to Dalhousie, 4 April 1960.

203. AM, 1960, p. 54, p. 62 and p. 66; Proceedings of Legislative Council, 3rd Meeting, 74th Session, 10–12 May 1960, p. 281.

204. *Nyasaland, Report for the Year 1960* (London: HMSO, 1961), pp. 115–6.

205. *Nyasaland, Report for the Year 1960* (London: HMSO, 1961), p. 4.

206. Ibid.

207. DO. 35/7477, Text of announcement by Armitage, 15 June 1960; see also PREM. 11/3077, Macleod to Macmillan, 2 June 1960, and Minute, Macmillan, 3 June 1960.

208. DO. 35/7477, Note, Macmillan, 3 June 1960, and Macleod to Macmillan, 2 June 1960.

209. DO. 35/7477, Macleod to Macmillan, 2 June 1960. See also DO. 35/7477, Armitage to Macleod, 30 May 1960.

210. Wood, op. cit., pp. 799–801; PREM. 11/3075, Brook to Macmillan, 10 February 1960; PREM. 11/3076, Watson to Monson, 23 February 1960.

211. *Report of the Nyasaland Constitutional Conference*, Cmnd. 1132 (London: HMSO, 1960).

212. PREM. 11/3077, Macmillan to Macleod, 6 August 1960.

213. Macleod to Welensky, 30 May 1960, cited in Wood, op. cit., p. 787 and p. 791.

214. Ibid.

215. Cmnd. 1132, pp. 5–8.

216. Cmnd. 1132, p. 9.

217. AD, 10 August 1960; and *Nyasaland Government Gazette*, 1960, p. 245. *Nyasaland, Report for the Year 1960* (London: HMSO, 1961), p. 5, gives the date as 11 August 1960.

218. Short, op. cit., p. 139.

219. *Nyasaland, Report for the Year, 1960* (London: HMSO, 1961), p. 6.

220. Ibid.

Sources

Primary sources

There are ten primary sources used in writing this book:

   1. Documents in the Public Record Office:

CO. 1015 – Central Africa and Aden: Original correspondence

1513: 1957–59 Situation Reports from Chief Intelligence Officer in Nyasaland.

1515: 1959 Disturbances in Nyasaland.

1516: 1959 Disturbances in Nyasaland.

1517: 1959 Disturbances in Nyasaland.

1518: 1959 Disturbances in Nyasaland.

1519: 1959 Measures against civil unrest in Nyasaland.

1522: 1959 Use of military aircraft during civil unrest in Nyasaland.

1524: 1959 Internal political situation during civil unrest in Nyasaland.

1526: 1959 Introduction of detention orders in Nyasaland.

1527: 1959 Counter measures against subversive publicity and propaganda in Nyasaland.

1533–1544: 1959 Commission of Inquiry into unrest in Nyasaland held by Lord Devlin.

1533: Establishment.

1534: Establishment.

1535: Appointment of members.

1536: Statement by Secretary of State on terms of reference.

1537: Order in Council authorising commencement of work.

1538: Rules for access to documents by Commission.

1539: Rules for evidence from witnesses attending Commission.

1540: Publication of Reports.

1541: Examination of detainees by Commission.

1542: Hearing of evidence by Commission from witnesses in the U.K.

1543: Publicity and articles in press on work of Commission.

1544: Action on Report.

1839: 1959 Reports by Governor on internal situation in Nyasaland.

1905: 1959 Detention of prisoners in Nyasaland .

1906: 1959 Statistics on prisoners held in Nyasaland.

1950: 1959 Visit by Secretary of State for Colonies to Colonies in Central Africa.

1976: 1959 Visit by Minister of State at Colonial Office to Colonies in Central Africa.

1977: 1959 Possible visit by Lord Perth, Minister of State in Colonial Office to Nyasaland.

1984: 1959 Record of meetings in Colonial Office with Governors of Northern Rhodesia and Nyasaland.

2054: 1959 Detention of Mr. O. Chirwa in Nyasaland.

2055: 1959 Detention of Dr. H. Banda in Nyasaland.

2063: 1959 Memorandum by Colonial Office on U.K. Policy in Central Africa.

2097: 1959 Detention Camps in Nyasaland.

2098: 1959 Inspection of Detention Camps in Nyasaland.

2116: 1957/58 Visit by Governor of Nyasaland to Colonial Office.

2118: 1958 Visit by Delegation from African National Congress of Nyasaland to U.K.

2119: 1959 Visit by Mr. O. Chirwa of Nyasaland to U.K.

DO. 35 – Original Correspondence

7476: 1959/60 Rioting in Nyasaland: reports and situation: position of Nyasaland detainees; ending of state of emergency.

7477: 1960 Rioting in Nyasaland: reports and situation: position of Nyasaland detainees; ending of state of emergency.

7478: 1959 Rioting in Nyasaland 1959; interdepartmental Central Africa Committee.

7479: 1959 Nyasaland Commission of Inquiry; question of showing Commission correspondence about Nyasaland constitutional reform.

7564: 1959/60 Consitutional development in Nyasaland: visits of Lord Home to Salisbury and of Mr. Macleod to Nyasaland; release of Dr. Banda.

7565: 1960 Constitutional development in Nyasaland: visit of Lord Home to Salisbury and of Mr. Macleod to Nyasaland; release of Dr. Banda.

7566: 1960 Constitutional development in Nyasaland: visit of Lord Home to Salisbury and of Mr. Macleod to Nyasaland; release of Dr. Banda.

PREM. 11 – Prime Minister's Office: Correspondence and Papers 1951–1964

3075: 1959/60 Constitutional development in Africa: Federation of Rhodesia and Nyasaland Part 6.

3076: 1960 Constitutional development in Africa: Federation of Rhodesia and Nyasaland Part 7.

3077: 1960 Constitutional development in Africa: Federation of Rhodesia and Nyasaland Part 8.

3078: 1960 Constitutional development in Africa: Federation of Rhodesia and Nyasaland Part 9.

3079: 1960 Constitutional development in Africa: Federation of Rhodesia and Nyasaland Part 10.

3080: 1960 Constitutional development in Africa: Federation of Rhodesia and Nyasaland Part 11.

3081: 1960 Prime Minister enquiries about press reports that Sir R. Armitage, Governor of Nyasaland, intended to resign.

3082: 1960 Situation in Nyasaland during visit of Dr. Banda to London for review conference.

3083: 1960 Proposal by Sir R. Welensky to establish closer defence cooperation between Federation and Portuguese East Africa.

3085: 1960 Correspondence from Lord Dalhousie, Governor-General, and Sir H. Gibbs on public opinion in Federation following visit by Prime Minister.

CAB. 21 – Visit of the Prime Minister, Mr. Harold Macmillan, to Commonwealth Countries in Africa

3155: 1959 October–December Visit of the Prime Minister, Mr. Harold Macmillan, to Commonwealth Countries in Africa.

3156: 1959 December Visit of the Prime Minister, Mr. Harold Macmillan, to Commonwealth Countries in Africa.

3157: 1960 January Visit of the Prime Minister, Mr. Harold Macmillan, to Commonwealth Countries in Africa.

CAB. 133 – Commonwealth and International Conferences from 1945

151: 1959 14 December–4 January – Briefs 1–9.
1959 14 December–31 December – Briefs 1–21.
1959 31 December – Briefs 1–8.
152: 1959 31 December 1960–15 January – Briefs 1–17.
1959 31 December 1960–1 January – Briefs 1–7.
1959 31 December – Briefs 1–6.
1959 31 December 1960–22 January – Briefs 1–22.

2. The Devlin Papers in Rhodes House Library, Oxford. These contain the transcripts of evidence taken by the Devlin Commission and the memoranda submitted to the Commission by individuals and groups, together with the papers which the Nyasaland Government submitted and correspondence to and from the Commission. In 1995 when the research for this book was undertaken, the Devlin Papers had not yet been catalogued. Reference to them, therefore, is made by Box number.

3. The transcripts deposited at Rhodes House Library, Oxford, by Granada Television, of interviews taken in 1982 and 1984 in preparation for their series *End of Empire*: Mss.Brit.Emp. s. 527/1 and s. 527/2.

4. The Kellock Papers in the Borthwick Institute of Historical Studies, University of York. The Kellock Papers on the Devlin Commission consist of 25 files in three boxes and contain a large number of statements taken by Kellock primarily from detained members of Congress but also from public officers; correspondence; memoranda; notes; publications; and press cuttings.

5. Documents in the Foreign and Commonwealth Office Research and Analysis Department Library.

6. An extensive correspondence with participants in the emergency – numbering over 300 – mainly government officials, both very senior and those more junior, but including British politicians, missionaries, military personnel and private citizens both African and expatriate.

7. Interviews, including those with Lord Perth, Sir Denys Roberts, Sir Peter Tapsell, Sir Peter Youens, Sir John Moreton, Sir Edgar Unsworth, Sir Henry Phillips, Sir David Hunt, Dr Wellington Chirwa, Paul Lewis, Richard Kettlewell, Humphry Berkeley, Julian Theunissen, John Codrington, Allan Lodge, James Skinner, Bryn Jones-Walters, Michael Harris, John Sheriff, Richard Chasemore and Nicholas Maxwell-Lawford.

8. The private papers of Sir Geoffrey Colby, Sir Robert Armitage particularly his letters and diaries, Sir Edgar Williams and Anthony Fairclough. Colby's papers are in Rhodes House Library, Oxford. Armitage's, Williams's and Fairclough's papers are privately held.

9. Memoirs of a number of participants including Sir Robert Armitage (in draft), R.W. Kettlewell, R.H. Martin, B. Jackson (in part), L.J. Foster, R.E.N. Smith (in part) and M. Gardiner. All privately held.

10. Privately held papers in the possession of former government officers, including the Zomba District Operations Committee Diary, 1959; FISB documents; a Fort Johnston Ulendo Diary; lists of detainees; and statements taken from detainees.

The extensive collection of Welensky Papers in Rhodes House Library, Oxford had not been catalogued and made open to the public at the time the research for this book was undertaken. Reliance was placed, therefore, on J.R.T. Wood's *The Welensky Papers: A History of the Federation of Rhodesia and Nyasaland* (Durban, 1983).

Secondary sources
Official documents

Cmnd. 8233 (1951) Report of the Conference on Closer Association in Central Africa.

Cmnd. 8234 (1951) The Central African Territories: Historical, Geographical and Economic Survey.

Cmnd. 8235 (1951) Comparative Survey of Central African Native Policies.

Cmnd. 8411 (1951) Closer Association in Central Africa: Statement by H.M. Government.

Cmnd. 8573 (1952) Draft Federal Scheme.

Cmnd. 8671 (1952) Report of the Judicial Commission.

Cmnd. 8672 (1952) Report of the Fiscal Commission.

Cmnd. 8673 (1952) Report of the Civil Service Preparatory Commission.

Cmnd. 8753 (1953) Federal Report of the Conference on Federation.

Cmnd. 8754 (1953) Federal Scheme prepared by a Conference held in London in January 1953.

CRS. 27–59 Beadle Tribunal (Review Tribunal (Preventive Detention Temporary Provisions) Act 1959) General Report (Salisbury, 1959).

Cmnd. 707 (1959) State of Emergency.

Cmnd. 814 (1959) Report of the Nyasaland Commission of Inquiry.

Cmnd. 815 (1959) Despatch from the Governor of Nyasaland commenting on the Devlin Commission's Report.

Cmnd. 1132 (1960) Report of the Nyasaland Constitutional Conference.

Nyasaland Reports for the Years 1959 and 1960 (London, 1960 and 1961).

The Southworth Commission Report, 1960 (Zomba, 2 May 1960).

Books

Alligan, G., *The Welensky Story* (London, 1962).

Baker, C.A., *Johnston's Administration* (Zomba, 1970).

Baker, C.A., *Development Governor, a biography of Sir Geoffrey Colby* (London, 1994).

Banda, H.K. and Nkumbula, H., *Federation in Central Africa* (London, 1951).

Brelsford, W.V. (ed.), *Handbook to the Federation of Rhodesia and Nyasaland* (London, 1960).

Brent, W.A., *Rhodesian Air Force: a brief history, 1947–1980* (Kwambona, R.S.A., 1987).

Brockway, F., *The Colonial Revolution* (New York, 1973).

Butler, Lord, *The Art of the Possible: The Memoirs of Lord Butler* (Aylesbury, 1971).

Burkinshaw, P., *Alarms and Excursions* (Leominster, 1991).

Chandos, Lord, *Memoirs* (London, 1962).

Chisiza, D.K., *Africa – What Lies Ahead* (New Delhi, 1961).

Chisiza, D.K., *Realities of African Independence* (London, 1961).

Chiume, M.W.K., *Nyasaland Speaks – An Appeal to the British People*, (London, 1959).

Chiume, M.W.K., *Kwacha* (Lusaka, 1975).

Clegg, E.M., *Race and Politics: Partnership in the Federation of Rhodesia and Nyasaland* (London, 1960).

Clutton-Brock, A.G., *Facing 1960 in Central Africa* (London, 1959).

Callaghan, Lord, *Time and Chance* (London, 1987).

Cohen, Sir Andrew, *British Policy in Changing Africa* (London 1959).

Cowderoy, D. and Nesbit, R.C., *War in the Air: Rhodesian Airforce 1935–1980* (Alberton, R.S.A., 1987).

Davidson, A.M., *The Real Paradise* (Edinburgh, 1993).

Devlin, Lord, *The Judge* (London, 1979).

Devlin, Lord, *Easing the Passing* (London, 1985).

Dickenson, R., *African Ambit* (Edinburgh, 1995).

Dunn, C., *Central African Witness* (London, 1959).

Evans, H., *Downing Street Diary: the Macmillan Years, 1957–1963* (London, 1981).

Fisher, Sir N., *Iain Macleod* (London, 1973).

Franck, T.M., *Race and Nationalism: The Struggle for Power in Rhodesia and Nyasaland* (London, 1960).

Franklin, H., *Unholy Wedlock: The Failure of the Central African Federation* (London, 1963).

Gray, R., *The Two Nations: Aspects of the Development of Race Relations in the Rhodesias and Nyasaland* (London, 1960).

Greenfield, J.M., *Testimony of a Rhodesian Federal* (Bulawayo, 1978).

Gupta, P.S., *Imperialism and the British Labour Movement, 1914–1964* (London, 1975).

Horne, A., *Macmillan, Vols I and II* (London, 1988).

Howarth, D., *The Shadow of the Dam* (London, 1961).

Hunt, D., *On the Spot: An Ambassador Remembers* (London, 1975).

Jones, G.B., *Britain and Nyasaland* (London, 1964).

Keatley, P., *The Politics of Partnership* (London, 1963).

Kilmuir, Earl, *Political Venture* (London, 1989).

Kirk-Greene, A.H.M. (ed.), *Africa in the Colonial Period, The Transfer of Power: the Colonial Administration in the Age of Decolonisation* (Oxford, 1979).

Kirkman, W.P., *Unscrambling and Empire: A Critique of British Colonial Policy* (London, 1966).

Lapping, B., *End of Empire* (London, 1989).

Leys, C. and Pratt, C., *New Deal in Central Africa* (London, 1960).

Lucas Phillips, L.E., *The Vision Splendid* (London, 1960).

Lwanda, J.L., *Kamuzu Banda of Malawi* (Glasgow, 1993).

Macmillan, H., *Pointing the Way* (London, 1972).

Macmillan, H., *At the End of the Day* (London, 1973).

McMaster, C., *Malawi: Foreign Policy and Development* (London, 1974).

Mason, P., *The Birth of a Dilemma: The Conquest and Settlement of Rhodesia* (London, 1958).

Mason, P., *Year of Decision* (London, 1960).

Masters, J., *Bhowani Junction* (Harmondsworth, 1960).

Mufuka, K.N., *Missions and Politics in Malawi* (Kingston, Ontario, 1977).

Mullins, P., *Retreat from Africa* (Edinburgh, 1992).

Munger, E.S., *President Kamuzu Banda of Malawi* (Hanover, New Hampshire, 1969).

Pachai, B., *Malawi: The History of the Nation* (London, 1973).

Pike, J.G., *Malawi: A Political and Economic History* (London, 1968).

Pike, J.G. and Rimmington, G.T., *Malawi: a Geographical Study* (London, 1965).

Rotberg, R.I., *The Rise of Nationalism in Central Africa: The Making of Malawi and Zambia, 1873–1964* (London, 1965).

Sampson, A., *Macmillan: A Study in Ambiguity* (London, 1967).

Sanger, C., *Central African Emergency* (London, 1960).

Shepherd, R., *Iain Macleod: a Biography* (London, 1994).

Shepperson, G. and Price, T., *Independent African* (Edinburgh, 1958).

Short, P., *Banda* (London, 1974).

Stonehouse, J., *Prohibited Immigrant* (London, 1960).

Taylor, D., *Rainbow on the Zambezi* (London, 1953).

Taylor, D., *The Rhodesian: The Life of Sir Roy Welensky* (London, 1955).

Thompson, C.H. and Woodruff, H.W., *Economic Development in Rhodesia and Nyasaland* (London, 1954).

Welensky, Sir Roy, *Welensky's 4000 Days: The Life and Death of the Federation of Rhodesia and Nyasaland* (London, 1964).

Wills, A.J., *An Introduction to the History of Central Africa* (London, 1973).

Wood, J.R.T., *The Welensky Papers: A History of the Federation of Rhodesia and Nyasaland* (Durban, 1983).

Young, K., *Sir Alec Douglas-Home* (London, 1970).

Index